Political Ideologies

Their Origins and Impact

Sixth Edition

Leon P. Baradat

MiraCosta College

 Prentice Hall, Upper Saddle River, New Jersey 07458

Library of Congress Cataloging-in-Publication Data

BARADAT, LEON P., (date)
    Political ideologies: their origins and impact / Leon P. Baradat.
—6th ed.
        p.   cm.
    Includes bibliographical references and index.
    ISBN 0–13–266370–8
    1. Political Science—History.   2. Ideology.   I. Title.
JA83.B248   1997
320.5'09–dc20   96-9491
                                                                CIP

Editorial director: *Charlyce Jones Owen*
Editor in chief: *Nancy Roberts*
Acquisitions editor: *Michael Bickerstaff*
Editorial assistant: *Anita Castro*
Director of production and manufacturing: *Barbara Kittle*
Managing editor: *Ann Marie McCarthy/Fran Russello*
Editorial/production supervision: *Kim Gueterman*
Manufacturing manager: *Nick Sklitsis*
Buyer: *Bob Anderson*
Cover designer: *Bruce Kenselaar*
Photo research: *Sherry Lee Cohen*
Illustrator: *Asterisk Group*
Copy editor: *Kathryn Beck*
Marketing manager: *Chaunfayta Hightower*

This book was set in 10/12 Palatino by NK Graphics
and was printed and bound by Courier Companies, Inc.
The cover was printed by Phoenix Color Corp.

 © 1997, 1994, 1991, 1988, 1984, 1979 by Prentice-Hall, Inc.
Simon & Schuster/A Viacom Company
Upper Saddle River, New Jersey 07458

Printed in the United States of America
10   9   8   7   6   5   4   3   2   1

ISBN   0-13-266370-8

Prentice-Hall International (UK) Limited, *London*
Prentice-Hall of Australia Pty. Limited, *Sydney*
Prentice-Hall of Canada Inc., *Toronto*
Prentice-Hall Hispanoamericana, S.A., *Mexico*
Prentice-Hall of India Private Limited, *New Delhi*
Prentice-Hall of Japan, Inc., *Tokyo*
Simon & Schuster Asia Pte. Ltd., *Singapore*
Editora Prentice-Hall do Brasil, Ltda., *Rio de Janeiro*

To Elaine
Wife, Partner, Friend;

To the memory of
Ellen Coté, Elaine's mother;

And to the memory of
Pete, my dad.

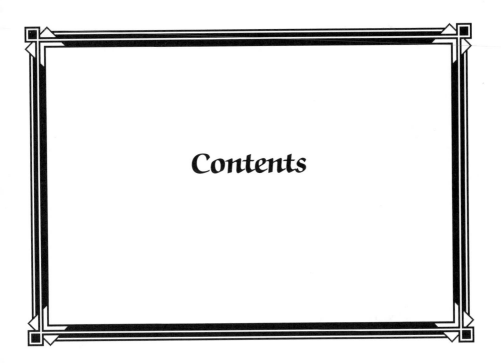

Contents

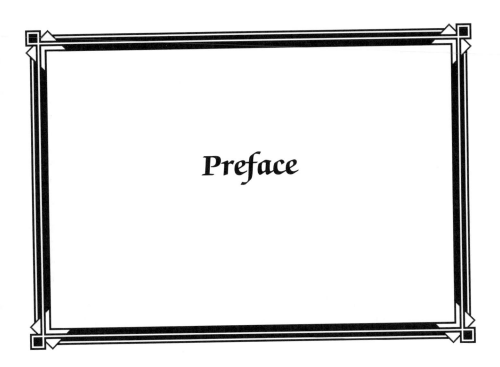

Preface

Since the first edition of this book, we have witnessed many changes in the tides of political turmoil throughout the world. The Cold War ended and much of the communist world collapsed. People were hopeful momentarily that the political climate would grow more temperate and tensions relax. However, although the frightening possibility of a nuclear confrontation between the superpowers has diminished, we still find ourselves confronted with a threatening environment. The Middle East continues to fester; religious fundamentalism engenders violence; political terrorism continues to threaten disruption; racism divides peoples against themselves; nationalism and neo-fascism emerge again, creating havoc and motivating paranoid Americans to join militant citizen militias in efforts to protect themselves from imagined adversity; famine emaciates millions in the underdeveloped world; air pollution is rampant; water everywhere is increasingly adulterated; the earth's protective layer of ozone is rapidly disintegrating; the globe apparently is warming in response to the chemicals released into the atmosphere; and the press of the world's population on available food supplies and other resources is now dangerously acute.

These problems, and many others demanding solutions, confront us and our political leaders. To resolve our difficulties, we realize that we must work together with other people in the world, since many of our problems traverse national boundaries and exceed the capacity of single states to successfully address them. In order to cooperate in the salvation of humankind, we must learn to deal with people who have values, biases, views, and ideas that are different from our own. Hence, we must confront a number of basic questions if we hope to successfully meet the challenges of the last few years of this century. What, for example, are the fundamental concepts in modern politics? What ideas serve as the foundation of our political system? How does our system differ from others? What is socialism, and how does it relate to democracy and to communism? Is fascism moribund, or does it survive, awaiting another chance to take hold in a society confused and disoriented by the complexities of modern life? Why don't people of the world see things *our* way? How do they view the world, and why do they value the things they do? What are their assumptions and objectives? And, perhaps most important, "What do *I* believe and how do my views relate to the politics of my time?" These and hundreds of other questions must be addressed if we are to face intelligently the political controversies that loom before us. These questions can be ignored only at great peril, and the study of political ideologies is perhaps the best context in which to begin to find answers. Ideological assumptions become the premises for the approaches different societies take to resolve their problems.

Traditionally, the American people have been impatient with theoretical concepts. Finding such notions abstract and uninteresting, they prefer more tangible, practical approaches to politics. Moreover, the American political tack has usually been unilateral. We have either tried to ignore the rest of the world—as in much of the early part of this century—or we have expected the world to conform to our attitudes and policies—as has been the case since World War II. But such a narrow view is no longer possible—if indeed it ever was. The United States must face the fact that it is only one player, albeit an important one, in global politics, and we must learn to cooperate with the rest of the world in the resolution of common problems. To do so, we must understand the other peoples of the world. We must comprehend their needs, their ideals, their values, their views. In this endeavor, there can be no better place to start than by coming to appreciate their political ideologies. A clear understanding of the current ideologies in the world is essential if one is to grasp the political realities of our time.

A NOTE TO THE STUDENT

I think of myself as a teacher, not an author. This book, therefore, is written as a vehicle for teaching some of the world's great ideas, and as such it reaches students whom the author will probably never meet and thus influences the lives of strangers, if only slightly. With pedagogy in mind, several features have been included in this book that will help the reader learn its contents more easily.

Each chapter is preceded by a preview of the material to be covered in that chapter. The preview is designed to alert students to the principal ideas developed in the text that follows. Thus you will find that, equipped with this overview, the details in the chapter become more meaningful. At the end of each chapter I have included a brief review of the major points so as to reinforce the material just learned. Later, the previews and reviews can be used to quickly refresh your memory about the chapters' contents. Please note, however, reading only the previews and the summaries is no substitute for reading the chapters in their entirety.

I have also included at the end of the chapters a brief bibliography of books that can be used in further pursuit of the subject. These lists are certainly not complete, but they can be used as jumping-off places for more detailed inquiry into the subject.

The text also includes *italicized* words and phrases. When encountering these words, take special note of them; it is my way of saying that material is particularly important. The glossary and the index at the end of the book should also be especially useful. In addition, the names and concepts appearing in **boldface** in the text can be found among the items in the glossary, and you should pay close attention to them as well.

As a final note to the reader, I would like to say just a few words about general education courses. Responding to economic and social pressures, students today are anxious to complete their studies so that they can begin to make a living. Courses that do not immediately translate into dollars are often viewed by students as superfluous impositions on their time. The course for which you are reading this text may be one of those offerings. Yet, there is more to life than materialism, and *we* must learn to appreciate and enjoy what we are and who we are while we make a living. In fact, it is likely that we will make a better living, or at least live better, if we appreciate and understand the world in which we live.

Education is the custodian of civilization. Its function is to transmit the knowledge of our civilization to each succeeding generation. General education courses are the principal vehicle by which this function is executed at the college level. They offer you the priceless treasure of society's wisdom. Immerse yourself in them, savor them, absorb them, enjoy them. Let general education courses expose you to the wonders of our world, expanding your vision and deepening your appreciation of life so that, as Stephen Bailey wrote, "Later in life when you knock on yourself, someone answers."

ACKNOWLEDGMENTS

While any inaccuracies in this book are completely my own responsibility, several people have made such substantial contributions to this work that I take pleasure in mentioning them here. My deepest gratitude belongs to my wife, Elaine. Her unselfish help and her unfailing support over the years have been instrumental to the book's success. I am also indebted to our sons Leon and René who, in the early editions of the book, sacrificed time we might have spent together, so that the book could be written.

For the lucidity the first edition enjoyed, all credit and many thanks go to Professor Julie Hatoff. Spending untold hours reviewing the manuscript, suggesting improvements, and correcting errors, Professor Hatoff was of invaluable assistance. I am similarly indebted to Professor Patricia Valiton and Mary Murphy for their services on the subsequent editions. Their conscientious attention to my misplaced modifiers, arbitrary punctuation, and eccentric spelling has been very helpful, and I am most grateful to them. I am also very grateful to my colleague and friend David Ballard for his help on this edition. Additionally, Professor Peter N. Kirstein of Saint Xavier College deserves special recognition for his many helpful comments and suggestions, and I am deeply indebted to Professor Monica Tagnoli of MiraCosta College and to the staff at the MiraCosta College Learning Resource Center, including Janet Megill, Patricia McClure, and Marion Forester. Their friendly and helpful attitude makes my work much easier. I would also like to thank Stan Wakefield, Mike Bickerstaff, Kim Gueterman, Kathryn Beck, Walter Welch, and Karen Horton of Prentice Hall. My thanks also to the reviewers Bruce Tuttle and Lyman H. Heine of Fresno State University and John Gerring of Boston University for their many helpful suggestions.

Besides those who did so much to make this book a reality, I would like to take this opportunity to express my gratitude to the people of California for providing an excellent and free public education system to its youth. Were it not for the opportunity to attend state-supported schools, I would almost surely not have received an education. In addition, I would like to single out three teachers who have had particular influence on my professional life and whose pedagogical and scholarly examples have been important inspirations. To N. B. (Tad) Martin, formerly professor of history at the College of the Sequoias, who has a grasp of history and a teaching ability worthy of emulation, my sincere appreciation. To Karl A. Svenson, professor of political science at Fresno State University, whose lectures were memorable and whose advice was timely and sound, my heartfelt thanks. Finally, and most important, to David H. Provost, professor of political science at Fresno State University, my lasting gratitude for the help, encouragement, scholastic training, and friendship he so abundantly extended. His example has been particularly meaningful to me.

Leon P. Baradat

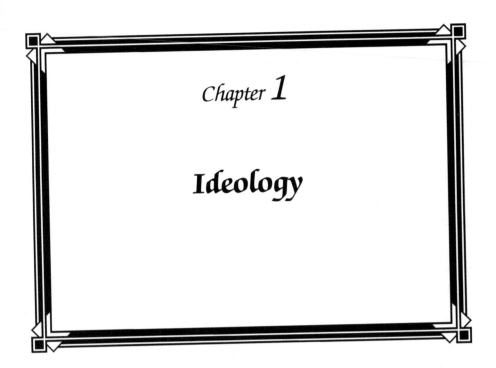

Chapter *1*

Ideology

PREVIEW

Ideologies were made necessary by the Age of Enlightenment belief that people could improve their conditions by taking positive action instead of passively accepting life as it came. This new belief was accompanied by the great economic and social upheaval caused by the mechanization of production (the Industrial Revolution). Indeed, one of the major themes of this book is that ideologies are the result of attempts to develop political accommodations to the economic and social conditions created by the Industrial Revolution.

Political scientists do not agree on the exact definition of the term ideology, *but their opinions have enough in common to allow us to develop a five-part definition for our purposes:*

1. *The term ideology can be used in many contexts, but unless otherwise specified, it is proper to give it a political meaning.*
2. *All ideologies provide an interpretation of the present and a view of a desired future. The anticipated future is invariably portrayed as materially better than the present and it is thought to be attainable within a single lifetime.*
3. *Each ideology includes a list of specific steps that can be taken to accomplish its goals.*
4. *Ideologies are oriented toward the masses.*
5. *Ideologies are simply stated and presented in motivational terms.*

THE DEVELOPMENT OF IDEOLOGY

Prior to the modern era, people were discouraged from seeking solutions to their problems. They were expected to do what they were told by their spiritual and temporal superiors. Politics had not yet become democratized. Ordinary people were not allowed to participate in the political system. Politics was reserved for kings heading a small ruling class. Indeed, the Prussian king and military genius Frederick the Great (1712–1786) once said, "A war is something which should not concern my people." Rather than enjoy a voice in government, the masses were expected to work, producing material goods to sustain the state, but they were not mobilized for political activity.

This attitude would be viewed as arrogant by contemporary observers, but only because every modern society is democratic in at least one sense of the word. *Every modern political system is motivational;* that is, the leaders attempt to mobilize their citizens to accomplish the political, economic, and social goals of the society. The United States, Great Britain, France, Russia, Japan, the People's Republic of China, and every other modern national political entity, regardless of the differences among them, share at least one major feature: They are all intensely interested in involving their citizens in efforts to accomplish the objectives of the state; and ideologies are among the major tools used by modern governments to mobilize the masses. Consequently, modern ideologies call upon people to join in collective efforts. The goals of each ideology and the precise methods used to reach these goals are different, but they each call for mass mobilization and collective efforts to accomplish desired ends.

The Source of Ideology

Knowledge, as it was commonly understood before the Enlightenment, was to be revealed by a superior wisdom; people were to understand and conform to such knowledge as best they could. Consequently, little questioning or challenging took place, and, naturally, change came very slowly.

Gradually, however, people began to challenge this intellectual straightjacket. Some, such as Galileo, were punished for doing so. Yet they persisted, and in time their efforts led to discoveries that revolutionized human existence. The net result of these accomplishments was the development of science and its application, technology. Success in early attempts to solve problems through the application of science, such as curing a disease or developing an important labor-saving device gave people a sense of liberation from ignorance. The world became rational, and could be approached in a systematic fashion. Invigorated by this secular epiphany, people were encouraged to apply human reason to an ever-widening range of problems.

In time, innovators developed machines that greatly increased productivity and drastically changed people's relationship to the things produced.

Galileo Galilei (1564–1642)
Engraving after painting by
Wyatt. Corbis-Bettmann

Whereas production was once limited to the quantity a person could fashion by hand, the new technology produced goods in quantities that no one had previously imagined. At the same time, however, the worker was no longer personally involved in the production process. Machines were weaving fabrics, forging steel, and carving wood. Workers found themselves tending the machines instead of making the goods.

These changes in productivity had enormous social effects. People who once led a relatively healthy, albeit poor, life in a rural setting were brought together to live in the cities. The workers' neighborhoods were crowded and unsanitary. Life became less social as people found themselves psychologically estranged from their neighbors at the very time when they were forced to cohabit the same city block. For millennia people had depended on a close relationship with the soil for the necessities of life. Now, suddenly, they found themselves divorced from the land. Urbanization and industrialization, accomplished by the brutal methods employed during the eighteenth and nineteenth centuries, caused massive confusion and insecurity among most people. Ordinary people became disoriented and frightened. No longer could they produce most of the things they needed themselves. They had become dependent for their well-being on people they did not know, in places they had never seen. Scholars, philosophers, and politicians launched themselves into efforts to comprehend these events, to explain them, and to rationalize them. Some of the rationalizations became political ideologies.

If the mechanization of production, the urbanization of society, and the separation of people from an intimate relationship with the land had been all that people had to face, the impact on human life would have been great indeed. However, even more turmoil lay ahead. Economic dislocation became a severe problem. Unemployment, depression, and inflation began to plague society and to disrupt the order of things to a degree previously unequaled. Workers became disoriented as the skills that had once been a major source of self-identification and pride were made unnecessary by automation. It became necessary to learn a new set of skills to fit the new technology. At the same time, the workers became divorced from owners. Capital investment necessary to buy machines, factories, and resources became so great that owners had to spend their time managing their money (becoming capitalists); they were no longer able to work alongside their employees. Hence, the workers, lulled by the monotony of the assembly line, became estranged from their work, alienated by impersonal managers, and separated from their employers.

Meanwhile, as family farms and businesses have disappeared, society has become increasingly mobile. Roots have disintegrated. Families, the most basic of all social units, have become dislocated from ancestral foundations, and the institution of the family itself seems to be dissolving before our eyes. While we are being crowded closer together, we seem to be losing concern for one another. We are becoming increasingly isolated in a world filled with people. Ironically, we are developing a self-oriented world at the very time that we are becoming more and more dependent on others for our most basic needs. As the pace of change quickens and the basic institutions of society are weakened, the generation gap, which must always have existed in some form, has widened.

Our economic success has tended to make our social problems worse. Industrialization has produced great wealth for those who are fortunate enough to profit from it. For others, however, it has produced a new kind of slavery. The new slaves, be they industrial workers or neocolonial suppliers of cheap raw materials, are exploited more fully than those of previous eras because of the efficiency of the modern system. The gap between the user and the used, between the haves and the have-nots, is also increasing, threatening frightful results for a world that remains insensitive to it. In addition, industrialized economies have become voracious consumers of natural resources. Some of these vital commodities are, in fact, reduced to very short supply. The competition for the remaining fuel and mineral resources increases the tension between industrialized and developing nations as well as among the industrialized nations themselves.

Not only have many technical advances increased the demand for resources, but they have also tended to increase the population and thus further escalate the demand for resources. Medical and nutritional discoveries have lengthened life expectancies and eradicated certain diseases so that today the world's population stands at over 5 billion, a figure that will certainly double within the next half-century. Housing, clothing, and feeding these multitudes aggravates the drain on basic resources, causing scarcity and stimulating greater competition for control of those goods.

Prior to the present era people relied on religion for answers to adversity, putting their faith unquestioningly in their God and in their priests. However, as rationalism developed and science seemed to contradict certain basic tenets of the Church, people began to rely on science for solutions to their difficulties. The world became increasingly materialistic, decreasingly spiritualistic. Unfortunately, however, science brought humanity mixed blessings. For each problem it solved, it created new difficulties. Automobiles give us mobility, yet they also visit air pollution on their owners; birth control pills prevent unwanted children, but now ancient moral scruples are rejected and society faces venereal disease and AIDS in epidemic proportions; preservatives keep food from spoiling for months, while cancer and other maladies plague users of the embalmed commodities; nuclear energy offers cheap and virtually inexhaustible energy, yet, as the accident at Chernobyl attests, a mishap at a power plant can be disastrous; furthermore, although nuclear deterrence kept an uneasy peace until the Soviet Union collapsed, and although the nuclear disarmament of the United States and Russia is proceeding, it will not be total, and the nuclear warheads still in the armories of the world's powers could, if unleashed, produce the ultimate holocaust.

As if these problems were not enough, their impact has been magnified because they have been forced on us over an extremely brief period. Most of the developments just mentioned have occurred during the span of a few generations. People have never before experienced the rate of change they face today. We find ourselves catapulted into the future before we can fully understand the present or the recent past.

Such fundamental change, to say nothing of the rate at which it is occurring, has tended to disorient and confuse people. Values and institutions have become temporary. The industrialization of our economy has caused social upheaval and political change. It is, of course, political change with which we are concerned in this study. However, the political developments of the past several centuries have been fostered by economic and social conditions. The political ideologies described in later chapters may be viewed as *attempts to find a political accommodation to the social and economic conditions created by the Industrial Revolution.* Madison, Marx, Mussolini, and others developed their ideas in response to the conditions confronting them. If those conditions had been different, political thought would have been different. The two factors most responsible for the world in which we now live are (1) *the belief that people can take active steps that will improve their lives* and (2) *the mechanization of production.* Almost every modern social condition and political idea is supported by these two factors. The phenomenon of political ideologies is unique to our era because it is a response to a unique set of circumstances.

IDEOLOGY DEFINED

The meaning of the word *ideology* is frequently debated. Dozens of different definitions have been suggested, and each has been challenged and contradicted. Indeed, political scientists cannot agree on whether ideology is a positive, negative, or neutral feature of modern society. While I have no hope of settling this controversy here, I do wish to discuss the origins of the term, explain the varying definitions of the word, and arrive at a definition that will be useful to us during the rest of this study.

The Origin of the Term

It is generally agreed that the term *ideology* was first used by the French in the early nineteenth century, but we do not know for sure who coined it. Most of the evidence, however, indicates that the French noble and scholar **Antoine Louis Claude Destutt de Tracy** (1754–1836) probably originated the word. Writing at the turn of the nineteenth century,[1] he used the word *ideology* in his systematic study of the Enlightenment. Like other thinkers of his time, De Tracy believed that people could use science to improve social and political conditions. To him ideology was a study of the process of forming ideas, a "science of ideas," if you will. *Ideas,* De Tracy believed, are stimulated by the physical environment. Hence, *empirical learning* (the kind that is gained through experience) is the only source of knowledge. Supernatural or spiritual phenomena play no part in the formation of ideas.

Although the thrust of De Tracy's thought is psychological, and hence not of immediate concern to us, two aspects of his theories should be noted. The first is *materialism.* Thought, according to De Tracy, is stimulated by material things only, and the formation of an idea is a physical rather than a spiritual or mystical process. The scientific and materialistic basis of ideology will be pointed out later. For now it is sufficient to note that materialism is a dominant theme in the concept of ideology.

The second important aspect of De Tracy's thought is that social and political improvement was its main goal. De Tracy wanted to apply the knowledge developed from his "science of ideas" to the whole society and thereby attempt to improve human life. Thus, ideology has been closely as-

---

[1]Interestingly, the first English version of De Tracy's most influential work, *Elements of Ideology,* was translated by Thomas Jefferson. It was published in English in 1817.

sociated with politics from the beginning. It is therefore appropriate to give the word a political connotation unless a different context is indicated.

Karl Marx (1818–1883) and **Friedrich Engels** (1820–1895), developed a second theory about what ideology is. In *The German Ideology* they contradict De Tracy on the subject. They argue that rather than a "science of ideas" ideology is nothing more than a fabrication used by a particular group of people to justify themselves. The concepts in an ideology were completely subjective, and they were used to justify the ruling class of society. Thus, the dominant political ideas, or ideology, of any society would always reflect the interests of the ruling class and, according to Marx and Engels, were based on incorrect interpretations of the nature of politics.

Karl Mannheim also studied ideology. While he basically agreed with Marx's conclusions, Mannheim contributed an analysis of ideology from a historical perspective. He compared the ideology of one historical era to that of another, arguing that no ideology could be fully understood unless this historical relationship was clear. No ideology, in other words, can be understood unless we grasp the ideas of the previous era and investigate the impact of the previous ideology on the current one.

Contemporary Definitions

Americans tend not to view political issues ideologically. Impatient with theoretical arguments, they consider ideologies idealistic and impractical concepts. Yet, political theory gives us statements of objectives by which to guide our actions and by which to assess our accomplishments. Without theory, political policy can be shortsighted and inconsistent. Hence, most political scientists readily agree that ideology is an important factor in our lives. Alas, they are no closer than earlier authorities to an agreement on exactly what the term means.

Frederick Watkins, in his insightful book, *The Age of Ideology,* suggests that ideology comes almost entirely from the political extremes. Ideologies, he argues, are always opposed to the status quo. They propose an abrupt change in the existing order; therefore, they are usually militant, revolutionary, and violent. Watkins goes on to point out that most ideologies are stated in simplistic terms, are utopian in their objectives, and usually display great faith in humankind's potential for finding success and happiness. Conservatism, because it defends the status quo and resists change, is an "anti-ideology," according to Watkins. Ideology emerged from the rationalist tradition, in which it was assumed that most problems could be solved if people applied reason rightly. As will be seen in the following chapter, however, the conservative rejects this optimistic assumption about the capacity of human reason. Hence, Watkins argues, the conservative is opposed to the basic assumption of any ideology.

This particular point occasions some difficulty. It is true that conservatives are very cautious about human reason. They are quick to argue that reason has its limits. Yet, they do not completely reject reason as a means by which a political problem can be solved. To argue, therefore, that conservatism is not an ideology may be to exaggerate.

Another modern commentator, David Ingersoll, suggests that each ideology includes an assessment of the status quo and a view of the future. The future is always represented as something better than the present or the past. Exactly what is better for the society is usually expressed in materialistic terms; for example, both Marx and Hitler envisioned a society of great bounty. In addition, Ingersoll asserts that each ideology contains a definite *plan of action* by which this better future can be attained. Indeed, the plan of action is central to any ideology, according to Ingersoll. Ideologies tend to convey a sense of urgency. Moreover, they are intended to stimulate people to achieve utopian objectives.

L. T. Sargent approaches the definition of ideology differently. He sees ideologies as based on the value systems of various societies. Yet, modern societies are complex and often contradictory. Hence, individuals within a society may not accept a single ideology; they may appropriate parts of several ideologies, or they may become completely attached to a single idea system. In any event, Sargent makes the point that ideologies are simplistic in their approach to problem solving. Ideology, he writes, "provides the believer with a picture of the world both as it is and as it should be, and, in so doing, . . . organizes the tremendous complexity of the world into something fairly simple and understandable.[2]

Finally, Terrence Ball cautions that developing too rigid a definition about what an ideology is would be to miss the point. Rather than a phenomenon composed of precise ingredients, Ball views ideology in more flexible and more academic terms. It is, he suggests, "an agenda of things to discuss, questions to ask, hypotheses to make. We should be able to use it when considering the interaction between ideas and politics. . . ."[3] For Ball, ideology exists whenever politics is motivated by intellectual rather than random impulses. Hence, the definition of ideology should not be construed narrowly or be understood to be dependent on any but the loosest criteria.

Clearly, the authorities do not agree on the definition of ideology. Opinions range widely, from the exclusive views of Watkins to the expansive perspective of Ball. Whatever the matter, it is clear that, at least for our purposes, five properties can be identified that are significant to the definition of ideology. It may be true, as Ball implies, that not all of these factors are essential

---

[2]L. T. Sargent, *Contemporary Political Ideologies*, rev. ed. (Homewood, IL.: Dorsey Press, 1972), p. 1.

[3]Terrence Ball and Richard Dagger, eds., *Ideals and Ideologies*, 2nd ed. (New York, Harper-Collins, 1995).

for ideology, but, at the same time, these factors are both common and important in the ideologies we will study.

Ideology is first and foremost a political term, though it can be applied to other contexts. Second, ideology consists of a view of the present and a vision of the future. The preferred future is presented as a materialistic improvement over the present. This desirable future condition is often attainable, according to the ideology, within a single lifetime. As a result one of the outstanding features of an ideology is its offer of hope. Third, ideology is action-oriented. It not only describes reality and offers a better future, but most important, it gives specific directions about the steps that must be taken to attain this goal. Fourth, ideology is directed toward the masses. If nothing else, John Locke, Karl Marx, Benito Mussolini, Vladimir Lenin, Mao Tse-tung, and Adolf Hitler had one thing in common: They directed their appeal to the masses. They were interested in mobilizing huge numbers of people. Finally, because ideologies are directed at the masses, they are usually couched in fairly simple terms that can be understood by ordinary people. For the same reason ideologies are usually motivational in tone, tending to call on people to make a great effort to attain the ideological goals. This mass appeal in itself implies confidence in people's ability to improve their lives through positive action. *All modern societies are democratic in this sense of the word.*

Applying these criteria to documents, seemingly so different from one another as the *Declaration of Independence* and to the *Communist Manifesto,* we

Thomas Jefferson (1743–1826)
Rembrant Peale portrait.
White House Collection

can see that the two tracts are not only ideological statements, but we also learn that they are very similar in important ways. Each of them is assuredly political. They each made statements about the world as seen by their authors and, implicitly at least, conjured how the world could be better. These observations were set out in common, assertive language for the times in which they were written, and they were each addressed to a wide readership. **Thomas Jefferson** wrote of the existence of certain inalienable rights and contended that governments were created to further these rights. He then went on to allege a large number of British violations of American rights. Similarly, Karl Marx focused on the essential equality of people and lamented that society had been divided into exploiting and exploited social classes. Finally, each document calls for action—the same action, interestingly enough: revolution. Each author claimed that the downtrodden have an inherent right to rise up and cast off their oppressors or exploiters.

In these terms, the two essays are virtually identical. They differ, of course. Jefferson asserted the authority of natural law, but he confined his statement to explaining why the Anglo-American colonies were in rebellion against the British government. Any invitation for others to engage in rebellion could only be inferred. Marx, on the other hand, invoked what he understood to be economic laws governing people and he called on workers *everywhere* to unite and to make themselves free. The theoretical differences and the intended focus of each essay aside, however, the two documents are very similar as ideological statements.

REVIEW

- Ideologies accompany humankind's increased effort to explain political and social phenomenon rationally.
- Ideologies are the result of efforts to make political accommodations to the conditions created by the Industrial Revolution.
- *Ideologies* was a term originally used in an objective way to explain the origin of ideas. Later, however, ideologies came to be understood as subjective political rationalizations.
- Today, ideologies are understood to be political statements that call upon the masses to act in some way in order to improve political life.

SUGGESTIONS FOR FURTHER READING

ABERCROMBIE, NICHOLAS, et al., *Dominant Ideologies*. New York: Routledge Chapman, 1990.

ADAMS, IAN, *Political Ideologies Today*. New York: St. Martin's Press, 1993.

BALL, STEPHEN J., *Ideals and Ideology*. New York: HarperCollins, 1991.

BALL, TERRENCE, and RICHARD DAGGER, *Ideals and Ideologies*. 2nd ed. New York: HarperCollins, 1995.

BELL, DANIEL, *The End of Ideology.* New York: Free Press, 1960.

CHRISTENSON, REO M., ALAN S. ENGEL, DAN N. JACOBS, MOSTAFA REJAL, and HERBERT WALTZER, *Ideologies and Modern Politics*, 3rd ed. New York: Harper & Row, 1981.

COX, RICHARD H., *Ideology, Politics, and Political Theory.* Belmont, CA.: Wadsworth, 1969.

EAGLETON, TERRY, *Ideology.* White Plains, NY: Longman, 1994.

HACKER, ANDREW, *The Study of Politics: The Western Tradition and American Origins*, 2nd ed. New York: McGraw-Hill, 1973.

INGERSOLL, DAVID E., and RICHARD K. MATTHEWS, *The Philosophic Roots of Modern Ideology*, 2nd ed. Englewood Cliffs, NJ: Prentice Hall, 1991.

JENKINS, THOMAS P., *The Study of Political Theory.* New York: Random House, 1955.

MARX, KARL, and FRIEDRICH ENGELS, *The German Ideology* (1846). London: Lawrence & Wishart, 1967.

SUSSER, BERNARD, *The Grammar of Modern Ideology.* Needham Heights, NY: Allyn & Bacon, 1994.

TINDER, GLEN, *Political Thinking*, 6th ed., New York: HarperCollins, 1995.

TORRANCE, JOHN, *Karl Marx's Theory of Ideas.* New York: Cambridge University Press, 1995.

WATKINS, FREDERICK M., *The Age of Ideology: Political Thought, 1950 to the Present*, 2nd ed. Englewood Cliffs, NJ: Prentice Hall, 1969.

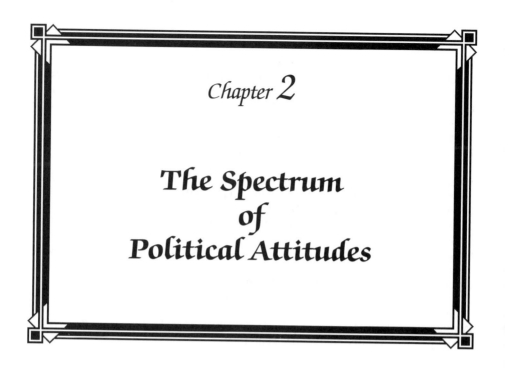

Chapter 2

The Spectrum
of
Political Attitudes

PREVIEW

The terms radical, liberal, moderate, conservative, and reactionary are among the words most often used in political discourse. The concepts of political change and political values must be discussed in relationship to these five terms in order to gain a clear understanding of what these words represent. Radicals, those farthest to the left, are people who find themselves extremely discontented with the status quo. Consequently, they wish an immediate and profound change in the existing order, advocating something new and different.

Considerably less dissatisfied than the radicals, but still wishing to change the system significantly, are the liberals. Liberalism enjoys a philosophical base which is divided into classical and contemporary eras. Although classical liberals tended to focus on the individual and on property rights while contemporary liberals view people in collective terms and emphasize human rights, both share a belief in the equality, intelligence, competence, and goodness of people.

Moderates find little evil in the existing society, and their reluctance to change it is exceeded only by that of the conservatives. Differing from liberals in almost every respect, conservatives have little confidence in human morality or intelligence. Consequently, though the world may not be as pleasant as the conservatives might wish, they are dubious about efforts to change it for fear that incompetent meddling might, indeed, make things worse. Only the reactionaries propose that institutions of previous eras be reinstated. Rejecting modern values, reactionaries would see society retrace its steps and adopt former political systems.

Being clear about the values people hold is usually more revealing about the place they occupy on the spectrum than simply knowing what policy changes they advocate. Basically, people on the right of the political spectrum revere authority, elitism, and property rights, while those on the left emphasize liberty, human equality, and human rights.

Beyond these philosophical convictions, there are several other motivations that cause people to lean to the left or right. Psychological factors about the need for change are important. Economic circumstances also play a part. Age is another factor. Finally, one's view of what human nature is is probably the most important determinant about with which side of the spectrum one will identify.

Each of these factors predisposes people's political advocacies to certain policy alternatives. The recent controversy in the United States over the conservative "supply side" economics as opposed to the "demand side" economics favored by liberals is an excellent case in point.

UNDERSTANDING THE SPECTRUM

Before going further in our discussion of ideologies, it is a good idea to develop an understanding of certain basic political concepts. The terms *radical, liberal, moderate, conservative,* and *reactionary* are among the most commonly heard words in political discussion. Being used in political debate, these terms are often employed to convey the speaker's or writer's bias. In these pages, however, no value judgments are implied in the use of any of the terms. Our objective is to understand the terms, not to label them as necessarily good or bad. Later, you may choose to ascribe your own values to each term, but for now let us satisfy ourselves with determining what each means in political contexts.

Actually, any coherent explanation of these political terms must include consideration of two basic concepts: *change* and *values*. We will begin with an analysis of the concept of political change. We shall then turn to an investigation of the meanings of these terms as they relate to intent, or political values. Before proceeding, however, we should arrange the terms *radical, liberal, moderate, conservative,* and *reactionary* along a continuum in order to gain a pictorial perspective on them. (See Figure 2–1.)

When they are arrayed from left to right in this fashion, we can see certain relationships among the terms with which we are concerned. For in-

FIGURE 2–1 The Political Spectrum

stance, the radical is at the far left of the spectrum, and the reactionary is at the opposite extreme. This alignment tells us something important. In politics the term *radical* means an extremist of the left but not of the right.[1] In everyday conversation, on the other hand, the term *radical* is usually used simply to refer to something extreme, with no reference to either side of the spectrum or any particular philosophical conviction.

CHANGE

People at each point on the political spectrum have an attitude about changing the existing political system (the *status quo*). Political change is fundamental to any society. By learning each group's attitude about change, we will be taking a large step toward understanding what the terms radical, liberal, moderate, conservative, and reactionary mean.

Political change can be a very complex subject. With reference to the spectrum of political attitudes, we must actually learn four things about change. First, we must determine the *direction* in which the proposed change would carry society. Is it progressive or retrogressive? Will it carry society forward or backward?

At this point the reader should be on guard. Our society generally has a favorable bias toward progress. This is so because our ideological origins are rooted in eighteenth-century British liberalism, which advocated progressive change. But, in fact, progress is not necessarily good or bad. It has no intrinsic value at all. *Progressive* change simply means a change from the status quo to something new and different. Conversely, *retrogressive* change refers to a return to a policy or institution that has been used by that society in the past. For instance, if one were to support the adoption of a compulsory public medical-insurance program, such a position (in the United States) would be a progressive attitude toward the government's role in the field of public health. On the other hand, one might favor returning the present United States Postal Service to its previous status within the President's cabinet. Such a position would clearly be retrogressive in this society. The watershed between progressive and retrogressive change lies between the conservative and reactionary sectors on the spectrum, and the line between these two sectors can be taken to represent no change at all, or continuation of the status quo. (See Figure 2–2.) In other words, everyone to the left of reactionary is progressive. Even conservatives are progressives in that, while they do not want a great deal of change to the status quo, the change they will allow is a transformation from what currently exists to that which the so-

---

[1]The terms *left* and *right* come to us from the French political tradition. Those who generally supported the policies of the monarch were seated to his right, and those who proposed changes in the system were arranged to his left.

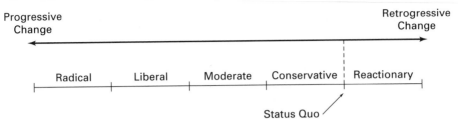

FIGURE 2–2   The Position of Status Quo on the Political Spectrum

ciety has yet to experience. Only the reactionary wants a change from the status quo to something that existed previously.

At this point some people might protest that they consider themselves conservative, but that on a given issue they prefer a previous institution to the present one. Does this make them reactionaries? Yes, it does—in relation to that particular issue. Although they might correctly consider themselves conservative as a general rule, they—like most of us—will find themselves at several different places on the spectrum in relation to a variety of specific issues. Few of us are absolutely consistent in our views, nor is there any particular reason to be so. Indeed, upon careful scrutiny most people will find it difficult to place themselves in any single category because their attitudes on various issues will range over two or even three sectors on the spectrum. Typically, however, we can identify a general pattern; that is, we might find ourselves supporting liberal policies more frequently than any other position on the spectrum, and consequently we might correctly characterize ourselves as liberals, even though our views on a few ideas might not be liberal.

The second thing one must determine is the *depth* of a proposed change. Would the desired change amount to a major or a minor adjustment in the society? Would it modify or replace an institution that is fundamental to the society as it now exists? If so, what is the likelihood that the proposed change will cause unforeseeable and uncontrollable effects once it is implemented? For example, a proposal at the state level to require a course in introductory political science for graduation from college would undoubtedly inconvenience and annoy some students. However, such a policy change would probably have almost no disruptive effect on the society as a whole. On the other hand, if a state were to greatly reduce its funding of the college system, the impact of such a policy would be enormous, changing thousands and perhaps millions of lives and eventually affecting the society as a whole. Further, although it is possible to anticipate some of the consequences of such a policy change, it is impossible to accurately predict all, or even most, of the subsequent changes, problems, or benefits that might result from such an action. As a general rule, the more basic the change, the more unpredictable, disruptive, and uncontrollable its effects.

Once again, as with the direction of change, the watershed for the depth of change is at the line between conservative and reactionary, or at the "status quo" point on the spectrum. The farther people find themselves from the status quo, the more dissatisfied they are with the existing order and the more intense their desire for change. (See Figure 2–3.)

With the questions of the direction and the depth of change settled, the third aspect we must consider is the *speed* at which people want change to occur. Obviously, the more upset people are with the status quo, the more impatient they are likely to be and, therefore, the more rapidly they would like to see the existing order modified. Hence, although it cannot be claimed that there is an absolute correspondence between the depth of change people desire and the speed at which they would like to see modification occur, it is possible to argue that there is often a general correspondence between the two. Because both attitudes relate to a common factor (the status quo), the intensity with which people feel alienated from the existing system usually corresponds with the depth and rapidity of the change that they desire.

The last factor we must consider regarding the concept of change is the *method* by which it occurs. Political change can take place in a multitude of ways: officially or unofficially; legally, illegally, or extralegally; smoothly or abruptly; peacefully or violently. It is tempting for some people to conclude that those who would use violence to gain their political objectives are extremists. This, however, is not necessarily the case. True, violence is a major tool of certain extremist political groups. However, *violence is used by people at practically every point on the political spectrum.* The death penalty, property expropriation, certain police techniques, and warfare itself are examples of forms of violence supported by people distributed all along the political continuum. Thus, it is unwise to jump to conclusions about the methods others use to accomplish their political goals.

It is possible, however, to make some generalizations about the methods employed for political change. For example, the farther we are from the status quo on the political spectrum, the more likely we are to find ourselves in opposition to the laws of the society. This is so because the law is a form of communication that sets forth the purposes, goals, and structure of the society. People who are opposed to those purposes, goals, or structure will necessarily be at odds with the law. Hence, it is usually easier for conservatives to be law-abiding and patriotic, since they are satisfied with the system. Radicals, liberals, or reactionaries, by contrast, find it much more difficult to

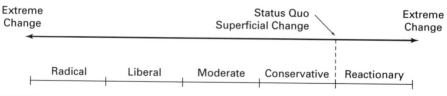

FIGURE 2–3   The Desire for Change as Shown on the Political Spectrum

abide willingly by all the laws or to wave the flag as enthusiastically as their conservative counterparts.

Nevertheless, one should not assume from this discussion that conservatives would never violate the law to gain their political objectives. It sometimes happens that even those who control the laws of a society may not benefit from them at a given time. In such circumstances it is not unlikely that an otherwise upstanding "pillar of society" would ignore or even violate the law. Examples include the incredible career of the "law-and-order-man" Richard M. Nixon, the refusal of corporations to comply with legislated health and safety requirements, and the scheme of landlords to paint their homes in the suburbs and write off the cost as maintenance for their rental properties in the central city. Even the administration of President Reagan, the most conservative in decades, chalked up a record—unequaled by any in our history—for people convicted of corruption in office: witness the exploits of Lieutenant Colonel Oliver North and National Security Adviser Admiral John Poindexter, public officials who admitted deliberate violations of the law to address what they regarded as more important principles. Thus, it should be clear that the methods people use to achieve political change are complex. It is inaccurate to conclude that certain methods are the monopoly of a single sector of the political spectrum. It is usually safe to say, however, that those who identify least with the existing order are most apt to resort to illegal and perhaps violent means to bring about change.

With the preceding general guide in mind, let us now turn to a consideration of each term on the political spectrum to determine the specific attitude of each group toward the concept of political change.

Radical

In general terms, a **radical** may be defined as a person who is extremely dissatisfied with the society as it is and therefore is impatient with less than extreme proposals for changing it. Hence, all radicals would favor an immediate and fundamental change in the society. In other words, *all radicals favor revolutionary change.* The criteria that distinguish one radical from another most clearly are the methods they would use to bring about a particular change. To illustrate this distinction, the radical sector has been divided into four sections in Figure 2–4. Note that these divisions are not intended to imply that there are only four different kinds of radicals. Rather, they are intended simply to point out the differences in degree with regard to the methods radicals might employ to get what they want politically.

Section A is, of course, the most extreme radical position. Individuals this far out on the political spectrum are extremely dissatisfied with the existing order and are probably greatly frustrated by it. Therefore, they propose not only that the system be *immediately* changed at its *foundations* but that it be changed by *violent* means. They believe that the society is so corrupt and

FIGURE 2–4 Radicalism on the Political Spectrum

so perverted that only fire will cleanse it. They argue that if change were to occur by any method short of violence, the reformers would have to compromise with the very people who are corrupting the present system, and that such a compromise would infect the new system with the same evils that made the previous one unacceptable. Hence, one must "burn [the system] down and rebuilt on its ashes."

Sections B and C are variations on the same theme. People in these sections are displeased and frustrated by the existing system. Yet, since their position on the spectrum is slightly less distant from the status quo, one can expect that the intensity of their frustration, impatience, and extremism is somewhat tempered. Each group proposes basic change in the society and argues that the change must occur immediately, but they differ with the people in Section A, and with each other, over the need for violence. People in Section B argue that although violence is not essential to meaningful change, it is probably necessary. Because the change they propose is so disruptive of the status quo, those in Section B believe that anyone who supports the existing order "would rather fight than switch." Yet, the people in Section B do not insist that violence is the only way of bringing about meaningful change; they simply believe that it is the most likely way.

Those who find themselves in Section C of the radical sector are very reluctant to use violence as a method of bringing about change. They would use it only as a last resort. In other words, they are also frustrated with the system, and they also propose fundamental and immediate change, but violence is to be used only if change is impossible by any other means. If, however, they were asked to choose between change with violence and no change without violence, they would opt for the former.

Many casual observers assume that all radicals are violent. This assumption is definitely not the case. *Not all radicals are violent; some are pacifists.* Considering the current values of most societies, refusal to fight for one's country constitutes an abrupt break with the norm and is therefore a radical position, but it is obviously not a violent one. Political *pacifists* are appropriately counted among the radicals because their refusal to use violence for political objectives is founded on an extreme belief in human rights. As you will soon learn, human rights is a value held sacred on the left side of the political spectrum.

Section D is where political pacifists are located on the spectrum. Like other radicals, pacifists propose fundamental and immediate change in the society, but they *refuse to use violence* to accomplish their political objectives.

Excellent examples of this kind of attitude can be found in the careers of Mahatma Gandhi, Dr. Martin Luther King, Jr., and farm labor leader Cesar Chavez. Each leader organized great social movements demanding immediate and profound change, yet each refused to use violence to reach his goals, even after he had suffered violence at the hands of supporters of the status quo.

Having established that people can be radical without relying on violence, we confront an apparent contradiction. Earlier I said that all radicals favor revolution. Yet, if some radicals are pacifists, how can all radicals be revolutionary? The answer can easily be found by clearing up another common misunderstanding. People normally believe that all revolutions are violent. But, this is not so at all. Violence is not inherent in revolution. The term **revolution** means a profound or fundamental change in a social, economic, cultural, or political system that occurs in a relatively brief period. Violence often accompanies revolution because fundamental change occurring over a short period of time is likely to stimulate deep-seated anxieties, which may erupt in conflict. Yet, bona fide revolutions have occurred which have not provoked widespread acts of violence. Hence, while the American, French, and Russian revolutions were violent transformations of the political order of those countries, the Renaissance and England's Glorious Revolution represented fundamental change in society without violence. Thus, they qualify as revolutions even though they were essentially peaceful.

Even though not all radicals are violent and not all revolutions provoke conflict, radicals tend to be received by their adversaries with inordinately severe reactions. Owing a great debt to the philosophy of **Jean Jacques Rousseau,** contemporary radicals make the establishment terribly uncomfortable. Extreme leftists challenge the most cherished values and assumptions of society. They reject the institutions of the establishment, calling for a more humane, egalitarian, and idealistic social and political system. In fact, they demand a society which many of us desire in the ideal but which, for practical reasons or for reasons of expedience or lack of commitment, we have been unable or perhaps unwilling to create. Put differently, the radical causes us to wonder if indeed we did not fail—if we settled for a less than perfect world because it was more convenient.

The radicals' contempt for society's values is so complete, their remedies so unorthodox, and, perhaps, the establishment's feelings of guilt at the thought that it may have failed so threatening, radicals are often feared with an intensity far beyond what is necessary to deal adequately with the challenge they pose. Accordingly, even though their numbers and influence do not demand such severe action, radical movements are often abjectly and totally crushed. The emotions prevalent among the establishment as a result of the New Left activities in the late 1960s and early 1970s reached levels far beyond those that should have existed given the meager size and power of the movement. This exaggerated response occurred not because the challenge threatened to succeed—far from it. The establishment's response, culminating in the Chicago "police riot" which put down the Yippies in 1968, the shooting at Kent State University in 1970, and the 1970 peace march on Washington, D.C., during which 10,000 people were arrested in a single weekend, assumed violent proportions for different reasons. The frightening thing about the New Left movement was that some of the nation's youth totally rejected the values of their parents. The young radicals drove home the horrifying specter that the establishment generation had built lives on a series of naive and shallow values: that the adults, worshipping materialistic idols, had wasted their lives in pursuit of false goals which the youth, the nation's sons and daughters, contemptuously rejected. Clearly, this proposition could not be quietly accepted, and it was too terrifying to ignore. The perpetrators of such a disquieting challenge had to be smashed!

Liberal

Since the liberal sector is closer to the status quo point on the continuum than the radical category, the **liberal** is significantly less dissatisfied with the existing society than the radical. Indeed, the liberal supports the basic features of that society. However, liberals are quick to recognize weaknesses in the society and therefore are anxious to reform the system. In general terms, liberals are not nearly as frustrated with the society as are rad-

In 1970, protesting students were fired upon by National Guard troops at Kent State University in Ohio.   Kent State University News Service

icals, but they are impatient with its deficiencies and therefore favor rapid and relatively far-reaching, progressive changes in the society.

One of the most fundamental differences between the radical and the liberal is the attitude of each toward the law. Since radicals are basically opposed to the political system that governs them, they are apt to see the law as one way in which those who dominate the society maintain their control. Hence, radicals find it hard to respect the law. Liberals, on the other hand, generally respect the concept of the law, and although they may want to change certain specifics of it, they usually will not violate it. Instead, they try to change the law through legal procedures. Liberals seek change in the system by several important means, but they reject any attempt to revolutionize the system because they support its essentials.

Liberalism is one of the intellectual by-products of the Enlightenment, of the scientific method, and ultimately of the Industrial Revolution. During the medieval era, people looked heavenward for Divine relief from their wretched earthly existence. Faith in human potential, as well as esteem for humankind in general, was very low. However, the discoveries of inquisitive people such as Copernicus, Galileo, and Bacon revolutionized people's attitudes toward themselves and their function in life. Through use of the scientific method, people began to make improvements in their material existence, and in so doing they began to develop confidence in their ability to solve many problems that they had previously borne with little complaint. It was not long before people began to conclude that if technological problems could be solved through the use of human reason, the same could be done with social and political problems.

This speculation led to the theory of liberalism. Optimism about people's ability to solve their problems through the use of reason is the keynote of liberalism. Accordingly, liberals are apt to apply reason to every problem and to be confident that, if a solution can be found, it will be discovered by rational exercise, rather than by other means. Liberals, therefore, tend to address social difficulties with a vigor that conservatives see as meddlesome and overly confident. The liberals' willingness to "trifle" with "tried and true" social institutions in efforts to improve them causes many conservatives, those who do not share such confidence in human reason, anxiety and disquiet.

Change has remained the major tool of liberalism throughout its long history. Consequently, its specific objectives have been revised from time to time. What was once desirable to liberals may be passé and unacceptable to them today, so that the exact meaning of liberalism has evolved over the years. For example, the original, or **classical liberals,** whose principal spokesman was **John Locke** (1632–1704), believed that all human beings were moral, competent, and intelligent. Further, Locke asserted that **natural law** (that is, certain rules of nature governing human conduct that could be discovered through the use of human reason) applied to all people in equal measure, thus assuring their fundamental moral equality. Revering the individual above all things in society, classical liberals believed that government oppressed people when it had too much power—therefore, the less government the better. In addition, private property was held in high esteem. Indeed, classical liberals believed that property was a *natural right* and that an individual's possessions were to be protected from government confiscation. More of this theory will be explained in Chapter 4, but for now it is sufficient to say that liberals have since moved beyond Locke's views.

Contemporary liberalism, as well be seen in Chapter 5, was fathered by **Jeremy Bentham** (1748–1832), and its followers continue to uphold several of the notions developed by their classical predecessors. Still viewing people as essentially good and intelligent, contemporary liberals remain optimistic about our ability to improve life through reason. Change, therefore, is still a major tool of the liberal. Human equality is another concept that the liberal continues to support, but the basis for the assumption of equality has changed. Few liberals still believe in the concept of natural law. Instead, the contemporary liberal is more likely to argue that although there is a wide variety of differences among individuals, all people are equally human, and their equality with one another is a matter of great importance. Therefore, since no person is more or less human than any other, and since equals have no moral right to treat one another unequally, all people have the right to expect certain treatment and consideration from other people. These are called the *human rights.*

In addition, contemporary liberals prefer to use government as a tool to help improve the conditions of human life, rather than insisting, as did the classical liberals, that government stay out of people's affairs. Moreover, finding that some people have used their control of property to unfair advantage over less fortunate individuals, contemporary liberals temper their belief in the individual's right to accumulate property with their concern for the happiness of the society as a whole.

Moderate

It is somewhat awkward to write about moderates because, unlike the other positions on the political spectrum, there is no philosophical foundation for the moderates' category. One could cite Aristotle's advice about seeking the Golden Mean of course, but even this attitude is more one of temperament than philosophy. One must be moderately something, either moderately right or moderately left; one is either moderately liberal or moderately conservative. I introduce the moderate category in this text only because it is so often used in political discussion to describe those who find themselves liberal or conservative about some things, but not really committed with any degree of intensity to either side of the spectrum.

Moderates are fundamentally satisfied with the society, although they agree that there is room for improvement and recognize several specific areas in need of modification. However, they insist that changes in the system should be made gradually and that no change should be so extreme as to disrupt the society. Because there is a bias toward moderation in our society, we must be vigilant in our study of this political sector. Moderation as a cultural predisposition, for example, has elicited biting criticism from the fascists, who maintain that tolerance rewards mediocrity and discourages the unusual or excellent. Meanwhile, some leftists argue that resistance to serious reform benefits the status quo at the expense of the downtrodden masses.

To say that being a moderate is only to take a mild stand on the issues is not to suggest that being moderate is always easy. Being moderate on an issue that engenders in most other people a highly emotional response can be very difficult indeed. For example, holding a moderate position on whether abortion should be legal could be problematical. Affirmative action, the death penalty, and feminism are other examples of issues on which the pro and con sides have so hardened that a less than absolutist stance can be unfairly seen as faint-hearted, ambivalent, and uncommitted. Whatever the case, it must be remembered that moderation, unlike liberalism, conservatism, reactionaryism, and radicalism, is a matter more of intensity of conviction than one of philosophical conviction.

Conservative

Conservatives are the most supportive of the status quo, and therefore are reluctant to see it changed. Being content with things as they are does not suggest that conservatives are necessarily happy with the existing system, however. Conservatives are often accused of lacking vision, but this charge is unfair. The difference between conservatives and liberals is not founded on the fact that the latter dream of achieving a better world while the former think the status quo is the best conceivable existence. In fact, conservatives may desire a future no less pleasant than the liberals—a future free of human conflict and suffering. The essential difference between the two viewpoints rests on their respective confidence in when (or, indeed, whether) the ideal can be accomplished. Thus, conservatives support the status quo not so much because they like it but because they believe that it is the best that can be achieved at the moment. Put differently, conservatives oppose change because they doubt that it will result in something better, not because they do not desire improvement.

Lacking confidence in society's ability to achieve improvements through bold policy initiatives, most conservatives support only very slow and superficial alteration of the system. The most cautious of them often resist even seemingly minor change. They tend to see an intrinsic value in existing institutions and are unwilling to tamper with them, claiming that to do so might seriously damage that which tradition has perfected.

To say that conservatives are satisfied with the status quo is certainly not to say that they are complacent. Indeed, conservatives are active not in seeking change, like their counterparts on the left, but in defending the system against those who they believe threaten it.

Of course, not all conservatives are equally resistant to change. Obviously, those closest to the status quo point on the spectrum are the least inclined to desire change. And, although it seems unlikely that many people are absolutely content with the system and are opposed to any change whatsoever, some people do take this position, and each of us could probably find some issues in which we would prefer no change at all. Still, most conservatives will accept some deviation from the status quo, be it ever so slight, and the change they will accept is progressive.

The primary reason conservatives are suspicious about the prospects of improving society through deliberate political policy is that they do not believe human reason is powerful enough to even completely understand, let alone solve society's problems. While they do not deny the existence of reason, they are wary of relying too heavily on it for solutions to human problems. Liberals and conservatives agree that people have complex natures composed of moral and immoral, rational and irrational impulses. They differ, however, on which attributes dominate. Liberals believe that human reason is powerful, that it can be successfully used to solve society's problems, and that it can also be employed by people to overcome impulses to do harm. Thus, liberals see human beings are trustworthy creatures that will normally behave themselves when left alone. Conservatives have less faith than liberals that people can use reason to restrain their animalistic impulses and their emotions; they mistrust human nature. Conservatives see people as relatively base and even somewhat sinister. Hence, the conservative view tends to favor authoritarian controls over the individuals in society.

Because they mistrust reason, conservatives often rely on irrationalist[2] rather than rationalist solutions to problems. For example, conservatives are more apt to found their religious beliefs on faith alone, while liberals seek more rationalistic bases for spiritual solace. Hence, the former are likely to

---

[2]The term *irrationlist* is not intended to imply that conservatives lack the rational or intellectual prowess of their opponents. In this book the term *irrationalist* only applies to persons who see severe limitations in people's ability to solve problems through the use of reason. While reason is thought useful for certain minor tasks, conservatives look instead to elements beyond their own control such as institutions, authority, tradition, and religion for answers to the most serious difficulties.

Our society is a product of the liberal tradition. The philosophies upon which our civilization is based imply confidence in human rationality to grasp the complexities of life and to improve conditions by using thought. Consequently, to be a *rationalist* is usually considered a positive trait and to be an irrationalist, a negative one. These, however, are value judgments that I do not ascribe to liberal and conservative camps. Indeed, no value at all is applied to the terms *rationalist* and *irrationalist* in these pages. They are used only to describe attitudes regarding the potential human reason.

gravitate toward fundamentalist faiths—witness the religious right-wing currently so prominent in contemporary American politics—while religious liberals tend toward less absolutist beliefs. One must seek long and hard to find a liberal fundamentalist or a conservative Unitarian. The former faith teaches that people are essentially evil and emphasizes that fire and brimstone await the unfaithful. The latter dwells more on the positive aspects of people, emphasizing that mutual human understanding offers rewards found in no other way.

To conservatives reason is of limited use in making life better. They believe that human reason is severely limited. While it can be used to deal with minor difficulties, technological improvements, for example, it cannot be counted upon to successfully solve ponderous problems, eliminating poverty in society, for instance. Therefore, conservatives tend to place great reliance for dealing with society's problems on the passage of time, authority, institutions, and traditions. They value longevity for its own sake and believe that one of the justifications for preserving a practice or an institution is the fact that it was worthwhile in the past. Obviously, this attitude encourages very little change in society.

Liberals and conservatives differ also with respect to the concept of human equality. Here again we find a difference in emphasis dominating the debate between two antagonists. Liberals recognize that people differ from one another: Some are stronger, more intelligent, better looking than others, and so on. But, the leftist argues, these are only superficial differences. The fact that all people are human—equally human—should be the condition that predisposes our conduct toward one another. "Cut a black man and he will bleed red," they argue, emphasizing that beneath the surface all people are alike. Conservatives take the opposite view. They are quick to recognize the biological similarity among people but argue that this fact is relatively unimportant given the enormous variation of qualities among people. To the liberal protestation about everyone having red blood, conservatives respond by asking, "So what?" Emphasizing that crucial inequalities have always existed among people, conservatives insist that to attempt constructing a society on any other assumption is pure folly.

Far from a simple academic debate, the question of the importance of human equality is fundamental to politics. Politics is largely caught up in the problem of how to justly distribute wealth and power in society. If one believes that human equality is fundamental, then there can be few moral arguments for distributing societies benefits unequally. If, however, human equality is inconsequential—or does not exist at all—it would hardly be just to insist on an equal distribution of wealth and power.

Liberals believe not only that all people are equal but they go on to insist that human equality is the most important factor. Thus, liberals, and leftists in general, favor an egalitarian political and social system. While most other conservatives agree with reactionaries that human equality is a myth, because of the heavy influence of classic liberalism in the United States, American conservatives accept the principle of human equality. However, they oppose society doing much to reward human equality because, while they agree people are equal, they do not agree that human equality is important. Life, they aver, is like a race or contest. Equality is only the beginning point and therefore should not be rewarded. Instead, people's accomplishments throughout life should be rewarded. Although people are equally human, the rightists say, they did nothing to become human or equal and therefore deserve no particular political or social benefits because of it. Each of these are powerful arguments, and indeed, the way you come down on this issue will go a long way toward determining where you might find yourself on the spectrum.

Conservatism has, of course, long been a prominent political position, but it was not until **Edmund Burke** (1729–1797) put pen to paper that it was given a formal philosophical base. The well-governed society, Burke argued, is one in which people know their place. "The rich, the able, and the well-born" govern, while the people of lower social rank recognize their betters and willingly submit to their rule. Should they refuse, should the ordinary people try to govern themselves, as in France during Burke's time, the ultimate result can only be disaster, for nothing noble can come from the mediocre.

Burke was not content, however, to see the elite rule with no admonition for temperance, for while they were the best in society, they too were human and afflicted with the same frailties as the commoners, albeit to a lesser degree. The elite, according to the venerable British Parliamentarian, are responsible for ruling benevolently and effectively. Power is not to be used by the rulers to suppress the masses. Still, nothing good will result if either group pretends that inferior people share equal political rights with the ruling group. Decrying the "false" values of liberalism, Burke put his case bluntly when he wrote:

> The occupation of a hair-dresser, or of a working tallow-chandler, cannot be a matter of honor to any person—to say nothing of a number of other more servile employments. Such description of men ought not to suffer oppression from the state; but the state suffers oppression, if such as they, either individually or collectively, are permitted to rule.

Interestingly, the present conservative position on private property is very close to the classical liberal attitude. The conservative believes that private property is an inalienable right of the individual and that it is one of the important factors that distinguish one person from another. As we will see later, conservatives believe that the property right dominates virtually every other right. Consequently, government has no legitimate power to interfere with the individual's accumulation or use of private property unless this activity causes injury, death, or the destruction of another's property, and even those conditions are allowable under certain circumstances. For example, conservatives have for years opposed government safety regulations for the automobile industry even though such regulations would reduce the number of fatal car crashes. Conservatives suggest that if people really wanted stronger fenders and air bags to protect them in collisions, consumers would demand such improvements in the marketplace. They argue that requiring such features by legislation constitutes an unnecessary intrusion by government into the lives of individuals and the private affairs of auto-makers.

On the other hand, liberals usually favor government regulation of business, arguing that likely irresponsible corporate behavior encouraged by the profit motive should be tempered by the law. In the case of air bags and other auto-safety devices, liberals might assert that most people of ordinary means when shopping for cars are apt to focus on more obvious factors than safety, such as price and styling, for example. This momentary lapse, however, should not be used as an excuse to allow auto-makers to sell the public unreasonably dangerous vehicles.

Just as there are two distinctly different kinds of liberals, classical and contemporary, conservatism can also be divided. Those that might be referred to as *Tories* closely follow the prescriptions of Burke. They make no bones about the fact that the excellent of society should rule, but at the same time, they should govern with dignity and enlightenment. Tories look for leadership in a ruling class, one that has a civil duty to govern the less able. They call upon the rulers to display a selfless *noblesse oblige* (obligation of the nobility), and to govern in the interests of society as a whole. As Burke's quotation above directs, the mediocre should certainly not rule, but neither should they be oppressed. A very paternalistic notion, toryism also demands that the elite rulers govern with a social conscience and strive to do what is "best" for all people in society.

The second group, who can be called the *entrepreneurs,* are much more individualistic and sometimes almost populist in their approach. While the Tories look to an elite class to rule, the entrepreneurs believe that the nation's leaders can come from any strata of society. "The cream rises to the top," they believe, and the government and other social institutions should allow the greatest latitude possible for individual accomplishment. Otherwise, it might impede the excellent from excelling. Unlike the Tories, the entrepreneurs demand less self-restraint and rather than seeing government as an obligation of one's station, it is viewed much more as an instrument by which superior individuals can better express their own authority. Instead of viewing government as a tool to shepherd society to noble goals, entrepreneurs want to limit government restraint on individual economic behavior so as to facilitate the elevation of the excellent and the devolution of the uncompetitive. Hence private enterprise, unregulated by the government, is the principal objective of the entrepreneurs. Columnist George Will, and to a much lesser extent, former President George Bush, are American examples of toryism. But the number of American Tories is very small. Much more numerous are the entrepreneurs who are led, at least symbolically, by former President Ronald Reagan, Speaker of the House Newt Gingrich, and talk-show host Rush Limbaugh.

Their differences aside, all conservatives share similar goals. They revere tradition, history, established institutions. Most important, because they are suspicious that human beings cannot make great improvements in society through rational and deliberate efforts, conservatives of all stripe are very reluctant to see substantial change fostered.

Conservative proclivity against change is in itself very comely to many people. In fact, it is not an exaggeration to suggest that of all the arguments made by conservatives to justify their ideology, the most attractive is the promise of political *order.* The preference for discipline alone attracts many people who might otherwise be drawn to other parts of the political spectrum. Radicals and liberals offer change, new ideas, different institutions; but even if these were to succeed, the process of change itself would disrupt the society for a time. As it happens, large numbers of people have very low thresholds for disorder. Thus, change—even though it might be for the better in the long run—disturbs them and they resist it. They are even willing to suffer a system that is somewhat harmful to their interests rather than go through any kind of abrupt dislocation in the pattern of their everyday lives. Order, then, is a powerful selling point for the conservative philosophy.

Reactionary

Of all the political positions discussed here, only the reactionary proposes retrogressive change; that is, **reactionaries** favor a policy that would return society to a previous condition or even a former value system. For example, we have witnessed a reactionary revolution with the overthrow of the Shah in Iran. Without going into detail about the nature of the movement formerly headed by the Ayatollah Khomeini, we can see that his advocacy of a return to a literal application of the ancient laws in the Koran was clearly a reactionary legal posture.

In the United States two movements with reactionary beliefs have recently become popular. The *Libertarian Party* lionizes the rights of the individual and thus calls for the reversal of the New Deal reforms of the 1930s and a return to the *laissez-faire* policies that preceded them. Laissez-faire and the New Deal will be explained in detail later, for now it is enough to point out that Libertarian philosophy advocates a kind of rugged individualism and the abolition of government policies that try to mitigate the ill effects imposed on the less well-off when the well-healed use their economic power. While the Libertarian Party itself has not succeeded in winning many elections, the extreme right in the Republican Party espouses the Libertarian philosophy, and that faction has recently come to dominate both the Republican Party and its efforts in Congress.

Extremist though they are, the followers of Libertarian philosophy do not threaten anarchism or the use of individual violence in defense of personal liberties. Such, however, is the posture of people even more reactionary than the Libertarians: the people associated with militant civilian militias. Again, this ideology is explained further on, but for now it is enough simply to point out that reactionaryism is a growing force in American politics.

Before we go further with the definition of *reactionary*, however, we should return to Figures 2–1 through 2–4 and note that they are distorted in one important respect. In these diagrams the reactionary sector is no longer than any other sector, leading one to believe that a person at the extreme right of the reactionary sector is not more dissatisfied with the system than a person at the leftmost point of the conservative sector. Actually, nothing could be further from the truth. In point of fact, the person farthest to the right among reactionaries is just as frustrated as the person at the left-most point of the radical sector. To be accurate in this respect, the reactionary sector should actually be extended so that it is as long as all the progressive sectors combined. (See Figure 2–5.)

As Figure 2–5 indicates, the intensity of feelings about the status quo and the actions proposed by people at different points on the spectrum demonstrate a huge range and an enormous variety. The progression in method is similar to the progression in intent. The closer people are to the status quo, the less impatient and frustrated they are and the more socially acceptable their methods. However, just as the Marxist at the far left insists that no change without violence is valid, so too the fascist at the extreme right argues that war is good in and of itself. All reactionaries reject claims to human equality and favor distributing wealth and power unequally on the basis of race, social class, intelligence, or some other criteria. By definition, reactionaries reject notions of social progress as defined by people to their left and look backward to other, previously held norms or values.

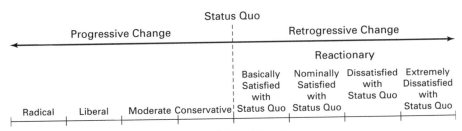

FIGURE 2–5   Reactionary Detailed on the Political Spectrum

VALUES

Having dealt with the concept of change, the reader is now prepared to distinguish a radical from a liberal or a moderate. But the perceptive reader has probably begun to wonder whether one must not know more about people than their attitudes toward change in order to understand their political orientation. For example, is it possible for a liberal and a reactionary to support exactly the same policy even when it proposes a basic change in the society? Yes, it is possible. The change itself is not important; what is significant is the anticipated result. Intent or expectation strikes at something much more fundamental in politics than simply the concept of change. It leads us to an investigation of basic political values and motivations.

For purposes of illustration, let us return to the question posed a moment ago: Can people on opposite ends of the spectrum favor the same change? The controversy surrounding abortion is a good case in point. On what grounds might abortion be supported or opposed? Although a prochoice stance is usually seen as a liberal position, some conservatives have supported abortion, arguing that such a policy would reduce the number of unwanted children among the poor, thus indirectly reducing welfare costs. Liberals supporting a woman's right to choose an abortion do so for an entirely different reason, claiming that deciding whether to have an abortion is a totally private matter, one in which the government has no business interfering. Some people's notion of morality, it is argued, should not be allowed so much authority that it denies the individual's right to privacy.

Yet, are there not opponents of abortion? Of course, there are many; they also come from both sides of the continuum. Taking a traditionalist stance, conservative opponents assert that pregnant women are morally obliged to bear their children to term and, except in extreme circumstances, they do not have the right to abort. Yet, liberals who oppose the death penalty because they reject society's right to take human life could oppose abortion for the same reason. Related issues, such as legalizing euthanasia, prostitution, and the use of heroin, can be argued on similar grounds by the various antagonists.

A slightly different variation of the same theme can be seen in the debate over the issue of public health insurance. Liberals who argue for altruistic reasons that all people should have adequate health insurance find themselves joined by the leaders of several large U.S. corporations in favor of creating a national health system. These companies, finding that the escalating cost of private health insurance policies are growing beyond the companies' abilities to pay for them, are beginning to support plans to create a national health system—something most other industrial countries have enjoyed for decades but until recently was strongly resisted as socialized medicine by corporate America. In this example, people at opposite sides of the spectrum support the same basic policy. Yet the motives of each side are quite different. The leftists argue that health care is a human right, whereas conservative corporate CEOs see a national health system as a means of reducing the costs borne by their corporations.

Clearly, then, intent, or political values, are important to our study and bear further inquiry. Unfortunately, the full complexity of the subject is beyond the scope of this book, but it must be dealt with, at least superficially, as a conflict between *property rights* and *human rights*.

Most people in our society have a fairly good understanding of human rights, since such rights appear in general terms in the Declaration of Independence and in specific terms in the Constitution of the United States, especially the Bill of Rights. Human rights include life; liberty; the pursuit of happiness; freedom of press, speech, and religion; *habeas corpus;* and so forth. These rights and liberties were incorporated into our political tradition by our country's founders, who were classical liberals.

The private property[3] right was originally thought to be a human right. Classical economists such as John Locke, Adam Smith, and David Ricardo were convinced that people could not be truly free unless they were allowed to accumulate private property. It was not long, however, before liberals observed that the control of property by some people could be used to deny liberty to others. Hence, the property right was quickly relegated to a secondary position in the priority of rights. Today it is considered a *social right*, but not a human or inalienable right, by liberals. Indeed, people as close to Locke's time as Thomas Jefferson and Jean Jacques Rousseau refused to recognize property as an inalienable right. One of the most hotly debated phrases in the proposed Declaration of Independence of 1776 was "life, liberty, and the *pursuit of happiness*" (emphasis added). People more conservative than Jefferson, its author, argued that the phrase should be changed to read "life, liberty, and *property*" (emphasis added), just as John Locke had originally written.[4] Jefferson prevailed in that debate, of course.

Liberals challenge private property as a human right on the basis that no necessary logical link exists between human well-being and *private* property. Human rights are those things that are necessary to the species in order to lead a decent human life. Consideration of the constituents of the phrase "life, liberty, and property" reveals that life is obviously an essential factor. Liberty is also fundamental if one accepts human equality as a reality. If people are equal, then no person has the moral right to subject another without consent. People, therefore, have the right to be free. Private property, however, does not enjoy similar status since it is not essential for people to lead a

---

[3]Please note that in this book the term *property* is being used in the broadest context. Hence, property refers not only to real estate but to all material items including money, clothing, furniture, and so forth.

[4]Locke actually used the word *estate* but *property* is commonly substituted for that term.

decent human life. Food, clothing, and housing are, of course, necessary for people to enjoy life, but these things need not be privately owned. Yielding to this logic, and impressed by the fact that some people use their control of property to the disadvantage of others. Jefferson penned the more general phrase "pursuit of happiness," and he successfully defended it against those who wished to substitute for it the term "property."

Later, however, in 1787, while Jefferson was serving as U.S. ambassador in France, a much more conservative group of men gathered in Philadelphia to write a new constitution. In it only scant mention was made of the rights of the people. Indeed, it was not until the Fifth Amendment was adopted that any general statement of inalienable rights appeared in the Constitution; that reference would read "life, liberty, and *property*" (emphasis added). Clearly, conservatives were in control of the country at the time.

As a general rule we can conclude that those toward the left on the political spectrum tend to give the greatest emphasis to *human rights,* while those on the right tend to emphasize *property rights.* For example, if one were to ask a liberal whether a person has the right to refuse to sell a piece of property to an African American, he or she would certainly say, "No! As long as the African American has the money to buy the property, the seller has no right to refuse to sell." Notice that liberals are not unappreciative of the property right. Clearly, they insist that the prospective buyer have the amount of money asked by the seller. With that condition satisfied, however, the liberal would require that the sale be completed. In this case the liberal's position is predicated on the assumption that an African American is morally equal to any other person. The emphasis here is definitely on human rights.

On the other hand, if the same question were put to conservatives, their response would be different. They would probably say that while racial prejudice is unfortunate, if property owners insist on refusing to sell their property to a particular person on the basis of racial prejudice, they have every right to do so. Why? Because it is *their property.* Here the conservative recognizes the conflict between human rights and property rights, but the property right obviously supersedes the human right; property holds forth over equality. The conservative, unlike the contemporary liberal, might even argue that the property right is one of the human rights. Even if that were the case, close scrutiny of the conservatives' attitude toward various human rights would show them insisting that the property right dominates all other human rights.

Let us put another question to the same test. Should you be able to shoot a person who is breaking into your home? The conservative would say yes, if that is the only way you have of defending your property. The liberal would argue that no piece of property is worth a human life and that with insurance and police protection the owner has less drastic ways to recover the property. Therefore, one does not have the right to shoot a burglar (unless, of course, the life of the owner is threatened).

The balance between human and property rights becomes increasingly one-sided as one moves toward the ends of the political spectrum until, at the farthest extremes, one side insists that there is no property right and the other totally denies human rights. On the far left, **Karl Marx** predicted that communism would be democratic, allowing absolutely no private property or inequality. **Benito Mussolini,** at the opposite extreme, denied human rights entirely, insisting that people had no justification, no rights, no reason for being that was not bound up with the nation-state. Indeed, the individual's only function was to produce for the good of the state, and anyone who failed to do so could be liquidated.

To further dramatize the differences between left and right, let us consider the various goals that arise from their respective values. As mentioned earlier, the left is inclined toward *egalitarianism*. Socialism, generally thought to be a leftist economic theory, tends to level the society and produce material equality because one of its main goals is to reduce the gap between the haves and the have-nots in a society.

Politically, leftists advocate an egalitarian society as well. Radicals tend to propose pure democracy. Both Rousseau, the founder of modern radicalism, and Marx demanded that political power be shared equally by all people. Liberals, on the other hand, accept representative government but insist that ultimate political power remain in the hands of the people.

By contrast, the right is unabashedly *elitist*. Capitalism is today a conservative economic system. This was not always so. Adam Smith, who fathered capitalism, was a classical liberal of the eighteenth century. Capitalism represented a liberal challenge to the mercantilist status quo of that time. Today, however, capitalism *is* the status quo; consequently, support of this system in a capitalist country is necessarily a conservative position.

Capitalism tends to stratify society. Those who are successful are respected and rewarded. Those who are not are abandoned as failures. The net result is that society becomes hierarchical, a circumstance thought desirable by people on the right.

Politically, rightists advocate an elitist structure as well. Believing that people are somewhat unequal, animalistic, and in need of guidance, conservative and reactionaries favor a society in which superiors command while subordinates obey. The farther to the right we look, the more structured and *authoritarian* is the desired society, until at the extreme right we come to Mussolini's fascism. Mussolini saw his society as a sort of social pyramid. At the base were the masses, whose duty was to perform their functions as well as possible. At the top of the pyramid was the party and, ultimately, the leader. The leader's function was to perceive good, justice, and right, and to rule the society accordingly. The masses were expected to obey without question because the leader was considered infallible.

Leftists, by contrast, want to maximize *personal liberties*. Believing that people will generally be well behaved when left alone, liberals tend to want government to use a light touch in regulating individual activity. Another reason liberals tend to want the police power restrained is that they usually defined acceptable human behavior in broader terms: They tend to view fewer things as being wrong than do conservatives. Many liberals, for example, believe that "victimless crimes" should not be crimes at all. Prostitution is an act between consenting adults and is no one else's business, some leftists argue. On the other hand, most conservatives insist that prostitution is morally repugnant and must therefore remain illegal. Similarly, most conservatives believe that unprescribed use of narcotics should remain illegal and the "drug war" should continue. By contrast, most liberals contend that education and treatment are more effective than is police intervention in fighting drug abuse. A growing number of leftists argue that the drug war clearly is not working and it is actually counterproductive, because in their zeal to discourage drug abuse, the authorities are trampling on the civil liberties of innocent people. They go on to suggest that the problem might be best solved by legalizing drug use. This, they aver, would take the profit away, thus removing drug pushes from the streets.

To say that conservatives use the police power more readily than do liberals is true in the area of criminal law, but in economic matters the two antagonists actually switch sides. As a general rule, conservatives are apt to believe that the wealthy deserve their bounty and that the government should protect them from attempts by the less well-off to take it from them. Government authority should not, however, be used to impede people using their property as they wish. Liberals, on the other hand, regard the wealthy with suspicion. They believe that people with economic power tend to use it to the disadvantage of the less fortunate. Accordingly, the liberals are quick to use government power to regulate individual or corporate economic behavior. Here we see the right being the more permissive of the two.

Uncharacteristically, the left has recently demonstrated that it can be even less tolerant than the right about the exercise of the civil liberties. Normally, the left accords people with the greatest latitude in free expression, for example. Yet, over the past few years, in an attempt to discourage expressions of racism, sexism, and homophobia, the left has demanded that universities adopt language codes for students and that the media and public persons avoid the use of words that certain people may find offensive. These efforts to enforce a certain *political correctness* (PC) on society has been stoutly resisted by the right, and the controversy has treated observers to a curious reversal of roles: the left trying to muzzle free speech, and the right defending it.

Finally, today's left tends toward *internationalism* and the right toward *nationalism*. Leftists speak of all people being brothers and sisters, arguing that national boundaries are artificial and unnecessary divisions setting people against one another. Marx, for instance, asserted that national boundaries would disappear between socialist systems because "working men have no country." Eventually the world would become a single socialist brotherhood. In an earlier generation French revolutionaries borrowed from Rousseau, demanding a system dedicated to "Liberty, Equality, [and] *Fraternity*" (emphasis added).[5] Conversely, fascists exalt differences between individuals within a state and dissimilarities among states. As people are ranked according to their value within a society, fascists argue, so too will state dominate state until one state rises above all others. Less extreme rightists do not necessarily demand imperialistic dominance, but they are clearly nationalists, believing that their nation is better than others and that their national interest can be placed before others. These ideas will be discussed more fully in the next chapter.

SOME GENERAL OBSERVATIONS

Before we end our discussion of political attitudes, a few general observations should be made regarding the various factors influencing individuals to take particular positions on the political spectrum.

Motivation

Many people suspect that economic pressures are the primary motivation for choosing a particular political position. This does indeed seem to be an important factor. People who are doing fairly well in a given society usually do not want to disrupt the system. On the other hand, the poor have lit-

---

[5]It is worth noting here that the fraternal, or social, aspects so prominent in the French Revolution were not very important in the American Revolution. Because America was blessed with an abundance of land and natural resources, opportunity was not as severely restricted in America as in the more stratified European societies. Hence, the American Revolution was almost completely political in nature. No serious attempt was made to realign the social structure or to redistribute the land in America. Because our revolution simply constituted a transfer of power from the English to the American elite, it has not been a model for European revolutions. It is true that the success of the American Revolution encouraged Europeans to seek change in their lives, but the changes needed in Europe were far more sweeping than those desired on the American side of the Atlantic. European revolutions became vehicles for economic and social change as well as for political transformation. Hence, the French Revolution, the world's most influential revolution, became the model for all subsequent European upheavals. Indeed, due largely to our unique social and economic environment, American politics has never been very similar to public affairs in Europe, a fact that sometimes causes serious misunderstanding on both sides.

tle to lose and much to gain from progressive change. Economics is not the only factor in the choice of a political philosophy, however. There are plenty of poor conservatives, and one can easily find rich liberals. In fact, there is no single motivation for people's political attitudes. The list of motivations is probably as great as the number of people with political attitudes. In the following paragraphs we will discuss the most important factors influencing people's political choices.

Age seems to be a significant factor. Although we currently find ourselves in an era in which the youth tend to be more conservative than any other age group, this is very rare historically. Usually, the youth is more likely to be liberal than the aged. This is probably because the older generations have a vested interest in the status quo that the younger generations have not yet acquired. Young people lack not only wealth but also a sense of commitment and belonging. Fifty-year-olds are likely to feel that they have a stake in the society, not only because they have become used to it, but also because they helped create it. The young have neither of these reasons to be committed to the system. The current conservatism of the nation's youth seems to stem from the society's emphasis on materialism, coupled with the nagging feelings among many that the economic future is unstable.

Some people are also more *psychologically suited* for liberalism or conservatism than others. To be a liberal, one must have a relatively high tolerance for disorder. Many people do not, so that while they may not benefit materially from the system, they resist change because they dislike disorder. On the other hand, some people seem to need almost constant change. The status quo never satisfies them simply because it *is* the status quo.

Perhaps the greatest single determining factor as to whether one will tend to the left or right is what he or she feels the *nature of people* to be. If one believes that people are essentially bad, selfish, and aggressive, then that person is likely to lean to the right of the spectrum. Anyone who thinks that people are inherently evil will tend to rely on strict laws and firm punishment for violators in the belief that such measures are necessary to control errant people. On the other hand, people who believe their fellows to be essentially moral and rational will lean toward the left. They will try to avoid impeding human liberty by "unnecessarily" severe laws and they will try to reason with offenders. People on the right tend to believe that prisons should be institutions for punishment, forcefully teaching transgressors to behave, whereas leftists see prisons as institutions for rehabilitation. Believing that denial of liberty is punishment enough, leftists hope to use penal institutions to school criminals in socially acceptable behavior and to give them skills that they can use to make a living honestly, thus avoiding a life of crime. The crux of the matter rests in assumptions about human nature: Are people impelled by greed and selfishness or are they motivated by more noble aspirations? How one comes down on this question will have a great deal to do with one's political views.

SPECIFIC POLICIES

At this point, it might be helpful to translate some of the previously discussed general ideological points into practical policy as related to United States politics. Basically, the politics of any country can be divided into two main arenas: foreign and domestic. Let us assume that the goals of our society can be generalized in the form of two major objectives: peace and prosperity. Since the Great Depression of the 1930s American politics has usually fluctuated along a rather narrow area of the spectrum, between mildly liberal and conservative policy alternatives. Given this fact, what specific policies might one expect from the establishment right and left in the United States in pursuit of the goals described above?

Foreign policy.   Believing that people are self-oriented and competitive, conservatives are likely to assume a relatively suspicious posture in dealing with foreign governments. Accordingly, they are apt to rely heavily upon a strong military capability to preserve the peace. Resorting to cliché, we can readily identify the slogan "The way to preserve the peace is to be prepared for war" as a distinctly conservative approach to foreign policy.

Given the propensity among conservatives to be suspicious, we can expect that the hallmark of their relations with other states will be a strong military posture buttressed by mutual defense alliances with their friends against those whom they perceive as adversaries. Their foreign aid programs will tend to emphasize military assistance, thus strengthening their allies. The thrust of their policies will be directed at guarding against the incursions of their foes. Essentially, the world is viewed in adversial terms, with the opponent seen as the aggressor. Since conflict is considered inevitable, little hope is held out for sustained amicable relations until the adversary conforms to the conservatives' views.

The liberal approach to foreign affairs is considerably different. Liberals hold that people are fundamentally moral and are capable of solving their differences rationally. Warfare is regarded as abnormal, while peace and cooperation are considered natural to human beings.

While liberals certainly do not ignore the martial aspect of foreign policy, they place much less emphasis on it than do their conservative counterparts. Their confidence in human reason is clearly apparent when they counter conservative militarism with the attitude that "the way to preserve the peace is to discover and eradicate the causes of war."

Deemphasizing military solutions, liberals tend to rely heavily on economic and technical aid to strike at what they conclude are the causes of war: poverty, disease, ignorance, intolerance, and so on. Further, liberals look to exchange programs among intellectuals, artists, and ordinary people as a means by which tensions can be reduced. This approach is based on the assumption that people will generally get along better if they understand one another; ignorance breeds fear, mistrust, anxiety, and conflict. Accordingly, liberals are likely to place great store on institutions such as the Peace Corps, the United Nations, and the World Bank, institutions which conservatives view with suspicion. Liberals support these organizations because they believe that they give the greatest promise of letting rational beings solve their problems peacefully.

Domestic policy.   As a general rule it can be assumed that, all other things being equal, liberals will spend more on domestic programs than will conservatives. This principle also pertains to foreign policy, but to a lesser extent. Liberals not only spend more money, but they release it on a broader base in the society, among people who are apt to spend it again quickly. For their part conservatives usually spend much less on domestic policy, and they release money among far fewer people—people who are also least likely to spend it again quickly. Consequently, liberal policies tend to place inflationary pressures on the economy by increasing the volume of money (the number of dollars in circulation) and the velocity of money (the frequency with which dollars are spent). Conservative policy reverses the liberal emphasis, thus exerting deflationary pressures on the economy.

A Peace Corps worker helps Nepal peasants build terracing for their fields.   Peace Corps

Specifically, conservatives argue that ours is an industrialized economy. The health of the country is therefore dependent on a sound industrial base. Hence, although government involvement in the economy should be kept to a minimum, government should engage in efforts to secure the industrial base.

This view, referred to as *supply-side economics,* calls for money to be funneled from the government directly to big business by various means, such as reduced government regulation of business, increased subsidies, increased tax write-offs, lucrative government contracts, guaranteed loans, free grants of government-funded research, high protective tariffs, low-level import quotas, and so on. The theory suggests that the captains of industry will use the added revenue to increase productivity through the purchase of new factories and machines and will also improve the condition of the workers by increasing wages, improving working conditions, and augmenting fringe benefits. Opponents refer to this as the *trickle-down* effect.

These policies, however, must be paid for by someone. Hence, conservative economic policies usually increase taxes on the poor and the middle class while reducing government services to them through cuts in social programs such as government aid to education, job training programs, social security, and so on. (See Figure 2–6.) A classic recent example of policies like these can be seen in the "Contract with America" and other initiatives of Speaker of the House, Newt Gingrich, and the Republican Congress of 1994–95.

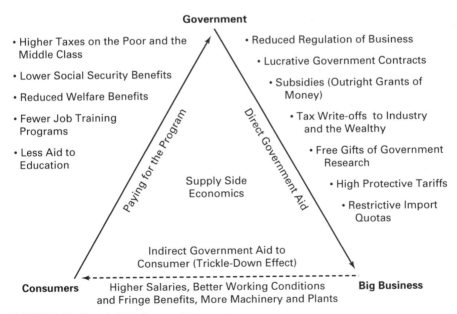

FIGURE 2–6   Supply-Side Economics

Liberals argue to the contrary, contending that people, not industry, are the nation's principle resource. The benefits of direct government support should go to the people as a whole rather than to the wealthy. Having their spending power increased by government programs, the people will purchase the goods produced by industry, thus affording it profits to increase wages and capital investments.

However, these policies must also be paid for. Hence, liberals would reverse the policies of the supply side technique, substituting what might be described as the *demand side*, which increases government regulation and taxation of big business. (See Figure 2–7.)

Interestingly, however, since liberal policies are so much more expensive than conservative programs, reversing the flow of money alone is not enough to cover the costs. Hence, besides increasing taxes on industry and the wealthy, liberals would ask the middle class to pay more taxes as well. Comprising the bulk of the taxpayers, and being less protected than the very wealthy or the very poor, the middle class would be asked to carry the bulk of the tax burden under either plan.

The arguments by each side against the other's programs are familiar. Conservatives assert that liberal programs put everyone on the government dole, destroying individual initiative and making the recipients wards of the state. Liberals respond by contending that if individual initiative is destroyed by the grant of government aid, what happens to initiative in business under the supply-side technique? Quoting George Bernard Shaw, who said, "American capitalism is really socialism for the rich," liberals ask

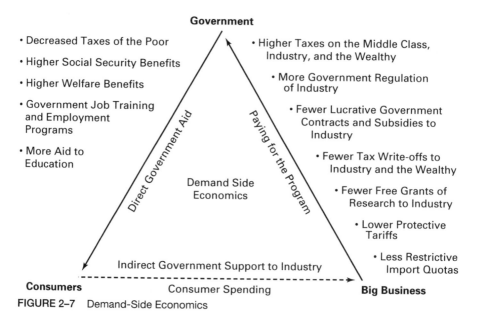

FIGURE 2–7   Demand-Side Economics

whether business is not made dependent upon government protection against competition by the supply-side model.

Liberals go on to argue that the trickle-down approach will not necessarily work. The government may release money to business in order to increase employment, for example, but business is likely to spend that money for its own purposes. Hence, the industrial owners may take greater profits from money the government meant for increasing jobs. After all, was it not just such a malfunction of the supply-side approach that caused the Great Depression?

"Ah," the conservatives respond, "if the supply-side is an inefficient method of releasing money into the economy—what of the demand side? The government may give the poor money with which to buy milk for the children but, all too often, it is spent on beer and cigarettes!" Round and round go the arguments. Each of us must decide which, if either, is right.

As a final note, the illustration shown in Figure 2–8 is offered in hopes that it will give you a more complete picture of the spectrum and thus help you understand the material in this chapter.

REVIEW

- The twin concepts of change and values must be considered when determining the placement of people on the political spectrum.
- Leftists—radicals and liberals—are discontented with things as they are and advocate progressive change.
- Conservatives are satisfied with things as they are, largely because they lack confidence in peoples' ability to use reason in order to accomplish change for the better.
- Reactionaries are not progressives; they wish to return society to previously used institutions and values.
- Leftists are rationalists. They believe human equality demands that wealth and power be distributed equally in society, and they support individual liberty and internationalism. Rightists tend to rely on irrationalism, and they believe that property and power should be awarded to the excellent, and that authority should be used to direct people.
- Many things dispose people to one place or another on the political spectrum, including economics, age, psychological proclivities, and beliefs about human nature.
- In translating ideological abstractions into specific political policy, rightists tend to support supply-side economics and a strong national defense, whereas leftists move to protect the demand-side in economics and believe in cooperative relations among all peoples of the world.

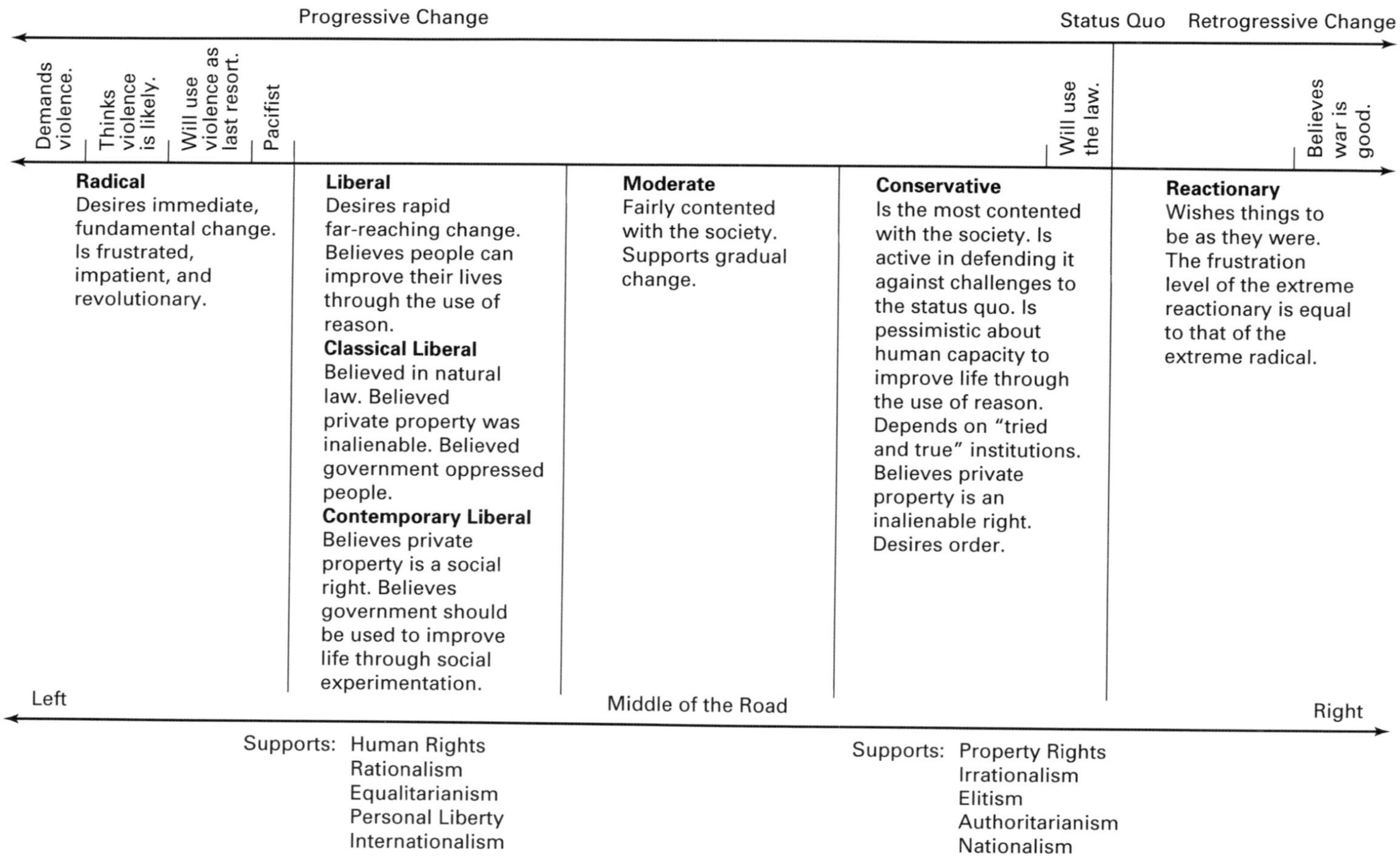

Progressive Change   Status Quo   Retrogressive Change

Radical
Desires immediate, fundamental change. Is frustrated, impatient, and revolutionary.

Demands violence.
Thinks violence is likely.
Will use violence as last resort.
Pacifist

Liberal
Desires rapid far-reaching change. Believes people can improve their lives through the use of reason.

Classical Liberal
Believed in natural law. Believed private property was inalienable. Believed government oppressed people.

Contemporary Liberal
Believes private property is a social right. Believes government should be used to improve life through social experimentation.

Moderate
Fairly contented with the society. Supports gradual change.

Conservative
Is the most contented with the society. Is active in defending it against challenges to the status quo. Is pessimistic about human capacity to improve life through the use of reason. Depends on "tried and true" institutions. Believes private property is an inalienable right. Desires order.

Will use the law.

Reactionary
Wishes things to be as they were. The frustration level of the extreme reactionary is equal to that of the extreme radical.

Believes war is good.

Left   Middle of the Road   Right

Supports: Human Rights
Rationalism
Equalitarianism
Personal Liberty
Internationalism

Supports: Property Rights
Irrationalism
Elitism
Authoritarianism
Nationalism

FIGURE 2–8   Spectrum of Political Attitudes

SUGGESTIONS FOR FURTHER READING

ASHFORD, NEGEL, and STEPHEN DAVIS, eds., *A Dictionary of Conservatism and Libertarian Thought.* New York: Routledge, 1991.

BOWLES, SAMUEL, and HERBERT GINTIS, *Democarcy and Capitalism.* New York: Basic Books, 1986.

BUCKS, PHILIP W., *How Conservatives Think.* Harmondsworth, Middlesex, England: Penguin Books, 1975.

BUCKLEY, WILLIAM F., JR., *Up From Liberalism.* New York: Hillman Books, 1961.

BURKE, EDMUND, *Reflections on the Revolution in France.* Chicago: Henry Regnery, 1955.

CARNOY, MARTIN, and DEREK SHARER, *Economic Democracy.* White Plains, NY: M. E. Sharpe, 1980.

DOLBEARE, KENNETH M., and LINDA J. MEDCALF, *American Ideologies Today.* New York: Random House, 1988.

FRIEDMAN, MILTON, and ROSE FRIEDMAN, *Freedom to Choose.* New York: Harcourt Brace Jovanovich, 1980.

GILLESPIE, ED, and BOB SCHELLHAS, eds., *Contract With America: The Bold Plan by Rep. Newt Gingrich, Rep. Dick Armey and the House Republicans to Change the Nation.* Westminster, MD: Times Books, 1994.

GREEN, KAREN, *Women of Reason: Feminism, Humanism & Political Thought.* New York: Continuum Publishing, 1995.

KIRK, RUSSELL, "Prescription, Authority, and Ordered Freedom," in *What Is Conservatism?,* ed. Frank S. Meyeer. New York: Holt, Rinehart & Winston, 1964.

———, *A Program for Conservatives.* Chicago: Henry Regnery, 1954.

KLEHR, HARVEY, *Far Left of Center: The American Radical Left Today.* New Brunswick, NJ: Transaction Press, 1990.

MURPHY, KENNETH, *Conceived in Liberty: The Rise and Transformation of Modern Conservatism.* New York: Free Press, 1994.

NISBIT, ROBERT A., *Conservatism.* Minneapolis: University of Minnesota Press, 1986.

ORTEGA Y GASSET, JOSÉ, *The Revolt of the Masses.* New York: W. W. Norton, 1960.

SIGLER, JAY A., ed., *The Conservative Tradition in American Thought.* New York: Capricorn Books, 1970.

VOLKOMER, WALTER E., ed., *The Liberal Tradition in American Thought.* New York: Capricorn Books, 1970.

YOUNG, JAMES P., *The American Liberal Tradition: A Reinterpretation.* Boulder, CO: Westview Press, 1995.

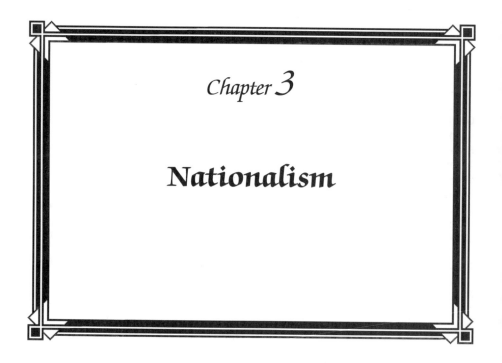

Chapter 3

Nationalism

PREVIEW

Nationalism is the theory of the nation-state, and as such it has had an enormous impact on the modern world. The terms nation and state are often confused. Nation is a sociological term referring to a group of people who have a sense of union with one another. State is a political term that includes four elements: people, territory, government, and sovereignty.

The state probably evolved when societies exchanged their nomadic lifestyle for farming. Yet, several theories of the origin of the state have had an important impact on nationalism as an ideology. The natural theory actually based its definition of humanity on the existence of the state. The divine theory suggested that a particular people was chosen by God, while the divine right of kings theory regarded the monarch as the personification of the state. The social contract theory equated the nation-state with the individuals in it, suggesting that the people are the source of legitimate political power; the force theory went further toward viewing the state as an amoral institution with few, if any, limits.

Each of these theories contributed to nationalism as the most powerful of contemporary political ideas. While patriotism is an act, gesture, or expression of loyalty to the state, nationalism is the theoretical definition and basis of the nation state. Nationalism is used as a frame of reference as well as a yardstick by which to measure and assess people and policy. It is a principle form of self-identification and thus it can both unite and divide people.

Nationalism calls on people to identify with the interests of their national group and to support the creation of a state—a nation-state—to support those interests. Nationalism has become increasingly popular since the French Revolution. Leftists have supported it as a vehicle to improve the well-being of citizens, while rightists use it to encourage unity and stability. The end of the Cold War has seen many people who were formerly controlled by the Soviet Union assert their right to national self-determination. At the same time, however, Western European countries and North American states have taken steps toward international unions, and the Muslim world has toyed with the idea of a huge, reactionary Pan-Islamic state.

THE IMPORTANCE OF NATIONALISM

Nationalism is among the oldest, and it is unquestionably the most virulent, of all ideologies. It is a phenomenon that has influenced and affected most of the other important ideologies. It would be difficult to exaggerate the importance of this concept in contemporary politics. *Nationalism is the most powerful political idea of the past several hundred years.* It has had a great impact on every person in every modern society. People who have applauded policies pursued in the name of country would have condemned the same acts if committed for any other reason. Millions of people have been sacrificed and died, property has been destroyed, and resources have been plundered in the name of the state. Yet, individuals have also risen to noble heights and made great contributions to humanity for the sake of the state. As we will see in later chapters, nationalism is so powerful that it has dominated almost every other idea system. Indeed, only anarchism rejects the state, and the only certain extreme forms of anarchism do so completely. In all other ideologies the state is given a role, and in some cases it is given the dominant place. Moreover, the appeal of nationalism has recently reasserted itself in some places, and former countries now find themselves split asunder by the conflicting and competing demands of different, once united, people. Hence, it is essential that we take up the study of nationalism early in this book. Before we consider nationalism itself, however, let us examine two terms that are essential to understanding nationalism: *nation* and *state*.

Nation and State

The term *nation* is often used as a synonym for *state* or *country*. This is not technically correct, but the mistake is commonly made by political leaders as well as by ordinary people. To be precise, the term *nation* does not have any political implication at all. Indeed, the concept of a nation is not political, but social. A nation can exist even though it is not contained within a particular state or served by a given government. A nation exists when there is a union of people based on similarities in linguistic pattern, ethnic relationship, cultural heritage, or even simple geographic proximity.

Probably the most common feature around which a nation is united is ethnic background. One's *nationality* is often expressed in terms of ethnic background rather than citizenship. Thus, while some people will respond "American" when asked their nationality, it is not uncommon for loyal United States citizens to answer "Dutch" or "Spanish" or "Latvian." These individuals are thinking of nationality as a social or ethnic term, not making a political comment. The fact that ethnic background can be the basis of a nation does not, however, mean that people must be related by blood to the members of the same nation. Switzerland, the United States, and Russia all include several ethnic groups. In fact, Russia contains almost 100 separate and distinct ethnic groups.

Even when a nation is clearly identified by its ethnic makeup, the people of that nation can be divided into any number of different states. The German people is a good example. Basically, German people make up the bulk of the populations of Germany, but the Austrian and Dutch people are also Germanic, or Teutonic, to say nothing of the inhabitants of several Swiss cantons (provinces). On the other hand, the Jews are a good example of a nation of people who, for a long time, had no country to call home. For thousands of years Jews maintained their national identity, linked by strong cultural patterns as well as by ethnic relationships, but they had no state of their own, and thus they lived in countries dominated by other national groups. Although their folklore promised a return to the homeland at some future time, the movement to set up a Jewish state in Palestine (known as *Zionism*) did not develop until the nineteenth century. Finally, in 1948 the state of Israel was created, and many Jews left their former homes for the new country. Today there are about 4 million people in the *state* of Israel, yet many members of the Jewish *nation* are still living in other lands. Both Russia and the United States, for example, have large Jewish populations.

By contrast with the Jews, the Polish nation has a long history of being encompassed by a state. Yet, from 1797 to 1919, Poland ceased to exist as a political entity, having been partitioned among its neighbors, Russia, Prussia, and Austria. The elimination of the Polish state did not spell the doom of the Polish nation, however. Bound together by a common language, intellectual tradition, history, geography, and religion, the Polish people continued to identify themselves as distinct from others, and following World War I the Polish state was created once again. After a brief period of independence, Poland was conquered by the Nazis and the Soviet Union, and from World War II until 1989, Poland was governed by a Soviet dominated communist government. If anything, the political ambiguity and the foreign domination endured by Poland served to strengthen the people's feeling that they belonged to the Polish nation. On the whole, however, in this example, politics is a relatively insignificant factor in establishing and maintaining the Polish nation.

On the other hand, while a nation need not be organized into any particular state, it is indeed possible that a nation can evolve almost solely because its people identify with one another on the basis of residing in the same country. Few would argue that the people in the Untied States are not a nation. Indeed, we are a people who enjoy a very strong national identity. Yet, what factors draw us together? Being a people of enormous racial diversity, ethnicity certainly is not the focus of our nationhood. Though we speak a common language, English plays only a marginal role in making us one people. "Baseball, hot dogs, apple pie, and Chevrolet" are hardly cultural features upon which our common bond exists. In fact, the American *nation* is founded upon the *state* itself. It is forged by popular support of concepts that can best be assimilated in the notion of the state: flag, country, democracy, liberty, tolerance, and so on. Although most Americans do not consider themselves political beings, the fact that we tend to find unity with one another primarily through the context of the state makes us very political indeed.

In contrast to the United States, the Soviet Union is a good example of a failed attempt to create a nation of people by political means. From 1917 to 1991, the Soviet Union was a single state composed of about 120 distinct national groups. Using Marxism-Leninism as the adhesive, Soviet leaders tried to create from their cosmopolitan society a single nation of people: "the new Soviet man," it was called. However, the various national groups within the country stubbornly resisted assimilation, preferring to maintain their traditional unique identities instead. Finally, in the late 1980s, when the communist system began to disintegrate, Soviet leader Mikhail S. Gorbachev, loosened the Communist party's totalitarian grip on the society. Responding to the new freedom, dozens of the national groups within the state loudly asserted their separate identities and many even demanded the right to political independence. In 1991 the Soviet Union collapsed and was replaced by fifteen independent countries, but even within most of these new countries, smaller national groups have demanded independence, or at least autonomy, from the new states in which they now find themselves. The people of Chechnya have attempted to become independent from Russia, for example. Without doubt, it will take decades for these controversies to sort themselves out. What is important for us at this point, however, is to note that, unlike in the United States, politics alone was not sufficiently strong in the Soviet Union to overcome the identities of the various national groups, and it therefore failed to coalesce them into a single nation.

Clearly therefore, the term *nation* has no necessary political implications, but this is not at all true of the term *state*. A description of the state normally includes four elements: people, territory (a defined geographical space solely associated with a particular state), sovereignty (ultimate legal authority within a given territory), and government. A nation of people can find itself spread across the globe, and its existence is not necessarily determined by its association with any specific location. All states, however, have clear territorial boundaries. Moreover, these lands are served by governments that technically have final legal authority over all the people within their boundaries. The only characteristic necessarily shared by state and nation is people. When a nation of people manage to create a state of their own, however, the resulting political entity, the *nation-state,* is very important.

The Nation-state.   The nation-state has become the principal form of political organization among modern people. Indeed, in political terms, part of the definition of a modern society is that it is organized into a nation-state. The term *nation* symbolizes the unity of a people; the term *state* politicizes that union. In this century, *national self-determination* (the right of national groups to organize their own nation-states) has become one of the most universally accepted principles, although it is far from perfectly adhered to. Thus, since the turn of the century, the family of nations has more than tripled and today stands at about 190. The nation-state has become a focal point around which people unify and through which they identify themselves and assess political events.

It should be noted at this point that while it is dominant today, the nation-state is only history's most recent authoritative form of political organization. Human beings have rallied to several other political organizations before adopting the nation-state. Among these earlier forms are tribes, city-states, empires, and feudal baronies. Since the nation-state is only the latest in a long series of systems used as principal organs of political association, it is logical to expect that the usefulness of the nation-state will eventually become marginal, thus encouraging the evolution of yet another institution to replace it. At present, however, the nation-state remains dominant.

In the United States the terms *nation* and *state* have specific meanings other than those just explained. In this country as well as in several Latin American countries that have followed our example, the term *state* has two meanings. It can mean *country,* as it has traditionally, or it can be used as a synonym for *province.* To complicate matters further, we used the word *nation* to refer to the central government. Thus, we pledge allegiance to the flag, to the Republic, and to the *Nation.* Congress is our *national* legislature, and a *national* law takes precedence over the laws of the *states.*

Theories of the Origin of the State

We are now fairly certain that the state evolved because society had a practical need for it. As farming developed; people ceased their nomadic wandering and private property became important. The state probably evolved as a way of organizing society to maximize resources which had become limited when the people stopped moving. Further, the instruments of the state were used to define, protect, and transfer property. Yet, in previous eras, philosophers and theologians explained the origins of the state in several other ways. Many of these theories are probably true in particular cases;

most of them, however, are demonstrably inaccurate, and some are even fanciful. True or not, however, these theories have motivated people, causing enormous impacts on political theory and on modern ideologies. Hence, we should at least consider the most important of them here.

The natural theory.   Aristotle, the father of political science, is an early prominent proponent of the *natural theory* of the origin of the state. He believed that people are basically good and that they constantly seek moral perfection, which they probably will never reach. Still, the quest for moral perfection is the noblest of human pursuits. Humans, according to Aristotle, are social beings by nature; that is, they naturally gather together and interact with one another, thus forming a community. This congregation takes place for reasons which go beyond simple biological necessity. The formal organization of the community is the state. The formation of the state is a result of people's natural inclinations to interact. Aristotle believed so firmly that the state was a society's natural environment that he claimed that people were human only within the state. An individual outside the state was either "a beast or a god," the state being the only environment in which one could be truly human. The state was the central institution in Aristotle's philosophy; it was not only the manifestation of our natural inclination to interact but also the vehicle through which the individual could achieve moral perfection. Expressing the same idea differently, Pericles (c. 495 B.C.–429 B.C.), Athens' most esteemed statesman said, "We alone regard a man who takes no interest in public affairs, not as a harmless but as a useless character."

To the ancient Greeks the state was not merely a natural phenomenon, it took on a much more important characteristic. While it was made up of interacting individuals, it was actually greater than any single person or any group. It became an entity with a life, rights, and obligations apart from those of the people it served. This **organic theory** of the state was later supported by diverse people such as Thomas Aquinas, Rousseau, and Mussolini. Today's leftists also often refer to the organic society.

The force theory.   The *force theory* actually embraces two schools of thought: a negative and a positive approach. The original school, the negative approach, goes back to ancient times. In this theory the state was created by conquest and force; it grew out of the forceful imposition of the strong over the weak. Therefore, the state was an evil thing that could be resisted in a righteous cause. As one might imagine, this particular attitude has been dogma to revolutionary groups through the ages: to the early Christians resisting the Roman Empire, to medieval theologians trying to make the temporal authority subject to the spiritual, to democratic insurrectionists leading the struggle against monarchical tyranny, and so forth.

The positive expression of the force theory developed in Germany during the nineteenth century. Internal political divisions and external pressures had prevented the consolidation of Italy and Germany into modern political units. A nationalistic spirit had been growing in Germany, however, since the Napoleonic wars. It became exaggerated as a result of the frustration encountered by its proponents.

The theory of the forceful origin of the state was maintained principally by **Georg Hegel** (1770–1831) and **Friedrich Nietzsche** (1844–1900). Their theories form the basis of what is now called *statism*. They argued that the state was indeed created by force, but that rather than being evil, this feature dignified the state. Force was *not* something to be avoided. On the contrary, it was the primary value in society. It was its own justification: "Might makes right," as Nietzsche put it. The state, institutionalizing the power of the strong over the weak, simply arranged affairs as they should be. According to force theorists, the weak *should* be ruled by the strong.

Some students of Hegel and Nietzsche have argued that the state is the most powerful form of human organization. As such it is above any ordinary moral or ethical restraint and it is greater than any individual. It is not limited by something as insignificant as individual rights. Although certainly neither Hegel nor Nietzsche would have been termed fascist or Nazi, Mussolini and Hitler used the force theory for their own purposes; so we shall return to a discussion of the ideas of these nineteenth century philosophers in Chapter 11. For now it is enough to remark that this version of the force theory is probably the most extreme example of nationalism. It puts the state above the people, giving government a status that cannot be equaled or surpassed. Hence, the institution itself has power separate from that of the people under it. The state is a self-contained being, an organic personality in and of itself, all-powerful and total.

The divine theory.   The *divine theory* is probably the oldest theory of the origin of the state. It is based on a fairly common assumption: Some people are God's chosen ones.

Saul, for example, was annointed by Samuel, the prophet of God, and Saul led the "chosen people" in the conquest of the Philistines. The Arabs conquered a vast empire, the Crusaders invaded the Middle East in the name of the "true religion," and Islamic fundamentalists still claim that they are the chosen ones. Similarly, the Japanese, believing they were favored by the sun goddess (Amaterasu) and convinced their emperor was her direct descendant, willingly died in the emperor's cause, thinking salvation awaited them for such martyrdom.

Early Christian theologians used the concept of the divine origin of the state to their own advantage. The early fathers of the Church, St. Ambrose (340–397), St. Augustine (354–430), and Pope Gregory the Great (540–604), argued that spiritual and temporal powers were separate but that both came from God. Each of these thinkers was ambivalent about the relationship between the state and the Church. Augustine and Ambrose implied that the state was subject to the spiritual leadership of the Church, but neither pressed the point too far. Gregory, on the other hand, believed that the Church should bow to the state in all secular affairs. Pope Gelasius I (492–496) first interpreted the **theory of the two swords** as it was to be applied during the Middle Ages. The spiritual and secular powers were both essential to human life, but they could not be joined under a single person. The primary function of each was to contribute to the salvation of people. The state helped pave the way to paradise, providing peace and order and creating the atmosphere in which people could best serve God. The Church was responsible for developing the true spiritual doctrine and giving people guidance toward their heavenly goal.

None of the early Christian fathers would have disagreed with any of these propositions. Gelasius I, however, went on to claim that the Pope should take precedence over the state. He was the first to argue that the Pope should be uncontradictable on questions of dogma. Further, he insisted that since the primary duty of both Church and state was to help people reach their eternal reward, the Church, being the *spiritual sword*, should prevail in disputes between these two basic institutions. John of Salisbury (1120–1180), a noted scholar, went even further than Gelasius I, stating that all temporal power actually came from the Church. Anyone who supported this theory would not question the superiority of the Church over the state.

The Church was generally regarded as the greater of the "two swords" throughout the medieval period, and princes normally accepted this notion, often reluctantly. Gradually, however, the intellectual advances of the Renaissance led to religious and political changes. National monarchs began to claim authority over secular affairs. At the same time, the Reformation challenged the Pope's spiritual absolutism.

Closer to home, the notion of *manifest destiny* was used to imply God's sanction for the United States conquering the North American continent and portions of the Pacific Ocean. Mormon doctrine teaches that the United States Constitution was divinely inspired, and a popular patriotic song suggests "God shed his grace on thee." Even President Reagan's 1983 assertion that the Soviet Union was an "evil empire," which threatened our survival, smacked of the divine theory born anew.

As you can see, the divine theory of the origin of the state has, at one time or another, had wide appeal. Perhaps the time in which it enjoys the greatest prominence is during war. It would be difficult to find a warring society that was not buttressed in its marshal resolve by its leaders' suggestion that God was on its side. Indeed, it is common to find that each side in a war claims for itself divine imprimatur.

Whatever the circumstances, three generalizations can be drawn about the divine theory: (1) Virtually every nation of people has, at one time or another, seen itself as chosen above all others in the sight of God; (2) Divine selection has invariably been self-recognized—the chosen people have usually discovered their privilege by themselves, rather than having it pointed out by less fortunate folk; (3) The discovery of such exalted status has usually preceded activities against other people—such as conquest, which could scarcely be justified without self-proclaimed superiority.

The divine right of kings theory. Inevitably those supporting absolute monarchy and those challenging the centralization of spiritual power joined forces in the *divine right of kings theory.* This contention was put forward as a counterproposal to the ancient theory of the two swords. Jean Bodin (1530–1597), gave this idea philosophical respectability when he developed his theories about the origin of the state and sovereignty.

Some early Christians believed in the **original donation theory,** which is somewhat compatible with the divine right of kings theory. It was contended that Adam and Eve's fall from grace and their banishment from the Garden of Eden resulted in God granting Adam the right to rule the temporal state and that all later kings were his heirs.

Like the ancients, adherents of the divine right of kings theory believed that all power came from God, but they differ from the churchmen by suggesting that God specifically chose the king and gave him absolute power (authority unrestrained by the monarch's subjects). Here these absolutists were joined by the Protestant reformers Martin Luther (1483–1546) and John Calvin (1509–1564), who proposed the theory of *passive obedience.* The Reformation and absolutist factions agreed that political power came from God

Martin Luther (1483–1546)   Philip
Gendreau Collection. Corbis-Bettmann

and that those who were chosen to exercise it were higher on the social scale than ordinary people. Consequently, people were duty bound to obey the prince, even though he be a tyrant, because he was God's magistrate on earth. Sinful kings would be held accountable by God.

This theory had a tremendous impact. Claiming legitimacy from divine authority as well as from civil right, monarchs became extremely powerful in this religious era. Popular refusal to obey the king was seen as heresy as well as treason. The absolute monarchy of Louis XIV of France was based on this theory, and the Stuart house of England was purged because of it. Indeed, the divine right of kings theory was important even in this century. Believing that he had a special covenant with God to rule Russia, Tsar Nicholas II (1894–1917) resisted popularly imposed limitations to his power because he believed that it would violate God's trust. Had the Tsar been more flexible, the 1905 and 1917 Russian revolutions might have been averted.

As the basis upon which the national sovereign built his power, the divine right of kings theory was central to the development of the nation-state system. Perhaps equally important, the theories of popular sovereignty and democracy were developed in opposition to the divine right of kings theory.

The social contract theory.   The idea that government was created by a *social contract* is an old one. The notion that ruler and ruled agreed on their respective roles and had obligations to one another can be traced back through millennia. Interpretations of the contract varied from time to time, but the ruler generally benefited from the theory more than the subjects. Still, the idea that the ruler governed by the consent of the governed was always implied by this theory.

The divine right of kings theory was used by monarchs to claim that there should be no limits on their political power. Opponents of absolute monarchy needed arguments to use against this powerful theory. The social contract theory as it developed in the seventeenth and eighteenth centuries was based on the concept of *popular sovereignty,* in which the ultimate source of the legitimacy and authority of the state is the people.

The contract, it was argued, was established when the all-powerful, or sovereign, people made an agreement that created the state and gave the ruler of the state certain powers. Note here that this theory suggests that rather than being created by natural human impulse or being empowered by God, the state was created by a deliberate and rational act of the people in society. On this matter social contract theories agree, but they disagree as to the exact form of government the contract created and the limitations placed on the powers of government by the sovereign people.

The social contract theory will be discussed more fully in Chapter 4. It is now important to note, however, that this theory is a major contributor to the ideology of nationalism. Under the social contract theory the state is created by all the individuals within it. Therefore, the state is of them, and at the same time they are part of it. This close interrelationship between the people and the state is fundamental to nationalism. The social contract theory gives the individual an important role. At the same time, it describes the combination of individuals into a whole that is different from, yet related to, its individual parts and, according to some theorists, has a greater power and justification than the simple sum of its parts.[1] Because of its close relationship with individual rights in some theories of the state, some scholars argue that nationalism is in the liberal tradition. In fact, nationalism is also comfortably situated on the right of the political spectrum, for the reasons developed in the next section.

THE HISTORY OF NATIONALISM

Nationalism is a relatively new phenomenon. While nationalism began to emerge as long ago as the twelfth century, it did not become an established political institution until much later. Developing at the same time as the Age of Enlightenment, nationalism was a political response to the growth of trade and communications accompanying the era, but it was not until the French Revolution that nationalism became an irrepressible idea.

The French Revolution is unquestionably the most important political stimulant of modern times. Its twin ideological goals, *nationalism* and *democracy*, were given substance and formed during the tumultuous events beginning at the end of the eighteenth century. The reverberations of the French Revolution quickly spread across Europe, and it can be fairly argued that the revolution's impact continues to resonate throughout the world today, because nationalism and democracy have become goals of an ever-increasing percentage of the world's people. The two ideas are not only historically related but they are also intellectually joined because they share similar philosophical foundations. Most particularly, each is rooted in the concept of popular sovereignty. Democracy will be examined in detail later, for now we shall focus on nationalism.

Prior to the French Revolution, political loyalties were not so much vested in abstract concepts as they were devoted to personalities. People thought of themselves more as subjects of the monarch than as members of a nation or even as citizens of a state. Inspired by the radical ideas of Jean Jacques Rousseau, however, the French revolutionaries rose against their king and called upon people to assert themselves as French men and women whom the government should serve, rather than the reverse. Social rank and titles were abolished, and each person was to take the common title of *citoyen*

---

[1]This refers to the organic theory already mentioned in this chapter and developed further in subsequent chapters.

(citizen) as a symbol of their *liberty* from monarchist oppression, their *equality* with each other person in the state, and their *fraternity* in belonging to the French nation.

The Napoleonic Wars (1799–1815) saw French troops march across Europe, spreading their revolutionary ideas as they went, and soon people in every European society, in the United States, in many European colonies in the Americas, and in Japan were infused with the ideas of national identity and self-determination. Throughout most of the remainder of the nineteenth century (called by some historians the Great Age of Nationalism), Europe's monarchs resisted the growing appeal of nationalism, viewing it as a challenge to their own power. Gradually, however, the idea of national unity began to appeal to conservatives as a useful mechanism for encouraging political stability at home and for galvanizing support for their imperialist designs abroad. Napoleon III (1852–1870) and Premier Otto von Bismarck, the first chancellor of the German Empire (1871–1890), were two early practitioners of *rightist nationalism.*

By the close of the nineteenth century, nationalism—a very pliant doctrine, as it turned out—was espoused by elements of both the left and the right. To the left, nationalism (*leftist nationalism*) was seen as a tool that could loosen the grip on people of monarchist oppression. Liberal philosophers such as Jeremy Bentham and Guiseppi Mazzini advocated it for improving the material well-being of people in society. Free trade, universal education and conscription, and popular journalism were advanced as things that could be done to foster national prosperity and strength. On the right, politicians and thinkers saw nationalism as a vehicle by which to forge stronger, more disciplined political unions and to expand the nation's economic interests through a new burst of colonialism across Africa and Asia.

World War I, early in the twentieth century, was at least partially caused by the imperialistic competition of Europe's powers that had been fostered by rightist nationalism. The war's end saw a general disenchantment with nationalism from the right. Indeed, led by U.S. President Woodrow Wilson, the world flirted again with leftist nationalism—a concept to be tempered, curiously enough, with internationalist safeguards. Thus, Wilson's Fourteen Points were a pledge to support *national self-determination* and a proposal to create the League of Nations. Each of these principles was present in the **Treaty of Versailles** (1919), ending the war. Ironically, national self-determination was allowed vent only in Europe, where several new states (Poland, Czechoslovakia, and Yugoslavia) were created, but European colonialism in Asia and Africa was perpetuated. As for the League, despite the cacophony of internationalist pacifist pledges to support it by the world's powers, and excepting a few minor successes by the League, it failed miserably. The United States refused to join the world body, and the conflicting national interests of Europe's states prevented serious sustained multinational cooperation on the problems of the day.

Very quickly in fact, the cooperation and positive aspects of leftist nationalism became overwhelmed by reinvigorated nationalistic impulses from the right. In the 1920s, Mussolini rose to power in Italy, truculently calling for the recreation of the Roman Empire. The following decade saw the emergence of Japanese militarism, Nazism in Germany, and fascism in Spain and in several East European states. Leaders of these states encouraged their people to brood about lost glory, and they belligerently asserted that their particular nation of people was somehow better than others and should therefore subject lessor peoples to their national wills. These policies led inevitably to World War II, the destruction of vast areas of the world, and a second general rejection of rightist nationalism.

The 1945 founding of the United Nations was accompanied by renewed calls for international cooperation. Although it can rightfully be said that the UN has sometimes been used as an instrument of U.S. foreign policy and at other times as a platform for anticolonialist hyperbole, the world body has also been successful at encouraging international efforts to fight disease, to tackle global environmental problems, and to maintain peace among antagonistic peoples.

Yet nationalism has never been far from the forefront in world affairs. Among the Afro-Asian colonial people, nationalist urges drove movements for independence that have spawned dozens of new states. In the developed world, the struggle between the ideologies of East and West masked the nationalistic impulses of many people, but the recent collapse of communism in the Soviet Union, Eastern Europe, and Yugoslavia have seen nationalism emerge afresh, threatening world peace. Indeed, as will be pointed out in a later chapter, exaggerated nationalism in these areas threatens to foster the reemergence of fascism in states where it was popular before World War II, and in other lands where the idea has not yet been tried.

While exaggerated nationalism—sometimes called *chauvinism*—can lead to fascism, more temperate attitudes of national unity are often espoused by less fanatical people. Indeed, nationalism has developed a broad-based political currency. Since the French Revolution it has been adopted on a previously unprecedented scale and today *nationalism is the most potent political idea in the world.*

THE THEORY OF NATIONALISM

Nationalism is an abstraction. Rather than giving loyalty to a person like a noble or a king, people are asked to commit to an idea, to a tradition, to a history, to a notion of fraternity. Nationalism represents the union of a political phenomenon with the identity of the human being. As a frame of reference for individuals and their societies., it dominates the modern world. This is especially true of Western civilization. While Asian societies tend to see social phenomena—family for example—as the primary institutions, we in the West are much more political in our viewpoints. People in Western societies identify very strongly with their home countries.

The ideological components in nationalism, its worldview, its vision of a better life, and its perceptions for actions to improve society, are largely implicit rather than—as in the case of most other ideologies—explicit. Nationalism focuses on the national group as the principal political unit and it demands that the national group be served by a state—a nation-state. Nationalism can be a unifying factor in that it demands the subordination of all identities, values, and interests to those of the national group. Hence, the interests of society and the interests of the state are equated with the national interests. Differences among the genders, social classes, religious beliefs, provincial concerns, political parties, and so forth, are expected to be consistent with the national interests, or they are to be suppressed.

Nationalism is also exclusivist. It demands that each individual give loyalty to only one nation-state. Furthermore, nationalism asks people to place the national interest ahead of other concerns and ahead of the interests of other national groups. In the United States, for example, a very nationalistic society, it is not uncommon to see bumper stickers, or to hear people say, "Love it or leave it," or "My country right or wrong," or "Speak English, or get the hell out." These slogans express deep-seeded feelings of belonging to a unique national group, one that will broach no contradictions.

As these slogans imply, nationalism calls for unity within the national group, and the national group insists on an extraordinary degree of loyalty. "My country right or wrong," for example, goes so far as to suggest that personal morality and integrity are to be subordinated to the nation-state. It clearly argues that the state deserves support and unquestioned loyalty even when its policies may be incorrect or even morally offensive. Such sentiments, if truly felt, exhibit an uncommon degree of personal identification with the state, for there are few other things, including family and religion, that people would openly support even in the face of moral contradictions. Such patriotism is, indeed, a fundamental and essential phenomenon in the concept of nationalism.

Several attempts have been made to differentiate between *nationalism* and *patriotism*. None of these has been very successful, however, because none has taken into account the theoretical nature of nationalism as opposed to the activist nature of patriotism. Simply put, nationalism is the theory of the modern nation-state. It is the theoretical basis for the organization of the world's people in about 190 political units, each claiming to be sovereign.

Patriotism, on the other hand, is not a theory but an act or gesture of loyalty or commitment to the nation-state. Nationalism describes the nation-state and offers a theoretical justification for it. Patriotism is saluting the flag or singing the national anthem; it is a feeling of commitment to the institution that is expressed by nationalism. Put differently, patriotism is to nationalism what religious worship is to theology. Patriotism is a form of secular worship of the nation-state, and, as such, it is generally considered a noble thing. Patriotism, however, can be taken to an absurd extreme—as in the slogans listed above—or it can be used to justify very ignoble objectives, such as the 1995 deadly bombing of a federal office building in Oklahoma City by a self-described patriot. As Samuel Johnson warned us, "Patriotism is the last refuge of scoundrels."

The emotional attachment to nationalism is so strong because nationalism gives the individual an identity and extends that identity into something greater than the self. Nationalism does more than simply describe a political entity. It creates a mirror in which individuals see and define themselves. It is also a prism through which individuals observe, assess, and react to events and to other people. Consequently, nationalism encourages people to identify almost exclusively with the national interests. Those things that compliment the national interest are thought good, whereas those things that contradict it are to be resisted. The identification of the self-interest is not to be viewed as different from the national interest. Or, at least, the self-interest must never contradict the national interest.

Nationalism has certain transcendental qualities, evoking a sense of history and purpose for its followers. As Edmund Burke put it, the state "becomes a partnership not only between those who are living, but between those who are living, those who are dead, and those who are to be born." Nationalism requires that if necessary its followers sacrifice everything—family, fortune, even life itself—for the good of the nation-state.

L.T. Sargent points out that the emotional nature of nationalism makes it the most powerful of all political ideas. It affects the individual more deeply and needs less reinforcement than any other political idea system. It unifies people and gives them a common basis for identifying themselves and one another. It sets up a value system and provides a mechanism through which the needs of the society can be met. And as mentioned earlier, it has stimulated some people to perform extraordinary deeds.

However, just as nationalism unites some people it also divides others, establishing artificial barriers between various national groups. This divisiveness is true even within a state, if more than one national group inhabit it. In such a situation, almost inevitably, the minority national groups become infected with the same feeling of exclusivity that influence the majority national group. Thus, the Soviet Union, Yugoslavia, and Czechoslovakia disintegrated and splintered into several smaller nation-states when the opportunity for disunion availed itself. Predictably, many other minority national groups in Russia, Georgia, Moldova, and in the new, smaller Yugoslavia, are agitating for independence, as they are also doing in Canada, Spain, Britain, Iraq, Turkey, China, and elsewhere.

Extreme forms of nationalism can also lead to imperialism—that is, when one nation becomes dominant over others. When the national interest becomes the justification for government policy, it can lead to interpretations that call for the subjugation of one nation by another. Thus, the colonial powers of Western Europe built vast empires in Asia, in Africa, and in the Americas to feed their industrial appetites. More recently, fascist Italy, Nazi Germany, and militarist Japan subjected millions of people in their drives to exert their national wills over "less deserving" peoples. The United States has also used arguments of national interest to involve itself economically and militarily in Latin America, Asia, the Pacific, and the Middle East. In short, although nationalism can be a valuable unifying factor, it also encourages people to define their interests and values in terms of something less than the good of humanity as a whole.

With the end of the Cold War and the collapse of the Soviet Union, the East-West confrontation evaporated, and, while some Western leaders called for a "new world order," international affairs became even more complex and contradictory than before. Nationalism has tended to become less a factor among the advanced states but more important among some less-developed societies.

Eastern Europe and the former Soviet Union are seething with nationalist separatism. Unfortunately, the nationalistic impulse is accompanied by negative aspects, including racism and anti-Semitism. Similarly, even within advanced countries like Belgium, Italy, and Canada, separatist nationalistic minority movements tug at state unity.

By contrast, the imperatives of communications and technological advances combine with economic factors to draw many of the world's leading industrial powers into closer association. The North American Free Trade Agreement among Canada, the United States, and Mexico calls for unprecedented economic cooperation. On an even wider scale, the European Community is inching toward an economic and political union that would result in the merger of Europe's leading industrial states into the most powerful economic unit on the globe. These two trends are not continuing without nationalistic complications, however. Nationalists in Germany and Britain loudly question the wisdom of ceding to the larger group their economic and political sovereignty. Chauvinistic elements in France, Italy, and Germany gain political stature domestically as they vehemently and even violently oppose the arrival of foreigners into their societies. And the people of the United States, recoiling from economic decline and competition from Europe and Japan, demand protectionist legislation to shelter their economy and try to stem the flow of immigrants into the country.

Finally, a new brand of internationalism may be on the horizon. Internationalism is usually equated with the left of the political spectrum, but this movement is quite reactionary. Rejecting modernization—or Westernization—many in the Muslim world are calling upon their co-religionists to forsake petty national differences and join in a single nation of Islam. This *Pan-Islamic movement* was given fresh impetus with the collapse of the Soviet

Union. Suddenly, a vast area in Central Asia divided into six independent Muslim states: Azerbaijan, Kazakhstan, Uzbekistan, Kirgzistan, Turkmenistan, and Tadzhikistan. Naturally, these new states turned to their co-religionists for help in becoming viable independent states since they had not before enjoyed such status in modern times. Their political fluidity and their formerly suppressed nationalism encourage some Muslim leaders to hope that these areas might eventually be folded into a larger state spanning Central Asia, the Middle East, and North Africa.

Whether the allure of Pan-Islam is strong enough to overwhelm nationalistic loyalties in the Muslim world, or whether the industrialized world will be able to overcome its attachment to national sovereignty are, of course, questions that only time can answer. If indeed nationalist movements are overcome by uniting economic or religious imperatives, the political power of nationalism will have to be reassessed. Until then, however, the extraordinary authority that nationalism exercises on people must be recognized and appreciated.

REVIEW

- *Nation* is a term referring to a people who have strong bonds of kinship with each other, while *state* is a political term implying people or peoples under a certain government, within a certain territory, which has sovereignty over its affairs.
- *Nation-state* is a term that refers to a nation of people who enjoy the existence of a state that sees to their interests.
- The origins of the state are probably quite pragmatic, but philosophers and rulers have often suggested more emotionally compelling reasons for the state, thereby hoping to increase the loyalty of their people to the state.
- Nationalism is the ideology of the nation-state. It asserts the right of a nation of people to be served by a state that complements their interests. It maintains that the national interests are paramount over individual interests and above the interests of other national groups.
- Nationalism can unify people, but it can also divide people and lead to conquest and imperialism.
- Today, nationalism is the world's most powerful political idea, but it is being challenged by internationalist movements that are driven by economic and religious imperatives.

SUGGESTIONS FOR FURTHER READING

BARON, S., *Modern Nationalism and Religion*. New York: Meridian Books, 1960.
BREUILLY, JOHN, *Nationalism and the State*. Manchester, England: Manchester University Press, 1982.
GELLNER, ERNEST, *Nations and Nationalism*. Oxford, England: Basil Blackwell, 1983.

GILLIS, JOHN R., ed., *Commemoration: The Politics of National Identity.* Ewing, NJ: Princeton University Press, 1994.

KOHN, HANS, *The Idea of Nationalism: A Study in Its Origins and Background.* New York: Collier Books, 1967.

KOHN, HANS, *Nationalism: Its Meaning and History.* Princeton, NJ: Van Nostrand, 1955.

NIMNI, EPHRAIM, *Marxism & Nationalism: The Theoretical Origins of Political Crisis.* Boulder, CO: Westview Press, 1991.

SEERS, DUDLEY, *The Political Economy of Nationalism.* New York: Oxford University Press, 1983.

SMITH, ANTHONY D., *Nationalism in the Twentieth Century.* New York: New York University Press, 1979.

SYMMONS-SYMONOLEWICZ, K., *Nationalist Movements: A Comparative View.* Meadville, PA: Maplewood Press, 1970.

TAMIR, YAEL, *Liberal Nationalism.* Ewing, NJ: Princeton University Press, 1993.

TINEY, LEONARD, ed., *The Nation State.* Oxford, England: Morton Robertson, 1981.

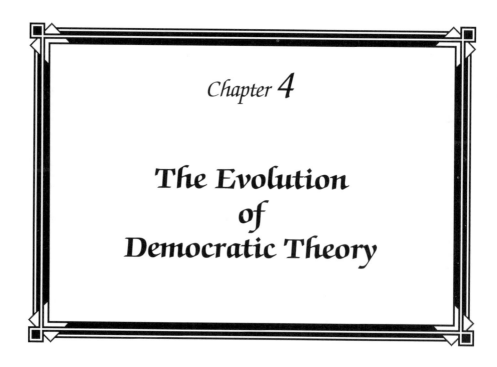

Chapter 4

The Evolution
of
Democratic Theory

PREVIEW

Modern democracy began to develop during the Age of Enlightenment. Some contemporary political scientists think of democracy in procedural terms only, while others insist that it also includes important philosophical content. Perhaps the most basic idea in democracy is that political power comes from the people and that government, therefore, is legal only by consent of the governed. The act of popular consent to government is explained by the theories of popular sovereignty and the social contract.

In the seventeenth century, political conditions in England reached a critical juncture. As often happens, the trying political times of this period resulted in a flurry of creativity, producing the works of Thomas Hobbes and John Locke. Almost a century later the momentum had shifted to France, where Jean Jacques Rousseau made his important contribution.

Hobbes, Locke, and Rousseau had much in common. Each believed that people had lived without government at one time and that they had been governed by natural law in the state of nature. Each also believed that people were capable of understanding natural law and of organizing a government that served their interests better than the state of nature. In addition, they believed that people were essentially equal under natural law and that political power was derived from the people.

Nevertheless, while these philosophers agreed on many points, there were also many areas in which they differed. They agreed that the individual should be free, but they disagreed on the definition of freedom. The conservative Hobbes suggested that freedom was possible only when the individuals in society subordinated themselves completely to the monarchs. The liberal Locke, on the other hand, thought that freedom was greatest when the individual was left alone. The radical Rousseau believed that human freedom would be achieved only through the creation of a new society in which equality was the dominant principle. Like Hobbes, Rousseau argued that freedom was possible only when individuals subordinated themselves to the sovereign authority.

The three philosophers also varied in their attitude toward government itself. Hobbes thought that an absolute monarchy would best suit the needs of the people. Locke favored a parliamentary republic in which the government did little except arbitrate disputes between citizens. Rousseau, adopting the most radical point of view, believed the community created an infallible general will by a direct democratic vote of all the people in the society.

Although Hobbes said little about a person's right to private property, Locke argued that private property was vital to people, yet he was clearly opposed to unlimited accumulation. Rousseau, on the other hand, opposed unequal distribution of property because that would make people unequal politically.

THE MEANING OF DEMOCRACY

Modern democracy evolved only after a very long period of development. The basis of democratic theory came from liberal philosophers, many of whom were not at all democratic but whose ideas could be extended logically to democratic conclusions. In this chapter we will study the thought of three early philosophers: Thomas Hobbes, John Locke, and Jean Jacques Rousseau. First, however, we should contemplate the nature of democracy. The inherent features of democracy are, even today, not completely agreed upon by the experts. Some political scientists argue that democracy is simply a way of making decisions. These scholars, sometimes called *process democrats,* claim that there is no real philosophy, or theory, of democracy. They believe that democracy is nothing more than an agreement among citizens that the majority vote will carry the issue or that one branch of government will not reach too far into the functions of another branch.

The process of democracy is, of course, very important and will be discussed in a later chapter. For now, however, let us study the ideas of a second group, the *principle democrats.* Principle democrats argue that democracy has a very important theoretical base. Although the procedure of democracy is important, they believe it is secondary to the basic intent and objectives of democracy as expressed in democratic theory. For instance, the basic principles of modern *liberal democracy* include the ideas that the individual is of major importance in the society, that each individual is basically equal to all other individuals, and that each has certain inalienable rights such as life and liberty. In the United States—a liberal democracy—we make political decisions by voting, but we use other specific legal and administrative procedures (the right not to be forced to incriminate one's self, the right to a defense, the right to a trial by jury, and so forth) to safeguard peoples' liberties. These procedures are called *due process of law*. Accordingly, even if a majority of the people voted to imprison someone, it could not be legally done because the *process* of majority rule is subordinate to the *principle* of individual liberty.

While certainly not uninterested in process, principle democrats regard the ultimate philosophical goals of democracy as more important than the procedures used to meet those goals. At the very least, principle democrats insist that a democratic government be dedicated to improving the conditions of life for all its people and that some mechanism exist by which the people in the society can exercise a degree of control over their leaders and express their wishes and needs.

On its face, liberal democracy would certainly seem to meet the principle democrats' standards. Assuming that freedom will make people happy, its goal is to make people as free as possible. Liberal democracy includes a large list of freedoms, including freedom of press, speech, religion, assembly, and so forth.

Yet, critics of our system contend that while it allows a wide range of political liberty, liberal democracy ignores the economic needs of its citizens to the point where any effort at real democracy is destroyed. However, this view is foreign to many Americans who satisfy themselves that simply securing political liberties is enough to create a democracy. Indeed, many of our citizens equate democracy with our system and see other forms of government, those without our cherished liberties, as undemocratic.

The Soviet Union is a good example of a system that claimed to be democratic while arguing that our system was not. Soviet authorities readily admitted that their citizens did not enjoy the same right to criticize the government as we do. Yet, they contended that their system was far more democratic than ours because it was dedicated to freeing people from economic bondage to an ownership class. It guaranteed its citizens jobs, free education, free medical care, low cost housing, and so on. Ideally, all people were supposed to enjoy equal economic conditions. Our society does not guarantee any of these "economic freedoms." In answer to a question about free expression in the USSR, a high Soviet authority once told me, "People who define democracy solely on the basis of being able to criticize the government have never been hungry." Obviously, we do not agree with this analysis. We contend that political freedoms are the very heart of democracy. We deemphasize the importance of economic freedom as the Soviets defined it, preferring to equate economic freedom with being able to work where one wishes and to accumulate goods as best as one can. Our system offers great economic diversity, but it also allows much greater economic disparity.

Clearly, the Soviet Union and the United States differed as to which procedures best define a democracy. Yet the dispute was based on something much more fundamental than process. The real argument revolved around the question of which principles are inherent in democracy. What is the philosophical content of democracy?

It is obvious that both process and principle are important to the meaning of democracy. Accordingly, we shall study both concepts in the next three chapters.

THE EARLY HISTORY OF DEMOCRACY

There are about 190 national constitutions in the world today, and almost all of them claim to be democratic. Democracy is currently a very popular term, but people have not always found it so attractive. Indeed, until about a century ago it was decidedly unpopular. To Plato, for example, it meant rule by the masses. Plato argued that there are few people of high quality in any society and that if all the people were allowed to rule, those of low quality, who were more numerous, would dominate the state. This group would establish a government that would reflect their meanness, and the result would be a "tyranny of the majority." Further, Plato warned that democracies were usually short lived and that the mob would soon surrender its power to a single tyrant, thus destroying the popular government.

Aristotle, whose attitude toward democracy was somewhat less negative than Plato's, still clearly preferred a different form of government. He reasoned that under certain conditions the will of the many could be equal to or even wiser than the judgment of a few. When the many governed for the good of all, Aristotle accepted democracy as a "true" or good form of government. To even the best democracy, however, Aristotle preferred what he called *aristocracy,* by which he meant rule of the upper class for the good of all the people in the society. The upper class contained the people of greatest refinement and quality in the society; therefore they were best equipped to provide sound government for the society as a whole.

Eventually the ancient Greeks abandoned democracy, and serious interest in it did not arise again until the Protestant Reformation set in motion a major challenge to the Catholic Church, the authority that had brought order to medieval Europe.

THE SOCIAL CONTRACT

The slow progress out of the Middle Ages, into which Europe had been plunged by the collapse of the Roman Empire, was accomplished largely through the use of the scientific method, leading ultimately to the develop-

ΠΛΑΤΩΝ

Plato (428 B.C.–347 B.C.)
New York Public Library
Picture Collection

ment of the Industrial Revolution itself. As I have already pointed out, success in solving their material problems gave people the confidence to take positive steps in search of solutions to their social, political, and economic problems. This new optimism, based on science and reason, led some thinkers to an exaggerated notion of individualism. Under individualism all people were essentially equal. If this were so, no one had a greater right to rule than another; hence, dynastical monarchy seemed to lose its relevance. Yet, society needed governors to maintain order, and these leaders were chosen by the community as a whole. Since people were essentially equal, no person enjoyed the moral right to govern an equal without some expression of consent by the governed. Legitimate political power, therefore, came from the people; the people were the source of ultimate legal and political authority. This theory of *popular sovereignty* led to much speculation about democracy during the seventeenth century. The theory that resulted, involving the actual grant of power by the people to the government, is called the *social contract theory*; that is, the social contract is the act of people exercising their sovereignty and creating a government to which they consent.

Calvinists and Jesuits

The first important utterances of the social contract theory came from two unlikely sources. The Calvinists in France, called Huguenots, were unhappy under the burdensome Catholic rule. Eventually they abandoned John Calvin's policy of passive obedience and adopted a doctrine that justified resistance to the Bourbon monarch, who claimed his authority on the grounds of the divine right of kings theory. The basic ideas in the opposing theories of popular sovereignty and the social contract are found in the writings of Francis Hotman (1524–1590) and of Theodore Beza (1519–1605), a protégé of Calvin himself, and in the pamphlet *Vindiciae Contra Tyrannos*, whose author is not definitely known.[1] Their basic thesis suggested that spiritual doctrine and truth come from God, but political power emanates from the sovereign people. The people elect a king to serve them. Two contracts are then entered into. The first, between God and the society, requires that all people maintain spiritual truth. The second, between the king and the people, provides for civil order. The first agreement requires that both king and people abide by God's law and calls for punishment of either for any failure to do so. The second contract binds the king as well as the people to the laws of the state. If the king governs justly, the people are bound to obey him; but if he is unjust, the people may—and indeed are obliged to—put him out. The ouster of such a king, however, can only be done indirectly and only as a last resort.

Although the democratic implications of this theory are clear, these Calvinists did not have democracy in mind. They discouraged any direct popular effort to overthrow the monarch. Such an act was to be carried out by the people's representatives. Nor was tyranny to be replaced by a democracy. These Calvinists were opposed to absolutism, but they believed it should be replaced by a limited monarchy.

Implausible as it seems, the Calvinist assault on monarchical absolutism was embellished by Jesuit theological writers. The rise of absolutism and the Protestant Reformation had combined into a powerful attack on the Church and the power of the papacy. The Jesuit Order, established by Ignatius Loyola in 1534, led the Catholic Church in reforms that arrested the progress of the Protestant Reformation. The Jesuits believed, however, that all spiritual power and authority should derive from the Pope. Conse-

[1]*Defense of Liberty Against Tyrants*, printed in 1594, was probably written by Hubert Languet or Philippe Duplessis-Mornay. It was published under the pseudonym Stephen Junis Brutis in an obvious and successful attempt to avoid the penalty for sedition in sixteenth-century France.

quently, since the absolute monarch wanted the state to control the Church, the Jesuits were opposed to the king.

The Jesuits were no more in favor of democracy than were the Calvinists, yet their ideas contributed greatly to the concept of popular government as well as to the notion of separation of church and state. Robert Bellarmine (1542–1621), Juan de Marisna (1536–1623), and Francisco Suarez (1548–1617) were the most important Jesuit writers. Suarez made a significant contribution by developing, with Hugo Grotius and others, the meaning of natural law, which would later be used by the classical liberals in their statement of democratic principles.

Like the Calvinists, these three Jesuits did not entirely agree on details but did agree on a basic theme. Generally, they distinguished between God's law and natural law, which was subordinate to God's law. Political organization and government, two natural phenomena, were granted to a ruler by the people; God did not grant such authority. God directly invested power only in the Pope. Thus, the Pope was chosen by God and was superior to all. By contrast, the king was chosen by the people and was therefore inferior to them. The Pope could overthrow a tyrant or grant the people the right to resist an evil ruler.

The Jesuits, like the Calvinists, were careful to recommend that the people depose a ruler only indirectly, through their representatives. The Jesuits

Elizabeth I (1533–1603)
Courtauld Institute of Art

also recommended that a tyrant be replaced with another monarch who was limited by the Pope and by Parliament. Even though these religious writers were not democrats, their ideas helped create the intellectual atmosphere in which democracy took form in the centuries that followed.

Thomas Hobbes

During the seventeenth century England went through a period of serious civil disorder. Two forces competed: *absolutism,* allied with Anglican traditionalism, versus *Puritan reform,* in league with Parliamentary assertiveness. When Elizabeth I died in 1603, the Tudor line, England's most popular and powerful ruling house, also ended.

James Stuart succeeded Elizabeth to the throne. Unattractive and bookish, he believed vehemently in the divine right of kings. His unpleasant personality and unpopular politics led to conflicts with the assertive Parliament. The situation was not helped by James's death in 1625, since his son, Charles I, shared his unpopular political attitudes. Charles I pursued arbitrary and foolish policies until a civil war broke out, ending in 1649 with Charles's execution. The execution of Charles I was an important step. While many monarchs through history had been killed in palace coups, they were usually removed from power in the name of the "rightful monarch." By contrast, in this episode the *people* of England held the king to account. Claiming that the king was supposed to serve the people, they assumed the right—for the first time in history—to try and execute an oppressor.

For the next eleven years England was ruled by Oliver Cromwell and the Puritan religious minority. Upon Cromwell's death Parliament decided to restore the Stuart monarchy by placing Charles II, the son of the executed monarch, on the throne. **Thomas Hobbes** (1588–1679), a mathematics tutor for the exiled prince, developed his theories in part to justify the Stuart restoration.

Hobbes believed that monarchy was the best possible form of government, yet he rejected the theory of the divine right of kings. Instead, he claimed that the social contract was the source of royal power. Though Hobbes believed that royal power came from the people, he placed few limits on the monarch.

Hobbes's view of people is not a happy one. He thought that people were basically self-serving. Although they were rational, they were not in control of their own destinies because they were driven by an overwhelming fear of death. This caused people to be aggressive toward one another. Hobbes, like all subsequent social contract theorists, assumed that there had been a time when government did not exist. In this *state of nature* people were free to act as they wished. No law governed them save natural law, and that law had no enforcement agency. Given his pessimistic views about the nature of people, it is not surprising that Hobbes believed that the state of nature was a wretched condition. Unregulated by law and government, people had given in to their baser instincts and acted aggressively toward their neighbors. They committed every kind of violence and deceit in order to raise their own status.

In *Leviathan*, his major work, Hobbes eloquently describes the hopeless chaos of the state of nature. In this hideous state there was only human conflict, a constant "war of each against all." Hobbes complained that there was "no knowledge of the face of the earth; no account of time; no arts; no letters; no society; and which is worst of all, continual fear, and danger of violent death; and the life of man, solitary, poor, nasty, brutish and short." Clearly, Hobbes viewed the human condition in the state of nature as chaotic, irresponsible, and devoid of freedom.

Though he viewed people as prisoners of their own avarice, Hobbes believed they were rational. As rational beings, they realized the futility of their existence and hit upon a way of creating order out of the chaos endemic to the state of nature: the social contract. In exchange for order they agreed to surrender all their natural rights to a monarch and render to him complete obedience. Obviously, Hobbes did not consider natural rights inalienable as did later natural law theorists; but he did assert that the sole function of the king was to keep order. As long as the monarch did so, his subjects were bound to obey his laws. However, since the social contract was an agreement among ordinary people, the king was not a party to it and need not be bound by it. Only he could make the law; and because he made the law, the king could not be bound or limited by it. Only if he failed to keep the peace could the people resist him.

Hobbes believed that freedom, though limited, was possible only if people surrendered their liberty to a monarch—hardly a democratic point of view. Since people were driven to excess by their insecurity, they could experience freedom only when they were restrained by a superior authority. Without such authoritarian checks people would become victims once again of their own fright-induced impulses and would return to the chaos of the state of nature. Thus, human reason, according to Hobbes, was powerful enough to devise a solution to chaos, but not strong enough to allow people to become part of the solution. Only the all-powerful monarch could do that.

By asserting that legitimate political power comes from people rather than from God, Hobbes made an important, but unintentional, contribution to the development of democratic thinking. His theory led subsequent English philosophers to the concept of the separation of church and state just as the Jesuits and Calvinists had done on the continent. Yet, Hobbes never intended his ideas to be used as the basis of popular government; quite the reverse. Even though he employed concepts normally thought to be liberal (for example, popular sovereignty and the social contract), his interpretation of these ideas led him to very conservative conclusions. Moreover, you will recall from Chapter 2 that liberals are optimistic about people, believing that they are basically good. Conservatives, on the other hand, hold the opposite attitude toward humanity. Clearly, Hobbes's view is closer to the conservative position. In short, Hobbes used a liberal vocabulary, which was in vogue among the intellectuals of his time, to express a conservative philosophy. The next natural law philosopher we will study, however, enjoyed indisputably liberal credentials.

John Locke

The death of Charles II brought to the throne James II (1685–1688). Less politically wise than his brother Charles, James II was not content to let his ministers bargain with Parliament; instead, he tried to be an active executive. Worse than that, he wanted absolute power. Such royal ambitions were not welcome in seventeenth-century England under any circumstances, but the fact that James was a Catholic sealed his fate.

In 1688, the English rose up against the "Catholic tyranny" and James II fled to France. This episode, known as the *Glorious Revolution* because it was practically bloodless, brought to a close the long struggle between king and Parliament for dominance in England. Although virtually free of violence, the Glorious Revolution was a true revolution because it visited major changes upon the English government, changes which ultimately led to the development of democracy in that land.

Before allowing a new king to ascend the throne, Parliament adopted a document, the *Bill of Rights*, that limited the power of the English monarchy

John Locke (1632–1704)   New York
Public Library Picture Collection

as it had never before been limited. It guaranteed Parliament the right to hold free elections, to meet frequently, to petition the king, and to legislate. The king was not allowed to suspend an act of Parliament, and he was forbidden to tax or to keep a standing army in peacetime without Parliament's approval. These restrictions had to be accepted by the new monarchs as the "true, ancient, and indubitable rights of the people of this realm."

Just as Hobbes had tried to justify the restoration of the Stuart dynasty, so **John Locke** (1632–1704) tried to give a philosophical base to the Glorious Revolution and the limitations placed on the monarch as a result. Of all his works, the one with the greatest political importance is his *Second Treatise.* In it are a series of arguments that, because of their simplicity and common-sense approach, captured the imagination of Locke's fellow citizens as well as people of later generations. As George H. Sabine has written, "His sincerity, his profound moral conviction, his genuine belief in liberty, in human rights, and in the dignity of human nature, united with his moderation and good sense, made him the ideal spokesman of a middle-class revolution."[2] Though his work obviously had substantial impact on British government, his philosophy found greatest application in the principles of the American Declaration of Independence and the United States Constitution.

Natural law. History's leading classical liberal, Locke believed in natural law and that people could discover its principles by using reason. Natural law, according to Locke, guaranteed each individual certain rights that could not legally be taken away, or *alienated,* without due process of law. He summarized these inalienable rights as "life, liberty, and estate." However, he was much more explicit than this generalization suggests. He held that *individual freedom* was an essential right; indeed, its importance to his theory would be hard to overestimate.

While Hobbes and Locke agreed on many points, they also contradicted each other. As we have seen, Hobbes was very pessimistic about human nature. He believed that people were basically evil and that they would harm each other if they were not subject to the control of an outside authority. Hence, Hobbes equated individual freedom with restraint by the government. Locke, by contrast, was very optimistic about human nature. He believed that governmental restraints on people were largely unnecessary. In fact, he argued that people were most free when they were left unfettered by government. Thus, to Locke, freedom was found in the absence of restraint. He felt that people would behave decently when left alone and argued that they should be free to exercise their rights without hindrance or regulation as long as they did not interfere with the rights of others.

Individual equality, in Locke's view, was another right guaranteed by

[2]George H. Sabine, *A History of Political Theory,* 3rd ed. (New York: Holt, Rinehart & Winston, 1961), p. 540.

natural law. Locke did not claim that all people were equal in all ways. He recognized that people differed widely in intelligence, physical prowess, and so forth; but regardless of the obvious differences among people he argued that they all had the same natural rights because the natural law, from which the natural rights flow, applies to all people in equal measure. Thus, no one had a greater claim to liberty than anyone else. Nor did anyone have more, or less, of any other kind of natural right, including the right to estate (private property).

Private property.   Locke was most specific about the individual's right to private property. Like all the early English classical liberals, he believed that private property was essential to people's well-being. The high status he gave to private property rests on two major assumptions. First, he assumed that the accumulation of private property allowed people to provide for themselves and their families the necessities of life. Once freed from the pressures of survival, people could turn to the task of developing their characters. If a society is in the throes of famine, its people care little whether the sun revolves around the earth or the earth orbits the sun. They are not likely to create an important art form, an advanced architecture, a subtle literature, or a sophisticated governmental system. We will see later that Marx adopted this idea, calling for the liberation of people from *compulsive toil* as a major theme of his own theory.

How property was regarded is of the utmost importance to our study. Property was seen by the English liberal as a means to an end, not as an end in itself. Locke saw private property as a vital first step to an improved human race. Locke's main interest was the individual, and he hoped for a society that would free its people to perfect their characters and their human qualities. The accumulation of property was important to him for the life it made possible, not as an absolute value in itself. Further, the accumulation of private property by any given individual was not to occur unchecked. Locke believed people should be allowed to accumulate only as much as they could use. He did not support amassing huge fortunes in the hands of some people while others lived in poverty. Thus, while he favored a market economy, thinking it most conducive to individual freedom, he would almost surely object to the great disparities in property ownership that exist in today's capitalist societies.

The second assumption of the early English liberals in support of private property involved individual identity. Locke believed that property ownership was more than a simple economic fact. A person's property reflected the individual who owned it. People were identified in part by the things they owned. What they were was modified by what they had.

Although we do not state this concept as often or in exactly the same way as Locke, it is still with us today. A statement such as "the clothes make the man" is worth some analysis. In this phrase property and personality are closely related by the implication that owning a particular item can change one's personality. This close link between the self, or the personality, and material items is a very strong feature of Western civilization; indeed, many modern commercial advertisements rely heavily on persuading consumers of this theory. Further, the equation of personality and property ownership helps explain why most important political ideologies have come from the West. You will recall that ideologies tend to offer a better material existence, the promise of a happier or better life. Such values dominate Western thought, whereas Eastern philosophies tend to focus on developing the inner self or finding spiritual contentment. Thus, ideologies are more Western than Eastern.

As one might expect from the importance Locke gave private property, he developed an elaborate theory to explain its origin and value. Not only did these ideas make a vital contribution to democracy, but subsequent thinkers adopted them and applied them to vastly different philosophies. Locke's influence can easily be found in the work of capitalist economists such as Adam Smith and David Ricardo, but as we will see later, it can also be found in the economic theory of Karl Marx.

Locke argued that all resources were originally held in common and that people could use them as needed, but he believed that common property became private property when human labor was applied to it. He believed that when people made things from natural resources, they transferred something of themselves into the items produced. The newly created product, the result of a union between human creativity and natural resources, actually became part of the worker and naturally belonged to that person. Thus the right of private property was born. Locke also believed that the value of any item was roughly determined by the amount of labor necessary to produce it. This idea, known as the *labor theory of value,* may be seen in Marx's famous theory of surplus value, discussed in Chapter 8.

As we have seen, Locke assumed that there had been a time when there was no organized society. During this time people interacted with nature, creating private property. Clearly, then, Locke assumed that private property existed before society was organized. In other words, private property was not created by society; society had no special claim on or control over private property. Private property was created by the individual. It was created when individuals passed part of their essence to an object through the process known as work. Thus, we return to the crucial point: *Private property is not important for its own sake.* It takes on importance when part of the essence of a human being has been transferred to it. While this theory seems to make private property equal to life and human equality, actually property is important only because it has been imbued with the essence of human beings.

That Locke considered property less important than human values is clear from his attitude toward the accumulation of property. Though he thought that people should normally be allowed to gather property without interference from outside agencies, he clearly believed that *property accumulation should be limited.* To begin with, Locke held that no person should be allowed to accumulate more property than could be used before it spoiled. A second restriction on property ownership was more general. Locke argued that people should not be able to exercise their economic rights to such an extent that others were denied the same rights. Since private property helps people define themselves, since it frees people from the mundane cares of daily subsistence, and since it is finite, no individual should accumulate so much property that others are prevented from accumulating the necessities of life. If such a restriction did not exist, it would be possible for one person, through the control of property, to deny others their identities and even their ability to be fully human. On this basis an agency of the society could interfere with an individual's accumulation of property if in so doing the right of others to accumulate property would be protected. Though Locke did not intend it in this way, this principle forms part of the bridge between classical liberalism, which is linked to capitalism, and utopian or humanitarian socialism, discussed in Chapter 9. *The roots of both capitalism and socialism spring from common intellectual soil.*

The last principle of natural law about which Locke was very specific has to do with the individual's collective interests. Locke assumed that the basic interests of all people in a given society were the same. Hence, while there might be some minor variations, whatever was beneficial for the society as a whole was probably ultimately beneficial for any particular individual, another belief that can also be found in socialism. This principle led Locke to look toward the majority vote as the most important feature of political decision making. His attitude toward majority rule will be discussed in more detail later; for now it is enough to remark that although Locke considered the individual very important, he viewed people as being united by common interests.

The social contract. Locke and Hobbes also differed in their views on the condition of people in the state of nature. Rejecting the proposition that people were evil and selfish in the state of nature, Locke believed instead that people were essentially good. Consequently, the state of nature prior to society and government was rather pleasant. Indeed, Locke suggested that the dominant themes in the natural state were "peace, good will, mutual assistance and preservation."

Yet, even though the state of nature was usually peaceful, there were two sources of unrest. Though Locke believed people were basically good, he did not think them perfect. Hence, from time to time some people might try to take advantage of others. Moreover, even when no malice was intended, two people might come into conflict while exercising what they considered to be their just liberties.

Conflict between people, then, could occur in the state of nature; and because there was no third party to arbitrate the dispute, individuals were forced to defend their own liberties. This clash presented a further problem because people were not equal in their ability to defend their rights from attack. Hence, injustice could occur in the state of nature because the person who manages to prevail over another may succeed only because he or she is stronger and not because he or she is right.

Believing that people were rational, Locke went on to theorize that people saw the need for an agency to dispense justice among them. This led the individuals in a community to make a contract among themselves, thereby creating society and removing themselves from the state of nature.

Hobbes, you will recall, insisted that the king was not a party to the contract that formed the society and thus could not be bound by it. Hobbes held that society and government were distinct elements, thus putting the power of the king above that of the individual and the society.

Locke made the same distinction as Hobbes, but for exactly the opposite reason. The people create the society through the social contract, and then government is created as an agent of the society. Consequently, government is two steps removed from the true source of its power, the individual, and is subordinate to the society, which is, in turn, subordinate to the individual. Also, since government and society are not the same thing, the fall of a government need not mean the end of the community. The community could create a new government to serve it if its original government was unsatisfactory.

The nature and function of government.   Though Locke believed that government ought to be strictly limited, he thought it performed a vital function: To serve the people. Hobbes, by contrast, thought that people should serve the government. Locke thought that some things could be done better when people were left alone and that other things were done better by society as a whole or by society's representatives. He believed that most people could act fairly and efficiently by themselves and insisted that government should not interfere with the individual in such cases. Yet, there were times when governmental activity was necessary to protect the rights of the people. Locke saw government as a passive arbitrator. Normally it would simply let people pursue their own best interests. When, however, two or more individuals came into conflict over the extent of their liberties, government was required to step in, arbitrate the dispute, and then step out again and let people go about their business without further interference.

Unlike Hobbes, who had people giving up almost all their rights to government, Locke believed that people should keep most of their freedoms. The only right that Locke expected people to surrender to government was the right to decide how extensive their individual liberties would be. Even there, however, the only time government should use its power was when individuals came into conflict over the use of their rights. Any other power was denied to government and reserved for the people.

Unlike some political theorists, Locke believed that the state or government should never become more powerful than the individuals it served. The government was created by society; society was created by a contract among all the individuals who wanted to join the society. In making the contract, the people agreed to accept the arbitration of the government. Since the power of the government was derived from and therefore dependent on the power of the individuals in the society, the government could not impose its authority on an unwilling individual. That individual would remove himself or herself from the society and from the authority of the government. In so doing, however, the individual would have to return to the state of nature and would forfeit the protection of the government.

Locke was also very particular about the structure and form of government. As pointed out earlier, he assumed that what was good for the society as a whole was good for the individual as well. Further, he believed that people were rational and capable of knowing what was good for them. Consequently, he assumed that the society could use the will of the majority as a formula for deciding correct policy. Moreover, individuals were expected to accept the decision of the majority even if they disagreed with it.

Besides believing in majority rule, Locke thought that people should be governed by a parliament elected by citizens who owned property. Though he argued that the people were sovereign, Locke thought it best that they not rule themselves directly. He saw members of a parliament as representing their constituents, and he believed that they should vote as their constituents wanted. Hence, the relationship between the government and the governed remained close. Though the people did not actually make the law themselves, the law was a product of their preferences.

Locke also called for separation of the executive and legislative powers. Most important, he believed that the legislature, which was the direct agent of the people, should take precedence over the executive branch. The legislature should decide on the policy of the government, and the executive should dutifully carry out the mandates of parliament.

Even though he argued that only property-owning citizens should vote and that the people must obey the government as long as it did not abuse their rights, Locke contended that the people were sovereign and that they had the right to rebel against an unjust government. The government's sole purpose was to serve the individual in such a way as to increase individual rights and liberties. At all other times it was to stay out of the people's business. If the government ever acted otherwise—that is, if it involved itself too much in the affairs of the people, thus reducing their rights and liberties without good reason—then the people had the right to put that government out and to create one that would serve them better. Once again we see Hobbes and Locke on opposite sides. Hobbes opposed popular rebellion against the king, whom he considered the sovereign, or the highest law in the land. Yet, since the king was given power by the people for the sole purpose of keeping order, the people were justified in ousting him and creating a new sovereign only if he failed to keep order. In other words, while Hobbes would have the people overthrow the government for failing to keep order, Locke believed such an action was justified when the government tried to regulate people too much. A glance at the spectrum of political attitudes described in Chapter 2 will show that Hobbes's concern for order and Locke's preference for individual liberty are quite consistent with the values of conservatives and liberals, respectively.

Liberal though Locke's ideas were, they too fell short of democracy. Locke was the "spokesman of a middle-class revolution." During Locke's time British government was controlled by the aristocracy. Yet a large and wealthy middle class, composed of merchants, manufacturers, bankers, and professionals, emerged on the eve of the Industrial Revolution to demand a share of political power in the society. Although Locke claimed that all people were equally possessed of natural rights, he advocated that political power be devolved only far enough to embrace the middle class by giving Parliament, which the middle class controlled through the House of Commons, the right to limit the monarch's power. He did not advocate that the masses of ordinary people, the poor, be given the right to elect members of Parliament; thus, he denied them political power.

Still, his philosophy was essential to the development of liberal democracy. Although he chose not to enfranchise the poor, his justification for giving the middle class political power were equally applicable to people of lower status; indeed, his theories were so sweeping that they could logically be applied to all people. Locke was probably prevented from extending his ideas only by the unquestioned bias for privilege endemic to his era. Thus, democracy had to await a more egalitarian epoch, an era parented when the mass production of goods created the necessary economic and social conditions. Still, it cannot be disputed that Locke's ideas came very close to being democratic; in the next generation, contemporary democratic thought was born.

Jean Jacques Rousseau

After the dramatic political events that stimulated the ideas of Hobbes and Locke, England settled into a period of consolidation and France became the new center of radical thought. Louis XIV (1638–1715) had established an absolutist monarchy and passed it on to his great-grandson, Louis XV. France had made great advances in science and literature. Yet, its political system was harsh, its social structure exploitative, and its government corrupt and unresponsive to the people's needs. These conditions stimulated a surge of literary activity that produced some of the period's best writers. Most were satirists and commentators rather than philosophers. But one thinker, **Jean Jacques Rousseau** (1712–1778), made such a creative impact as to set himself apart from the others, and he is generally considered to be the founder of modern radical thought.

The community.   Like other social contract theorists, Rousseau believed that there had been a time when neither government nor society existed. But Rousseau believed that people in the state of nature were simple, shy, and innocent. Unlike Hobbes, Rousseau suspected that before society was created people were timid, and that they avoided conflict rather than seeking it out. Such a condition was not unpleasant. Life was peaceful in the state of nature, *but it was not fulfilled.*

Rousseau believed that people wanted to improve themselves, to make themselves better. This goal, he argued, could not be achieved in the state of nature because, while it was an innocent condition, it was not a moral life. Rousseau was deeply influenced by the ancient Greeks who, you will recall, regarded people as human only if they actually participated in the affairs of state.

Rousseau agreed that morals could be developed only in an environment in which people related to and interacted with one another. This relationship did not exist in the state of nature; hence, he concluded that moral life was impossible in that condition. Yet, because people wanted to improve themselves, they were compelled to form a community that destroyed the state of nature. The community then established a moral code that made human perfection (and even *becoming* human) possible. In the state of nature people were more animal than human. "We begin properly to become men," Rousseau said, "only after we have become citizens."

Nevertheless, the formation of the community does not necessarily lead to a good life; it only makes a moral life possible. Indeed, Rousseau was convinced that while people had the capacity to be good, they were more likely to become immoral as the community became more sophisticated.

Private property, which Rousseau believed developed only after the community was formed, encouraged greed and selfishness. The most aggressive people in the community gained control of most of the property, and they set up a government to help them maintain that control. Hence, people become prisoners either to their own greed or to that of their rulers. "Man is born free," Rousseau wrote, "and everywhere he is in chains." As we will see later, Marx and other radicals developed similar ideas.

The organic society.   Rousseau offered a solution to the dilemma just described. He could not advise a return to the state of nature because that would require people to give up the chance to live moral lives. Instead, people must build a new community that is structured so that a moral existence is possible.

Jean Jacques Rousseau
(1712–1778)   Giraudon

According to Rousseau, people should form a new society to which they would surrender themselves completely. By giving up their rights and powers to the group, they would create a new entity. The society would become an *organism* in which each individual contributed to the whole. By giving up their individual powers, people would gain a new kind of equality and a new kind of power. They would achieve equality because they would all become full contributors to the group. Enhanced power would also accrue to the community, the sum greater than its individual parts.

This new society would actually be a person, according to Rousseau— a "public person." The public person would be directed by the *general will, that is the combination of the will of each person in the society engaged in the enterprise of doing what was good for all.* As such the general will could do no wrong because it would create the right. It could not be bad because it would determine what was moral.

The general will also made individual freedom possible. Freedom, according to Rousseau, meant doing only what one wanted to do. When people join the community, they voluntarily agree to comply with the general will of the community. The general will, created by the majority in the interests of all in society, cannot be wrong. If a person votes with the minority, he or she must still accept the majority decision. If the majority creates the general will, and if the general will can do no wrong, then the minority must be wrong; and since the individual agreed to live by the general will, those who are in the minority are expected to comply with the will of the majority, thus enhancing their freedom. If those in the minority refuse to follow the general will, they are violating their own will and thus are refusing to be free.[3]

People who refuse to comply with the general will, and thus with their own best interests, can be *forced* to comply. Thus, Rousseau argues that the community has the right to *force its members to be free.* As he put it, "Whoever shall refuse to obey the general will must be constrained by the whole body of his fellow citizens to do so; which is no more than to say that it may be necessary to compel a man to be free."

By asserting that the general will cannot be wrong, Rousseau completed the circle begun by Hobbes more than a century before. It will be recalled that the English philosopher separated the monarch from the agent of moral authority—the Church. Here Rousseau claims that the community, which controls the state, actually creates moral authority itself, thus rejoining moral authority and the state, this time in a secular setting. This theory gave a philosophical justification to the anticlerical features of the French Revolution. It was also used later by Mussolini in developing his notion of the totalitarian state.

An important lesson learned from the example of Rousseau and Hobbes is that sometimes two different ideas, carried to opposite extremes, can result in similar conclusions. Hobbes, on the right of the spectrum, would have society bound to the absolute power of a monarch. Rousseau, on the left, demanded that people subject themselves to the general will in no less absolute fashion.

Economic and political systems. Like Locke, Rousseau gave importance to property, associating it with the foundation of society itself. "The first man who," he wrote, "after enclosing a piece of ground, bethought himself to say 'This is mine' and found people simple enough to believe him, was the real founder of society." Yet, to Rousseau, private property was not a sacred com-

---

[3]Note the step toward *moral relativism* here. Moral relativism suggests that there are no absolute principles of right and wrong, but rather, the society determines moral values. The concept of *moral absolutism*—that there existed a set of absolute truths that humans are bound to obey but are powerless to influence—was prominent at Rousseau's time, and before. Natural law is a moral absolutist principle, after all. In fact, Rousseau's belief in the natural law is testament to his own acceptance of moral absolutism. His theory of the general will, however, while it is no less absolutist than other natural law theories, does suggest that people play a part in determining what the absolute principles are. This is an important step toward establishing the philosophical tenets justifying popularly controlled government.

modity. In fact, he was the first natural law theorist to regard private property as something other than a natural right. Instead, he argued that it was a *social right*. Hence, no one has an unlimited right to accumulate property. Much as Marx would argue later, Rousseau thought that private property could be used to exploit people because it was a source of inequality among individuals. While he never actually supported the elimination of private property, Rousseau objected to an unequal distribution of property among the members of the society. Private property, he believed, should be distributed equally among the individuals in the state. However, Rousseau's motive for supporting equal ownership of private property had nothing to do with the material well-being of citizens. It was purely a political convenience; his goal was individual equality, not material well-being.

Rousseau was even more particular about the governmental form he thought the community should use. To begin with, he believed that each individual's will was inalienable; it could not be transferred to another. Consequently, he opposed representative government, since no one could represent another individual. This led him to favor a direct form of democracy, that is, one in which the citizens vote on the laws themselves instead of sending representatives to a legislature. However, because of the limited technology of his time, the direct democracy recommended by Rousseau required that the state be very small. Like the ancient Greeks of whom he was so fond, Rousseau believed that the city-state was the only political entity small enough for all citizens to meet and vote on every law or policy.

Rousseau was also very careful to distinguish between executive and legislative functions and powers. First, he insisted on complete separation of the two. He also demanded that the legislature be more powerful than the executive. The legislature was all of the people, or the community, making the general will. Hence, it was the sovereign or all-powerful body. The executive, according to Rousseau, was merely the government. Rousseau, like Locke, carefully distinguished between the community and the government. The government only served the community. It had no special rights or privileges and, as in Locke's theories, could be changed at any time while the community remained unchanged. The sole function of the executive (the government), in other words, was to carry out the wishes of the community (the general will).

Even as Rousseau established the theoretical basis for radical, or pure, democracy, more conservative thinkers were beginning to modify the ideas of Locke and others, creating a political-economic system known as democratic capitalism. While Rousseau's theories greatly influenced politics on the continent, the more conservative doctrines had an immense impact in England and the United States, only to be followed by the leftist modifications of democratic socialism. In the next chapter, we will study these two variants of democratic theory.

REVIEW

- Democracy has both procedural and philosophical aspects. Liberal democracy, the type practiced in the United States, holds that the philosophical aspects of democracy are more important than its procedures.
- Democracy is based on the theory of popular sovereignty (legitimate political power comes from the people) and the theory of the social contract (an agreement among citizens to create, cooperate with, and control government).
- Thomas Hobbes, a social contract philosopher, was no democrat, but his ideas became important to later democratic thinkers. He believed that people empower government, that church and state should be separate, and that the monarch should be given almost total power so as to keep order.
- John Locke, the founder of classical liberalism, saw people creating government in order to increase the liberties of the individuals within society. He favored representative government and the accumulation of private property. Locke would, however, limit the accumulation and use of private property in the interests of all citizens.
- Rousseau, the founder of modern radicalism, wanted private property distributed equally to all people so as to maintain political equality. Rejecting representative government, he called on all citizens to make the laws themselves. He felt that laws made by the majority in the interests of all citizens constituted the general will and therefore could not be disobeyed.

SUGGESTIONS FOR FURTHER READING

ARBLASTER, ANTHONY, *Democracy*. Minneapolis: University of Minnesota Press, 1987.

BARBER, JAMES DAVID, *The Book of Democracy*. Englewood Cliffs, NJ: Prentice Hall, 1995.

DUNCAN, GRAEME, ed., *Democratic Theory and Practice*. Cambridge, England: Cambridge University Press, 1983.

DUNN, JOHN, ed., *Democracy*. New York: Oxford University Press, 1994.

HOBBES, THOMAS, *Leviathan*, ed. Michael Oakshott. New York: Collier, 1962.

INGERSOLL, DAVID E., *Communism, Fascism, and Democracy*. Columbus, OH: Charles E. Merrill, 1971.

LOCKE, JOHN, *The Second Treatise of Government (An Essay Concerning the True Original Extent and End of Civil Government) and a Letter Concerning Toleration*, ed. J. W. Gough. New York: Macmillan, 1956.

MCDONALD, LEE CAMERON, *Western Political Theory*, Part 3. New York: Harcourt Brace Jovanovich, 1968.

MACPHERSON, C. B., *The Life and Times of Liberal Democracy*. Oxford, England: Oxford University Press, 1977.

MACPHERSON, C.B., *The Political Theory of Possessive Individualism: Hobbes to Locke*. Oxford: Oxford University Press, 1962.

MACPHERSON, C. B., *The Real World of Democracy*. New York: Oxford University Press, 1969.

NELSON, WILLIAM M., *On Justifying Democracy*. London: Routledge & Kegan Paul, 1980.

RITTER, ALAN and JULIA CONAWAY BONDANELLA, ed., *Rousseau's Political Writings*. Trans. Julia Conaway Bondanella. New York: W. W. Norton & Co., 1988.

SABINE, GEORGE H., *A History of Political Theory*. 3rd ed. New York: Holt, Rinehart & Winston, 1961.

SCHULTZ, ERNST B., *Democracy*. New York: Barron's Educational Series, 1966.

WEALE, ALBERT, *Political Theory and Social Policy*. London: Macmillan, 1983.

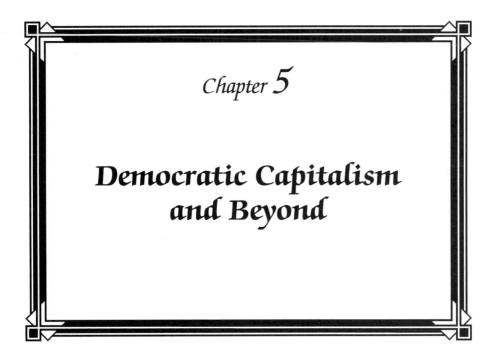

Chapter 5

Democratic Capitalism and Beyond

PREVIEW

Economics and politics are inextricably linked in modern society. Hence, two major variants of democracy have developed: democratic capitalism *and* democratic socialism. *Democratic capitalism combines the economic system developed by Adam Smith, David Ricardo, and Thomas Malthus with the political theories of the neoclassical democrats Edmund Burke, James Madison, and John C. Calhoun. Taking a rather bleak position regarding the nature of people, these democrats favored an economy based on free individual commercial activity, a strong central government, and a relatively paternalistic representative political system.*

Contemporary liberalism developed in the tradition of Jeremy Bentham, John Stuart Mill, Thomas Hill Green, and John Dewey. This school equates individual happiness with the happiness of society as a whole. Government should not act in such a way as to restrict individual liberties, but governmental action is not necessarily equated with restriction of individual liberty. Because private control of the means of production has been used to oppress large numbers of people, the liberal democrats favor government action, a mild form of socialism if you will, to prevent such oppression. Believing that people can devise institutions that will serve their needs better than institutions that already exist, they practice social engineering. The victories and defeats of such experiments can be found in the policies of the New Deal and the Great Society, and the reactionary policies of Ronald Reagan and Newt Gingrich.

CAPITALISM

One of the distinguishing features of modern ideologies is that, since the Industrial Revolution, politics and economics have become inextricably joined. Modern democracy, like all other contemporary ideologies, cannot be divorced from its accompanying economic system. Thus, we find that modern democracy is divided into two major variants, *democratic capitalism* and *democratic socialism*. Accordingly, our study of modern ideologies must necessarily include consideration of economic theory.

Adam Smith

Rejecting **mercantilism,** the economic system current in his time, **Adam Smith** (1723–1790), a Scottish scholar, developed the ideas that are today understood to be rudiments of **capitalism.** In his 1776 book, *The Wealth of Nations,* Smith asserted that a nation's wealth was not determined—as had previously been thought—by the amount of gold found in its treasury. Rather, the wealth of nations is determined by their productivity.

Accordingly, Smith advocated the principle of *laissez-faire,* which demanded that the government should pursue no economic policy. Instead, the government should remain aloof of economic matters, thus encouraging competition. He reasoned that the resources of a nation would be most effectively distributed when each individual in the society could demand and use them as he or she thought best. In this way, Smith suggested, there would be optimum economic development. The "invisible hand" of supply and demand would assure that the best possible quality would be offered at the lowest possible price.

Competition was seen as the engine of the new economic system. People would array themselves against one another in a form of economic combat. Those who offered quality goods at reasonable prices would prosper, while those who did not would find themselves forced out of the market.

The net result of this uninhibited competitive process would be an economic system of unparalleled prosperity, or so it was reasoned. This happy conclusion rested on the assumption that *the good of the whole is best served when each person pursues his or her own self-interest.* Herein lies one of the basic differences between capitalism and socialism. While capitalism assumes that society's best interest is maximized when each individual is free to do that which he or she thinks is best for himself or herself, socialism, as we shall see in Chapter 9, is based on the attitude that the individual's interests are maximized when each person suppresses selfish objectives for the greater good. Socialism asks people to cultivate a social consciousness; capitalism does not, because it assumes that the social good will be achieved automatically.

In the early stages of the Industrial Revolution, the age during which Smith lived, confidence in the therapeutic value of pursuing self-interest may well have been justified. The national economies of the day were badly warped by arbitrary, government-sanctioned monopolies, and it was thought desirable to free economic systems from governmental restraint. The "dead hand of feudalism" still dominated much of the land, even as money began to assume greater importance in the society. Inventions and the application of machinery to production promised to vastly expand the availability of goods, if only people could be persuaded to invest enough capital to make use of them. Indeed, the freewheeling system Smith proposed may have been, as Marx later concluded, the very step necessary to catapult Europe into a new era of human history.

Capitalism after Smith. Smith, however, was followed by a new generation of economists who were forced to deal with the bleak side of capitalism as well as with its more pleasant aspects. The Industrial Revolution and the need to accumulate capital had visited terrible hardships upon the working class, forcing workers and their families to live in the most miserable and oppressive conditions.

In the early 1800s **David Ricardo** (1772–1823) and **Thomas Malthus** (1766–1834), two English economists, became capitalism's leading intellectual lights. Ricardo assumed that while human labor created value, it was perfectly appropriate for those who controlled capital to force labor to surrender a large part of the value it created. Otherwise, additional capital would not be forthcoming. On this assumption Ricardo developed the theory of the **Iron Law of Wages,** in which he suggested that the owner of the factory and the machines would be driven by the profit motive to pay the workers only enough to bring them to the factories to work another day. Though this process might be perceived as cruel, Ricardo argued that only in this way would enough capital be created to find future production. Hence, although the workers' conditions were admittedly miserable, they would degenerate even further unless additional capital was created.

Even gloomier than his colleague, Thomas Malthus became alarmed by the impending disaster he foresaw. He suggested that food might be expected to increase in arithmetic proportions—from quantities of one, to two, to three, to four, and so on. Population, however, could grow geometrically—from quantities of one, to two, to four, to sixteen, and so on. If such a progression were allowed to take place, the result would soon be catastrophic. Assuming that the population was most likely to increase in good times, Malthus concluded that it was more prudent, and indeed more humane in the long run, to deny the masses more than the bare essentials, thus discouraging a potentially ruinous population explosion. These arguments justified the accumulation of massive amounts of wealth in the hands of a very few, while the suffering among the workers, those who produced the wealth, mounted.

Then, toward the end of the nineteenth century, a new and "scientific" rationale for the possession of great wealth by a few in the face of the misery of the masses was advanced by another Englishman, *Herbert Spencer* (1820–1903). Loosely extrapolating Charles Darwin's theory of natural selection, Spencer applied it to a concept of social development that became known as **Social Darwinism.** Coining the phrase "survival of the fittest," a phrase often mistakenly attributed to Darwin himself, Spencer suggested that the wealthy were so favored because they were superior to the poor. Thus, according to Spencer, the possession of great wealth set the owner apart as a particularly worthy individual. It also encouraged the rich to redouble their efforts to expand their fortunes, thus asserting their advanced natures over the less worthy poor.

American capitalism.   Spencer's theory became most popular in the United States, where capitalist competition and "rugged individualism" had assumed exaggerated proportions. Harkening to the pompous lectures of William Graham Sumner (1840–1910), a Yale professor and the nation's leading proponent of Social Darwinism, American moguls—the robber barons, as they came to be called—steeped themselves in righteous justification while they plundered those less fortunate.

Happily, this brutal phrase of capitalism was abandoned with the reforms of the Progressive Era (1901–1920) and, most important, with the **New Deal** of Franklin Delano Roosevelt (1933–1945). Yet, the doctrine of untempered individualism came into vogue once again in the 1980s when Ronald Reagan became president. He limited government involvement in the economy and celebrated the "free marketplace" as the appropriate arbiter of the distribution of goods and the dispenser of social justice. Ronald Reagan presided over a reactionary revolution which saw businesses deregulated and social programs emaciated by lack of public financial support. The freewheeling entrepreneurial system advocated by Reagan encouraged people to suppress their social consciences, and urged individuals to seek their own advantage. On the positive side, inflation was reduced dramatically, and interest rates and unemployment also fell. But at the same time, homelessness increased disgracefully; the gap between rich and poor widened seriously, the civil rights movement was set back in several important areas, and civil liberties were narrowed. Meanwhile, Reagan's policies of deregulation and his neglectful approach to administering policy saw natural resources pillaged for profit; the toxicity of air and water reached unprecedented levels; and the stock and commodity exchanges descended into unethical and illegal practices that had not been seen since the 1920s. At the same time, the national debt tripled, and the interest on the debt catapulted to the third largest category in the national budget. In only four years, the United States fell from the world's greatest creditor nation to the world's greatest debtor nation.

The 1980s passion for raw individualism appeared to have run its course without destroying the foundations of the social and economic system forged by the New Deal. Moderates like George Bush and Bill Clinton pursued centrist policies during the late 1980s and early 1990s. At the same time, however, the economic and social uncertainties accompanying cybernetics, the most current stage of the industrial revolution, created anxiety and uncertainty among the American public. Consequently, a new wave of individualism, even *Libertarianism*, has swept the country and brought into Congress an unprecedentedly conservative, even reactionary, group headed by Speaker of the House of Representatives, Newt Gingrich. This new congressional majority holds government involvement in the individual's life responsible for virtually every serious problem the country faces. A new round of reactionary assaults appears to be in the making, and the infrastructure of the New Deal's welfare-state seems again to be threatened. Clearly, however, the needs of society have long since outstripped the potential of Smith's rather simple prescriptions.

All the same, founded on the principle of unlimited accumulation, American capitalism, most would agree, has been a terribly successful and productive economic system over the years. However, close scrutiny reveals problems and contradictions worthy of consideration.

While affording great opportunity to its citizens, American capitalism reserves many of its greatest advantages for those with enough wealth to buy into the system. The adage "It takes money to make money" is indeed prophetic. For example, the greatest tax advantages to the middle class are usually available through buying a home. Yet, with skyrocketing prices and interest rates, fewer and fewer people can afford the initial amount necessary to buy a house and thus qualify for the tax deductions. The wealthy, on the other hand, can easily afford to buy a home or two—thus receiving this advantage as well. The wealthy enjoy many other tax and financial advantages of which the poor and lower middle class cannot avail themselves. They can make investments that can be sheltered by capital gains tax reductions. If they lose their investments, they can deduct the loss from their taxes. The most wealthy among us pay a tax rate of 33 percent, barely twice the rate assessed the poorest taxpayer.

The advantages afforded the wealthy in our system are even more startling when one becomes aware of the tendency for wealth to accumulate in fewer and fewer hands. Recent statistics indicate that the nation's wealth has become more concentrated in the hands of the few than at any other time in this century, including the 1920s—the decade leading to the Great Depression. In 1995, astonishingly, 39 percent of all the wealth in the country was owned by the richest one percent of the U.S. population.[1] As a measure of the rate at which wealth is concentrating, consider that in 1980 the top 1 percent of the population owned only 25 percent of the wealth. In 1992, its share had jumped to 35 percent, an increase of 0.833 percent of the total wealth annu-

[1]NBC News, April 17, 1995, 5:30 P.M.

During the Great Depression of the 1930s, millions of proud but unemployed people reluctantly queued up to receive life-saving food from charity organizations.   National Archives

ally. Between 1992 and 1995, however, the rate at which wealth concentrated among the nation's richest 1 percent has accelerated to a full 1 percent annually. Meanwhile, between the beginning of 1993 and the end of 1994, the nation's productivity grew by 2.1 percent while real wages fell by 3 percent, reinforcing a twenty-year decline in the standard of living of the middle class and below.[2]

Some people argue that the economic system is malfunctioning when it gives greater advantages to the wealthy than it gives to the poor. "The rich get richer and the poor get poorer," they grimace. In fact, however, the capitalist system is not malfunctioning when it favors the wealthy—indeed it is doing exactly what it is supposed to do by such bias. Capitalism depends on *private* enterprise. It must have private capital investment if it is to function adequately. The most efficient way of creating private capital is to concentrate huge amounts of money in the hands of a tiny minority of the people rather than spreading it out more equally among the masses. The fortunate few—the wealthy—then put their amassed fortunes into capital investments,

[2]James Risen, "Reich Cites Fallings Wages as Administration Failure," *The Los Angeles Times,* June 23, 1995.

increasing productivity. The increased productivity is then divided among the masses in improved living standards and among the wealthy in increased profits. The trick is to divide the nation's productivity properly. If too much money is siphoned off in profits, consumers will lack funds with which to buy, causing a depressed economy and unemployment. If, on the other hand, too much of the productivity goes to the consumer, too little money will be left for capital investment, resulting in aging plants and machinery, reducing efficiency and productivity, and causing inflation.

It is clear, therefore, that capitalism depends on the existence of a tiny, enormously wealthy class. Hence, laws in capitalist societies are structured so as to give their wealthy greater economic benefits than are enjoyed by the rest of their people. Taking advantage of these privileges, the same families are apt to remain wealthy through time. The Rockefellers, Guggenheims, Mellons, Fords, and other families of great wealth, having amassed fortunes at the early stages of our industrialization, are likely to remain wealthy because the law is tilted in favor of their doing so.

This is not to suggest that other people cannot become wealthy or that large amounts of capital investment are not provided by small investors. Clearly, the capitalist system provides enough opportunity to allow for significant social and economic mobility. Yet, the fact remains that over 90 percent of all the stock in the United States is owned by less than 3 percent of its people. In short, capitalism depends upon the monopolization of wealth.

Nevertheless, the negative aspects of capitalism, of which the foregoing are only some examples, should not be dwelled upon at the expense of attention to its positive features. The United States has risen from a relatively poor agrarian country to become the greatest industrial power in the world. Its people enjoy a standard of living unequaled in history. Perhaps even more remarkable, these economic successes have been achieved in a political and economic environment that remains open to personal free expression, affording its citizens a latitude of activity envied by people around the globe. The worst excesses of individualistic aggrandizement have been tempered by government regulation and social welfare programs. In developing programs that mitigate the economic impact on the "losers" in capitalistic competition, however, we have introduced socialist policies. Capitalism, in its purest form, rewards and protects only the "winners." Hence, ours is a mixed economic system.

In any event, capitalism and democracy developed coincidentally, both having been nurtured by confidence in human potential spawned by the scientific method, the Industrial Revolution, and the resulting liberal individualism. Indeed, it was very difficult to distinguish between capitalism and democracy during what one might call the neoclassical period of democratic theory.

NEOCLASSICAL DEMOCRATIC THEORY

The group of political theorists who followed Hobbes, Locke, and Rousseau differed from them in a number of ways, though they had much in common with them as well. One of the differences is highly significant, however. The early philosophers were trying to justify a political system that they hoped would become a reality. The *neoclassical democratic philosophers* were trying to design governmental schemes in an environment that was *already* democratic. This single fact made their political views quite different. While Locke and Rousseau were definitely on the left of the political spectrum and were optimistic and hopeful about people, the second wave of democratic theorists tended to be more conservative and pessimistic about human nature, although they did not go to the extreme Hobbes reached.

Locke and Rousseau were never faced with the problem of applying their theories. Later thinkers, by contrast, had to implement their ideas in the real world, a circumstance that made them more conservative. As time passed, the idea of natural law became less and less credible among scholars and politicians alike. Egalitarianism as well as majoritarianism were set aside in favor of distinctions based on social class. The new generation of thinkers substituted limited voting rights for equal representation, probusiness policies for absolute *laissez-faire*, and in some cases organicism for individualism. Still later, liberal democratic principles reemerged and, as we will see, evolved into one of the two major strains of contemporary democracy. Here, however, we will examine the theories of the second wave of democratic philosophers more closely.

Edmund Burke

There were three major neoclassical democrats. Interestingly, each of the three was a distinguished politician in his own right, and each developed his political theory in response to a political issue that he faced in his public life. The first of the three was **Edmund Burke** (1729–1797). Although he was an Irishman, Burke had no trouble being accepted into English society and became an articulate spokesman for the ideals of the English state, crown, and church. Burke was noted for his eloquence in Parliament, where he served for almost thirty years.

Conservative philosophy.   As mentioned in Chapter 2, Burke was the father of modern conservative philosophy. Conservative positions have always existed, to be sure, but Burke was the first to address conservatism as a philosophy, the first to analyze the basic principles and motivations of conservatives.

Burke's attitude was Hobbesian in several ways. Social and political stability were the major goals of his theories. Hence, he believed that a good government is one that keeps the peace. Although Burke was a conservative, he did not always object to change; indeed, he regarded it as a necessary feature of life. However, he felt that any change should be gradual, well thought out, and consistent with the prevailing social environment. He opposed changes that might disrupt the society, believing that the only modifications that should be made are those that will keep things much as they are.

Examples of how Burke applied this theory are found in his positions on the revolutions in England, the United States, and France and in his attitude toward the British East India Company. Burke defended the 1688 revolution in England and the 1776 revolution in the Anglo-American colonies[3] on the grounds that each was an attempt to restore to a society constitutional principles that an aggressive king had destroyed. By the same token, however, Burke is famous for his passionate objection to the French Revolution. In his classic work *Reflections on the Revolution in France,* he argued that since the revolution had abruptly cut France off from its past development by replacing its monarchy with a republic, it posed a dire threat to French civilization itself.

Burke's resistance to change stemmed from his assumption that human reason is not competent to improve social or political systems. Burke believed that the institutions of any society are the products of the accumulated wisdom of centuries. No single generation has the ability to produce abrupt changes that will improve the society. Indeed, by meddling with institutions that have been perfected over centuries, people may destroy them completely. Burke viewed civilization as a fragile thing that could be ruined if it were not protected from human folly.

Burke believed that any existing institution had value; that is, an existing institution, a product of the wisdom of successive generations, has proved its value by surviving and should therefore not be trifled with. If they were not useful, institutions would disappear, Burke reasoned. In addition, Burke believed that part of the strength of an institution comes from the fact that it is accepted by the citizens in a society. This popular acceptance could occur only after an extended period. Any proposal for change, regardless of the soundness of the thought that produced it, could not attract the same commitment that an institution could develop over time. Hence, according to Burke, a new institution can never be as valuable as an older one.

Surprisingly, Burke's conservative philosophy led him to develop an attitude toward society similar to Rousseau's. Burke, like Rousseau, believed that there had been a time when people existed as solitary individuals without a society as we know it. They came together, however, out of a need to interact with each other, and in so doing, they formed an institution that has

---

[3]Burke's career in Parliament (1765–1794) spanned the period of the American Revolution. British policies in the American colonies had been very controversial. Many members of Parliament opposed the government's attempts to force the American colonies to comply with its will. The British people were also divided on the issue, and their reluctance to fight their American cousins made it necessary for England to hire Hessian mercenaries to fight in the colonies.

become part of the definition of humanity itself. Burke believed that goodness, morality, even civilization itself became possible only when people had created society. Society thus becomes the context in which people can refine their characters and develop their human traits. Moreover, the society develops an organic character. It becomes a personality in its own right, a "political personality."

Although Burke did not emphasize this point as much as Rousseau, he believed that absolute power came from the society and the state. The society may be a collection of "foolish" individuals, but when those individuals join to form a society, their collective judgment becomes "wise" and "always acts right." Burke's respect for tradition and history, coupled with his assumption that society had almost mystical powers, contributed to an attitude toward society that approached religious devotion. Here, too, he not only followed Rousseau but anticipated the ideas of Georg Hegel (1772–1831), whose political ideas we will study in subsequent chapters.

Theory of government. As already mentioned, Burke had a conservative attitude toward government. The primary purpose of government, he believed, was to keep order. He was also uneasy about the concept of popular rule. Hence, he made a strong defense for representative government. He argued that the proper governing agency of England was Parliament. Yet, Parliament should not necessarily be controlled by the people. Rather, it was an institution through which the minority would rule the majority, albeit in a benevolent fashion.

Burke maintained that a good ruler must meet three qualifications. *Ability* was of course necessary if the government was to be managed efficiently. Second, Burke believed that only people with *property* should be allowed to govern, since they would be less likely to desire the possessions of others. Burke believed that it was quite natural for property to be distributed unequally among the people in the state. Because people without property are never content, they constantly try to deprive the wealthy of their property. This disruption of society could be avoided if power was granted solely to property holders.

Burke's third qualification for government was *high birth*. While Burke did not argue that the upper class would always rule better than other classes, he pointed out that the nobility tended to have a greater stabilizing influence than any other class and should therefore rule. Note the overriding importance given to stability in each of the last two qualifications. You will remember that the conservative desires order more than anything else.

Burke rejected Locke's belief that members of Parliament should be bound by the wishes of their constituents. Those wishes should be considered, of course, but members of Parliament should not let such pressure sway them from their better judgment. Legislators were elected to make policy for their constituents, but they were not to be thought of as "ambassadors" who could act only on the instructions of their constituents. As Burke put it, "While a member of the legislature ought to give great weight to the wishes of his constituents, he ought never to sacrifice to them his unbiased opinion, his mature judgment, his enlightened conscience."

Burke also rejected another liberal democratic position. *He denied the basic equality of people.* People, he argued, are obviously unequal. They have different abilities and intellects. Consistent with his conservative views, Burke believed that the most important distinctions among people are property and social status. Those who have property and status are simply more important than those who do not. Consquently, the well-to-do, being more influential than the poor, deserve more representation in government.

Burke was also a nationalist. Indeed, his ideas did much to integrate nationalism with conservative philosophy. As a nationalist, however, Burke rejected the local autonomy of federalism in the United States. He argued that when people were elected to Parliament, they were not required to represent the narrow interests of their constituencies. Parliament, he believed, was a national legislature, not a meeting of local representatives. "You choose a member, indeed," he said in a speech to his constituents, "but when you have chosen him, he is not a member of Bristol, but he is a member of Parliament."

To Burke, then, democracy is a system in which the people choose representatives who will rule them in their best interests. This attitude stems from a pessimistic view of human potential founded on a lack of confidence in the power of human reason and on a denial of the existence of human equality.

James Madison

James Madison (1751–1836) is the second major neoclassical democratic philosopher. Madison had a long and distinguished political career. His most important political writings, like those of Burke, were responses to the dramatic political events of his day. Though still a young man in 1787, Madison was an experienced statesman by the time of the Constitutional Convention. It was at this meeting that he made his greatest contribution to government, even though he continued a brilliant career long afterwards.

Because he brought to the Constitutional Convention the fundamental structure on which the United States Constitution was based, Madison is often called the Father of the Constitution. He is also one of our best sources of information on the political intent of the drafters. Sharing the authorship of a collection of essays known as *The Federalist Papers* with Alexander Hamilton and John Jay, Madison treats us to a beautifully written, well-reasoned explanation of the political theory upon which the Constitution is based. Following the Constitution's ratification, Madison wrote and carried through Congress the Bill of Rights.

James Madison (1751–1836) President James Madison Thomas Sully portrait. Corcoran Gallery of Art.

Madison's view of politics. Madison was a very complicated character whose political attitudes vacillated from right to left on the spectrum, depending on the circumstances. With regard to popular government, Madisonian philosophy is definitely conservative. His studies convinced him that the history of democracy was rather unsuccessful. When faced with a crisis, popularly controlled governments usually degenerated into "mob rule," finally ending with the people giving power to a tyrant of some sort. Hence, Madison, like almost everyone present at the Constitutional Convention, had little respect for pure democracy.

Though Madison probably believed in popular sovereignty in theory, he did not trust the people themselves. In fact, Madison's attitude toward people was somewhat Hobbesian. In *The Federalist* (no. 55) he expressed mixed feelings about the nature of people.

> . . . As there is a degree of depravity in mankind which requires a certain degree of circumspection and distrust, so there are other qualities in human nature which justify a certain portion of esteem and confidence.

In *The Federalist* (no. 10), however, he describes human nature in unambiguous Hobbesian terms. "So strong is this propensity of mankind to fall into mutual animosities that where no substantial occasion presents itself the most frivolous and fanciful distinctions have been sufficient to kindle their unfriendly passions and excite their most violent conflicts."

Despite his Hobbesian disposition toward people, Madison did not share the English philosopher's confidence in strong government as a remedy for human shortcomings. Quite the contrary. Like Locke, he believed that individual liberty was the main goal of a political system. Yet, unlike Locke he was not at all confident of the individual's ability to achieve and maintain liberty in a democratic society. This conflict involved Madison in a dilemma. He believed that people ought to govern themselves in some way, but at the same time experience taught him that popular governments soon degenerated into dictatorships.

Therefore, Madison was convinced that government was necessary, and he preferred a popularly controlled political system. Still, his studies showed that neither the people nor the government could be counted on to maintain "liberty, which is essential to political life." He had observed that government, when left unchecked, was oppressive and cruel. At the same time, however, he believed that human nature was not only aggressive and selfish but *unchangeable* as well. He therefore wanted to construct a system that would play the oppressiveness of government against the avarice of people, hoping that each would check the negative aspects of the other. This mutual negation, he speculated, would result in good government and the greatest amount of individual liberty possible. This, as you will see shortly, is at once the genius and perhaps the greatest failing of James Madison and the American political system.

Madison's political system.   Madison did not fear the individual; indeed, he supported individual rights and liberties. What concerned him was not solitary individuals but groups of individuals in politics. These groups he called *factions.*

Madison noted that in politics people had a habit of combining into factions to pursue mutual interests. This grouping he considered unfortunate but unavoidable. The faction about which he felt the greatest trepidation was the majority. You will recall that he believed people were essentially selfish and that if, in a democratic system, a group was in the majority for a sustained period, it would use its power to oppress the minority.

Using the Constitution to protect minorities, *Madison's system of government is largely an attempt to divide and frustrate the majority.* Madison envisioned a political system with the broadest possible power base. For example, he rejected the common belief that a democracy could work only in a very small area, arguing that it could succeed in a large country like the United States. A large population spread over a huge area would make it difficult to create a permanent majority. Such a society would probably divide into varied and fluctuating minority factions, making a long lasting majority unlikely. Instead, majorities would be created out of combinations of competing minorities. Thus, any majority would be temporary, and new ones would be elusive. This system, which political scientists now term *pluralism,* will be discussed in more detail in the next chapter.

Economic disparity was also a necessary component of Madison's scheme. Not unlike Karl Marx, Madison believed that economic factors move people to political activity more than any other single factor. Madison was not as absolute on this subject as Marx; he believed that religion, culture, ideals, and geographic factors also influence people. Still, he argued that economic concerns are the most powerful force in people's lives. "A landed interest, a manufacturing interest, a mercantile interest, with many lesser interests," Madison wrote, "grow up of necessity in civilized nations, and divide them into different classes, actuated by different sentiments and views." Madison's wish for a diverse and competitive economic system, together with his belief that people are by nature combative, led to the conclusion that capitalism is the economic system best suited to the political structure he had in mind.

Madison's view of the nature of a democracy was almost identical to Burke's, with one very important exception. Madison expected that the legislators would represent their districts or their states. Unlike Burke, he wanted to localize rather than nationalize politics, since this process would institutionalize tens, or even hundreds, of local factions and hopefully discourage the emergence of a permanent national majority faction. Madison was very pessimistic about the chance of a successful democratic government. His studies indicated that pure democracy is usually unsuccessful and "can admit of no cure to the mischiefs of faction." On the other hand, he wrote in *The Federalist* (no. 10), "A republic, by which I mean a government in which the scheme of representation takes place, opens a different prospect and promises the *cure* for which we are seeking" (emphasis added).

In short, Madison believed that the people should rule themselves, but only through elected representatives. What he called a "republic" is more accurately termed a *representative democracy.* Madison also expected that the representatives would be free to use their judgment rather than being bound to the wishes of their constituents, as Locke had expected. Echoing Burke, Madison wrote in *The Federalist* (no. 10) that a republic would:

> . . . refine and enlarge the public views by passing them through the medium of a chosen body of citizens, whose patriotism and love of justice will be least likely to sacrifice it to temporary or partial considerations. Under such a regulation it may well happen that the public voice, pronounced by the representatives of the people, will be more consonant to the public good than if pronounced by the people themselves, convened for the purpose.

Thus, Madison expected that the United States would be governed by an enlightened and benevolent aristocracy that would protect the *interests* of the people but would not necessarily be bound by the people's *will.*

Checks and balances.   Madison's best-known and most creative contribution is the system of *separation of powers* and *checks and balances.* In developing this system, he owed a great deal to two earlier students of government, James Harrington (1611–1677) and Charles Montesquieu (1689–1755). Both of these men were interested in a democratic republic and in developing a way of limiting the power of the government over the people. Using their ideas as a base, Madison created a complex system of institutional and popular restraints.

By separating the powers of government, Madison hoped to make it impossible for any single branch of the government to gain too much power and use it to dominate the others. No person could serve in more than one branch of the government at a time, and each branch was given its own separate and distinct powers. The legislature, divided into two houses, was to make the law, the executive was to carry out the law, and the judiciary was to adjudicate legal disputes and interpret the law. Yet each branch was given some powers that overlapped with those of the other two branches. The legislature controlled the purse strings, and it was also allowed to ratify appointments to the executive and judicial branches. The executive appointed judges and could veto laws. The courts were expected to nullify any law or executive action that violated the Constitution.[4] These are just a few examples of the checks and balances provided for in the American system of government; there are many others, and we shall discuss them in the next chapter.

Another way Madison diffused power was by creating *federalism.* The powers of government were divided between the state and the national governments. In this way Madison hoped to prevent either level of government from gaining too much power. Federalism also divided the people of the United States into several compartments. He hoped that although majorities might develop at the state level, the various majorities would check each other, thus preventing a permanent majority at the national level. "The influence of factitious leaders may kindle a flame within their particular States," he wrote, "but will be unable to spread a general conflagration through the other states."

The mechanisms mentioned above are the *institutional checks and balances,* but Madison reserved his ultimate impediments, the *popular checks and balances,* for the people. This effort to frustrate a permanent majority was built into the electoral system itself. To begin with, only members of the

---

[4]It is true that the Constitution does not grant the power of judicial review to the courts in so many words, but there can be little question that the founders intended such a power to exist. In *The Federalist* (no. 78) Hamilton wrote: "No legislative act, therefore, contrary to the constitution can be valid. . . . Where the will of the legislature, declared in its statutes, stands in opposition to that of the people, declared in the constitution, the judges ought to be governed by the latter rather than the former. They ought to regulate their decision by the fundamental laws rather than by those which are not fundamental."

House of Representatives were elected directly by the people. Until the Seventeenth Amendment was passed in 1913, senators were elected by the state legislatures. The president and vice presidents were, and still are, elected by the electoral college, and although the voters elect the electors, the electors are not required by the Constitution to vote for the presidential candidate to whom they are pledged. Judges are even more removed from popular control, since they are appointed to the bench for life.

The people's hold over government is complicated even more because officials are elected to staggered terms from different constituencies. While House members are elected from congressional districts every two years, senators are elected on a statewide basis to six-year terms, with only one-third of the Senate being elected every two years. The president, by contrast, is chosen in a national election to a four-year term. Hence, it takes six full years for voters, in 536 different constituencies, to fill every national elective office. This arrangement was deliberately contrived to soften the effect of popular "passions."

Popular control is also reduced by the fact that the terms of office of elected officials are fixed by law and cannot be interrupted except under very unusual circumstances. The people elect many officials, but only when the law calls for election and not necessarily when the people wish to vote on a particular office. Elections take place on the first Tuesday following the first Monday of November in even years. Why? Because that is when the law calls for them to be held.

It is clear that the American political system, as developed by Madison, is not very democratic in the participatory sense of the term. In fact, it severely limits the ways in which people actually rule themselves. The people cannot pass laws; they cannot repeal laws. They cannot legally remove a person from office before the expiration of the term. Officials may be impeached, of course, but even this is not done by the people. Congress impeaches; the people do not.

To cap the irony, popular sovereignty, which means that the people are the source of all law and power, is supposed to be the central feature of democracy. Yet, the Constitution of the United States may not be amended directly by the people of the United States. It may be amended only through their representatives in Congress and the state legislatures.

One should gather from these comments that our political system was not designed to be very democratic in the literal sense of the term. The people formally participate in their government very rarely; their direct control over government officials is limited to election day. It is true that popular control and participation are much more significant than a simple statement of the people's formal powers indicates, but the fact remains that the system was not intended to be very democratic. Even so, the American political system has been liberalized considerably since the Constitution was written.

However, the theoretical justifications for these changes are founded more in the ideas of Thomas Jefferson than in those of James Madison.

Jefferson's alternative.   A man of reason, **Thomas Jefferson** (1743–1826) was America's Voltaire. Yet, Jefferson was a man of action as well as a man of thought. His most famous work, the Declaration of Independence, articulated the Spirit of '76, which justified the American Revolution and became a beacon, leading freedom-loving people throughout the world to their goal. America's most articulate statesman, Jefferson may be placed between Locke and Rousseau on the left of the political spectrum. Though he generally leaned toward Locke's version of the social contract and natural law, he shared Rousseau's respect for the common people and for participatory government. More than most of the other natural law theorists, Jefferson favored revolution as a way of bringing about meaningful political change. Arguing that 20 years without a rebellion would be too long if government officials were to remain servants of the people, Jefferson wrote: "The tree of liberty must be refreshed from time to time with the blood of patriots and tyrants."

To Jefferson the Spirit of '76 was a declaration that all people were created equal, that "the Laws of Nature and Nature's God" had given every person a set of rights that could not be legally alienated, and that among those rights were "Life, Liberty, and the pursuit of Happiness."[5] As a social con-

---

[5]You will recall from Chapter 2 that in drafting the Declaration of Independence, Jefferson amended Locke's phrase "life, liberty and property" to read "Life, Liberty and the pursuit of Happiness." This distinction is important, since it was intentional. Jefferson put up a spirited defense of the phrase against the Second Continental Congress delegates who wanted to change it back to Locke's more familiar one. Though Jefferson was a classical democratic theorist in the tradition of Locke, he, like Rousseau, lived a full generation after the English philosopher and saw a different reality. Locke, the philosopher of a capitalist class that was challenging the dominant feudal class, saw private property as a means of achieving greater freedom. However, by the time of Rousseau and Jefferson the capitalist class had moved much closer to the source of power; some capitalists were actually beginning to use their control of property to deny equality and liberty to others. It will be recalled that Rousseau, the radical, suggested equal distribution of private property as a means by which the equality and liberty of all citizens in the community could be guaranteed. Jefferson sought a milder solution by simply deleting property from the inalienable rights and substituting a more abstract phrase. In either case, however, it is clear that an important change had occurred in leftist thinking about private property. Instead of considering private property a *natural right,* they gave it second-class status as a *social right.* And so it remains today. The left generally deemphasizes the importance of private property and values it only as a contribution to the welfare of the society, while those toward the right of the political spectrum take a more traditionally Lockean position and equate private property with individual well-being and liberty.

One should note, however, that even Locke opposed unlimited accumulation of private property by any individual. The American capitalists' argument in support of unlimited accumulation of private property is actually a perversion of the theories of Locke and Adam Smith rather than a true reflection of their ideas.

tract theorist, he believed that government was the product of an intentional act by the people in the society. He agreed with Locke that all "just powers" of government accrue to it from the people and that the government is supposed to serve the people, not the other way around. If the government does not serve the interests of the people, its masters, "it is the Right of the People to alter or abolish it, and to institute new Government, laying its foundation on such principles, and organizing its powers in such form as to them shall seem most likely to effect their Safety and Happiness."[6]

Jefferson's most outstanding characteristic was his love for and confidence in the common individual. No other political theorist has expressed such deep faith in ordinary people. Like Rousseau, Jefferson idealized the common people, yet somehow Jefferson's vision of the sturdy, self-reliant yeoman seems more appealing than Rousseau's "noble savage." True to Rousseau's basic theme, Jefferson avoided the sophisticated society of the cities for the more peaceful and simple rural life of his home in Monticello.

Jefferson's faith in the common people went beyond the romantic notion of an uncomplicated lifestyle, however. His confidence in the strength and wisdom of the ordinary folk was unshakeable. Unlike Hobbes, Burke, Madison, or Hamilton, Jefferson believed that the people were the only competent guardians of their own liberties, and as such they should be in firm control of their government. Discussing the role of the people in a republic, he wrote to Madison from France in 1787 that "they are the only sure reliance for the preservation of our liberties."

Jefferson's democratic ruralism is very close to an early form of populism (an ideology dedicated to the common people). Its impact on our political system has been great. Jefferson's liberal democratic theories have acted as a counterweight to Madison's conservative democratic ideas; indeed, the interplay between these two basic attitudes has dominated American political history. During the American Revolution and under the Articles of Confederation, Jefferson's ideology prevailed. However, for many reasons, not the least of which was the low priority given private property during this period, opposition to the Articles of Confederation began to build, culminating in the adoption of the Constitution of the United States. *The Constitution was, in fact, no less than the culmination of a conservative counterrevolution to the dominant theme of the American Revolution.*

Put differently, the Spirit of '76 was, for its time, radical and revolutionary. However, because of the apparent failure of the Articles of Confederation (1781–1789), under which it seemed that the economic and political situation was leading the country to disaster, James Madison, Alexander Hamilton, Benjamin Franklin, George Washington, and other delegates to the Constitutional Convention deliberately stifled the Spirit of '76, replacing it with a much more conservative, less democratic, and more paternalistic system of

---

[6]From the Declaration of Independence.

government. Although most of the nation's founders believed in popular checks on government, they were opposed to *direct* popular control of the basic government institutions. Hence, they created a government in which power was much more centralized than it had been under the Articles of Confederation. They also severely limited popular control over the government.

When the Constitution was adopted, the "revolution" was ended, the Spirit of '76 snuffed out, the radical experiment brought to a close, and a different, more conservative, less idealistic experiment begun. What might have existed had the revolution been allowed to run its course is impossible to know. History seems to indicate that we gained a great deal by ending it. One loss, however, was an optimistic attitude toward humanity. Thomas Paine, who understood revolution as did few other people, had expectations for the American Revolution much like Jefferson's, if not even more utopian. "We have it in our power to begin the world all over again," he wrote in *Common Sense*. Even with all our materialistic progress, we must be a bit saddened that Paine's idealism was lost.

The conservative victory was not as absolute as one might think, however. Since 1789, the year the Constitution went into effect, the system has gradually been liberalized. Indeed, George Mason, Jefferson, Samuel Adams, and others insisted, in return for their support, that the conservative Constitution be amended to mention the specific rights of the people under the new system. The original document was concerned primarily with the structure and powers of the central government. Little reference was made to the rights and liberties of the people, and the radicals insisted that they be added. This addition, of course, was the *Bill of Rights*.

Since the passage of the Bill of Rights the country has gone through a series of liberalizing eras that have gradually relaxed the restraints imposed on the people by the new political order. The changing social and economic effects of industrialization demanded political democratization. In the early nineteenth century the administrations of Thomas Jefferson (1801–1809) and Andrew Jackson (1829–1837) extended the vote to almost every adult white male citizen. And the Lincoln epoch (1861–1867) not only liberated the slaves but also brought about the Homestead Act, which made free land available to poor farmers. Other legislation during Lincoln's era promoted federal aid to education and made possible the construction of the transcontinental railroad. The Progressive Era amended the Constitution to provide for women's suffrage and for popular election of United States senators, enacted the progressive income tax, and established the procedures of initiative, referendum, and recall (otherwise known as *direct democracy*) in many states. The New Deal (1933–1941) brought social security, collective bargaining, and many social-welfare programs. The Great Society (1964–1969) launched a war on poverty and racial bigotry, while the past two decades have witnessed drives to liberate women and gays. Each of these eras produced great change. Nevertheless, each was followed by a period of reaction in which many of the changes were dismantled. The net result is that the liberties of individuals in the system have been gradually, if not completely, equalized and increased. Although much remains to be done, the nation has evolved to something closer to the Jeffersonian political ideal than perhaps Madison and his colleagues intended.

John C. Calhoun

John C. Calhoun (1782–1850) had one of the most distinguished careers of public service in United States history, holding high office almost continuously for nearly forty years. Devoted to the Union—but also to the principle of *states' rights*—he greatly expanded on a theme earlier initiated by Jefferson and Madison and developed the theory of *nullification* in *The South Carolina Exposition,* written in 1828. In this tract Calhoun argued that the states had created the national government and that the latter was therefore subordinate to the states. Accordingly, no state could be bound to a national law if its state legislature voted to nullify the statute. Thus, in an attempt to define the relationship of the states to the national government, Calhoun insisted that the Constitution was confederate in form and so inadvertently developed the philosophy used by the South in its secession from the Union ten years after his death.

Concurrent majorities.   In the last few months of his life Calhoun, though tired and ill, wrote a brilliant treatise on political philosophy. In this document, entitled *A Disquisition on Government,* he analyzed the essence of democracy, raising questions that have not yet been answered fully.

Calhoun took the social nature of people as fact. People, he argued, instinctively group together. He also assumed that government is necessary when people form groups. While he believed that people are naturally social beings, he argued, not unlike Hobbes, that individuals feel greater concern for themselves than for others in the group. This self-concern causes them to attack one another; hence, the need for government is clear and universal. Yet, Calhoun pointed out that even though government is intended primarily to protect individuals from each other, it is run by people who have the same selfish impulses as other people. Therefore, they can—if unchecked—use the power of government to oppress the very people the government is supposed to protect. Accordingly, government must be limited, and the mechanism by which a government is limited is what Calhoun called a constitution.

Calhoun believed that the people's most important political function was to limit governmental power. He did not concern himself greatly with the concept of government itself because he believed that government was divinely inspired. The job left to mortals was to maintain their liberties by effectively limiting government. "Constitution is the contrivance of man," he wrote in the *Disquisition,* "while government is of divine ordination. Man is left to perfect what the wisdom of the Infinite ordained as necessary to preserve the race."

Because he believed that the governors would naturally use their power to take advantage of the governed, Calhoun saw the governor and the governed as adversaries: "Those who exercise power and those subject to its exercise—the rulers and the ruled—stand in antagonistic relations to each other." As a result he argued that the people must be able to defend themselves against oppressive rulers. Thus, the vote was necessary, he thought, because it gave the people control over the length of time the ruler could rule.

At this point Calhoun turned what appears to be a relatively standard justification of democracy into a piercing analysis of freedom and oppression. In so doing, he filled in many details about the rights of the minority and the nature of majority oppression that Madison had not elaborated.

According to Calhoun, although popular suffrage gave the people some control over the government it did not guarantee justice and good government, as Locke, Rousseau, and Jefferson had believed. All the popular vote did was to transfer power from the few to the many, thus changing the source of governmental authority without changing the tendency of government to oppress. Since every individual has an urge to take advantage of others, government by the many can be just as oppressive as government by one or by a few. The only difference is that government by the majority oppresses the minority, while government by a few oppresses the many. Hence, democracy, while it was the best form of government available, was no guarantee against oppression. Calhoun agreed with Madison that a tyranny of the majority was just as dangerous as any other form of tyranny.

Some philosophers argued that an existing majority would be kept from oppressing the minority because it could find itself out of power and at the mercy of a new majority after the next election. Calhoun rejected this argument on the grounds that the selfish nature of the rulers would force them to oppress all the more when they felt themselves threatened with the loss of their power.

For a solution to this dilemma, Calhoun turned to a Madisonian structure of government. He advocated a system in which society should be divided into groups based on economic, religious, regional, and ethnic lines, thus forming several local majorities. At this point, however, Calhoun exceeds Madison's separatism by rejecting the Virginian's belief that national government should hold sway in disputes with local authorities. Instead, Calhoun insisted that each of the local majorities would have to agree to a national law before it could become effective.

This system of *concurrent majorities* would, Calhoun believed, result in an effective government. The vote would make those who governed responsible to the voters, and the need for a unanimous agreement by the several majorities would prevent government oppression. A perfect government would give representation and a veto to every interest group in the society. This safeguard, however, would be difficult if not impossible to guarantee. Yet, Calhoun reasoned, even if the society were only divided into its major interest groups, each having a veto over the actions of the whole, a goal of protection against oppression might well be achieved. Getting the agreement of several majorities would, Calhoun thought, probably require overwhelming popular approval, leaving a minority too small for the rulers to exploit profitably. As he put it in the *Disquisition,* "For, in such case, it would require so large a portion of the community, compared with the whole, to concur, or acquiesce in the action of the government, that the number to be plundered would be too few, and the number to be aggrandized too many, to afford adequate motives to oppression and abuse of its powers."

Calhoun further justified the system of concurrent majorities by analyzing it in relation to the *numerical majority* used in more standard forms of democracy. As had Burke, Calhoun rejected human equality as sufficient justification for political equality. He argued instead that the numerical majority accounts only for raw numbers and thus implies that everyone in the society has essentially the same interests. This concept, according to Calhoun, is unrealistic. A society, he rightly ventured, is composed of people with many varying interests. Since the numerical majority does not account for these differences, it does not reflect the society in all its complexity.

Concurrent majorities, Calhoun believed, would not only weigh the numerical value of people but also measure people in terms of their interests, thus giving a more accurate accounting of the popular will. The first error that naturally arises from overlooking the differences among individuals is to confuse the numerical majority with the people themselves, and to do this so completely as to regard them as identical. "This *radical* error" Calhoun wrote, ". . . has contributed more than any other cause to prevent the formation of popular constitutional governments, and to destroy them even when they have been formed" (emphasis added). Here the South Carolinian makes clear his unwillingness to accept the equality of all the people in the society. Because any single majority could veto the action of the whole, he would obviously give the veto power to a very small number of people. Like Madison, he does not seem to be concerned about the tyranny of the minority, but is it not a tyranny when a tiny part of the whole can prevent the majority of the people from doing what they wish?

Calhoun also argued that a permanent numerical majority would form if his system of concurrent majorities was not used. This seems doubtful, especially in the face of his own correct assertion that the society is made up of a myriad of varying interests. It is more likely that while there could be a group that would find itself always in the minority, the membership of the majority would change from one issue to the next to reflect the varied interest patterns in the society. Moreover, Calhoun seemed to imply that while the society is made up of individuals with various competing interests, each person in the society has only one major interest, and each can be conveniently fitted into one majority or another. But is it not more likely that each person has several interests, and that two or more of those interests may sometimes conflict with each other? How can such a person be represented in the system of concurrent majorities? Can that person vote as a member of each group that reflects his or her interests? In such a case it seems likely that Calhoun's system of concurrent majorities displays at least as many distortions as the simple numerical majority, to say nothing of the possibility that the majority view would often be frustrated by a very small minority.

Calhoun continued his analysis by suggesting that a constitutional democratic government is impossible without the system of concurrent majorities. A constitutional government, which is synonymous with a limited government, allows action by the numerical majority. Such action is positive and is therefore equated with government itself. Apparently forgetting that the numerical majority could vote against a policy just as easily as it could vote in favor, Calhoun further suggested that only the concurrent majorities can veto anything. Moreover, he equated this power of negation or limitation with constitution. "It is, indeed, the negative power which makes the constitution," he wrote, "and the positive which makes government. The one is the power of acting; and the other the power of preventing or arresting action. The two combined, make constitutional governments."

Calhoun argued that a government acted unfairly when it took actions that were unfavorable to any interest group in the society. Those in the minority within their own interest group could be consoled, since, at least, they were overruled by people with similar interests; and perhaps the majority knew best. However, a simple numerical majority measures quantity, not quality, and thus can abuse the best interests of any part of the society. Calhoun believed that this would be a gross misuse of the power of government and saw it as a form of tyranny no less than any other dictatorship. "The numerical majority is truly *single power*—and excludes the negative as completely as the absolute government of one, or of the few. The former is as much the absolute government of the democratic, or popular form, as the latter of the monarchical or aristocratical. It has, accordingly, in common with them, the same tendency of oppression and abuse of power."

The neoclassical democrats differ most clearly from the classical democrats in two areas. Locke, Rousseau, Jefferson, and even Hobbes argued that people were basically equal. Further, Locke, Rousseau, and Jefferson agreed that, while property rights were important, they should not be used to deny equal political and economic rights. This assumption of human equality is absent among the neoclassical democrats. Burke and Calhoun were the most clearly elitist, but elitism, or rule by a superior group, is implied by Madison as well. Unlike their predecessors, the neoclassical democrats all agreed that people should have a representative government, but they differed as to the level of government to which the representative should owe greatest allegiance. Burke argued for a national view, but Madison was less adamant about it, and Calhoun was unalterably dedicated to a local (state) control of legislation.

Each of the three neoclassical democrats may be considered a democrat because each believed in some kind of popular control over the rules. Yet, they all rejected direct democracy and favored an elite governing class. Indeed, they even rejected the principle of government by the majority. Burke said least about the concept of rule by the majority; clearly, he did not consider this concept vital, since he supported the preservation of the noble class as a governing group. Madison and Calhoun were opposed to majority rule as an absolute principle. They feared that the majority would abuse the rights of minorities, and each devised a system for frustrating the majority's wishes. Further, believing people to be essentially self-oriented and rejecting human equality as an important factor, the neoclassical democrats reasoned that capitalism was the most appropriate economic system since it tended to reward people in relation to their contributions. In short, by emphasizing property rights above human rights and by denying majoritarianism and human equality, the neoclassical democrats carried democracy toward the right of the political spectrum. But the passage of time and the evolution of liberal theory eventually restored democracy to the left.

THE EMERGENCE OF SOCIAL DEMOCRATIC LIBERALISM

During Locke's time people had begun to think that they could use reason to improve social conditions. After all, through science, reason had improved their material existence. They all speculated that if there were natural forces guiding all other creatures, there might also be natural forces guiding people. Hence, liberalism was born swaddled in the theory of natural law.

Jeremy Bentham (1748–1832) belonged to a later generation, however. Indeed, he was in the forefront of the second wave of English liberal thinkers. Like earlier liberals, he was a product of the scientific and technological progress achieved since the Enlightenment. He too believed that people could use reason to improve themselves, but he thought that the natural law theory led to a philosophical dead end. Bentham held that as long as the people in a society were confident that there was "right conduct" that could be found through the active pursuit of "right reason," society would be dynamic and changing. However, as soon as those in power thought that they had found the answer, all the citizens would have to conform to the leader's idea of right conduct. At that point the society would lose its vitality and become stagnant.

Utilitarianism

Bentham did not argue that there was an absolute, eternal, and universal rule in nature by which people should govern their conduct. Instead, he based his liberalism on belief in the value of human self-reliance. He disagreed with the idea of *moral absolutism,* the principle that there was a single source of right and wrong in nature, a good and bad beyond human authority. However, Bentham did not reject the standard of natural law without suggesting his own measure by which to evaluate human activity and conduct: the *moral relativist* philosophy of *utilitarianism.*

"Nature," Bentham wrote in *An Introduction to the Principles of Morals and Legislation,* "has placed mankind under the governance of two sovereign masters, *pain* and *pleasure.*" Human happiness would be achieved when pain was at a minimum and pleasure at a maximum. The value or *utility* of any policy, therefore, can be measured by the amount of pleasure or pain it brings to an individual or to society as a whole. Rejecting elitism, Bentham assumed that one person's happiness is equal to the happiness of any other. Further, Bentham believed that the well-being of society would be maximized by any policy that brought "the greatest happiness to the greatest number." The principle of utility, or utilitarianism, was Bentham's major interest. Almost everything he did or wrote was a variation on that theme, and he developed a theory of law by which to implement it.

Positivist law resulted from the combination of Bentham's rejection of natural law, his utilitarianism, and his conviction that government should take *positive* steps to maximize the happiness of the society. "The business of government," he wrote, "is to promote the happiness of society." The authority of a given law, in Bentham's view, had nothing to do with any concept of eternal good or justice, as natural law theorists believed. As long as the law was made by the legally established authority, it was a valid law. It did not have to meet any other standard. Law was not based on an absolute, unchanging truth. It was *not* a semisacred thing that people should worship and never change. Law, in Bentham's view, was a tool by which the society could modify its social conditions in order to increase its happiness. Thus, Bentham's theory of positivist law took down the pedestal on which law had been placed by the early liberals. It brought law back within reach of the society by calling for change and reform.

While Bentham viewed as valid any law that was made by the proper authority, he did not regard every valid law as good law. To assess the wisdom of law, Bentham applied his theory of utilitarianism. But if a society were to adopt a policy that gave the greatest happiness to the greatest number, it would need a way of measuring utility. To satisfy this need, Bentham developed his *hedonistic calculus.* This elaborate formula included a list of fourteen categories of human pleasure, twelve categories of pain, and seven standards of measurement. These, Bentham suggested, should be used by a *scientific legislature* to determine the wisdom of a proposed policy. Though his hedonistic calculus is impractical and even a bit ridiculous, it stems from a genuine concern for improvement and democratization of the government and the legislative process. Moreover, one should bear in mind that this formula, suggested in a time when people were enchanted with science, was a well-meant attempt to scientifically measure the worth of any policy or law.[7]

Bentham's contribution was important. He had the foresight to lead Western thought out of the trap inherent in natural law. In utilitarianism he gave us a practical standard by which to measure the value of a particular policy. With these ideas he set liberalism on a new course, one that could significantly improve the condition of society. In calling for positive legal and governmental steps to improve the society, he provided motivation for many reforms that were adopted in England between 1830 and 1850: the civil service, the secret ballot, equal popular representation in Parliament, expanded educational opportunities, humane treatment of animals, and much more. It is perhaps not too much to say that Jeremy Bentham and his followers gave England a new social conscience. In short, Bentham was the founder of contemporary liberalism (see Chapter 2).

Democratic Socialism

The introduction of utilitarianism and positivist law into democratic theory led to a whole new concept of popular government. The relationship of people to their government had changed drastically since Locke's era and even since the time of Madison. In the seventeenth and eighteenth centuries the most likely oppressor of the people was indeed the government. Few other institutions were powerful enough to oppress the masses. Those that were strong enough, such as the Church or the landowning class, almost always used government to dominate the people. Democracy itself was relatively untested at that time. What democracy there was often degenerated into mob rule and eventually turned into a dictatorship of one kind or another.

In the nineteenth century, however, democracy was more successful, and its development was accompanied by the growth of industrialization and capitalism. The new political system was praised as government by the people, yet the economic system seemed to squeeze ownership into the hands of fewer and fewer people. This process continued until a single company became the major employer in a given locale or even owned the town

---

[7]Bentham's confidence that science would lead to the solution of social problems was not uncommon among intellectuals of the nineteenth century. Several scholars of the last century besides Bentham, including—as you will see—Marx, held the same hope for science.

outright. Wages were kept low, hours of work were long, safety features were ignored, and men, women, and children were exploited.

It became clear that people could be controlled by economic forces the way they had been controlled by government in the past. Capitalism, which had long been supported by liberals because it tended to increase individual freedom and equality, became suspect because of its ability to exploit people. Gradually those on the left of the political spectrum began to wonder why, if the government was supposed to be democratic and if the economic forces in the society were exploiting the people, the people did not use their control of government to regulate the economy. *This new emphasis revolutionized liberal democracy, making it more socially oriented and less individualistic.* Although Bentham was the first modern liberal, his thinking only prepared the way for the new attitude toward democracy. It took several later thinkers to bring these new ideas to maturity.

John Stuart Mill.   John Stuart Mill (1806–1873) was a student of Bentham, but his scholarship, logic, and clear writing allowed him to go beyond his teacher. So great were his intellectual powers that he is generally recognized as one of the most important philosophers of the nineteenth century. Like Bentham, he was a political activist, and he even spent three years in the House of Commons. From an early age he supported contemporary movements, such as free education, trade unionism, equal apportionment of Parliamentary seats, and repeal of the corn tariffs. Moreover, he was among the first modern thinkers to advocate the equality of women.

Mill was interested in many areas of thought, including philosophy, logic, morals, and economics. His most important work, *On Liberty* (1859), is perhaps the most eloquent treatment of individual freedom in the English language. In it he argued that although democracy was the preferable form of government, even democracy had a tendency to limit individual liberty. Hence, freedom of speech and thought should be given absolute protection under the law because individual liberty was the surest way of reaching happiness.

Obviously influenced by Bentham's ideas, Mill became a utilitarian. He reasoned that happiness is the principle objective of the society and that happiness can best be achieved when people do good for each other. The original motivation for kindness toward another person, Mill argued, was *enlightened self-interest.* That is, individuals do good deeds because they know that they themselves will ultimately benefit from such acts. However, Mill took his analysis one step further and in so doing was led toward a very different conclusion than that reached by others who supported the enlightened self-interest theory of motivation. Mill argued that, in time, people can become used to doing good and will continue to do so even if they do not expect any particular reward. In other words, Mill came very close to arguing that people are not necessarily selfish, or that if they are, they can change or control that part of their nature. This optimism about human character is typical of leftist ideologies.

Mill's conclusions gradually led him to attack *laissez-faire* capitalism and made him the first liberal democratic philosopher to attack the "enslaving capacity of capitalism." Mill's arguments were so effective that few liberals have supported *laissez-faire* since his time. Before Mill, *laissez-faire* had been opposed only by the extreme left—by Marx and other socialists and radicals. Under Mill the liberal democrats began a movement to the left that led many of them to prefer socialism over capitalism.

Thomas Hill Green.   Thomas Hill Green (1836–1882), a professor of moral philosophy in England, became a leading liberal thinker. Like Mill, he was concerned with individual liberty. "We shall probably all agree," he wrote, "that freedom, rightly understood, is the greatest of blessings; that its attainment is the true end of our efforts as citizens." Green was careful, however, to point out that freedom did not mean the right to do whatever one wished without regard for others. It was not the same as the absence of restraint, as Locke had suggested. Reacting to the economic and political impediments imposed on most people by industrialization, Green defined freedom as the "liberation of the powers of all men equally for contributions to a common good." Thus, Green's call for freedom in a *positive* and *social* sense represents another major leftward shift in liberal thought.

Green suggested that individual freedom comes not from people being able to contribute to their own welfare but from people being able to contribute to the society as a whole. He argued against a government playing the role Locke envisioned, that is, merely serving as a passive arbiter of disputes between individuals. Instead, he believed that government should take definite steps to increase the freedom of the people. One of the elements in the society that he saw being used to restrict the individual's liberty was private property. The Industrial Revolution had seen great wealth concentrate into the hands of only a tiny group of fortunates, while ordinary people, driven from the land to the factories, became increasingly dependent on others: on a system of production and distribution over which they had no control. Thus, people became subject more than ever before to the power of the ownership class. Viewing these trends as undemocratic, Green urged people to use the institutions of government to protect themselves from the powerful economic forces over which they had no other control. This position, of course, is an early philosophical justification of the *welfare state*. Hence, he gave forceful support to a government that would take *positive* steps to improve the lives of the people through policies promoting free education, labor laws protecting women and children, sanitary working and living conditions, and much more.

Poverty can be a prison as confining as any penitentiary, Green believed. If this assumption is correct, and if the state is responsible for increasing the individual's freedom to the greatest possible degree, as Locke had argued, then it is clear that a government must take responsibility for the material well-being of its citizens. In short, Bentham, Mill, and Green led liberalism beyond the conviction that government had only a political obligation to its citizens. Government must not limit itself to sweeping streets and catching burglars. On the contrary, government has social and economic responsibilities to its citizens besides its strictly civic functions.

Green's ideas were of great importance to the liberal movement. They not only added to the philosophical foundations for positive governmental action to protect the citizens from powers against which they were otherwise helpless, in the tradition of Bentham and Mill, but they also did much more. Green's work directed liberalism away from solitary individualism toward a social conscience and collectivism. This trend will build until eventually liberals support an organic theory of society similar to but less extreme than Rousseau's. Still, Green based his liberalism on Bentham's utilitarianism and Mill's enlightened self-interest, not on any moral view of human rights. It was left to another philosopher to give liberalism the moral depth it has enjoyed in the twentieth century.

John Dewey.   The leading American philosopher of contemporary liberalism, or social democracy, was John Dewey (1859–1952). He stated its goals more clearly than anyone else, putting the final touches on the philosophical principles that find liberals trying to change political institutions for the good of society. Dewey strongly believed in the intelligence and dignity of people and in the power and wisdom of individual contributions to the collective good.

Dewey brought liberalism back to its central theme. He argued that all people were equal in their humanity. This does not mean that there are no differences among people's physical or mental abilities. Such an argument would be foolish. Yet, regardless of the differences among people, no individual is more human than the next, and each person contributes to the society. Consequently, each has a right to equal political and legal treatment at the hands of the state. To deny such treatment would be an abuse of the human rights to which each individual has equal claim. Importantly, he argued that precisely because there are physical and intellectual differences among people, equal political and legal treatment becomes necessary. Otherwise, Dewey argued, those who do not have great strength or intellect could be tyrannized by those who do.

Having reestablished this basic assumption, Dewey extended the logic of Bentham, Mill, and Green. Dewey agreed that the happiness of the individual is the primary goal of the society. However, he held that no definition could remain unchanged. Our understanding of all things is determined by our environment and our experiences. This empirical attitude, which of course is the foundation of *pragmatism,* which Dewey supported, tended to

John Dewey (1859–1952)   Library
of Congress

make all knowledge tentative and conditional. Hence, the meaning of happiness, society, and human rights, and even of the individual itself, is constantly changing as our perception of the environment changes: "An individual is nothing fixed, given ready-made," Dewey wrote to emphasize his moral relativism. "It is something achieved, and achieved not in isolation, but [with] the aid and support of conditions, cultural, and physical, including in 'cultural' economic, legal, and political institutions as well as science and art."

Yet, Dewey did not suggest that we are at the mercy of the environment simply because it creates our definitions. He believed that people could make their lives better by applying their intelligence to the problems they faced.

Dewey's belief in the changing nature of truth and his confidence in human reasoning led him to advocate *social engineering*. Unlike conservatives, who believe that existing institutions have value in themselves and should not be meddled with, Dewey was an enthusiastic supporter of social experimentation. He encouraged people to modify and adjust institutions so as to increase the happiness of the society. He rejected Burke's argument that an institution is the product of the collective wisdom of successive generations and that no single generation is competent to improve that institution by changing it. In contrast, Dewey wrote that liberalism "is as much interested in the *positive construction of favorable institutions* legal, political, and economic, as it is in the work of removing abuse and overt oppressions" (emphasis added). Hence, not only are people able to modify institutions that oppress them, but they should go further by creating institutions that will increase their happiness.

People, Dewey asserted, should study their society and not hesitate to make institutional changes that would improve their lives. They were not to stop there, however. He encouraged them to try to mold individuals themselves, thereby improving human beings and making them more socially compatible. This concept is indeed a far cry from Madison's rather bleak view that human nature is base and unchangeable. "The commitment of liberalism to experimental procedure," Dewey explained, "carries with it the idea of continuous reconstruction of the ideas of individuality and of liberty in intimate connection with changes in social relations."

This dedication to the concept of *social engineering* by the most influential American philosopher of this century had important effects. Dewey's ideas inspired liberals to create the policies of the New Deal, the Fair Deal, and the Great Society of the 1960s.

This chapter and Chapter 4 have dealt with the theory or principles of democracy. Yet, as indicated in Chapter 4, democracy includes specific procedures as well as principles. In the following chapter we shall consider the most important procedures and institutions found in contemporary democratic systems.

REVIEW

- Politics and economics have become inextricably linked in modern social understanding. Hence, democracy cannot stand alone as a concept, but is better understood as democratic capitalism and democratic socialism.
- Capitalism is founded on classical liberal principles of individualism. It is dependent on a passive government and competition among individuals.
- American capitalism was at first extremely exploitative of ordinary people, but its worst excesses were tempered by the New Deal. Although the policies of President Ronald Reagan in the 1980s and Speaker of the House Newt Gingrich in the 1990s threaten them, so far, the fundamental institutions of the New Deal remain intact.
- The neoclassical democratic philosophers, Edmund Burke, James Madison, and John C. Calhoun, believed in some kind of popular control of government. Yet, they rejected human equality and were content to see the elite rule benevolently. Madison's distrust of the people and mob rule led him to create the separation of powers and a system of checks and balances, but since its adoption the Constitution has been modified along the liberal lines of Jefferson's theories.

- Jeremy Bentham, the founder of contemporary liberalism, rejected the moral absolutism of natural law. Through his theories of utilitarianism and positivist law he led the demand for social and political reform in England.
- John Stuart Mill and Thomas Hill Green followed the logic of Bentham and increased the call for social consciousness, thus leading the way toward democratic socialism. John Dewey called upon people to constantly question the values upon which society is based and to boldly try to improve the human condition through social engineering.

SUGGESTIONS FOR FURTHER READING

BARBER, JAMES DAVID, *The Book of Democracy.* Englewood Cliffs, NJ: Prentice Hall, 1995.

BENTHAM, JEREMY, *An Introduction to the Principles of Morals and Legislation.* New York: Harper & Row, 1952.

BURKE, EDMUND, *Reflections on the Revolution in France.* Chicago: Henry Regnery, 1955.

CALHOUN, JOHN C., *Disquisition on Government and Selection from the Discourse.* Indianapolis: Bobbs-Merrill, 1953.

EDWARDS, RICHARD C., MICHAEL REICH, and THOMAS E. WEISSKOPF, *The Capitalist System.* 2nd ed. Englewood Cliffs, NJ: Prentice Hall, 1978.

FAIRFIELD, ROY P., ed., *The Federalist Papers: Essays by Alexander Hamilton, James Madison, and John Jay.* New York: Anchor Books, 1961.

GALBRAITH, JOHN KENNETH, *The Age of Uncertainty.* Boston: Houghton Mifflin, 1977.

GARFORTH, F. W., *Educative Democracy: John Stuart Mill on Education in Society.* Oxford, England: Oxford University Press, 1980.

HELD, DAVID. *Models of Democracy.* Minneapolis: University of Minnesota Press, 1982.

HEILBRONER, ROBERT L., *The Worldly Philosophers.* 5th ed. New York: Simon & Schuster, 1980.

INGERSOLL, DAVID E., *Communism, Fascism, and Democracy.* Columbus, OH: Charles E. Merrill, 1971.

LEVINE, ANDREW, *Liberal Democracy.* New York: Columbia University Press, 1981.

MACPHERSON, C. B., *The Real World of Democracy.* New York: Oxford University Press, 1969.

MILL, JOHN STUART, *On Liberty and Considerations on Representative Government.* Fairhaven, NJ: Oxford University Press, 1933.

———. *Principles of Political Economy.* Toronto: University of Toronto Press, 1965.

PORTER, STEVEN, *The Ethics of Democracy.* Endwell, NY: Phantom Publishers, 1994.

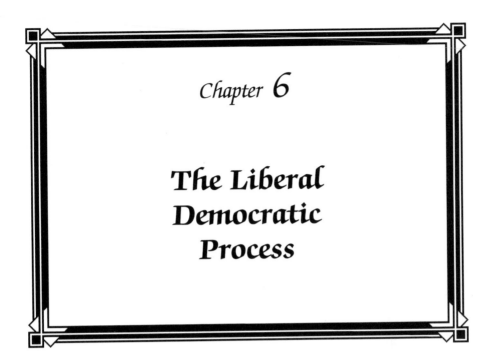

Chapter 6

The Liberal Democratic Process

PREVIEW

The two preceding chapters dealt with democracy's philosophical content. In this chapter we examine the procedures used in democratic systems.

Direct democracy exists when the people make the laws themselves. When representatives make the laws for the people, the government is called a republic. Pluralism is a variant of the republican form in which pressure groups are the primary link between the people and the policymakers.

Democracy must work within a governmental system. Two systems of government are particularly noteworthy: American and British. The American system divides power between two basic levels of government: state and national. The American government also uses the presidential-congressional system. The most prominent features of the presidential-congressional system are the election of the legislators and the executive to unrelated, uninterruptable terms and the prohibition against serving in more than one branch at a time. Powers are separated among the branches, but some responsibilities overlap and form the basis for the system of checks and balances.

The British system concentrates all governmental power at the central level, and the central government then establishes and empowers local governments. Within the national government, power is further centralized in Parliament through the use of the parliamentary-cabinet system. Here Parliament embodies the legislative, executive, and judicial branches. The legislature, specifically the House of Com-

mons, is at least technically superior to the executive and judicial branches and can pass any law it deems appropriate. The only popular elections held in this system are elections to Parliament. Parliament chooses its leader who forms a government, the cabinet, which shares administrative powers and responsibility.

Democratic systems, regardless of their structure, are largely products of the electoral system they use. The U.S. system uses the single-member district, discouraging the existence of more than two major parties. On the other hand, the multimember district tends to encourage the existence of more than two major parties because it gives minor parties a better chance of victory, but this system usually fails to produce a majority in the legislature.

Directly related to the type of electoral district used is the political party system that evolves. A single-party system exists when only one party has a reasonable chance of gaining control of the government. The two-party system tends to produce a majority for the winner and therefore encourages strong government. The multiparty system, a third alternative, tends to give voice to the various opposing points of view in a political system, but this system can be unstable because it usually fails to produce a majority party.

Representation is another complicated subject in any democratic government. Several theories about representation have been developed, but none has prevailed. These theories range from reactionary autocracy, to conservative paternalism, to liberal representative government, to radical pure democracy. Regardless what form is used, democracy suffers severe criticism today. Friend and foe alike question its continued viability in a modern technological setting.

SYSTEMS OF DEMOCRACY

Popular government is the essence of a democratic system. Early liberal thinkers understood this principle, and they saw the policy-making process as the most important democratic procedure. Consequently, they regarded the legislative process as the core of democracy. The executive and judicial functions were thought of as service agencies that carried out the laws made by the people. Accordingly, the democratic process was equated with the policy-making or legislative process, and the relationship between the people and the legislative process became the most important criterion for distinguishing among the various democratic systems.

Democracy and the Legislative Process

The three major democratic procedures are based on the relationship of the people to the legislative, or policy-making, process. In the simplest form, called **direct democracy** or pure democracy, the people act as their own legislature. (See Figure 6–1.) There are no representatives; in other words, the people make the laws for themselves. You will recall that Jean Jacques

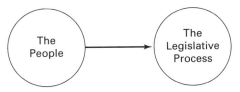

FIGURE 6–1 Direct Democracy   The relationship between the people and the policy-making process is direct.

Rousseau favored this kind of governmental system. He argued that no one could truly represent another person's will. Hence, all the individuals in the society must represent themselves.

This form of democracy has been used by several societies. Ancient Athens practiced direct democracy, and even today one can find it in some Swiss cantons and in some New England town meetings. Before the advent of modern technology, direct democracy was not possible in an area larger than a city-state; therefore, it has not been very popular. Today, however, it is possible for a society, using computers, television, and the telephone, to govern itself in a much more direct way than was possible in the past. However, any society that has the technological capacity to create a direct democracy through electronics is so complex that the problems it faces may be beyond the understanding of ordinary citizens, given the limited amount of time they could reasonably be expected to devote to matters of public policy.

A second form of popular government is called indirect democracy, representative government, or **republic.** Each of these terms refers to the same system. However, the word republic originally did not necessarily refer to a democratic system. It simply meant government without a king. The Roman Republic, for example, was governed by the aristocratic class (patricians) through the Senate, but most of the citizens of Rome (plebeians) could not serve in the Senate or choose its members. Though it was certainly not a democracy, this system was a republic simply because it was not ruled by a king.

The term republic has taken on a somewhat different meaning in the United States. The word is used in the Constitution and was explained by James Madison in *The Federalist* (no. 10). Madison made it clear that republic referred to a government of elected representatives who were responsible to the people to some extent. Hence, the term republic actually means "democratic republic" in American constitutional law, and the courts have ruled accordingly in the past. A democratic republic is an indirect form of democracy. Instead of the people making the laws themselves, they elect legislators to do it for them. Thus, the people are removed one step from the legislative process, and their relationship to the policy-making process is less direct than under the pure form of democracy. (See Figure 6–2.)

One of the interesting facts about this particular form of government is

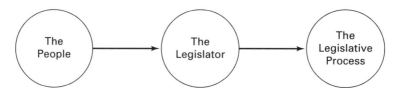

The legislator is added, making the people's
relationship to the legislative process indirect.

FIGURE 6–2   Republic

that there is a negative correspondence between the terms *republic* and *democracy;* that is, the more republican the government, the less democratic it becomes, and vice versa. Put differently, the more a society gives its representatives to do, the less the people have to do for themselves. Conversely, the more the people participate in their political system, the less power their representatives have.

For instance, a system molded along the lines that Thomas Jefferson favored would be very democratic and only slightly republican. Jefferson thought that the popularly elected representatives should be bound to vote the way their constituents wanted. A very republican and only slightly democratic form might be one in which the elected representatives were allowed to vote as they wished on any issue and the people could only defeat them in the next election if they disagreed with the way they had voted. This is the procedure desired by Edmund Burke and James Madison.

Using the definition we have just developed, one must conclude that the United States' form of government is highly republican but only slightly democratic. United States citizens do not have a great deal of *formal* control over their political system. We have already learned that we have no direct formal power over who will serve as our judges. We only elect electors, who, in turn, choose the president, and they are not bound to vote for the candidate the people favor. We do have direct electoral control over the members of Congress, but even so we can vote for these officials only when their terms expire, and some of those terms are as long as six years; none is shorter than two years. Further, elections are not held when the need for them arises; they are held only when the law commands.

You will recall that in a democracy the people are supposed to be sovereign, meaning that they ultimately control the law of the society. Yet, as mentioned in Chapter 5, the people do not propose or ratify amendments to the Constitution of the United States, the country's highest law. The people may not pass or repeal federal statutes, nor may they legally remove federal officials before their terms expire. All these responsibilities are granted by the Constitution to the elected representatives.

To suggest that the political system used in the United States is not very democratic is not necessarily to criticize it, however. It is simply a statement of fact, not a value judgment. Several states have more democratic systems than the national government. Some state constitutions cannot be amended without a direct vote by the people; state voters can often pass law, repeal it, or remove elected officials by the ballot before their terms expire. These states give their people much more direct control over government than is allowed at the national level. Yet, few serious students of government would argue that the state governments that give their citizens such powers make better laws or have finer officials than the national government.

The third major form of democracy, **pluralism,** is not really a different system. Rather, it is a variant of the republican system. Yet, pluralism is such an important variation on republicanism that it should be studied separately.

Pluralism is actually the kind of system foreseen by Madison. He realized that a country as geographically large and as economically, socially, politically, and culturally diverse as the United States cannot attain a single majority on most issues. At the same time, the population of this country is so large that a single ordinary individual is powerless to affect the system. The individual's only hope of protecting his or her interests is to join groups.

The American people have been called a nation of joiners, and so we must be if we expect to further our interests. If, for instance, a person wanted to have a stop sign installed at an intersection, he or she could go to the local officials and petition for the sign. While this procedure might get results, the officials probably would not accede to a request by a single person. Usually, the individual would have to mobilize many other people before the officials felt enough pressure to act.

Pluralism recognizes that the individual must join with the other people to achieve his or her political goals. Consequently, in this system the *interest group* is sandwiched between the people and the legislature. (See Figure 6–3.)

Pluralism has certain problems. To begin with, it removes the individual a step further from the policy-making process, creating important philosophical difficulties. As you know, liberal democratic theory argues that the individual is the most important and valuable part of the society; yet, our political practices seem to take the decision-making process further and further from the direct control of the individual—a potentially dangerous situation.

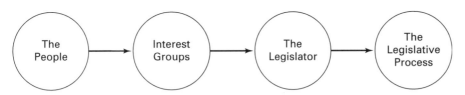

The interjection of the interest group between the people and the legislator removes the people one step further from the legislative process.

FIGURE 6–3   Pluralism

If our political theory and practice are contradictory, we run the risk of encouraging public dissatisfaction.

There are other problems with pluralism. Even if there were no contradiction between democratic theory and pluralistic practice, pluralism would be an imperfect form of representation. For instance, not all the interests in the society are represented equally well. The best-organized and best-financed interest groups can represent their points of view most effectively. The National Rifle Association, for example, is a very well-organized and amply funded group of like-minded individuals; it has been very successful in achieving many of its goals. On the other hand, farm labor, because of its migrant nature, its poverty, and its politically disaffected people, tends to be poorly represented. Moreover, even if our major interests are represented by one group or another, it is unlikely that all our concerns are represented. Consequently, pluralism, though it may be necessary in a modern democratic society, is a very imperfect form of representation.

A final aspect of pluralism should be analyzed before we end this discussion. We have seen that the legislative process is affected by a considerable number of interest groups. When a particular issue arises, however, only a small number of groups take an interest in it. (See Figure 6–4.) Let us assume that only the groups that have a plus or minus sign are interested in a

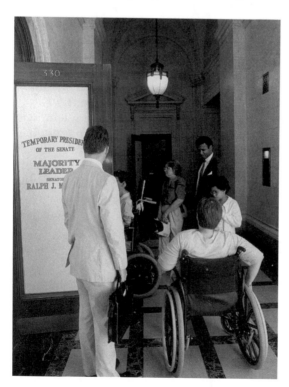

People enter a legislator's office to lobby for their cause. Corbis-Bettman

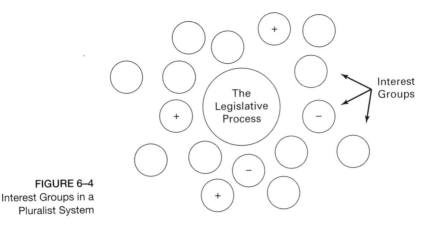

FIGURE 6–4
Interest Groups in a
Pluralist System

given issue. Let us assume further that those with a plus sign are in favor of a certain policy for dealing with the issue and those with a minus sign are opposed to it. The interested groups are obviously a minority of the total number of interest groups, and they probably do not represent anything near the majority of the people in the country. Yet, they will be the most influential in determining the fate of the policy. Moreover, we can assume that the number of pressure groups in favor or opposed to the policy will not necessarily determine what will become of it. Hence, we cannot assume that a policy will pass simply because three interest groups favor it while only two oppose it. We can also safely assume that the interest groups that represent the largest number of people will not necessarily have their way.

The victorious side of any issue will not necessarily be the side with the largest following; it will be the side with the greatest power. In other words, pluralism has taken the "body count" out of democratic politics. No longer are issues settled by simply counting those in favor and those opposed to a question, if indeed they ever were decided that way.

Pluralism, to summarize, is a method of decision making that is popularly based and therefore democratic; but in a pluralist system choices are not necessarily determined by the number of people for or against a given question. Many other factors contribute to the power of interest groups in relation to political issues.

Money is, of course, a major source of power for most successful interest groups. In fact, money is essential for any interest group that hopes to succeed for a sustained period of time. Yet, money is not the only, or even necessarily the most important, source of power for interest groups. Some groups are sustained by *charismatic leaders* such as Dr. Martin Luther King, Jr., Ralph Nader, or Pat Robertson. Others benefit from *an efficient organizational apparatus* or an unusually *large number of active members.*

Of all sources of interest group power, *knowledge* is undoubtedly the most important most of the time. Politicians often know little about the issues they must resolve and usually look for information that will help them make wise decisions. If an interest group can establish credibility on a given issue, it can do a great deal to influence policymakers.

Elite Theorism

Among the most persistent and insightful critics of the American political system are the *elite theorists.* As the name implies, these critics argue that the United States government is not a democracy. It is at best an *oligarchy,* or a system ruled by a relatively small number of people. The rulers of this country, the elite theorists contend, are the people who control the large industrial firms and the various pressure groups.

C. Wright Mills, the most influential of the elite theorists, wrote of a *power elite* that controls the political system. He argued that these people maintain their dominant position through economic, social, school, and family relationships. Robert Michels, another elite theorist, suggested a different dynamic when he set forth his theory of the *iron law of oligarchy.* This theory holds that in any organization only a small percentage of members will be active. Hence, the leadership of any body will come from a tiny group of activists. Because the general membership is usually dormant, the leadership will actually control the organization.

Regardless of how the members of the elite rise to their position of control, the elite theorists agree that they, and not the people as a whole, actually run the country. Interestingly, most elite theorists and pluralists do not disagree on the basic structure of the political system. They concur that the system is responsive to interest groups. The difference between them rests in their definition of democracy. Although pluralists admit that the leadership of various interest groups has great power, they believe that the general membership has enough control over the leaders to make them responsive, and hence to make the system democratic. The elite theorists see essentially the same reality as the pluralists, but they are not satisfied that the people's power over their leaders is strong enough to make the system democratic.

Conspiratorial theories. Just as the pluralists must be understood as distinct from the elite theorists, care must be taken that the elite theorists are not confused with those who espouse conspiratorial theories. Conspiratorialists are phobic about politics. They believe that someone, usually a small group of unseen people, is secretly and diabolically controlling things from behind the scenes. Among the suspected master manipulators are communists, international bankers, Jews, and satan worshipers. The various militant civilian militia groups around the country that have come to prominence since the 1995 bombing of a federal building in Oklahoma City are deeply embroiled in conspiratorial suspicions. They see the federal government as the sinister culprit, constantly maneuvering to deny innocent patriots their liberties.

In the 1960s, Pulitzer Prize winning historian Richard Hofstadter analyzed the conspiratorial approach to politics, referring to it as the *"paranoid style."* While Hofstadter concedes that some secret planning accompanies virtually every political movement, the paranoid style imagines a plot of colossal proportions affecting millions and threatening the very nation itself. Using isolated facts together with a curious leap in imagination to prove to their own satisfaction the existence of the conspiracy, persons asserting the paranoid style mentally catapult from the "undeniable to the unbelievable." They are convinced that their imagined opponent is totally evil and that their own motives are pure, but often misunderstood. Public rejection of their point of view is often interpreted as persecution and so their stance becomes increasingly militant as they see their situation becoming more and more hopeless.[1]

The suggestion that the nation, or indeed the world, is controlled by such secret and evil power is not infrequently found very attractive. It brushes aside the immense complexity of modern politics and substitutes for it a very simple scenario. If people can believe that they are manipulated by unknown and uncontrollable forces, they can escape any responsibility for understanding or solving social problems. Politics is thus reduced to a very simple equation. There is a single source of our difficulties and if only we can get at the source and root it out, all will be well.

Yet, the very simplicity of such theories makes them suspect. It stretches credulity beyond rational limits to suggest that a few masterminds could, without our knowing about it, be pulling the strings that make the rest of us dance like puppets. No less bizarre is the belief that the federal government has somehow become the tool of megalomaniacs whose mission it is to enslave the hapless citizenry. Indeed, so far as the militant civilian militias are concerned, the *rights* that are supposed to be in jeopardy (to bear arms without condition or regulation, to refuse to pay taxes, or to resist government authority with deadly force) are liberties solely in the imaginations of these extremists and have never been even marginally sanctioned in law. To some people, however, believing in an evil force is preferable to coming to grips with the intricacies of reality, and accepting such fantasies represents the ultimate abdication of the personal responsibility so necessary to a successful democracy.

Unlike the conspiratorial theorists, the elite theorists do not claim that all fateful decisions are made by a single group of unseen ogres. Rather, they believe that each issue generates a different elite. Those with great power on one issue, aerospace for instance, may have relatively little impact on another, such as farming.

Elite theorists contend that the political system is composed of thou-

---

[1]Richard Hofstadter, *The Paranoid Style In American Politics.* (New York: Knopf, 1965), Chapter 1.

sands of elites who coalesce and dissolve alliances with each new issue. The point is not that a single group dominates every issue; rather, it is that, for better or for worse, there are several thousand extremely powerful people who populate the elite of the country and who are able to join in alliances to have their way on particular issues.

SYSTEMS OF GOVERNMENT

No study of the process of democracy would be complete without considering the systems of government in which the process is applied. Although a multitude of governmental systems exists, two forms are particularly important. We will focus on the United States and Great Britain because each developed political systems used, in modified form, in many other democratic societies.

The American System

The original structure of American government was **confederate** under the Articles of Confederation (1781–1789). Each state was sovereign (the highest legal authority within its territory) and independent but voluntarily joined in a compact with the other states for purposes of defense and trade. Traditionally, confederacies are not very successful. Since each participant is sovereign, the central government has no legal way to enforce compliance with national law. Consequently, cooperation among the constituent members is the only adhesive of a confederate compact. Ironically, however, the usual reason for creating a confederate compact of several sovereign and independent entities, instead of forming a single union with sovereignty located in the national government, is that the partners do not completely trust one another—thus making voluntary cooperation difficult. For this and other reasons the Articles failed and was replaced by the *federal* Constitution in 1789.

Federalism.   Although Calhoun and his supporters argued to the contrary, the United States Constitution initiated an entirely different form of government than that known under confederacy. A federal government is one which divides powers between the states and the national government. Each level is guaranteed certain rights, including the right to exist, so that the states cannot legally destroy the national government or another state government, and the national government may not dissolve the states. Thus, the Union is "one and inseparable."

The states and the national government enjoy certain powers exclusive of each other while sharing other powers concurrently. Making war and peace is an example of an *exclusive power* for the national government; education is exclusive to the states. Taxation is a *concurrent power* because it is exercised by both levels of government. As you can see, the division of powers is a complicated matter.

The presidential-congressional system. Yet another invention of the American founders is the presidential-congressional system. In this arrangement the legislature and the executive are elected separately. Moreover, they are elected to *fixed terms* that cannot be interrupted. You will recall that the president and vice president are elected to four-year terms, while the members of the House of Representatives serve two-year terms, and the members of the Senate serve for six years.

The American electoral process affects our system of government in several important ways. First, although the constituencies of the executives, senators, and representatives are different, each public official is chosen in a popular election. Since public officials are elected separately, they are not indebted to each other for their election. Also, since only the president and vice president are chosen in a national election, they are the only officials who can claim to represent the nation as a whole.

Separate election of principal officials in the United States results in another interesting situation. The people may elect an executive from one party and a majority of the legislature from another. While this circumstance, called *divided government,* appeals to the desire of some people for balanced government, it can also cause a serious problem. If the two party platforms reflect definite ideological differences, members of different parties are unlikely to reach agreements readily, a condition that could lead to legislative stagnation, with Congress passing bills and the president vetoing them. Even if the executive and legislative majority are from the same party, the fact that they are elected separately and serve uninterruptable terms tends to diminish the need for party discipline and loyalty. The legislature cannot require the executive's resignation by a vote of no confidence; similarly, the executive cannot suspend the legislature and force elections. Hence, legislators from the president's party can oppose bills sponsored by the executive because they know that the president will not resign if the bills fail to pass. By the same token, the president does not feel compelled to appoint cabinet members from the ranks of the legislature as the British prime minister must.

Nevertheless, the fact that elected politicians serve terms of office that cannot be interrupted except by extraordinary procedures tends to give stability to the system. That is to say, under the presidential-congressional system officials serve out their terms regardless of what happens (barring death or resignation). True, Congress can impeach officials, but impeachment is an awkward and slow process that has been used only a few times.

Except under very unusual circumstances, then, our elected officials will complete their terms, come what may. As a result the government does not change suddenly during times of crisis. While this stability is usually considered an advantage of the presidential-congressional system, critics argue that the government seems unresponsive at times. Elections are not called when issues demand them or when the people want a change of leadership; the people get to vote only when the law provides for an election. During the constitutional crisis over the Watergate controversy, many people turned envious eyes toward the parliamentary-cabinet system because it allows that at almost any time unpopular officials can be removed by a parliamentary vote of no confidence or by a direct vote of the people.

As appealing as the quick-turnover feature of the parliamentary-cabinet system may seem, it can cause serious instability. One wonders what turmoil might have erupted if the United States had had a parliamentary-cabinet system between 1966 and 1972. During that period the Indochina War so divided the country that no position on our involvement in the war seemed to enjoy majority support. The question dominated our political system, yet it defied solution. In times of such strife the parliamentary-cabinet system can be dangerously unstable, and often the governmental instability brought on by a controversial policy makes the situation even worse, so that a solution is increasingly difficult to achieve.

Other distinctive features of the presidential-congressional system are **separation of powers** and **checks and balances.** As mentioned earlier, separate elections make the two branches independent of one another. In addition, the law specifically separates the branches of government from each other. For instance, no person may serve in more than one branch at a time. A member of Congress elected or appointed to the executive branch would have to resign his or her congressional seat.

Further, the executive, legislative, and judicial branches are each given separate powers that only they may exercise. The courts are responsible for adjudicating disputes; they also are the final authority on the interpretation of the law. Only the legislature can pass fiscal legislation—that is, approve expenditures—while the executive is solely responsible for the administration of policy and is virtually unrestrained in foreign affairs.

As Figure 6–5 shows, the basic powers of the three branches are indeed separate and unique; however, some of the powers of each branch overlap with those of the other two. These overlapping powers are called the checks and balances. They are intended to prevent any branch from becoming too powerful and dominating the others. You will recall that James Madison, who devised this system, did not trust government, so he tried to make sure that each branch was relatively equal in power and that each acted as a guardian against abuses by the other two. Yet, we should remember that Madison, like Thomas Hobbes, also had little trust in the people, so he wrote in a number of checks against the majority as well (see Chapter 5 for examples).

Most of us have a positive attitude about the separation of powers and checks and balances systems. We normally share Madison's apprehension

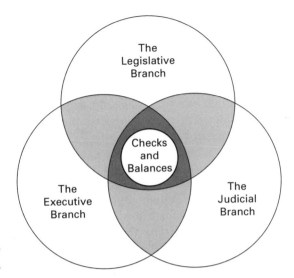

FIGURE 6–5 Separation of Powers and Checks and Balances

about government, although perhaps most of us are not as intense about it as he was. There are, however, some undesirable aspects of this feature of our system. By dividing and diffusing power and then causing each of the branches to compete with the others, the presidential-congressional system encourages conflict and even stagnation within the government.

This situation is aggravated by the vagueness of the U.S. Constitution. This lack of clarity sometimes results in a very combative atmosphere. When the built-in division of government is combined with the abstract wording of the Constitution, we find that each branch is encouraged to exercise its powers assertively while, at the same time, preventing the other two branches from gaining excessive influence. Such maneuvering leads to constant conflict among the three branches.

The British System

Unitary government. Britain has a unitary structure of government. Older than either federalism or confederacy, the unitary structure is used by most governments in the world. This arrangement centralizes all governmental power at the central level. Any local governments that exist are created and granted powers by the central government. Local governments, in other words, are dependent on the central government for their powers and have for themselves no direct constitutional justifications or guarantees.

The unitary structure seems strange to us because our government uses the federal form. However, the unitary arrangement should not be unfamiliar since it may be seen in the relationship between our state governments and local agencies. Only the relationship between the states and the national government is federal in the United States; that is, both the national government and the state governments are guaranteed by the federal Constitution. City, county, parish, township, and special-district governments are not mentioned in the Constitution and are therefore completely subject to the state governments. The same is true of any other local government in any other state. Local governments may be guaranteed by provisions of their states' constitutions, but they have no protection under the Constitution of the United States. The same relationship exists between the central and all lower governments in Britain.

The parliamentary-cabinet system.   Although there are now many variations on the theme, the parliamentary-cabinet system was first developed in England, and the British government still provides the best example of this institution. Unlike the presidential-congressional system, the parliamentary-cabinet system separates the positions of **head of state** and **head of government.** In the American systems, the president performs both roles, but in Britain the monarch is head of state—the symbol of the history and political continuity of the country—and the prime minister is head of government— the country's political leader. (Other countries that use this system but that do not have a hereditary head of state usually elect someone to the post for a relatively long term, often seven years. Elected heads of state commonly have the title of president.) The British head of state has little real power. She or he can dismiss Parliament and call for new elections, appoint ministers, and issue proclamations, but each of these acts is performed only after a request by the prime minister. While some constitutions, such as those of France, India, and Russia, give the head of state important powers, most give the office a purely symbolic role.

The bulk of the political power in the parliamentary-cabinet system is vested in the Parliament. The British system, which developed out of John Locke's political theory, never adopted Madison's structural changes. Hence, separation of powers and checks and balances are less prominent in the British system than in the American system.

A major principle of the British system is *parliamentary primacy.* You will recall that the classical democratic thinkers saw democracy as a process in which the people made policy and thus governed themselves. Therefore, they considered the legislature to be the chief agency of the government. The executive and judicial branches, while important, were only service agencies charged with administering and adjudicating the policies determined by the legislature. The legislature, the primary democratic institution and the agent of the sovereign people, cannot be wrong. Consequently, the British Parliament is, at least in theory, not subject to restraint by the other two branches. No act it passes can be declared unconstitutional. Indeed, some scholars argue that the Parliament *is* the constitution. On paper, then, the cabinet becomes nothing more than the executive committee of Parliament and is directly responsible to it. In practice, of course, the relationship between the cabinet and Parliament is quite different, but this is a matter of political practice rather than law.

The principle of parliamentary primacy makes impossible the equality of the three major branches implied in the presidential-congressional system. Hence, the checks and balances cannot work the way they do in the Madisonian model.

Figure 6–6 represents the parliamentary-cabinet system of government: The power of government is not distributed among three separate branches. Actually, each branch of the government is part of the same whole. Parliament, the whole, is made up of the legislature, which is dominant; the executive; and the judiciary. The House of Commons, part of the legislature, is the only body actually elected by the people. Consequently, it acts as the chief agent of the people, and as such it is the major democratic institution in the system. The cabinet, which consists of members of the legislature, is simply the executive committee of the legislature, as indicated earlier. Members of the cabinet need not resign their seats in the legislature before they enter the executive branch. On the contrary, cabinet members must usually be members of Parliament in order to be appointed to the executive body. The courts are also nominally part of Parliament: The Lords of Appeal in Ordinary, Britain's highest court of appeals, is actually a committee of the House of Lords. Its highest magistrate, the lord chancellor, presides not only over the Lords of Appeals in Ordinary but also over the House of Lords, and usually is a member of the cabinet as well. Obviously, no such office could exist in our system.

At the beginning of each new legislative term the House of Commons chooses someone whose leadership the members of it will follow. This individual is, of course, the leader of the majority party and will be *appointed* prime minister by the head of state. Note that there is no popular election for

FIGURE 6–6 The Parliamentary-Cabinet System

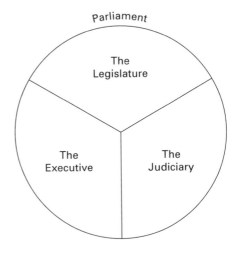

the chief executive in the parliamentary-cabinet system. The prime minister must meet only one requirement: He or she controls the majority of Parliament and can get any bill passed that he or she recommends. If Parliament ever fails to support the recommendation of the prime minister, he or she must resign. Parliament will either hold new elections or pick a new prime minister from the old majority. The decision as to whether or not new elections will be held is usually made by the head of state, who follows the advice of the prime minister.

The fact that Parliament actually chooses the prime minister and that the prime minister decides when elections will be held creates a unique relationship between the executive and the legislature. This relationship tends to increase party discipline and loyalty. The majority party obviously will not choose a member of the opposition to head the government. Also, voting against a policy recommended by the prime minister will not only help defeat the particular policy but may bring down the government as well. Not wishing to help destroy their party's government and loath to stand for reelection prematurely, members of the ruling party in Parliament are encouraged to vote with their executive's policies more regularly than in the presidential-congressional system.

Another important area in which the British and American systems differ is the executive branch. The presidential-congressional system has a *singular executive;* that is, the people of the United States elect only two executive officials, the president and the vice-president, and the Constitution gives executive powers only to the president. All other major executive officials are appointed by the president and are given executive powers to administer. Technically, therefore, all executive powers, regardless of who exercises them, are the president's powers.

The parliamentary-cabinet system, by contrast, has a *plural executive* because, like the prime minister, cabinet members are also appointed by the monarch and exercise his or her powers. Thus the status of the members of the British cabinet is much closer to that of the chief executive than is true in the American system. In the United States the president may give direct orders to cabinet members because they are appointed by the president and exercise the president's powers. In the parliamentary-cabinet system, however, the cabinet members are appointed by the same authority that appoints the prime minister: the monarch. The cabinet members are also more independent of the prime minister, since it is not the prime minister's power they are exercising but the power of the state itself. The prime minister may not give a cabinet minister a direct order because each minister is the sole head of his or her own department.

In the American system the cabinet is a body of advisers to the president. The president has the ultimate power and makes the decisions. If the president delegates this power, he or she is still responsible for policy. In the British system the cabinet is a body of equals headed by the prime minister.

The policies of the government are made by the cabinet as a whole. Instead of being flanked by subordinate advisers, the prime minister must get people appointed to the cabinet who can help hold the parliamentary majority together. Thus, at least senior cabinet members are powerful parliamentarians and are influential in party affairs in their own right; clearly, the prime minister does not dominate the cabinet completely.

Not only does the prime minister not dominate the cabinet, but, due to the principle of **collective responsibility,** he or she is not solely responsible for the policies of the government either. Under this principle a governmental decision is arrived at by a consensus of the cabinet. The decision then becomes a policy of the government, and all government ministers (that is, cabinet members) should support it. Although votes are not usually taken in cabinet meetings, a policy is not adopted until it has broad cabinet support. A policy would never be adopted if the members whose ministries were principally involved did not agree to it. Once a policy is adopted, however, any minister who still opposes it must remain silent, or resign.

Unlike our system, the parliamentary-cabinet system tends to centralize the power of government in the hands of Parliament. As already mentioned, the House of Commons can pass any law it chooses. It could end the monarchy, reshape the judicial branch, or suspend elections, thus ending British democracy as we know it. There is no opposing governmental power to prevent such actions, as there is in our system. Instead of encouraging competition and conflict, this system depends on cooperation and trust. If this system is to work well, the people in the country must be politically mature. The people's belief in democracy must be so strong that public expectation and opinion serves as the ultimate check on abuse of power.

In some ways the parliamentary-cabinet system is more responsible to the citizens, and therefore more democratic, than others. For instance, Parliament is elected to a maximum term; that is, parliamentary elections must be held at least once every four or five years. Yet, elections can be called at any time before the end of the term if the issues require such action. Since this often occurs and Parliaments seldom remain in office for a full term, issues, and not the calendar, force elections. Consequently, elections tend to be much more issue-oriented in the parliamentary-cabinet system than in the American model. In 1988, for example, the two major party candidates ignored the national debt—our most pressing contemporary problem. George Bush, the Republican, said nothing about it because it was an embarrassment for his party, which had tripled the debt in only eight years. But the Democratic candidate, Michael Dukakis, also ignored the issue because he knew that higher taxes must be part of the solution for reducing the annual deficit, and he realized that campaigning to raise taxes would cost him the election.

Such side-stepping of major controversies would be impossible in a parliamentary campaign, since an election would probably have been called to settle the issue. Ideally, elections are held in the British system whenever the government no longer has the confidence of the people or of Parliament. The prime minister will ask for elections when the government's policies seem to lack support.

The parliamentary-cabinet system is not without its problems, however. Perhaps the greatest problem with this system is that it can be very unstable. As indicated earlier, this system tends to be weak during times of controversy. Elections can be called and governments changed very often. Hence, just when a stable government is needed, this system can be at its most unstable.

The situation is made worse if no majority party is elected. When a single party wins more than half the seats in Parliament, there is very little trouble determining who will form the government. In some cases, however, the seats of Parliament are divided so evenly among three or more parties that no party controls the majority. Then, a **coalition government** must be formed in which two or more parties join to make a majority. They agree on the government's positions on the major issues and divide the various cabinet offices between them.

Coalition governments tend to be very unstable, however. Disagreements often occur between the coalition members, tempers rise, and one or more parties may pull out of the coalition and turn against the government. This reversal of loyalty causes loss of confidence in the government, which must then resign. New elections are held, and if a single party does not win the majority of the seats, a new coalition must be forged—only to begin the process all over again.

ELECTIONS

Perhaps nothing is more important in a democratic system than its electoral process. Through elections the people express their will on the issues and choose their leaders. One should not be surprised to learn that elections, vital as they are, are complex, multifaceted processes.

Nominations

People wishing to be candidates for local office usually just have to formally indicate their intention or secure a small number of signatures on a petition in order to be listed on a ballot. Those who seek high office usually face either nomination by **convention** or nomination by **primary election.** Delegates to a nominating convention may be elected or appointed at the local level to attend the party convention, where they adopt a party platform and nominate candidates for various offices. Criticized as being undemocratic, nominating conventions are used less and less these days.

Primaries are elections in which the voters choose the candidates they wish to have listed on the ballot of the November **general election.** While primary elections are more democratic than other nomination methods, there are some serious drawbacks to them. Primaries extend the election period over several months; costly campaigning must be carried on over this long period. Such added expenditures, it is claimed, have had the effect of limiting public office to the wealthy. Other critics mention the divisiveness of the primary. Partisan primaries (primaries in which candidates are hoping to become their party's nominee for office) tend to encourage fights within parties, causing wounds that sometimes do not heal before the general election. Such conflicts weaken the party structure and may cause needless defeats.

One final difficulty with the primary system deserves serious consideration. Any democrat must believe that when the people are informed, the majority's judgment is correct more often than any minority group. When the people are not well informed, however, the judgment of the many might not be as good as the opinion of the few who are well informed. The problem of voter ignorance is more serious in primaries than at other times. Nonincumbent candidates, contenders for an office that they do not hold, are usually not well known; moreover, many of them have little money with which to publicize their names and their positions on current issues. Consequently, voters in primaries are often poorly informed about the candidates. Under these circumstances the people's choice is not always a good one; the party regulars at the convention probably would be better qualified to pick candidates.

Electoral Districts

The kind of electoral district used largely determines the way a particular political system functions. There are two basic kinds of electoral districts: the single-member district and the multimember district. The **single-member district** is used in the United States in all partisan elections. Regardless of the number of candidates running, only one person will be elected within a single-member district. Members of Congress, for example, are elected from congressional districts, each district having only one seat. Thus, because Georgia, for example, sends eleven members to the House of Representatives, the state is divided or apportioned into eleven districts, each electing a single individual to go to Congress.

Since each state's two United States senators are elected at different

Figure 6–7 Elections in Single-Member Districts

Party	Vote Distribution
A	41%
B	39%
C	20%

times, the states are actually single-member districts for Senate elections as well. The states are also single-member districts in presidential elections because *all* the state's electors are awarded to the candidate who wins the most popular votes in that state.[2] Each state, therefore, gives a single prize consisting of a certain number of electoral votes to the winner of its presidential election.

To study the impact of the single-member district, let us assume that parties A, B, and C each ran a candidate for Congress in a particular district and that the popular vote in the district was distributed as indicated in Figure 6–7. Because only a *plurality* (the most votes) is necessary to win in most systems using single-member districts, party A's candidate is the clear winner. At first glance, winning by a plurality does not seem to present any problems, but several interesting features may be seen upon closer scrutiny.

As long as there is more than one candidate for the single seat, the seats will always be distributed disproportionately to the votes cast. In our example, although party A won the largest numbers of votes, a majority of the voters (59 percent) voted against the winner and therefore are unrepresented. Put differently, 41 percent of the voters won 100 percent of the representation. All those who voted for party B or C might as well have stayed home, since their votes do not count toward electing any representatives at all. Consequently, the percentage of congressional seats any party wins is probably not even approximately the same as the percentage of votes it earned. This fact can cause some serious distortions. For example, England, using single-member districts in its Parliamentary elections of 1992, showed returns as indicated in Figure 6–8.

The Conservative Party, led by John Major, carried a majority in Parlia-

Figure 6–8   Results of the 1992 British Parliamentary Elections

Party	Percent of Popular Vote Won	Percent of Parliamentary Seats Won
Conservative	41.9	51.6
Labour	34.4	41.6
Liberal Democrat	17.9	3.1
Other	5.8	3.7

[2]Only Maine and Nebraska divide their electoral votes. Each state gives two electors to the candidate who wins the largest number of popular votes statewide, and each state gives one elector to the candidates who win the largest number of popular votes in each of their congressional districts (two in Maine and three in Nebraska). But, since only one person can win election in the statewide poll and only one can win in each congressional district, these are single-member districts as well.

ment while falling far short of winning a majority of the popular vote. (In fact, no political party has won a majority of the popular vote in any of the 14 post-World War II British general elections, and yet only the election of February 1974 failed to give a party the majority in Parliament.) In 1992, the Labour Party managed to concentrate its popular vote so that it won a significantly greater proportion of Parliament than it carried as a percentage of the popular vote. The Liberal Democrat Party experienced the opposite. Because voters for it were spread across the country rather than being principally located in one section of the country, the Liberal Democrats went terribly underrepresented in Parliament. Each of these disproportionate results occurred because of the winner-take-all feature of the single-member district.

The same kind of distortion can occur in American presidential elections. In 1992, Democrat Bill Clinton won 43 percent of the popular votes, Republican George Bush won 38 percent, and Independent Ross Perot won 19 percent—the highest percentage taken by any third-party or independent presidential candidate in eighty years. Yet, because the candidate who wins the largest number of votes in the state gets *all* the states electors, Clinton was awarded 370 electors, Bush 168, and Perot none.

The single-member district also works to the advantage of a single-party or two-party system. Looking back at Figure 6–7, we can see that although party A won the election, party B came close. Since party B needs to increase its vote by only two or three percent to win, it will probably remain in existence and enter candidates in future elections. The circumstances are quite different for party C, however. Since it has to more than double its vote in order to win, it does not have much chance of survival. Failing to get even close to victory, all but the most dedicated members will probably soon leave party C for another party whose chances of victory are better, and the two major parties will soon find that they are the only serious contestants. American political history is replete with unsuccessful attempts by minor parties to rise to power, and the use of the single-member district is largely responsible for their failure.

The alternative to the single-member district is the **multimember district.** As the term implies, this system provides for the election of several officials from a given district. This electoral method is used in many countries, including Ireland. Most countries using multimember districts employ a system of **proportional representation** to distribute seats on an equitable basis. For example, let us assume that there are five seats open in an electoral district, and parties A, B, and C entered candidates in the election. If the vote were distributed as indicated in Figure 6–7, each party would win something. Parties A and B would win two seats each and party C would win one seat. Although it would not win dramatically, party C would gain something under this procedure and would undoubtedly remain in existence. In addition, new parties would be encouraged to form simply because the percentage of votes necessary to win is greatly reduced, just as the number of parties is increased. Thus, the multimember district encourages the existence of a multiparty system.

Political Party Structures

Political parties have several functions. Stating positions on issues, providing candidates, and holding officials responsible for their acts are only a few of their most important responsibilities. The goal of a political party is easily stated: to gain control of the government. Of course, in a democracy political parties gain and keep control of the government through the electoral process.

There are basically three kinds of political party systems. A **single-party system** exists when one party, over an extended period of time, controls the vast majority of legislative seats and its choice for the chief executive is assured of that office. There may be any number of other parties in the country, but none of them is able to win more than a tiny fraction of the vote.

Care must be taken not to oversimplify the character of the single-party system. Many people equate it with dictatorship. Although dictators often try to hinder their competitors by making opposition parties illegal, a single-party system need not necessarily be a dictatorship. Indeed, single-party democracies are not unheard of. During the Era of Good Feelings in the early nineteenth century, the Democrat-Republican Party had no effective opposition in this country. Yet, the period is considered to have been democratic, since leaders were still chosen by the people and the competition that ordinarily takes place between parties occurred within a single party.

A more contemporary example of a single-party democracy can be found in India. Before the usurpation of power by Indira Gandhi between 1975 and 1977, India was a single-party democracy. The Congress Party was favored by an overwhelming majority of the people, often winning as many as two-thirds of the seats in the national parliament and the state legislatures. India, however, provides a dramatic example of the greatest problem of a single-party system. Though such a system can be used in a democracy, the opposition is so small and weak that it can do little to hinder the dominant party if the country's leaders decide to destroy the democratic process. So it was with Gandhi. Feeling her personal power threatened, she imprisoned her opposition, censored the press, intimidated the courts, and eliminated popular liberties. When she had finished, the Indian democracy lay in ruins. To her credit, however, Gandhi restored democracy to India in 1977, accepting her own parliamentary defeat in the process. Displaying amazing political resilience, she was subsequently returned to power by the people of India after the failure of the opposition government, only to be later assassinated in 1984.

A **two-party system** exists when only two parties have a meaningful chance of winning control of the government. Used in several countries, including Australia and the United States, this system has the advantages of the single-party system without running the same risk of becoming a dictatorship. The greatest advantage of the single-party system is that it produces a strong government; its candidates always win with a majority vote of the citizens. If the system has two major parties instead of only one, elected officials also usually win with a majority; yet, the dominant party is checked by a substantial opposition party.

While the two-party system offers the advantage of a majority government checked by a strong opposition, this very factor tends to distort the complexity of politics. Having only two significant parties, such a system implies that there are only two important sides to any issue: the establishment "in" position and the establishment "out" alternative. In reality, there might be many different positions on each issue. Hence, by limiting the opposition to only one significant party, the two-party system tends to limit the full range of alternatives on the issues.

A **multiparty system** exists when there are several parties that have a significant number of seats in the legislature. It best reflects the various minority arguments. In fact, the multiparty system tends to divide the people into so many different factions that the majority is completely lost, leaving only a set of competing minorities. Many minority parties develop as the willingness or ability to compromise has been lost, and the parties tend to state their differences in very specific terms. This diversity gives the voter many clear alternatives among which to choose, but at the same time it makes producing a majority harder. The proliferation of alternatives and the specificity of debate in this system are admirable, to be sure. However, the lack of compromise as well as the inability to produce a majority party makes this otherwise attractive system less appealing than it might be.

After decades of weak governments occasioned by its use of the multiparty system, Italy is attempting to reorganize itself into a two-party system. On the other hand, the long period of consensus in Japan that assured a majority in parliament for its Liberal Democratic Party collapsed recently. The result is that the political party system has shattered and now a coalition comprised of several parties tenuously governs the society.

The multiparty system can function reasonably well in a parliamentary-cabinet form of government; it is less compatible with the presidential-congressional system, however. No party that fails to carry a majority of the seats in a parliament can govern without forming a coalition of minority parties that agree on policy and on selections for the various cabinet positions. Coalition governments are noted for their instability. They usually do not last long because the delicate agreements on which they are founded are soon outdated by new events. When the coalition self-destructs, a new one must be organized; and this process of forming a new government usually requires an election.

Unstable as this procedure may be, the parliamentary-cabinet system can accommodate it because in this system terms of office are not fixed by law. Not so in the presidential-congressional system. Even if there is no majority in the legislature, the executive and legislative officials must serve uninterruptable terms of several years. Governmental stagnation or worse may result.

Perhaps the most poignant example of the dangers of combining incompatible governmental and political party systems may be found in the events that ended the Allende regime in Chile in 1973. Salvador Allende had won the plurality of the popular vote but not the majority in the elections of 1970, so the election was thrown into the Congress. As a Marxist, Allende was a very controversial figure; the Congress hesitated to elect him. Finally, after much negotiation, an agreement, or coalition, was established and Allende was elected president. But after Allende's inauguration controversies developed over redistribution of farmland and nationalization of foreign-owned properties. Eventually the various parties in the coalition withdrew their support, denying Allende a majority of the Congress. Faced with the prospect of a deadlock that would last for years until his term expired, Allende began to rule by decree, issuing administrative orders that were fiercely opposed by the conservatives and reactionaries in the country. Economic hardship set in; boycotts, strikes, and demonstrations followed. Finally, for the first time in almost half a century, the Chilean army intervened, murdered the president, suspended civil liberties, executed thousands, and imprisoned many more. As would soon happen in India, the most stable democracy in all of South America was destroyed in the name of democracy.

Appealing as the multiparty system might look to people who are frustrated by the seeming lack of difference between the two major American parties, we should be very cautious about opting for the more diverse system. The lack of compromise inherent in the multiparty system bodes ill for a form of government that depends on pluralistic problem solving, as democracy does. The lack of a majority government also tends to make the multiparty system less than desirable; in fact, as we have seen, it is basically incompatible with the presidential-congressional system.

REPRESENTATION

The subject of representation in a democracy is almost as complex as the question of elections. Assuming that the system is not a direct democracy, as Rousseau preferred, the student of politics immediately confronts the question of what the basis of representation should be. Because ours is a democratic society, our natural inclination is to insist that population be the basis of representation. Further, we would probably agree that all people should be treated fairly by the law and that they should all enjoy equal representation. Yet, there are several foundations on which to base representation besides population. In fact, the United States system does not favor people as much as we assume it does.

Another basis for representation is territory. In the United States, each state—regardless of its population—is represented by two United States senators. As a result California, the nation's largest state with a population of over 30 million, has the same representation in the upper house of Congress as states one-fortieth its size. This is not very "democratic."

Functional representation is another variant of representation. In some countries institutions such as the church, universities, and labor unions are given representation in the national parliament. Ireland uses this system, as do several other countries. Just before its collapse, the Soviet Union reserved one-third of its 2,250 seats in its national legislature (the Congress of People's Deputies) for the Communist party, trade unions, the National Academy of Science, a women's group, and several other institutions. Some governments guarantee representation to their various ethnic groups. Switzerland, for example, ensures that its German, French, and Italian populations are each included in its plural executive. Similarly, Russia guarantees its numerous minority populations seats in one house of its legislature, in rough proportion to their percentage of the total population. On the other hand, the British government gives its nobles, a social class, representation in the House of Lords, while several African governments guarantee representation in their national legislatures to many of their tribes.

Another dilemma is the question of whether public officials should represent the national interest, as Edmund Burke argued, or whether they should reflect the interests of a more local area, as James Madison recommended. If the national interest receives the greatest attention, an unfeeling central bureaucracy can mandate policies that seem to make little sense to local areas. On the other hand, when local interests become paramount, policy tends to become provincial and narrow, working to the disadvantage of a modern state.

Of all the arguments concerning representation in a democracy, none is more controversial than the dispute over whether public officials should represent the people's *will* or their *interests.* This quandary returns us to the question of how democratic a republic should be. If the system is to be highly democratic, the representatives should make every effort to determine how their constituents want them to act and behave accordingly. The most republican attitude is that the representatives should use their judgment to determine the interests of the people and then select the course that is best suited to those interests.

The former position assumes that people are rational, able to understand their needs and the various programs that bear on those needs. Further, it assumes not only that people are able to understand the issues but also that they will make the effort to do so. The republican position implies that representatives are somehow better qualified to decide policy than are ordinary people. Because the people may not perceive their interests as clearly as their representatives do, and because they may favor an action that is actually harmful to them, the people's will is not always synonymous with their best interests. Thus, the representative should always vote according to the people's best interests regardless of whether those interests conform to the people's preferences.

Theories of Representation

The question of how the people should be represented is as old as democracy itself. Many political theorists have grappled with the problem, but none has been persuasive enough to dominate the argument. Although some of this information has already been dealt with in other parts of this book, perhaps a brief outline of the basic theories of representation would be helpful at this point.

The **reactionary theory of representation,** supported by Thomas Hobbes and Alexander Hamilton, is based on the need for order and authority. The executive, preferably a monarch, and the parliament serve the public interest as they perceive it. While they should be open to popular input, being of superior knowledge and judgment they should not be hindered by popular sentiment. The people, for their part, must support the state and accept the government's policies willingly in the confidence that the politicians have acted in the public's best interest.

This elitist position provides for no popular control. Indeed, many people might reject this theory as undemocratic; its only popular aspect is the assumption that the rulers are protecting and benefiting the public interest.

Less extreme is the **conservative theory of representation,** supported by Edmund Burke and James Madison. Conservatives grant popular control without encouraging public participation in the governing process. In this variant the people choose those who are to govern them from an elite group. Yet, the people do not have the right to compel their representatives to vote or behave in a particular way. If however, the officials do not satisfy the public, the people may replace them with other members of the elite at the next election. The federal system of government is similar to this model.

John Locke and Thomas Jefferson subscribed to the **liberal theory of representation,** the most democratic of all the republican theories. According to this theory, all people are essentially equal and all are therefore equally capable of ruling. This mass-oriented theory requires that the representative act as a messenger for his or her constituents rather than as a policymaker. Hence, public officials are obliged to vote the way their constituents want them to.

The **radical theory of representation,** advanced by Jean Jacques Rousseau and the New Left of the 1960s, calls for the greatest amount of popular input. Rejecting representative government altogether, this theory holds that only the people themselves are capable of representing their own views, at least on the important issues. Thus, this theory claims that pure or direct democracy is the most desirable form of government; indeed, it is the only truly democratic form.

SOME CRITICISMS OF DEMOCRACY

Democracy has many critics at every point on the political spectrum. It is attacked by the far left as well as by the far right. Some of the most biting criticisms, however, come from supporters of democracy itself.

Some critics argue that democracy is a hopelessly visionary idea based on a number of impossible principles that can never really work because they are too idealistic. They claim that ideas such as human equality or the actual practice of self-government are futile dreams that can never be carried out. At best, they say, the elite really rules in a "democracy." The fact that the general public believes it is running the system proves that the subtleties of government are beyond the understanding of ordinary people.

Another criticism of democracy is based on the belief that the majority of the people have only average intelligence and creativity. Therefore, a government controlled by the majority would probably be biased in favor of the average or the mediocre. Prejudice against the innovative, the unusual, or the excellent would dominate such a system; laws would be passed to move the society toward the lowest common denominator. The truly superior individuals would suffer as the ordinary people imposed their will on the country. Summing up this position, Russell Kirk, a leading conservative, writes: "Aye, men are created different; and a government which ignores this law becomes an unjust government, for it sacrifices nobility for mediocrity; it pulls down the aspiring natures to gratify the inferior natures."[3]

Democracy is also attacked as slow and inefficient. The mechanism for decision making, which we have just studied, is awkward, unable to make the speedy decisions necessary in a jet-propelled, electronically powered, cybernetic society. The critics also point out that while democracy might have been possible during a simpler era, our technology has complicated society to such an extent that popular government is no longer possible. Ordinary people with everyday concerns are simply not equipped to handle the complexities facing policymakers in the modern state. Our society has evolved

---

[3]Russell Kirk, "Prescription, Authority, and Ordered Freedom," in *What Is Conservatism?* ed. Frank S. Meyer (New York: Holt, Rinehart & Winston, 1964), p. 34.

faster than we have been able to adjust, and one of the casualties of this development must be democracy itself.

These are just a few of the criticisms of democracy. Many more specific criticisms could be made, but a catalog of these is unnecessary. The general comments made here should be considered carefully, however, because they are supported by some of our most brilliant thinkers. To think of democracy as the best possible form of government is not to make it so. Questioning the continued viability and usefulness of democracy is a healthy exercise in which all citizens should engage, if for no other reason than to better understand it and thus improve our application of it.

REVIEW

- Most people agree that liberal democracy includes both principles and procedure.
- Democratic procedure is distinguished largely on the basis of how directly the people are involved in decision making.
- In pure democracy, the people make the law themselves. A republic uses representatives of the people to make law, and in pluralism interest groups advocate before legislators in order to influence legislation.
- The American system of government uses federalism to divide powers between the national and state governments. The presidential-congressional system has the executive and legislators elected separately for fixed terms.
- The British use a unitary form that concentrates governmental power in the central government. The parliamentary-cabinet system provides that the people elect Parliament and that Parliament chooses the executive, the prime minister.
- Elections are used to decide issues as well as to choose officers.
- The single-member district encourages a single- or two-party system, while a multimember district fosters a multiparty system.
- The two-party system gives voters alternatives, and it usually produces a majority for the winner. The multiparty system features many alternatives, but it often fails to produce a majority and it may be incompatible with the presidential-congressional system.
- Representative government poses questions about who should be represented, and about what criteria the representatives should use when casting a vote: the will or the interest of constituents.
- Democracy has been criticized as being overly idealist, leading to mediocrity and to inefficiencies when coping with modern problems.

SUGGESTIONS FOR FURTHER READING

BARBER, JAMES DAVID, *The Book of Democracy*. Englewood Cliffs, NJ: Prentice Hall, 1995.
COULTER, EDWIN M., *Principles of Politics and Government*. Boston: Allyn & Bacon, 1981.

CURTIS, MICHAEL, *Comparative Government and Politics: An Introductory Essay in Political Science.* New York: Harper & Row, 1968.

DAHL, ROBERT A., *Dilemmas of Pluralist Democracy.* New Haven, CT: Yale University Press, 1982.

DAHL, ROBERT, *Who Governs?* New Haven, CT: Yale University Press, 1961.

HARRISON, REGINALD J., *Pluralism and Corporation.* London: Allen & Unwin, 1980.

HOFSTADTER, RICHARD, *The Paranoid Style In American Politics.* New York: Knopf, 1965.

KENNON, PATRICK, *Twilight of Democracy.* New York: Doubleday, 1995.

MACPHERSON, C. B., *The Real World of Democracy.* New York: Oxford University Press, 1969.

NORTON, PHILIP, *The British Policy.* New York: Longman, 1984.

RYAN, ALAN, *John Dewey and the High Tide of American Liberalism.* New York: W. W. Norton, 1995.

SCHREMS, JOHN J., *Principles of Politics.* Englewood Cliffs, NJ: Prentice Hall, 1986.

VAN DEN DOD, HANS, and BEN VAN VELTHOVER, *Democracy and Welfare Economies.* 2nd ed. New York: Cambridge University Press, 1993.

ZOLO, DANILO, *Democracy and Complexity: A Realist Approach.* University Park, PA: Pennsylvania State University Press, 1992.

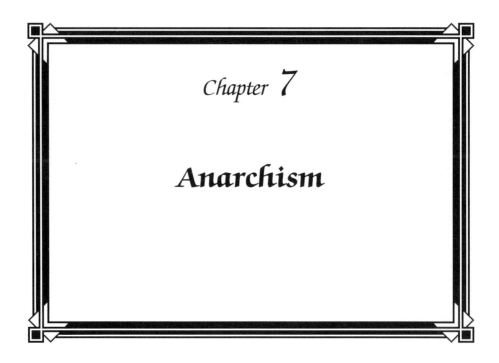

Chapter 7

Anarchism

PREVIEW

Arising from reaction to the growing power of government and the increasing influence of capitalism, anarchism developed among a small but highly motivated number of people. Poorly understood in our society, anarchism is the purest expression of individualism in political thought. Anarchists of all sorts see government as an impediment to human progress and wish to eliminate it in part, or even completely. Agreeing that government should be limited, anarchists tend to disagree on other matters of substance and tactics. Social anarchists, those on the left, wish to free individuals from governmental restraint so that the individuals can do the greatest good possible for society as a whole. By contrast, individualist anarchists, those on the right of the political spectrum, seek to limit government so that individuals can accomplish the greatest good for themselves alone. Anarchists can be pacifistic or violent, devout or atheistic, socialist or capitalist. Indeed, except for the reduction or elimination of government, there are few things on which anarchists agree. Currently, anarchism is becoming fashionable among certain elements in the American public. The militant civilian militias threaten insurrection in defense of their supposed liberties.

DEVELOPMENT OF ANARCHISM

Even as the imperatives of the Industrial Revolution motivated some people to seek more popular participation in government, others agitated for social organization without government. As Europe industrialized, wealth concentrated into the hands of the few, and power centralized in the state. Feelings of impotence and helplessness overcame workers who saw their skills made obsolete by machines and who therefore were put to mindless, repetitive tasks. When once they had actually produced whole products, they now found themselves on assembly lines doing jobs that required little skill and paid a pittance. The simple life of the peasant evaporated as people were forced to enter squalid ghettoes surrounding the factories. The government, once remote, began to play an increasing role in the lives of the individuals: promulgating restrictions, issuing regulations, giving orders, and making demands. Yet, as the institution of government became more pervasive, the people in government became almost anonymous. Growing with its new tasks, a faceless bureaucracy confronted the common people, imposing its will with vigor, even as it became abstract and ambiguous in form.

Although opposition to organized government can be traced as far back as ancient Greece, anarchism as an ideology and as a political movement did not take shape until the early part of the nineteenth century—with the rise of the Industrial Revolution and improved forms of communication. It was then that the means of social control were complete enough and political power adequately centralized to impose the weight of property and government to the extent that they were perceived as impediments to human development.

DEFINITION OF ANARCHISM

Woefully misunderstood in the United States, anarchism continues to hold a strong attraction for some people in the world. Indeed, anarchism, has recently become very popular among right-wing extremists and gun enthusiasts in the United States.

Anarchism is often equated with *anarchy.* This is an understandable mistake, but it results in an unfortunate misapprehension. Anarchy implies chaos, disorder, and confusion resulting from the absence of government. Few, if any, anarchists advocate such a state of affairs. Indeed, they contend that the opposite will result from the elimination of government. Essentially, anarchists believe that human beings have outgrown the need for government—if indeed they ever needed it in the first place. Government, it is assumed, was created to facilitate human development, but instead it actually impedes people from fulfilling their potential. Thus, believing that people will unilaterally conduct themselves appropriately without outside power systems enforcing conformist behavior, all anarchists want to see government reduced. Because of its reliance on human self-government, *anarchism is the purest form of democracy.*

No anarchist wants to eliminate government entirely. The most extreme anarchists do want to end all forms of *institutional government,* but they do not advocate anarchy because they believe that the most important kind of government will remain: *self-government.* Less fervent anarchists support the existence of local governments (villages, communes, syndicates), but they would greatly reduce, or eliminate entirely, national government systems.

More expansive than simple antagonism toward government, anarchism also opposes institutions that buttress the state, helping it to impose restrictions upon human behavior and development. Social class distinctions are rejected as an artificial and contrived barrier by which a society's power elite denies others privilege. Racism, it is alleged, is a similar device. Private property is criticized, since it is often viewed as an institution denying people freedom. According to some anarchists, property is used to exalt the few and belittle the many, thus becoming an instrument of oppression. Similarly, religion is sometimes condemned. Seen as a tool for mass control, the Church is eschewed. While most anarchists are atheists, denying the very existence of God, some, like Leo Tolstoy, remained devout but abandoned established religion for a less exploitative interpretation of Christianity.

Many anarchists resist any institution that tends to demand that people conform to accepted behavior. Consequently, schools are often seen as instruments of regimentation and oppression. All societies use education to socialize their young. Not only do schools teach traditional subjects like reading, mathematics, and music, but they also teach appropriate social behavior. For example, anarchists view teaching elementary students to line up before entering the classroom as an abomination. Such regimentation, anarchists believe, deforms children, squeezing from them their natural spontaneity and robbing them of creativity. Such discipline denies people freedom, forcing them to surrender their individuality and creating slavish automatons of once unspoiled creatures. But schools are only one example. Anarchists view most of society's institutions similarly, including labor unions, scouting, the law, peer group pressure, etiquette and manners, and so forth. All of these institutions are, in the broadest sense, government. The anarchist chafes at its authority, feeling that government places undue restrictions on people, crippling them and denying them the freedom inherent in the human spirit. Put differently, rather than helping people fulfill their human potential, government—and other authoritative institutions—dehumanize them.

In general terms, anarchists want to maximize human liberty. They view government and its supporting institutions as antithetical to freedom and deleterious to human development. Instead of being useful institutions that facilitate human progress, governments block its path. Viewed from this perspective, anarchism is perhaps not startling to some people. Indeed, although few of us are actually anarchists, many of us harbor some anarchist tendencies. Many of us see some elements of government as detrimental rather than helpful to our interests. Standing in line for hours to have a driver's license renewed, trying to have college transcripts forwarded, paying hard-earned money in exorbitant taxes to support impersonal bureaucracies whose regulations prevent us from doing as we wish, and dozens of other frustrating episodes can kindle within us the desire to see elements of the government reduced or eliminated.

While all anarchists oppose government to some extent, few other generalizations can be accurately applied to them as a group. There are, in fact, several misconceptions about the ideology; for example, in the United States anarchism is seen as a necessarily violent movement. This misconception is quite natural because so much violence was attributed to anarchists in this country at the turn of the century. The Haymarket Riot of 1886, the assassination of President William McKinley in 1901, the Great Red Scare of 1919, and the Sacco-Vanzetti hysteria of the mid-1920s were but a few dramatic episodes in which real or alleged anarchistic violence was blamed for the turmoil characterizing the era.

Although it is doubtful that anarchism deserved the full weight of blame ascribed to it in these events, many immigrants to the United States who came from Southern and Eastern Europe at the time were adherents of the violent anarchist theories of Mikhail Bakunin. Thus, the impression developed that all anarchists were bomb-throwing malcontents who should be suppressed for the good of society.

In point of fact, however, anarchism can be violent or nonviolent depending on the particular theory advocated. Indeed, the earliest anarchists eschewed violence and opposed government on grounds that it was itself the greatest perpetrator of violence in society.

Another misapprehension about anarchism is that it is solely a leftist ideology. In reality, anarchism can be found on either the far right or the far left of the political spectrum. All anarchists would see government reduced or eliminated, leaving the individual free to pursue his or her best interests. To this extent all anarchists are the same. However, a critical distinction among them is revealed when we investigate exactly why they wish the individual to be freed from governmental restraint. What, in other words, is the individual's relationship to society?

Leftists of all persuasions view the individual in relation to all other individuals. Indeed, they believe that the individual cannot be effectively evaluated apart from the group. Accordingly, anarchists on the left wish to free people from governmental control because they believe that government prevents individuals from making the greatest possible contribution to society as a whole. The state, they believe, is a tool of mass oppression and should be eliminated if humanity is to advance freely to its fullest potential.

The state is used by the ruling class to dominate the governed, thus unfairly and artificially restricting the progress of others. For example, laws giving one social class more economic and political rights than others are often found in stratified societies, and these rules invariably benefit those who make them—the ruling class.

Anarchists from the left, known as **social anarchists**, would reduce or eliminate the offending governmental institutions, stripping away the artificial restraints on individual freedom and thus allowing each person, regardless of social class, to make his or her greatest contribution to the society as a whole. Counted among the social anarchists are William Godwin, Pierre Joseph Proudhon, Mikhail Bakunin, Peter Kropotkin, Leo Tolstoy, and Emma Goldman. Some of these social anarchists (Bakunin, Kropotkin, and Goldman) advocated the use of violence, while Godwin, Proudhon, and Tolstoy denounced such practices as immoral or at least counterproductive.

Social anarchism is perhaps the best known form of anarchism because of the prolific literature produced by its adherents and because of their dramatic deeds for the cause. Yet, the anarchists of the far right are probably the most numerous, at least in the United States. Instead of favoring a society in which all individuals advance together, one in which the material differences between individuals are kept to a minimum, the anarchists of the right—**individualist anarchists**—envision a kind of Social Darwinism in which the society will advance best when each individual is encouraged to achieve what he or she can for himself or herself. This principle of "ownness," as Max Stirner called it, suggests that humanity is best served when people advance or fall back in relation to their individual abilities.

Individualist anarchists resist government policies such as welfare programs, affirmative action policies, and progressive income taxes, arguing that these policies protect the weak at the expense of the strong. Such policies artificially warp society, retarding progress, and should be eliminated. Individualist anarchist theories have been expressed by celebrated people such as Max Stirner, Henry David Thoreau, Josiah Warren, S. E. Parker, and Ayn Rand. The militant civilian militia movement, currently so popular in some quarters of the United States, is heavily laced with individualist anarchist objectives.

PARTICULAR THEORIES OF ANARCHISM

Anarchism has an almost endless number of variations. Some anarchist theories have heralded freewheeling individualistic societies, while others have advocated communist structures. Some anarchists have made atheism an objective; yet others have called for people to forsake government for societies based on religious unions. Violence has often been seen as the vehicle for instituting anarchism, while pacifism has also been counseled. Government has been accused of preventing human harmony, and it has also been challenged by those who see it as impeding the strong and artificially protecting the weak. Because of the diverse views of anarchists, it is difficult to construct generalizations which accurately describe this theory. Anarchism is, indeed, *the purest expression of individualism in politics.* Consequently, rather than generalizing any further, it may be useful to briefly examine the basic ideas of some of history's leading anarchist thinkers.

The Pacifists

William Godwin (1756–1836) is generally credited with founding modern anarchism. The son of stern Calvinist parents, Godwin followed many of his ancestors into the ministry.[1] Yet, his considerable familiarity with French and English rationalism persuaded him to leave the church to pursue a literary career instead. Godwin was truly a product of his era. Like his contemporary Thomas Paine, he had been schooled in the nonconformist philosophies of radical Protestantism and came to believe in the virtues of human individualism, seeing the church and later the state as conspiracies to benefit a few at the expense of many.

In 1793 Godwin published his most important work, *The Enquiry Concerning Political Justice,* which immediately established him as a leading social critic. Basically, he suggested that all people are fundamentally equal and rational. If left to their own impulses, people would naturally create a harmonious society in which all would benefit and none would suffer at the hands of another. Unfortunately, however, society had evolved institutions that subdued the natural human impulse, creating a biased and exploitative society.

As you have already learned, these libertarian ideas[2] were not unique to Godwin; Rousseau and other leftists shared this view. However, the English philosopher condemned not only the national government and its centralized institutions, but he also lashed out at schools, organized religion, the family, and other local institutions as purveyors of the biases which threatened individual goodness and accomplishment.

Godwin opposed most laws and institutional restraints imposed upon the individual. In their place he would see the creation of a society that he vaguely described as a community without rules, founded upon the belief that individuals, left to their own inclinations, would conduct themselves with mutual respect and compassion. Those who used social and political institutions for their own advantage—the "imposters," as he called them— were to be "reeducated" to change their values and attitudes.

---

[1]Godwin's daughter, Mary, became the wife of the English poet Percy Bysshe Shelley, and it was she who authored the story of Frankenstein.

[2]The term *libertarian* used in this context is meant to mean liberty loving. It does not refer to the ideas of the Libertarian Party of the United States.

Godwin's social criticism is far more important than his vague aspirations for a more compatible society. Indeed, his condemnation of the state and other institutions set the tone for subsequent social anarchists (anarchism on the left). Although he launched a spirited defense of the French Revolution in answer to Edmund Burke's criticism of it, he generally discouraged the use of violence as unnecessary to bring about needed change.

Incorporating most of Godwin's moralistic objections to the state and its institutions, **Pierre Joseph Proudhon** (1809–1865) gave anarchism the philosophical depth and economic perspective that made it a viable political ideology in the modern world. Largely self-educated, this son of a working man endeared himself to the French public for his modest lifestyle and his sincere devotion to humanitarian principles.

Proudhon professed the **Labor Theory of Value** (all value is created by the workers) and used it to answer the question in the title of his best known book, *What Is Property?*: "Property is theft," he responded on the first page. By this he meant that all unearned property (rent, interest, profits) was stolen from the workers who produced it.

Proudhon, the first person to call himself an anarchist, demanded the elimination of government and other institutions, which he claimed unduly denied the people earned property and human rights so that the governing class might flourish. Denouncing the established order, he advocated restructuring society into voluntary associations of workers. These institutions, *syndicates* they were called, would dispense the necessary services usually provided by government. Thus, *anarcho-syndicalism* was born; it remains to this day a potent influence in the labor movement of France as well as many other countries. Indeed, the "industrial unions"—the United Mine Workers, the United Auto Workers, and many others—in this country are organized on a syndical (industry-wide) basis as opposed to the skilled-crafts, or guild, model.

Syndicalism, Proudhon believed, should be voluntary and should be created at the expense of the state. It should liberate the worker from the twin masters of capitalism and government. Frustrated by the growing complexity of modern bureaucracy and decrying the lack of morality in state policy, Proudhon condemned authority as corrupt and decadent. Traditional political authority, he claimed, exists solely to "maintain *order* in society, by consecrating and sanctifying obedience of the citizen to the state, subordination of the poor to the rich, of the common people to the upper class, of the worker to the idler, of the layman to the priest." Since he thought the state exploitative and without moral justification, Proudhon would see it eliminated and replaced with an institution that more accurately reflected the economic and political rights of the people.

Still, however, Proudhon did not call for violent overthrow of the state. Instead, he would have the workers take it upon themselves to ignore traditional authority and organize the syndicates. Thus denied the support of the productive elements in society, the state would collapse, leaving only the voluntary associations of workers or syndicates.

Leo Tolstoy (1828–1910), Russian noble and literary master, was another noted anarchist. Following a frivolous youth, Tolstoy became troubled by the suffering of Russia's peasants. Equally disturbing to him was the realization that the peasant plight resulted from deliberate policies of the Russian Orthodox Church and the Tsarist regime.

Tolstoy developed a great admiration and respect for the individual and most particularly for the Russian peasant. He saw the peasants confronted with the tremendous power of the state that brutalized them. His sympathy for the peasant deepened when he saw them suffering so desperately, even as they were encouraged to bear exploitation by the Church, which Tolstoy felt manipulated the scriptures to serve the state and its ruling class. The great author's compassion and admiration for the peasant were expressed as early as 1869 in his magnum opus, *War and Peace*. In this exquisite novel about the 1812 Napoleonic invasion of Russia, Tolstoy develops the thesis that the hated aggressor was not turned back by Tsars and generals. Rather, Napoleon was defeated through the dedication, suffering, and sacrifice of millions of lowly individuals who stood to the defense of Mother Russia.

Tolstoy's anarchism stemmed from two fundamental and closely related convictions: his interpretation of Christianity and his commitment to

Leo Tolstoy (1828–1910)
Corbis-Bettmann

pacifism. Echoing the force theory of the origin of the state, Tolstoy believed that the state resulted from nothing more than the imposition of power by the strong over the weak. Physical violence, he contended, was the basis of political power. A devout Christian who was convinced that Christianity demanded peace and human justice, Tolstoy considered the state illegitimate on the basis of its presumed method of development: the use of force. Yet, beyond this conclusion the state continued its offense by perpetuating violence. Indeed, Tolstoy saw the state as the principal source of violence in society.

On the pretext of having to protect society from aggressive neighbors, the state organized armies. However, in Tolstoy's view, the armies were actually turned against the people they purported to protect. In other words, the state perpetrated violence against its own people. Why did the state use violence against its own citizens? To exploit them, to squeeze the last measure of energy and production from people while denying them the desserts of their labor. The state, then, in Tolstoy's view, was illegitimate from its beginning and continued to assault the individual with orchestrated violence and exploitation. In short, the state was evil and invalid.

To those who argued that the state was the context in which civilization developed, Tolstoy refused to concede the point. But, he argued, even if the state might have been necessary at one time to create the atmosphere in which religion, education, culture, and communication could develop, society clearly had evolved beyond its previous dependence. Arguing that modern people are quite capable of creating and maintaining civilized institutions without the state, Tolstoy indicted the state, charging that it actually hindered rather than encouraged civilized society.

Having thus challenged the legitimacy of this monstrous evil in society, Tolstoy called on the Russian people to destroy the state itself. Yet, he cautioned against the use of revolution for the cause. Instead, he encouraged people to abandon their commitment to the Russian Orthodox Church, which he viewed as the handmaiden of the state. Tolstoy rejected the ceremony, vestments, and clergy as irrelevant trappings of the true faith (he was excommunicated for these beliefs). Rather, he called on each individual to be dedicated to the principles of Christian peace and human fraternity.

He called on people to recognize only one law, the law of God; to be bound only to the dictates of their own consciences; and to ignore any other pretensions to authority. True Christians, he said, could not give their allegiance to the state, for that would mean abandoning their own consciences and the law of God. Christians, he said, were independent of the state because they recognize the law of God as the only true law. Further, they are bound by their faith to follow their own consciences relative to those laws, ignoring other mandates; if they do otherwise, they jeopardize their immortal souls. "Man," Tolstoy wrote, "cannot serve two masters."

The proper response to government, Tolstoy asserted, was simply to ignore it. When the state issues an order, the people should drop their hands and walk away. Tolstoy believed that this technique, today called *passive resistance,* would spell the doom of government. The power of passive resistance as a political tool was appreciated by many people over the years, but no one has understood its potential like India's great leader Mahatma Gandhi. With unshakable resolve, Gandhi entreated his people to resist the British colonial government, not with barricades and bullets, but with quiet, firm disobedience.

Gandhi's tactics were very effective in the long run. After much pain, his followers used stubborn but peaceful protest to demonstrate dramatically the immorality of using force. Eventually unable to justify the use of force against a pacifist adversary, the British finally relented and India became independent. As powerful a tool as it may be, passive resistance is not necessarily always going to reward its advocates. Suggesting that the British government bent before a moral imperative that would have left Hitler or Stalin unmoved, someone once quipped that Gandhi was very clever in his choice of opponents.

Russia, Europe's most oppressive state, produced several other important anarchists. Unfortunately, Tolstoy's passive resistance was not seen by many of his compatriots as a viable method for changing the system.

The Revolutionaries

Perhaps history's best known anarchist is **Mikhail Bakunin** (1814–1876), a Russian aristocrat. Preceding Tolstoy, he also resisted the church and the state as exploitative and oppressive institutions. Unlike the venerable author, however, Bakunin also advocated atheism and violence. Indeed, he is credited as being the founder of violent anarchism. Condemning the state as humankind's greatest obstacle to attaining liberty, Bakunin advocated terrorism, destruction, and revolution. More radical even than Marx, who at least called for revolution by honest working people, Bakunin contended that a successful revolution would come about by arming the underworld of society—its vagabonds, pimps, thieves, murderers—the **lumpenproletariat.**

Alternating between long periods of revolutionary activity, imprisonment, and exile, Bakunin was unable to reduce his ideas to systematic presentations until the last decade of his life. By then he had gained international notoriety as a revolutionary, and so his reputation remains today. Even so, his writing reveals a logical, if somewhat undisciplined, mind.

Basically, Bakunin rejected all forms of human conformity. He regarded most of society's institutions as devices to enslave the human spirit, denying it the freedom for which it was destined. For example, he rejected religion and belief in God. To believe in a superhuman power necessarily meant the abdication of the free human spirit and the enslavement of people to a supposed divine spirit. Placing total emphasis on human freedom, he challenged God to liberate people. "If God existed," he wrote, "only in one way could he serve human liberty—by ceasing to exist."

Bakunin had been strongly influenced by the Russian **Narodnik** (Populist) movement, which lionized the Russian peasant. The perfect social arrangement, he opined, would be composed of rural communes in which each citizen freely and voluntarily agreed to work. Unlike Rousseau, however, Bakunin would have nothing to do with the principle of majority rule. Seeing each individual as a free spirit, owing no debt to anyone else, he envisioned that each person in society would remain free either to give or to withhold consent from the norms of the group. Thus maximizing individual freedom, Bakunin expected to liberate people from societal restraints, expecting that they would then be able to make their contributions to the whole as free and willing participants rather than as slaves to the opinion makers of the community.

Although Bakunin failed to depose a government during his lifetime, he is indisputably the most influential anarchist history offers. His ideas are credited with stimulating assassinations, terrorism, and rebellion in many nations. His philosophy had a great impact on subsequent anarchists and other radicals; it was particularly popular among the peasants of Italy, Ukraine, and Spain. Indeed, Ukraine in 1917 and Spain in 1936–1939 hosted the only sustained anarchistic experiments, and both were based on Bakuninist theory.

Much less the activist and more the scholarly writer was Prince **Peter Kropotkin** (1842–1921). Like his Russian compatriots Tolstoy and Bakunin, Kropotkin was a noble who profited from the privilege his society afforded that rather arbitrary status. Trained as a scientist, Kropotkin made a number of important contributions to the geographical studies of the Russian Far East and Scandinavia. Captivated by the revolutionary energy of Bakunin, Kropotkin became an activist in the 1870s but returned to the scholarly life after being imprisoned for his illicit activities. From the mid-1880s until 1917 he resided in London, occupying himself with scholarly and philosophical writing. With the Tsar's overthrow in 1917, he returned to Moscow, living there in quiet and honored retirement until his death.

Kropotkin's scientific background encouraged him to dispute the then popular doctrine of **Social Darwinism,** as put forth by Herbert Spencer. He was convinced that higher animals, and man in particular, had met with the greatest success when acting cooperatively rather than aggressively.

Government, according to Kropotkin, tended to divide person against person, class against class, country against country, and was therefore destructive of human progress. It was the "personification of injustice, oppression, and monopoly" in his view and must therefore be eliminated and replaced with an anarchist society based upon communist principles and voluntary mutual aid among free individuals.

Kropotkin believed that people were essentially social beings and that the state tended to make them antisocial. With its elimination he expected people to seek one another's support and cooperation. Thus, a positive rather than negative atmosphere would evolve and would accrue to the ultimate benefit of all in the society.

Kropotkin's attitude toward revolution was ambivalent. An avowed Bakuninist during his early years, he did engage in revolutionary activities, but he later questioned whether revolution was the most effective method by which to transform society. Although he certainly never became a pacifist, Kropotkin tended to lean increasingly toward the belief that, nourished by the increasing capacity of industrialization to sustain a communist society, anarchism would evolve naturally from the human desire to be free.

Emma Goldman (1869–1940) was the most influential anarchist in United States history. Fleeing Tsarist Russia, she came to America in 1886, only to be brutalized in the sweatshops of the garment industry in Rochester, New York. Disillusioned by harsh economic conditions as well as by the prejudices of the moral strictures of American society, she found herself becoming increasingly radical. Alexander Berkman, who became her lifelong lover, introduced her to the theories of Bakunin and to the tiny American anarchist movement.

Soon Goldman became a leading advocate of radical causes ranging from atheism to the use of contraceptives by women. A fiery speaker, she often brought crowds to their feet and the police to her door. Arrested time and again for leftist agitation, Goldman came to be known as "Red Emma."

Emma Goldman (1869–1940)
Corbis-Bettmann

During most of her career, Goldman was an activist. She led protests, addressed rallies, advocated strikes, published the anarchist journal *Mother Earth,* and even sold her body to get enough money to buy the pistol with which Berkman tried to assassinate industrialist Henry Clay Frick. As World War I approached she became a leading opponent of the "capitalist's war," again finding herself in jail and finally deported to the Soviet Union. Her initial enthusiasm for the Soviet regime soon transformed into bitter disappointment, however, causing her to support the Russian navy's anti-Bolshevik rebellion on the island of Kronstadt in 1921, and ultimately inducing her to leave the country for London.

Continuing her radical activities throughout the 1920s and 1930s, Goldman became a vociferous opponent of fascism and Nazism. She joined the anarchists in Spain resisting the reactionary rebellion of Francisco Franco and ultimately died of a stroke in Canada while trying to raise money for the anarchist cause.

Although she remained an activist to the end, an advocate of "propaganda by the deed," Goldman gradually came to question the violent acts of her youth. Time found her increasingly drawn to the temperate approach of Kropotkin and away from the terrorist methods of Bakunin. In the end, Emma Goldman advocated the elimination of government to be replaced by a network of communes based on mutual trust and consideration among individuals who remained free to think and act as they chose.

Besides the relatively mild Kroptokin and the activist Goldman, history's most extreme anarchist movement also owes a great deal to Bakunin. Unlike their revolutionary mentor, the **Nihilists** remained in Russia, combating Tsarist oppression. Feeling the pressure for change in the nineteenth century, the Tsarist regime responded to demands for reform and modernization with reaction and brutal repression. The government's obstinate intransigence frustrated the radicals and encouraged them to resort to increasingly extreme activities, eventually including conspiracy, terrorism, and assassination.

The most frustrated group of radicals, the Nihilists abandoned all hope of reform and came to believe that society itself had to be brought down. The term Nihilists was first introduced in *Fathers and Sons,* a novel by Ivan Turgenev. Developing the most chaotic, violent, and destructive variant of anarchist theories, the Nihilists were prominent between the 1860s and 1880s. Their philosophy contended that government was so rotten, so corrupt, so decayed that it was beyond repair. The only constructive act possible, in the minds of these unhappy people, was the destruction of society. Anything that survived the violent onslaught would perhaps be worth saving. In a single sentence, Nihilist Dmitri Pisarev (1840–1918) captured the philosophy of these tortured radicals: "Here is the ultimatum of our camp: What can be smashed, should be smashed; what will stand the blow is good; what will fly into smithereens is rubbish; at any rate, hit out right and left—there will and can be no harm from it."

The most notorious Nihilist was Sergi Nechayev (1847–1882). A protégé of Bakunin, Nechayev schemed and plotted unscrupulously. Devoted to only one idea, the destruction of the state, he lied, cheated, and even murdered his own co-conspirators. Proclaiming his Nihilist convictions, he wrote: "We must devote ourselves wholly to destruction, constant, ceaseless, relentless, until there is nothing left of existing institutions." Though in practice the Nihilists were amateurish and bungling and were eventually wiped out, their blatant violence terrorized the Russian government and caused it some loss of esteem, since its brutal policies so obviously produced Nihilist extremism.

Individualist Anarchists

Easily the most solitary philosophy among anarchists is **individualist anarchism** (anarchism on the right). The people thus far discussed, whether violent or not, religious or not, socialist or not, were **social anarchists** (anarchism on the left); they opposed government because they believed that it limited people's freedom. However, they were not interested in individual freedom solely for the individual's own sake. Each of the social anarchists recognized that individuals within society are directly related to each other and are somehow responsible to each other. Such is not the case with the individualist anarchists. These ideologues recognize only the individual, denying any obligation or even much value to interrelationships among people. Exceeding the confines of what is usually understood as "individualism," these anarchists promote a concept which might better be termed "individualistism."

The founder of individualist anarchism is **Max Stirner** (1806–1856), a German philosopher and social critic. Stirner led a relatively undistinguished life except for a brief moment of notoriety in the late 1840s, when his most successful work, *The Ego and His Own,* was published. Within its pages Stirner portrays humanity as a completely *atomistic* group of individuals who owe no true responsibility to anyone save themselves.

According to Stirner, society's institutions, including government and religion, are artificial props unrightfully forcing the strong to sacrifice in support of the weak. Stirner suggests that all acts, though usually rationalized as being for the greater good, are actually committed out of selfish motives. Thus, he argues that contrary to what people say, they do not worship God for God's sake, but for their own benefit's sake. The worship of God is a protective device intended by the worshippers to save their souls. Yet, they piously represent it as an unselfish act. Stirner sees this pretense as a self-deception preventing people from openly and efficiently acting in their own interests.

Stirner demands that people abandon their feeble attempts at mutual responsibility and concentrate on themselves alone. Defiantly proclaiming his thesis of "ownness," Stirner wrote: *"My own* I am at all times and under all circumstances, if I know how to have myself and do not throw myself away on others." In another place in *The Ego and His Own* he restates the point even more bluntly: "I am everything to myself and I do everything on my own account."

Thus establishing to his satisfaction *"the sovereignty of the individual,"* Stirner encourages each person to act without regard to the society as a whole. People are justified to take what they wish simply because they desire it. The social good is a hoax created to limit the power of the strong. When society protects the weak, it destroys individual freedom. Stirner calls upon people to refuse recognition of their supposed obligation to others, thus liberating themselves from the artificial fetters unrightfully imposed upon them. Exalting in his own presumed freedom, he exclaimed, "The *people* are dead. Up with *me!"*

As previously indicated, individualist anarchist ideas can also be found in works by Henry David Thoreau, Josiah Warren, S. E. Parker, and Ayn Rand. Certainly one of this nation's most popular contemporary writers, Ayn Rand (1905–1982), a Russian-born thinker, advocated *objectivism* in novels and journals. This theory lionizes individualism and relegates collectivism to irrelevance. Reminiscent of Stirner, Rand claims that selfishness is good and altruism is decadent. She encourages her followers to focus on their own narrow interest in the belief that the only worthwhile accomplishment is one perpetrated by an individual purely motivated by selfish interests.

Rand's popularity in the United States stems from her *laissez-faire* economic ideas, but also because her atomistic approach is deeply rooted in the fabric of American society as well. Perhaps stemming from the frontier ethic under which people relied on themselves to carve a life out of the wilderness, the mystique of *rugged individualism* has enjoyed particular popularity in the United States. Thus, the "strong, silent type" who "goes it alone" has often captured the imagination of the American people. The tendency toward an atomistic society in which the individual comes first and society is secondary—almost incidental—has certainly been an important force in our history. The current popularity of the Libertarian ideology also is partially explained by its emphasis on the individual.

Yet, a very real danger is concealed in this approach to modern politics. While a measure of self-reliance is indisputably healthy, we do not live in a society in which people have only a slight relationship to each other. Our society is culturally, politically, and economically integrated. Indeed, the most striking development of the past few decades is the growing interdependence in the world. This state of affairs makes exaggerated individualism paradoxical and even dangerous, for if people in an interrelated context refuse to foster a social consciousness, they will tear at the fabric of society until it is severely damaged, or even destroyed.

At its greatest extreme, individualist anarchism can lead to an attitude of complete self-reliance and a frightening exclusivity. It can become reminiscent of Thomas Hobbes' vision of the natural state: "A war of each against all." Stirner's "ownness" and Rand's objectivism can become a kind of "one, true, and only meism," in which only the self counts. It can isolate people more than any other political theory.

Militant Civilian Militias

A shattering explosion at an Oklahoma City federal office building in April 1995 jolted a relatively complacent public. For a few hours rumors spread that the explosion was the work of foreign terrorists, but soon the ugly truth became known. The most deadly act of terrorism in American history was perpetrated by U.S. citizens who saw the federal government as a mortal enemy. Although not actually members of a militia, the suspected bombers espoused ideas similar to those of the militant civilian militias. Suddenly public attention was riveted on this previously little-noticed movement of governmentphobes whose fear of the motivation and intent of government policy stretches credulity beyond reasonable limits.

An estimated 15,000 to 30,000 American citizens have joined over 240 militia groups scattered across forty states of the Union. Although large differences separate many of these groups, certain similarities among them have become clear. They all see government as being captive of evil forces who are bent on enslaving them and abolishing their personal liberties. Their reading of the Second Amendment of the U.S. Constitution assures them the right to keep arms without government interference. Finally, violent confrontation is imminent between the government and those who feel they must righteously defend their individual liberties against the encroachment of federal laws and law enforcers.

The militia movement is deeply submerged in the conspiratorial theory as well as being anarchistic. Rallied by low-budget short wave radio programs originating in several states, militia listeners are harangued by Mark Koernke—the leading spokesperson for this budding ideology—and by several lesser radio personalities. Koernke works as a janitor at the University of Michigan during the day, but at night he becomes "Mark from Michigan," and is regarded by his followers as the leading sentinel against government tyranny.

Virtually every unpleasant policy or activity of the government is twisted and reshaped by these antigovernment crusaders until they are recast as evidence of the plots to deny the American people their liberties. The Brady Bill, requiring would-be gun owners to endure a waiting period of a few days before a gun can be sold; the North American Free Trade Agreement (NAFTA); the General Agreement on Trade and Tariffs (GATT); the Federal Reserve Board; agents of the FBI, the Internal Revenue Service (IRS), the Alcohol, Tobacco, and Firearms Agency (ATF); and so on are being used to rob Americans of freedom.

Militia movement leaders variously claim that the federal government, which is secretly controlled by sinister forces, is plotting to cooperate with a United Nations invasion of the U.S.; planted a bomb in Oklahoma City itself in order to discredit the militia movement; deliberately murdered innocent people who were trying to defend their just liberties at Ruby Ridge, Idaho,[3] in 1992 and at Waco, Texas, in 1993. Warning that a violent confrontation is imminent between thousands of armed citizens of the U.S. and their government, militia leaders have threatened U.S. senators in congressional testimony, warned that 15,000 Gurkha troops are hiding in the Michigan hills awaiting orders to swoop down on the unsuspecting Midwest, claimed that the backs of road signs are marked with coded instructions to guide UN invading columns, and announced that the federal government is controlled by satanic forces.

As bizarre as these charges are and as truculent as the militia movement has become, its leaders claim that the militias are defensive organizations and don't want a fight. Indeed, Norm Olson, one of the movement's most belligerent leaders, claimed that it was actually Japan that detonated the bomb in Oklahoma City in retaliation against the U.S. government—which, Olson claimed, released lethal gas in Tokyo's subways—and blithely told Congress that the militia movement was not a great deal unlike neighborhood watch.

The paranoiac ramblings of these extremists and the rather comical specter of aging militia members becoming America's defenders of liberty should not distract us from the fact that several thousand people find these images compelling. In a nation like our own, which has had a long romance with individualism, such ideas can indeed be very appealing to certain groups of people. For example, the membership of the militia groups actually increased significantly after the Oklahoma bombing.[4]

---

[3]Following an investigation of the Ruby Ridge encounter, the federal government agreed to give a large payment to Randy Weaver for the wrongful deaths of his wife and his fourteen-year-old son, but no responsible authority has claimed that the government deliberately assassinated the two Weavers.

[4]This material was taken from several articles in the *Los Angeles Times,* including "Militias Rely on Networks of Fiery Right," April 30, 1995; "Militia Promoters Draw a Crowd," May 8, 1995; "Militia Leaders Bring Their Fiery Talk to Capitol Hill," June 16, 1995; and "Militia Groups Growing, Study Says," June 18, 1995.

REVIEW

- All anarchists want to dramatically reduce the structure and power of government, but only the most extreme anarchists want all institutional government eliminated.
- Anarchists do not advocate anarchy. Rather, they believe that if left unimpeded by government, people will govern themselves appropriately. Thus, anarchism is the purest form of individualism and of democracy.
- Anarchists have varying views about property, religion, education, and violence, but most anarchists believe the government and its supporting institutions (the church and the educational system, for example) prevent people from being completely free.
- Anarchists on the left, social anarchists, want government and its supporting institutions reduced in power and form, so that people will be free to make their greatest contributions to society as a whole.
- Individualist anarchists, those on the right, would limit government and its supporting institutions, so that individuals are free to make their greatest contributions to themselves.
- The nihilists, the most extreme anarchists, believe that all of society's institutions must be reduced to rubble.
- The militant civilian militia members are the most numerous American anarchists today.

SUGGESTIONS FOR FURTHER READING

BOWIE, NORMAN E., and ROBERT I. SIMON, *The Individual and the Political Order.* Englewood Cliffs, NJ: Prentice Hall, 1977.

CARTER, APRIL, *The Political Theory of Anarchism.* New York: Harper & Row, 1971.

CROWDER, GEORGE, *Classical Anarchism: The Political Thought of Godwin, Proudhon, Bakunin and Kropotkin.* New York: Oxford University Press, 1992.

FORMAN, JAMES D., *Anarchism.* New York: Dell, 1975.

KELLY, AILEEN, *Mikhail Bakunin.* Oxford, England: Clarendon Press, 1982.

MAY, TODD, *The Political Philosophy of Poststructuralist Anarchism.* University Park, PA: Pennsylvania State University Press, 1994.

RAND, AYN, *Atlas Shrugged.* New York: Random House, 1957.

RITTER, ALAN, *Anarchism.* Cambridge, England: Cambridge University Press, 1980.

SHATZ, MARSHALL S., ed., *The Essential Works of Anarchism.* New York: Bantam Books, 1971.

TAYLOR, RICHARD, *An Introduction in Freedom, Anarchy, and the Law.* Englewood Cliffs, NJ: Prentice Hall, 1973.

WARD, COLIN, *Anarchy in Action.* London: Freedom Press, 1982.

WOLFF, ROBERT PAUL, *In Defense of Anarchism.* New York: Harper & Row, 1976.

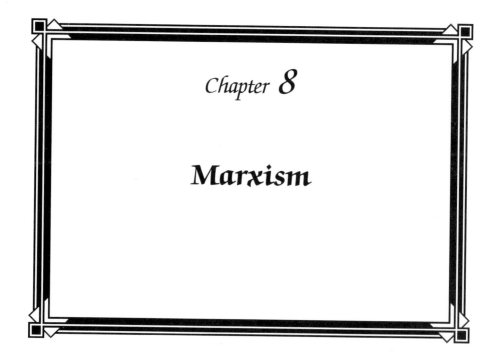

Chapter 8

Marxism

PREVIEW

At the time in which Marx lived, Europe was going through a period of reactionary repression that was made even worse by the conditions resulting from the Industrial Revolution. Yet, the academic community was optimistic about the potential of science and actively sought the formula for understanding human history.

Believing that he had discovered this formula, Marx thought that people's ideas are conditioned by their economic environment and that economic change stimulates a dialectic conflict between those ruling and those ruled in society. The rulers use every available resource to keep themselves in power, but this effort is doomed to failure. Eventually the social class controlling the new dominant means of production will win the struggle to create its own political and social conditions. According to Marx, the final conflict will find the capitalist and proletarian classes engaged in a struggle that the proletariat will win because, while the capitalist system is productive, it is also exploitative and parasitic. When the proletariat class comes to power, it will establish a dictatorship, which, in turn, will create a socialist economy and eliminate all nonproletarian classes. This development will lead to greater productivity and the elimination of poverty; peace and happiness will prevail. When the last nonproletariat has been eliminated from the society, the state will have "withered away," its few remaining institutions acting only as administrators of the economy. As each country becomes socialist in its turn, national boundaries will disappear and eventually a single utopia will replace the divided, exploitative, and cruel world of capitalism.

BACKGROUND

Communism is a very old concept, dating back to the beginning of recorded history. Many primitive societies practiced some form of communal ownership, work, and consumption. Communist tendencies in modern Europe can be found in as early a work as Plato's *Republic,* in early Christian life, in Sir Thomas More's *Utopia,* in the German Anabaptists, and in the English Levelers and Diggers.

The concept of communism, as it was originally meant, did not imply a national economic system. Rather, it meant a local, communal relationship among small groups of people. With the Industrial Revolution, however, two factors evolved that made collective production, distribution, and consumption of goods on a national scale seem feasible. First, the mechanization of production increased output so greatly that some people began to believe hunger and poverty could be eliminated for the first time in history. Second, improvements in technology and communications made it possible to organize, administer, and control a national economic system.

The realization that technology now made communism possible on a national scale, combined with genuine humanitarian compassion, led to the first major "socialist" movement. While communism was originally thought to mean communal living and sharing on a local basis, the term **socialism** was coined by **Robert Owen** (1771–1858), the father of English socialism, to refer to communal living and sharing on a national scale.

Owen was one of a small group of people who thought that simple humanitarianism required the development of a society in which no one would starve while others prospered. These **utopian socialists** were among the first true socialists. The utopian movement will be discussed in more detail in the next chapter; here it is enough to point out that by the middle of the nineteenth century the utopian socialist movement had lost its vitality. People no longer responded to its humanitarian appeal. Its numerous experimental socialist communities in Europe and America had all failed.

Karl Marx was *not* a utopian socialist. Although he was concerned about people's inhumanity to one another, Marx did not believe that people would adopt socialism merely because it was a nice way for one individual to treat another. Marx's theory claimed that socialism was an inevitable result of the Industrial Revolution. Marx's view rescued socialism from oblivion and turned it into one of the most powerful ideas of this century. Marx was also responsible for adding to the meaning of communism. In his introduction to the *Communist Manifesto,* A. J. P. Taylor tells us that Marx used the word *communism* not as a descriptive term but as a polemic intended to arouse people. It excited some and frightened others. *Socialism,* on the other hand, had come to be regarded with indifference. Hence, while Marx espoused *socialism,* that is, a national collectivized economy, he used the word *communist* for the title of his call to revolution, hoping that the substitute term would arouse his audience. For that reason, communism has come to be associated with Marxist socialism.

The complexity of Marx has not been fully appreciated, partly because of the contradictory character of the man himself. Marx was, at the same time, a revolutionary and a Victorian gentleman, a political activist and a sedate scholar, a philosopher and an ideologue, a historian and a futurist.

Marx's Life

Karl Marx (1818–1883) was the oldest son in a Jewish family. Born in Trier, Germany, he came from a prosperous middle-class home. His father was a lawyer who somewhat cynically converted to Christianity for commercial reasons. Yet, his mother remained a strict orthodox Jew and became estranged from her son upon learning he had become an atheist.

In 1836 Marx entered the University of Berlin where he came under the powerful influence of Hegelian philosophy. The young scholar quickly became a serious student, fired by radical ideas of materialism and social justice. Later Marx moved to the University of Jena, where he completed his doctorate in philosophy.

Prepared for a life in academia, the young scholar found the Prussian

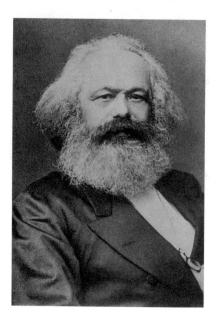

Karl Marx (1818–1883)   New York Public Library
Picture Collection

hand of political oppression heavy indeed. Denied teaching positions by the government because of his radical political views, Marx finally became the editor of a leftist newspaper. The many articles he wrote criticizing the reactionary government incurred its wrath. Unable to tolerate the paper's opposition, the government closed it down in 1843, and Marx was driven into exile.

Paris was the capital of socialism at that time. It hosted dozens of radical groups and was the home of some of the leading socialist thinkers of the day. The young German scholar was immediately comfortable in this setting where he met many leftists and even debated with **Pierre Joseph Proudhon** and **Mikhail Bakunin,** two leading social anarchists. In 1844 he met **Friedrich Engels** (1820–1895), and they quickly became friends.

Engels, the son of a wealthy Prussian industrialist family and a scholar in his own right, not only became Marx's lifelong benefactor, supporting him while he studied and wrote, but also collaborated in Marx's work and made several important contributions to it. After Marx's death his loyal friend carried on the work, editing and publishing the second and third volumes of Marx's *Das Kapital* and finally taking up the leadership of the international socialist movement.

Marx's radical political activities between 1844 and 1848 resulted in his being forced out of one European country after another. At the same time, the political situation in Europe grew increasingly tense until rebellions broke out across the continent in 1848. Thinking that the proletarian revolution they awaited was at hand, Marx and other socialists belonging to the Communist League feared that the opportunity might be wasted for want of a doctrine directing the revolutionaries. Hence, Marx was commissioned to write a brief essay setting forth the ideology of the impending revolution. This tract, hastily written in Belgium, is the *Communist Manifesto*. It contains a brief sketch of Marx's ideas and includes several important thoughts that Marx adapted from the work of his friend Engels.

The year 1848 was indeed a year of revolution. Uprisings flared in several countries from France to Hungary, but each was suppressed in turn. Pursued by police for his revolutionary activities, Marx once again found himself looking for a place to live. At last, in 1849, he took his family to England, where he remained for the rest of his life except for occasional visits to the continent. For the next thirty-four years he studied and wrote in the British Museum. In all of Europe, only England was free enough and sufficiently secure about its political institutions to host this unorthodox and radical thinker.

Despite his scholarly interests, Marx remained active politically. He once wrote, "The philosophers have only *interpreted* the world, the point is to *change* it" (emphasis added). Committed to the revolution he felt sure would soon erupt, Marx corresponded with socialists throughout Europe and in 1864 helped found the International Association of Workingmen, commonly known as the *First International*.

Nevertheless, Marx was not very successful as a revolutionary. Ill at ease in the pragmatic world of applied politics, Marx's revolutionary goal eluded him. Throughout his life he anticipated a great proletarian conflagration, which never materialized. Yet, although he modified his theories with the passage of time, until his death he remained convinced of the validity of his analysis. Indeed, his intellectual prowess was so great that he came to dominate the socialist movement. It was only after his death that major variations of his thought attracted substantial followings among socialists.

Europe in the Nineteenth Century

Before we can fully understand Marx, we must acquaint ourselves with the world in which he lived. Europe in the nineteenth century was dominated by three major influences. First, the Scientific Quest, was scholarly; the second, the Concert of Europe, political; and the third, the Industrial Revolution, economic.

The scientific quest.   Marx lived during a time when belief in science was at its peak. It had revealed secrets of life that were previously unimagined. There was growing confidence that the mysteries of the universe would soon be solved and that humanity was on the verge of a new era of knowledge and understanding of things about which earlier generations could only speculate. Battling with ignorance and superstition, science was close to victory, or so it seemed.

As mentioned earlier, people began to suspect that just as there were laws governing other natural elements, there might also be natural laws governing human beings. A large part of the scholarly community of Europe—including Jeremy Bentham, Herbert Spencer, Auguste Comte, and Sigmund Freud—was indeed persuaded that such laws existed, and Marx was only one of many who sought the "secret" of human motivation. The greatest inspirations in the field of scientific determinism came from Sir Isaac Newton (1642–1727) and Charles Darwin (1809–1882). Newton, with his theories of universal gravitation, terrestrial mechanics, and mass and movement, gave us the tools with which to rationalize the universe. Physical phenomena became understandable as well as predictable, and from this foundation, developments in science and technology launched the present era. Darwin, in turn, gave us a theory of natural selection which provides for biology the foundation that Newton's ideas establish for physics.

For his part, Marx believed that he had discovered the laws—economic laws—that governed human social development; hence, his supporters call his theory **scientific socialism.** Engels, convinced that Marx had done for social history what Darwin had done for biological science, made the following comparison: "As Darwin discovered the law of development of organic nature, so Marx discovered the developmental law of human history."

The Concert of Europe. The Napoleonic conquest of Europe had completely dislocated the established order. When Napoleon was finally defeated and sent into exile in 1815, the leading statespersons of Europe gathered in Vienna. Although delighted to be rid of their longstanding rival, they were deeply concerned about the legacy he had left them. The Europe they had fought to restore was changed beyond recognition. The map was redrawn, the ancient royal families had lost their domains, and the people of Europe were openly demanding democratic reforms. Major decisions had to be made. Either Europe could be brought closer to the radical goals of the French Revolution or it could be forced to reestablish the old dynastic monarchies. Predictably, Europe's leaders agreed to reestablish autocratic rule and to cooperate in defending it against demands for democratic reforms. Thus, three years before Marx's birth, one of the most reactionary periods in history began.

Yet, the demand for reform would not be quieted. Time and again the flag of rebellion was raised. In 1821, again in 1830, and yet again in 1848, the barricades were thrown up in Belgium, Germany, Poland, Austria, Hungary, Italy, Bohemia, Spain, Portugal, and especially in France. Each time these violent demands for reform were repressed so thoroughly that the next rebel-

Charles Darwin (1809–1882)
Corbis-Bettman

lion was made inevitable. All the strength of monarchy was set against the irrepressible forces of history. Though democracy won out over monarchy in the end, this inevitable result was postponed for a century at great cost in terms of human frustration, misery, and death.

This was the political environment Marx encountered during his formative years. Hounded by the police, he fled from one country after another in search of a place that allowed freedom of thought and expression. Little wonder that in his early life he believed that only violence could bring about meaningful changes in society.

The Industrial Revolution. The scientific method had given people a new framework for thought. It also brought on a new technology that mechanized production and replaced human or animal energy with steam. Yet, as machines and energy sources became more sophisticated, their costs exceeded the resources of the individual. Consequently, cottage industry was replaced by the factory system. Family ownership of industry was eventually displaced by stock market investors and professional managers. Each of these developments removed ownership from production and estranged the workers from the owners.

This new economic system allowed people with money to buy up the machinery and factories needed to produce goods. People who had been self-employed, or who at least had worked closely with their employers, found themselves forced to work in huge factories. The resulting depersonalization of labor was increased by the new machinery, which tended to make old skills obsolete. Workers were put behind machines to perform monotonous and menial tasks requiring no skills beyond those needed to keep the machine functioning properly, even as wages were suppressed because skilled jobs disappeared.

The factory system brought with it a whole new way of life. People were herded into the cities where housing was cramped and squalid. Sanitation facilities were so woefully inadequate that people were forced to live in filth. The factories themselves were dark, damp, and unventilated. Having isolated the workers from anything that might reduce their productivity, the owners sealed them in stuffy, dimly lighted workrooms. Thousands died of asthma and tuberculosis because the air they breathed was contaminated by smoke, steam, dust, and filth. Many people toiled as long as sixteen hours a day in the summer and thirteen and a half hours in the winter, sometimes seven days a week. At times workers could not even leave the factories and were forced to sleep beneath the machines to which they were enslaved.

Women and children were the most desirable laborers because they could be paid less and were least likely to resist the harsh discipline, beatings, and other cruelties imposed on them. The family unit disintegrated. A working mother might seldom see her children unless they also worked in the factories. Small children were left completely unattended for long periods. Men, usually the first to be fired, sometimes had to depend on the earnings of their wives and children for subsistence. The disgrace and humiliation of these circumstances often drove men to leave home, to dissipate in drunkenness, to perpetrate cruelties on their families, or even to commit suicide.

The owners were often indifferent to the suffering in their factories. Some capitalists rationalized the wretched conditions of the laborers by claiming that industry saved these people from idleness, the greatest sin of all. Others used Social Darwinist arguments, claiming that the laborers were obviously inferior to the owners and *should* be worked hard. They resolved that eventually the inferiors would die out, leaving only the strong. The owners imposed heavy fines and even corporal punishment for whistling or talking at work, for working too slowly, or for being late. The law gave the workers no protection and demanded a heavy penalty for theft. When a woman was put on trial for stealing a few coins to feed her starving children, Thomas Hood, a poet of the time, wrote in anguish, "Oh God, that bread should be so dear and flesh and blood so cheap!" Charles Dickens, however, is probably the best-known author inspired by the plight of the worker. Just a glance at *David Copperfield, Hard Times,* or *Oliver Twist* impresses the reader with the hopeless circumstances of the poor during this era. Given these conditions of political oppression and economic exploitation, and the social evils that accompanied them, it is not difficult to understand how someone as perceptive as Marx could seek nothing less than radical change in the society.

CAPITALIST DEVELOPMENT

Whatever the ultimate validity of his theories, history has shown Marx to have erred in a number of important respects. Our understanding of Marx will be enhanced if we consider a few of his greatest mistakes before studying his theories.

Marx firmly believed that his generation came at the very end of the capitalist era, and he fully expected the socialist revolution to occur at any moment. Given the despicable conditions of the working class during his life, Marx can be forgiven for expecting that the masses would rise up to cast off their chains should things continue to deteriorate. Perhaps they would have done so had capitalists been as blind as Marx imagined. He was quite wrong, however, in his estimation of both the productivity of capitalism and of its capacity to adjust to threatening conditions. In fact, capitalism far outproduced even the wildest predictions of its nineteenth-century enthusiasts, and the Western capitalists responded to proletarian threats of violence with policies that shared with the worker enough of the newly created wealth to put off a disastrous conflagration.

As it turned out, Marx was seeing the beginning of the capitalist era rather than its end. Preindustrialized (that is, premechanized) economies are usually incapable of producing enough to satisfy all the economic needs of their people. Hence, productivity usually falls below the level we shall call *subsistence*. In these conditions scarcity is a fact of life, causing anxiety. To escape depravity, a few people in such societies—the wealthy—manage to accumulate enough, or more than enough, to satisfy their needs, thus leaving even less to be consumed by the masses. Thus, the portion of production left for ordinary people to consume falls even farther below subsistence, aggravating the suffering of the majority.

Industrialization of an economy can eventually increase productivity, but first money must be found to buy the factories, resources, and machines. Where does the money come from? Some undoubtedly comes from the coffers of the wealthy, but historically the wealthy have demanded sacrifices from the poor to pay for most technological advances. Wages are suppressed and working conditions tend to decline, thus creating capital to invest in mechanization. Consequently, if the masses are already suffering because they must consume at less than the subsistence level and are asked to sacrifice more to create enough capital for industrialization, their conditions of life and work must be terrible indeed.

Such sacrifices do not come voluntarily. To enforce these deficits for the workers, the owners of production used the powers of government, forcing workers to labor for meager wages under terrible conditions. Labor unions were suppressed; strikes were broken by thugs, the police, or the army; and unemployment compensation, workers' compensation, and social security were nonexistent. Collusion between government and the owners of production occurred in every society that industrialized, including England and the United States. The reason for such collusion was that force had to be used to induce the workers to make sacrifices which they would not otherwise make voluntarily.

This stage of the Industrial Revolution—its most exploitative period—was witnessed by Marx and by Dickens. Marx's error was not in decrying these conditions but rather in concluding that the workers' conditions would continue to disintegrate rather than improve. What actually did occur is that, with industrialization, production began to climb, creating capital. Marx anticipated that, driven by the need to increase profits, the capitalists would intensify their exploitation of the workers until the latter could no longer stand their misery: Revolution would then erupt. This bleak prediction has not yet come to pass in the West. Industrial productivity grew to such an extent that it brought huge profits to the owners and, at the same time, vastly improved living and working conditions for the common people. Perhaps realizing that Marx was indeed correct in predicting their doom if they did not provide improved conditions for the workers, the capitalists have grudgingly accepted collective bargaining, fringe-benefit packages, wage increases, and social protection programs. Each of these benefits, however, followed great struggles by workers for their rights. Interestingly, with the recent decline of the labor unions and the rise of conservativism, American workers are again experiencing a reduction in real wages and the loss of fringe benefits, even as corporate profits climb.

Whatever the reason, capitalism has not forced its own doom. Far more flexible and pragmatic than Marx anticipated, capitalism has survived the centennial of his death. Although it has received some very serious blows, the worst of which were the rise of fascism and the Great Depression (1920s–1945), capitalism, albeit in modified form, survives today as a vital economic system showing few signs of the demise predicted by its nemesis, while socialism currently appears to be in retreat.

THE BASIC PRINCIPLES OF MARXISM

Wretched as things had become, Marx was still optimistic about the future of humanity. He saw people in historical terms. Individuals, he believed, were destined for freedom and creativity but had been prevented from developing completely because they were slaves to their own basic needs. Before the Industrial Revolution human productivity had not been great enough to provide a sufficient supply of the necessities of life to free people from **compulsive toil** (a term coined by Marx to express Locke's concept of the necessity to work incessantly just to survive). With the emergence of capitalism, to which Marx gives due praise, people became—for the first time—productive enough to provide an abundance of goods. They could now devote more time to the development of their own humanity. Yet, capitalism failed to distribute its abundance fairly. Indeed, Marx saw that it tended to take away from the workers more and more of the products they created, giving them instead to the capitalist, a nonworker who exploits toilers.

The irony of the dilemma that Marx witnessed is clear: For the first time in history humanity has created an economic system that produces enough for all people so that they may enjoy the spare time necessary to refine their humanity—to be free, in other words. Yet, that very economic system distributes its bounty to a few wealthy people, thus artificially perpetuating the enslavement of the masses. What history had denied people for millennia was now being withheld from them by their fellows. Clearly, in Marx's view, capitalism was to be appreciated for its productivity, but it was also to be despised for its oppression, and it should be abandoned for a more equitable system. Marx was convinced that capitalism was but a necessary step to a new era of social justice. Hoping to guide people to a new, more perfect era, he laid down the doctrines we call Marxism.

Marxist Sociological Theory

The most fundamental assumption in Marxism is **economic determinism.** On this premise Marx built the rest of his theory. Economic determinism suggests that the primary human motivation is economic. "It is not the consciousness of men that determines their existence," Marx argues, "but their social existence that determines their consciousness"; that is, what we value and what we do politically is determined by our economic circumstances. Hence, it stands to reason that people in similar economic circumstances will have much in common.

This idea is not unique to Marx. He was introduced to the concept at the University of Berlin, where it enjoyed considerable support. Indeed, even James Madison proceeded from a similar assumption about human motivation. Consider this statement from *The Federalist* (no. 10):

> But the most common and durable source of factions (political adversaries) has been the various and unequal distribution of property. Those who hold and those who are without property have ever formed distinct interests in society. Those who are creditors and those who are debtors, fall under a like discrimination. A landed interest, a manufacturing interest, a monied interest, with many lesser interests, grow up of necessity in civilized nations, and divide them into different *classes, actuated by different sentiments and views.* (Emphasis added.)

As a matter of fact, economic determinism has gained general currency in the world today, with most people believing that economics plays an important part in determining political behavior. In this respect at least, Glen Tinder posits that we are all now Marxists.[1]

Marx saw all societies as composed of two basic parts: the *foundation* and the *superstructure*. The foundation of any society, according to this theory, is material. In other words, the economic system is at the base of the society. Marx further divided the economy into two basic factors: the means of production and the relations of production. The *means of production* are the resources and technology at the disposal of a particular society, and their interrelationship determines the kind of economic system the society enjoys. The *relations of production* (or social classes) are determined by the affiliation between human beings in the society and the means of production. The owners of the means of production enjoy the most beneficial position in the economy, and thus become members of the most influential social group—the ruling class. (The validity of this part of Marx's proposition becomes clear if one tries to imagine a wealthy class that does not have great influence in society.) Thus, in a pastoral society the ruling group would be those who own the

---

[1]Glen Tinder, *Political Thinking*, 4th ed. (Boston: Little, Brown, 1986), p. 184.

most livestock; in an agrarian society the greatest land owners would dominate; and in an industrial society the capitalist class rules.

The foundation of society (the economic and social class systems) determines the nature of society's superstructure which rests upon the foundation. The superstructure is composed of all nonmaterial institutions in the society, and each is arranged in a way that suits the ruling class. Included in the superstructure are values, ideology, government, education, law, religion, art, and so forth. (See Figure 8–1.) *The function of the superstructure is to assure the rulers continued dominance and to keep the ruled in their place.*

Consequently, Marx conceived of government as a tool of class oppression that manipulated all the cultural elements in the society to the advantage of those who controlled the economy. "Political power," he wrote, "properly so called, is merely organized power of one class for oppressing another." Marx called religion "the opiate of the people" because he believed that it drugged them, numbing their senses and disposing them to put up with their wretched existence so that they would be rewarded in a "mythical" afterlife. The aphorism "That's the cross I have to bear" illustrates the kind of attitude to which Marx objected. He wanted people to abandon the rationalizations with which they had been programmed by their rulers. When they did, they would become aware of their plight. They would then have taken the first step toward the revolution and freedom.

Marx suggested that two societies with similar economic systems would develop similar superstructures (similar political and social systems). For example, societies with feudal economic bases (that is, agrarian societies in which the land is owned by a tiny elite and the bulk of the population

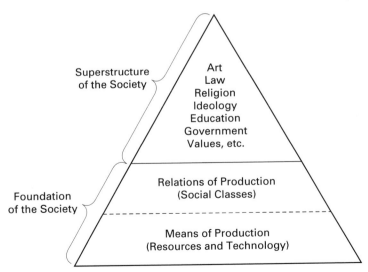

FIGURE 8–1 Marxian Abstract of Society's Structure

works the land of the great nobles) will develop similar social and political institutions in their superstructures. Their political systems include monarchies supported by a powerful aristocratic class of landowners. The values, laws, ideologies, and educational systems tend to justify these political and economic systems. The dominant religion tends to be structured in a hierarchical fashion similar to the Catholic Church, and the Church also acts to support the system.

On the other hand, according to Marx, capitalistic systems (those whose economies are based on money and industrial production controlled by a small elite) evolve different institutions in their superstructures. Representative democracies give the illusion of popular control, but the governments are actually captained by the moguls who own the means of production. The values, laws, ideologies, and educational systems encourage sympathetic public attitudes toward these political and economic systems. Protestantism, with its individualistic and egalitarian doctrines, becomes the dominant religious form. Being free of the former Catholic bias against usury and commerce, Protestantism is more compatible with capitalist values. Further, espousing the ethic that hard work, industriousness, and frugality result in individual progress, social good, and even (perhaps) eternal reward, Protestantism anoints capitalist activity with moral justifications and would therefore replace Catholicism as the dominant creed.

Although it is certainly not difficult to find circumstances that contradict Marx's views about how economics predisposes society, one would be remiss not to recognize that indeed there is much to be learned from this analysis. It is true, for example, that the areas which developed extensive capitalist systems—England, Holland, Switzerland, northern Germany, Scandinavia, and the United States—also accepted Protestantism as the dominant religious form. Even in Catholic France, which also built a substantial industrial base, the Huguenots (French Protestants) own a disproportionately large percentage of the capital wealth.

It is also true that societies make concerted efforts to socialize their citizens. That is, they take great pains to inculcate in their people the dominant values and norms of society, and these attitudes invariably accrue to the benefit of the people who control the system. In the United States, for example, American Government is a required course in most states at elementary, high school, and college levels. Why is this subject thought to be so important? Other than creating jobs for political scientists (your author included), the study of government assumes that democracy depends upon a well-informed citizenry; thus the requirement. Yet, these courses (especially in the lower grades) do more than simply inform students. Great effort is expended to develop a positive attitude among students about their system of government.

Clearly, the above example illustrates the conscious attempt by society's leaders to instill in each generation the values that society espouses. Some may justify this phenomenon as an attempt to help young people become productive and happy citizens, while others may condemn it as propaganda. Whatever the case, the example tends to indicate that Marx is at least partially correct about the function of the superstructure. However, whether or not his assumption about the character of the society's foundation is sound remains debatable.

Marxist Historical Theory

Dialectic materialism is the essence of Marxism. To be a Marxist, one must accept this theory. As the Marxist theory of history, it is the basis for the belief that Marx created a "scientific" theory of socialism.

The dialectic. Part of this theory, the concept of the dialectic, was taken from the thinking of **Georg Hegel** (1770–1831), one of the most important political philosophers of modern history. Hegel developed a theory of history in which change is the central theme. Hegel believed that the world was progressing toward a goal that was predetermined by God. He called the goal the *Idea*. History, in other words, was the unfolding of God's Idea.

Since the Idea (or the course of history) was predetermined by God, people could not hope to understand it completely. Nor should they try to adjust the progress of history because that too, for the same reason, was beyond their power. Individuals can, however, be free, and they can find truth. Truth is found when people understand and accept their place in history, or in the divine plan. When they find truth, they will also be free because they will not imprison themselves in a futile struggle against the will of an all-powerful God. These ideas, far from being liberal, form part of the basis for German nationalism and, more particularly, for fascism. Marx, an atheist with political views on the far left of the political spectrum, obviously did not draw inspiration from Hegel's definition of the Idea.

The concept that Marx did borrow from Hegel was that of the dialectic. Both Marx and Hegel saw the dialectic as a means of achieving historical *progress through struggle*. Hegel believed that history was spiritually motivated. He suggested that the dialectic was a divinely created force by which the Idea (history) was caused to unfold. He believed that any reality is two things. It is itself, and it is part of what it is becoming. Thus, the only consistency Hegel saw was change itself. To Hegel, history was simply the process of change brought on by struggle. In this process no truth was ever lost, since today's reality would become part of a more perfect truth tomorrow.

To better understand Hegel's theory, let us consider the following example. Let us call the existing state of affairs the *thesis*. Eventually any thesis will be challenged by a new idea, which we will call the *antithesis*. A conflict between the thesis and the antithesis will follow; this is called the *dialectic process.* The result of this conflict will, according to Hegel, be a *synthesis* of all the good parts of the thesis and of the antithesis. Then the synthesis becomes the new thesis to which another antithesis eventually develops. Struggle between them ensues, and a new synthesis, and eventually a new thesis evolves, and the process begins again. Hegel believed that the dialectic process always led to something better than what existed previously. He argued that good features were never lost in the dialectic process; rather they became part of a new, more complete good. Negative aspects of the thesis and antithesis, however, were destroyed in the dialectic process. This, Hegel called the "negation of the negative." Hence, Hegel saw history as inevitably progressive, with each new era improved over the last. And he expected the dialectic to continue refining and improving human institutions until the Idea was fulfilled. (See Figure 8–2.)

Dialectic materialism. Marx rejected Hegel's metaphysical assumptions, of course, but he adopted the dialectic as the fundamental logic of history. He agreed with Hegel that humanity would eventually reach the end of the process of change. In other words, both Hegel and Marx were idealists, each believing that people could develop a perfect social and political existence. However, Marx did not accept Hegel's version of the dialectic but changed it to suit his own view of historical progress. Hegel had argued that the dialectic was a struggle between divinely inspired ideas and that it led to changes

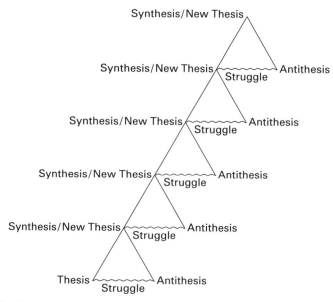

FIGURE 8–2   Hegelian Dialectic

in the earthly social or political environment. Marx, it is said, stood Hegelianism on its head by suggesting the opposite. Citing economic determinism, Marx claimed that the dialectic was a conflict among worldly interests. Rather than stimulating struggle, ideas were actually the result of the dialectic conflict. *Materialism,* not *spiritualism,* inspired the dialectic, according to Marx. He then went on to name the characters in the dialectic drama.

Marx believed that human conflict was caused by social-class differences. In addition, he held that the struggle which occurred at the end of one historical era and led to the dawn of a new one was a struggle between opposing social classes. Further, he believed that humanity had passed through four historical stages and was about to enter its fifth and final era. Each historical era had been characterized by a particular economic system (the means and relations of production) leading to a specific political system (superstructure).

The first era of human history, Marx believed, was based on *primitive communism.* People were unorganized and unsophisticated during this age. There was no occupational specialization, or division of labor. Every person worked at producing, and people necessarily shared their produce with one another in order to survive. The antithesis to this system developed as people began to specialize in the production of certain goods. This *division of labor* resulted in more abundant and better quality goods, but it also caused a major division within society. As people focused on producing their specialty, the original collectivism of society was lost. The spears an artisan produced became *his* spears, and he traded them for products which other people produced. Thus, the concept of *private property* was born and with it the nemesis of humankind. Society tended to value various objects differently and the value of the individual was equated with the things he or she owned. This fatal differentiation resulted in the beginnings of a class structure that created strife in the society. This strife led to a new era. As the members of a tribe began to differentiate among themselves, they also began to develop prejudices against other tribes. Eventually, after much strife, a new order was born because one tribe, or group of people, came to dominate others. The dominant people forced the dominated people into servitude. Hence, *slavery* became the basis of the economic system in the next era.

Empire was the dominant political system based on the foundation of slavery. The antithesis to the era of slavery and empire was the challenge from the barbarian hordes. When the barbarians finally prevailed over the empire, a new political-economic system had emerged, called *feudalism.* Feudalism was a system in which a landed aristocracy provided police and military protection to the peasants, who soon became *serfs* (people legally bound to the land—"land slaves") and farmed the nobles' lands. Since feudalism depended on a large number of self-sufficient manors, trade was almost completely stopped for a time. Gradually the stability provided by the nobles and the demand for luxury items stimulated a rebirth of trade. The aristocrats, however, usually looked down on commerce, so trade and its profits were left to a new class, the **bourgeoisie**.[2]

The bourgeoisie antithesis grew in strength until it finally toppled the feudal aristocracies in a series of revolutions; the English revolution in the 1640s and the American and French upheavals of the late eighteenth century are among the earliest and best-known examples. The new era initiated by those revolutions featured *capitalism* as its economic system. Marx called the new political systems *bourgeois democracies*. The term *democracy* was given to these political systems because, as Marx explained, there was a pretense of popular government through legislative representation; in reality, however, the capitalists always controlled the system.

Capitalism fostered factory workers, the **proletariat** (or wage slaves), a class that would act as the antithesis in the fourth historical era. Marx believed that the tension between the two classes would build into a new, and this time final, dialectic struggle. Capitalism had increased human productivity to the point at which all basic material needs could be satisfied. Nevertheless, it was exploitative in nature, so that the goods produced were not equally distributed; in fact, the reverse was true. Marx assumed that the victory of the proletariat was inevitable; it would be a victory of the exploited over the exploiter. He also believed that the proletariat itself would not be exploitative. If all other classes were eliminated, the source of all human strife would disappear and a new, classless society holding its goods in common would emerge. In this communist society all people would find peace and happiness. (See Figure 8–3.)

Marx, however, spent most of his time analyzing capitalism rather than discussing socialism; consequently, his theory is very hazy in places. For instance, he never described the communist utopia in detail. He did say that it was to be democratic, but, as we have already learned, that could mean any number of things. Practically the only specific he mentioned about the utopia was that its economic system would be totally socialist. In other words, in the new society there would be absolutely no private property except for personal effects. Marx is also vague about what part he expected the peasantry to play in the final revolution. This question is vital to students of Marxism

---

[2]*Bourgeoisie* is a French term that means "middle class" in English. However, one must be careful not to draw any false conclusions from this translation. In the United States almost everyone is considered to be in the middle class. It is true that there are some who are poor and a few who are very wealthy, but traditionally most of the people of the United States see themselves as somewhere between these two extremes. This feeling of economic homogeneity has undoubtedly contributed to the country's political stability, but one wonders if it is not, after all, based on a conveniently broad definition of the label "middle class;" that is, most people are middle class in this country because the definition of the term is purposely expanded until all but the very rich and the very poor are included. The term *bourgeoisie* should not be understood in the same way. Marx meant the word as it is defined in French. The French bourgeoisie was a class of educated, wealthy merchants and tradespersons that developed as commerce increased.

FIGURE 8–3 Marxian Dialectic

because they note, without exception, the countries that developed Marxist systems as a result of indigenous political movements (for example, Russia, Yugoslavia, China, North Vietnam, and Cuba) have populations consisting largely of peasants. Understandably, there is a great deal of disagreement on this question. Some scholars believe that Marx expected peasants to become an agrarian proletariat and to participate fully in the dialectic. Others think that he did not foresee any significant role for them at all. Vladimir Lenin and Mao Tse-tung, as we will see in Chapters 9 and 10, filled in some of the details of peasant participation in the building of socialism. They also answered many other crucial questions about the practical application of Marxist theory.

Marxist Economic Theory

Marx studied capitalism and the ideas of Locke, Smith, Ricardo, Malthus, and others very carefully, analyzing them perceptively in *Das Kapital*. In this work he concludes that "capitalism has within it the seeds of its own destruction." In short, Marx believed that the fall of capitalism was inevitable and that it would lead to socialism.

The theory of work.   Marx, like John Locke, believed that work could be the way in which people might express their creativity. Indeed, both men believed that work is the process through which people develop their humanity and fulfill themselves. By interacting with nature in what is termed labor, individuals develop and change their own character. The essence of human beings, therefore, becomes closely related to their work. To Marx work was a form of "self-creation." Describing the laboring process, Marx wrote, "Man is constantly developing and changing—creating his own nature." In other words, the product of our labor is part of us, and something of us is in the things that we produce through our work. This attitude might appear naive or perhaps even mystical at first glance. Yet, which of us has not felt great satisfaction at having made something by hand? Do we not feel a closer relationship with objects we have made ourselves?

The theory of self-alienation. Marx's theory of work and his attitude toward capitalism led him to his theory of human self-alienation. This alienation occurs because of three factors. First, since it can be a form of "self-creativity," it should be enjoyable, Marx reasoned. Yet, because the capitalists squeeze every possible cent of profit from the workers, they make the conditions of work intolerable. Consequently, instead of enjoying work or the act of self-creation, the members of the proletariat grow to hate the very process by which they could refine their own nature. Consequently, they become alienated from a part of their own selves. Second, Marx believed that capitalists *must* exploit the workers in order to produce a profit. The capitalists force the workers to sell their product and then use that product against the workers to exploit them further. This, Marx claimed, forces the workers to regard their own product, something that is actually part of them, as alien and even harmful to them; thus, it becomes another form of self-alienation. Third, and here Marx is truly paradoxical, the capitalist is criticized for mechanizing production because this process robs laborers of their skills and reduces them to little more than feeders of machines. Hence, all the creativity is taken out of work, making it impossible for people ever to develop their humanity fully: This is the ultimate alienation. Marx is indeed contradictory at this point. Clearly, he saw himself as a prophet of the future. He claimed that socialism was the coming economic system and that it would produce even more than capitalism. Yet, in this theory he seems to resent mechanization and its effects on the proletariat and even appears to look back nostalgically to an earlier era. In a passage from *Das Kapital,* Marx, often a laborious writer, displayed unusual eloquence while discussing human self-alienation.

> Within the capitalist system all methods for raising the social productiveness of labor are brought about at the cost of the individual laborer; all means for the development of production transform themselves into means of domination over, and exploitation of, the producers; they mutilate the laborer into a fragment of a man, *degrade him to the level of an appendage of a machine, destroy every remnant of charm in his work and turn it into a hated toil; they estrange from him the intellectual potentialities of the labor-process in the same proportion as science is incorporated in it as an independent power;* they distort the conditions under which he works, subject him during the labor-process to a despotism the more hateful for its meanness; they transform his lifetime into working-time and drag his wife and child beneath the wheels of the Juggernaut of capital. (Emphasis added.)

Ironically, the capitalists seem to have learned the lessons of Marx's alienation, whereas the Soviets never did. Capitalists spend millions of dollars each year in efforts to make the assembly line and office more pleasant places in which to work and therefore to make labor more productive. Studies are made of worker satisfaction, walls are painted vivid colors, music is piped in, and workers are frequently rotated on the assembly line in attempts to combat boredom. Yet, until the Soviet Union collapsed, its factories there were drab and labor was monotonous. Working conditions were shabby and dangerous and workers were clearly alienated. Absenteeism, tardiness, careless or deliberate mistakes, and alcoholism plagued Soviet plants. Clearly, the workers' paradise was not achieved in the land that had claimed devotion to Marxist ideals.

The labor theory of value.   As you have already learned, the **labor theory of value** was not invented by Marx. It was generally accepted during the eighteenth and nineteenth centuries; in fact, it was openly supported by the great classical economists Adam Smith and John Locke and by no less a figure than David Ricardo. Living as he did at the end of the period dominated by classical economists, Marx is probably the last major economist to support the labor theory of value. In fact, Marx was once called "a Ricardo turned socialist" because he shared so many assumptions with the great capitalist economist yet adapted them to a different conclusion.

The labor theory of value is concerned with the *intrinsic worth* of an object. Value is a complex concept. The value most modern economists are concerned with is the *exchange value* of an item, that is, the amount of money one can get for an item on the market. *Sentimental value* is another kind of worth. Though the market value of one's dog may be high, one may not wish to sell the dog because its sentimental value is greater than anything anyone will offer for it. *Use value* is a third measure of worth. Though the sentimental value one attaches to an old car used to drive back and forth to work may be low and the exchange value little higher, the usefulness of the car might be quite high since it adequately performs a needed function. *Esthetic value* is yet another measure. The gracefulness or beauty of an old building may far exceed its commercial value or its usefulness.

By contrast, the labor theory of value is concerned with establishing a standard for measuring intrinsic value. This concept assumes that there are two kinds of value brought to the production process. Resources, machinery, and finance are termed *constant value;* that is, these factors, when applied to the production of an item, cannot add any value to the item greater than their own intrinsic worth. Only labor is a *variable value* because only labor produces something of greater worth than itself.

Here Marx pays tribute to the genius of human creativity. The materials necessary to produce a watch, for example, can be placed next to the tools and machines used in watchmaking; nevertheless, a watch will not be produced until human creativity—labor—is applied. Similarly, the components of an unassembled piece of clothing have an aggregate value, but when they are combined through labor to become a shirt, something new has been produced, and its value far exceeds the sum of its individual parts.

The intrinsic value of any object, Marx assumed, is therefore determined by the amount of labor—human creativity—needed to produce it. The *price* of the object, the amount of money it will fetch on the market at any given time, is determined by supply and demand. However, the *value* of the object is determined by the labor time needed for its production.

The theory of surplus value. The *theory of surplus value* is based on the labor theory of value and, according to Engels, is Marx's most important discovery. Marx argued that capitalism enslaves the proletariat because people have to work to survive while the capitalist has a monopoly on the means of production—that is, factories and machinery. Thus, the workers must sell their labor at whatever price the capitalist will pay. Marx also adopted Ricardo's **iron law of wages.** You will recall that Ricardo suggested that capitalists, driven by the need to make profits and capital, will pay their workers only subsistence wages—enough to feed themselves and their families—because that much is necessary to bring them back to work the next day. Hence, not only are the workers slaves—"wage slaves"—but their masters pay them only the most meager wages, regardless of how much value they may produce.

Thus, the capitalists force workers to produce an excess, or *surplus value,* and they keep that sum for themselves as a profit. According to this theory, the workers' intrinsic value is the money needed to feed themselves and their families. Anything they produce above the subsistence level is surplus value. Since under Ricardo's iron law of wages the capitalists pay only a subsistence wage, they keep the surplus value produced by the workers as their profit. For example, let us say that it takes six hours of work to produce the necessities of life for a laborer and his or her family. If the employer forces the laborer to work for thirteen hours, yet only pays a subsistence wage, the capitalist has forced the laborer to surrender seven hours of surplus value. Because the surplus value can be produced only by labor, Marx goes on to argue, it belongs to the laborer by right. Accordingly, any profit the capitalists make from the labor of their employees is ill-gotten and exploitative. The capitalist is, therefore, a villain, a parasite who lives by sucking the economic lifeblood of the proletariat, and must be erased from society when the proletariat takes over. Needless to say, Ricardo, who was a capitalist economist, would not have agreed with this conclusion. Ricardo believed that the capitalists' control of property distinguished them from other people and justified their exploitation of the worker, for such exploitation created capital thus assuring further productivity.

At this point you might be wondering how Marx expected capital to develop if profits, or surplus value, were not allowed. The answer is simple: Marx did not oppose capital per se, he rejected the capitalist. He did not condemn profit, he opposed private profit. The German scholar knew that capital was necessary for production, but he rejected the notion that it should be controlled by private individuals. Capital, he suggested, was created by all and should be owned by all. Marx certainly did not oppose creating surplus value to be used to invest in increased productivity. What he objected to was that private citizens should be allowed to monopolize the means of production and use that power to force workers—the creators of value—to surrender their goods in order to survive. Put differently, no one should be allowed to profit from the labor of another. On this point, Marx's differences with Ricardo are more moral in nature rather than economic.

Marxist Theory of Revolution

Marx vacillated over whether violence was necessary to achieve socialist goals. During the early part of his professional life he clearly suggested that one could not hope for a change from a capitalist system to a socialist one without violence. Gradually, however, he began to weaken this position until finally he admitted that certain systems (such as those in England, Holland, and perhaps the United States) might be responsive enough to adopt socialism by nonviolent means. Violence was still necessary elsewhere, however. Later, Lenin would again insist that no meaningful change could occur without violence.

The basis of Marx's argument for violence was his perception of the dialectic process. He believed that technological change cannot be stopped: Resources will become depleted, and new means of production will inevitably evolve, resulting in economic change. When the economy changes, economic determinism dictates that the entire foundation of the society must be transformed, forcing a change in its superstructure as well. In other words, economic change cannot be prevented. Economic change forces social change, which, in turn, drives political change. Violence is necessary in this process because the rulers who control the economy feel their economic and political power threatened by the uncontrollable changes taking place in the means of production. Vainly trying to resist the inevitable, they use their governmental power to keep themselves in control. However, they are resisting the progress of history. History is therefore propelled from one era to another. A series of revolutions punctuates the dialectic dynamic; each new era is born in the victory of those who control the new dominant means of production. In the final struggle the proletariat will confront their capitalist exploiters. The capitalists will have to use force, but their resistance is doomed to defeat at the hands of the irresistible pressure of history.

More specifically, Marx predicted the demise of capitalism. Competition, he argued, would force the capitalists to buy more machinery. Yet, only human labor can produce a surplus value; thus, the capitalists' profits would decline as they employed fewer people. At the same time, unemployment would increase among the proletariat as competition forced increasing numbers of former capitalists into the proletarian ranks. On the one hand, the size of the proletariat and the depth of its misery would increase; on the other, the wealth in the society would be controlled by fewer people. Marx predicted that every capitalist society would be subject to increasingly frequent and ever more serious economic convulsions. Eventually the misery of the proletariat would increase to a point that could no longer be endured and a revolution would erupt, bringing the system to its knees. "The knell of capitalist private property sounds. The expropriators are expropriated."

Marx's attitude toward revolution is of critical importance, since he believed it to be virtually inevitable in most cases. But what kind of revolution did he anticipate, and what did he regard as the proper role for himself and other revolutionary leaders?

Using the French Revolution as his model, Marx envisioned a spontaneous uprising of the workers. Conditions for the common people in prerevolutionary France had degenerated to miserable levels. Yet, little was done in the way of advanced planning for a popular revolt prior to its eruption in Paris in 1789. The precise cause of the French Revolution remains a mystery, but what is clear is that after centuries of aristocratic abuse, the people of France had quietly reached the breaking point; on a hot day—July 14, 1789— some ordinarily trivial event sparked a public fury that culminated in a frightful period of social and political chaos, and the world was changed forever.

Expecting that the proletariat would rise up spontaneously to cast off its capitalist oppressors just as the French had vanquished their aristocratic rulers, Marx saw a rather passive role for those who first realized the course of history. Marx, Engels, and most other revolutionaries of the period were progeny of middle-class families, not proletarians. Yet, they presumed to herald the advent of a proletarian succession to power. How could this be?

Marx suggested that there were certain people who, by virtue of their perceptive minds, could understand the forces of history long before others. Thus, he and his colleagues were able to predict the new era even before those who were to be its beneficiaries were conscious of their happy future.

The principle of *class consciousness* is critical. Marx assumed that the workers had not yet fully comprehended that they were a group completely separate and distinct from the bourgeoisie. When the proletariat became fully aware of its unique situation in society—when it developed class consciousness—it would realize the full extent of its oppression and the parasitic nature of its rulers. It would then spontaneously rise up in revolution.

Helping to develop class consciousness is the role Marx saw for himself and his revolutionary colleagues. Calling his followers the *vanguard of the proletariat*, Marx advised that their function was to do what they could to instill in the worker the true nature of a class-ridden society. Importantly, Marx did not advocate that revolutionaries should organize and lead the revolution. He saw their function as more educative than participatory. Once aware of their circumstances, the proletariat would take care of the revolution themselves. Marx's attitude toward revolution and revolutionaries is particularly important because, as we shall see in the next chapter, Lenin, who was supposedly a disciple of the German master, abandoned this rather passive role for a more activist one.

The Marxist Political System

Of all the subjects on which he wrote, Marx is probably least clear in discussing the political system that would exist after the revolution. Basically he conceived of the proletarian state as developing in two steps. First, he expected that the proletariat would create a dictatorship. The purpose of the **dictatorship of the proletariat** would be to eliminate all but a single proletarian class. Since all human strife emanated from social class difference, according to Marx, human harmony was possible only if class differences would be eradicated. This goal could be achieved through a process of reeducation. If that failed, the dictatorship would be justified in removing from the society anyone who opposed it.

Although the purpose of the dictatorship of the proletariat is quite clear, the exact nature of the institution remains shrouded in ambiguity and has been the subject of considerable debate. Lenin, who took an elitist attitude, insisted that the dictatorship should be *over* the proletariat as well as superior to all other elements in the society. He argued that not only should the Communist Party (the Bolsheviks) lead the revolution, but that it should also become the dictator of the proletariat.

Since Marx insisted on a democratic format in all other things and since he never attempted to form a communist party as Lenin later did, it is highly unlikely that he meant to imply the model Lenin employed. Indeed, Michael Harrington, a noted American socialist scholar, suggested that Marx actually intended something approaching a democracy when he called for the "dictatorship of the proletariat." Marx expected that the overwhelming number of people in society would be among the proletariat when the revolution occurred. Hence, if he meant that the dictatorship was to be *by* the proletariat, the situation would indeed be different. The huge majority of people—the proletariat—would impose its egalitarian policies on the tiny corps of remaining capitalists. In numerical terms, at least, such a system would be more democratic than that which Lenin used.

In any event, as the dictatorship succeeded in redirecting the society toward the socialist utopia, more and more people would adopt the **socialist**

ethic, meaning willingness to work to one's capacity and to share the fruits of labor with the rest of society. This concept is clearly the most revolutionary aspect of Marx's thought. Like all leftists, he believed people could change, redirecting their lives and actions toward more desirable goals. To this end Marx expected the dictatorship to encourage people to abandon their selfish, atomistic ways, adopting collective, or organic, values which accrue to the good of society as a whole. The new society would operate on the principle "From each according to his ability, to each according to his needs."

If people could be encouraged to enjoy their labor, they would become more productive than was possible in a capitalist system. If the productivity was shared equally by all, social anxieties and frustrations would most probably abate, creating a happy, contented populace. Thus, crime, war, and human turmoil would disappear. As strife and anxiety declined, a gradual change in society's foundations would lead to the second Marxist state. The need for the dictatorship would disappear. Eventually, when the last nonproletariat was gone, the state would have "withered away": The police state would have ceased to exist. Then, all the individuals in society would be "free" to *govern themselves* responsibly for the good of all, and the system would have evolved into a *democratic utopia* similar to that desired by many anarchists. Only a skeletal shell of the former state would be left, and it would simply administer the economy. As Engels put it, "In the final stage of communism, the government of men will change to the administration of things."

Internationalism

Since Marx believed that dialectic materialism was a law of historical development, he expected that socialism would be adopted in every country in the world sooner or later. He never suggested a timetable for this development, but there can be no doubt that he believed it was inevitable. The exact schedule for the adoption of socialism in any country depended on its economic development. Though he made no specific predictions, Marx clearly expected that the most industrialized nations of his day (England, Germany, France, Belgium, and Holland) were on the verge of the proletarian revolution.

During Marx's lifetime, the nation-state system was an important political fact, as it is today. Indeed, since the nation-state system had developed along with capitalism, Marx believed that it was part of the capitalist superstructure. He argued that nation-states were organized by the capitalists to keep people who really had a great deal in common separated from one another. People of the same social class from different countries, he reasoned, actually had more in common with each other than people of different classes within the same country. National boundaries were only artificial separations designed to reinforce the capitalist system. Indeed, Marx declared that "workingmen have no country." Consequently, he believed that as various countries became socialist they would recognize the divisiveness of national boundaries and would erase the lines that separated them until finally all national boundaries would have "withered away" and the entire world would be a single socialist utopia.

Throughout his life, Marx dominated the socialist movement. Yet, socialism existed long before Marx was born, and, following his death, other thinkers developed socialist theories quite different from those of Marx. We shall now turn to a discussion of the various non-Marxist socialist theories.

REVIEW

- Marx lived during an extraordinary time. The scholars of the day sought scientific laws governing human conduct. Societies were ruled by reactionary monarchs who repressed demands for reform. The beginning stages of the Industrial Revolution visited great hardship on ordinary people, as capitalism was used to extract profits from hapless workers.
- Economic determinism suggests that the social and political realities of any society are predisposed by its economic system. The political and social institutions and values of society are controlled and used by the ownership class.
- Dialectic materialism posits that history is progressively motivated by the evolution of economic systems, evoking violent struggles between social classes who dominate different powerful economic systems.
- Marx believed that work was a form of self-expression and creativity. However, since the capitalists controlled the means of production, the owners of the means of production wrongfully forced the workers to surrender large portions of the value that the workers alone had produced.
- Marx expected that the living conditions of the workers would continue to decline as the capitalists exploited them more and more, until finally, the workers would spontaneously rise up and vanquish their exploiters.
- When the workers gained power, they would create a dictatorship of the proletariat that would gradually eliminate all but the proletariat class. As class difference disappeared, the state would wither away, until finally a communist utopia evolved.
- Each society would go through the various historical stages in its own time. When each reached the socialist stage, it would eliminate its artificial national boundaries and a one-world communist utopia would eventually exist.

SUGGESTIONS FOR FURTHER READING

CARVER, TERRELL, ed., *The Cambridge Companion to Marx.* New York: Cambridge University Press, 1991.

COHEN, CARL, *Communism, Fascism and Democracy,* 2nd ed. New York: Random House, 1972.

COLLINS, PETER H., *Ideology After the Fall of Communism.* New York: Marion Boyars, 1993.

FABRA, PAUL, *Capitalism vs. Anti-Capitalism: The Triumph of Recardian over Marxist Political Economy.* New Brunswick, NJ: Transaction Press, 1994.

FORMAN, JAMES D., *Communism.* New York. Dell, 1974.

HEGEL, GEORG WILHELM FRIEDRICH, *Reason and History,* trans. Robert S. Hartman. New York: Liberal Arts Press, 1953.

HEILBRONER, ROBERT L., *Marxism: For and Against.* New York: W. W. Norton, 1980.

HOOK, SYDNEY, *From Hegel to Marx: Studies in the Intellectual Development of Karl Marx.* New York: Columbia University Press, 1994.

INGERSOLL, DAVID E., *Communism, Fascism, and Democracy.* Columbus, OH: Charles E. Merrill, 1971.

MARX, KARL, and FRIEDRICH ENGELS, *The Communist Manifesto.* Baltimore: Penguin Books, 1967.

MCLELLAN, DAVID, *Karl Marx.* New York: Viking Press, 1975.

MCLELLAN, DAVID. *Karl Marx: His Life and Thought.* New York: Harper & Row, 1973.

MONGAR, THOMAS, *The Death of Communism and the Rebirth of Original Marxism.* Lewistown, NY: Edwin Mellen Press, 1994.

SHORTALL, FELTON, *The Incomplete Marx.* Brookfield, VT: Ashgate, 1994.

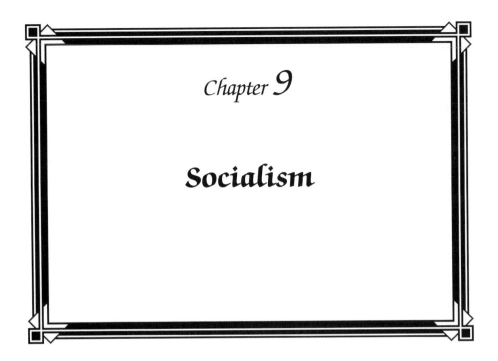

Chapter 9

Socialism

PREVIEW

*Socialism has three basic features: (1) public ownership of production, nationalized
or cooperative; (2) a social welfare system, with which the society cares for its needy
members; (3) the intention of abundance, equality, and sharing that will free people
from material want. Combined with one or both of the first two characteristics, the
third (the social intent) is required to create an authentic socialist state.*

*Rooted in the Industrial Revolution, the origins of socialism can be traced to
prerevolutionary France. Jean Jacques Rousseau, though not a socialist, gave leftists
the foundation of egalitarianism on which socialism is based. François Noel Babeuf
anticipated Marx and Lenin with his conspiratorial method and his ideas about class
identification. After the French Revolution, utopian socialists deplored the suffering
caused by early capitalism and claimed that humanity was destined to live commu-
nally. But utopian socialism failed, and Marx's "scientific socialism" came to dominate the movement.*

*After Marx's death the socialist movement shattered into three distinct and
competitive variants. The orthodox school rejected any significant change in Marx's
works and rapidly became obsolete. The revisionists and the Fabians challenged most
of the fundamental Marxist theories, preferring more gradual and peaceful development of the socialist goals. Their ideas have had a great impact on almost every modern non-Marxist socialist movement in Europe and America.*

Marxism-Leninism is the third major socialist variant that developed after

Marx's death. Basically a revolutionary and a practical politician, Lenin proposed a more activist though less consistent ideology than Marx had envisioned. Arguing that capitalist institutions such as imperialism discouraged the spontaneous proletarian revolutions that Marx had predicted, Lenin created an elite group of dedicated revolutionaries who would lead the rebellion and govern after the capitalist system collapsed. When the bourgeois rulers had been replaced by the dictatorship of the proletariat, a system that rewarded people according to their work would be established. Through education, material rewards, and elimination of the worst dissidents from society, the proletariat would grow until it was the only economic class in the society. Then the system would evolve into the classic Marxist utopia.

THE MEANING OF SOCIALISM

Socialism is a complex idea system, one that is often misunderstood. It is perhaps the most complete political ideology because its goals are all encompassing. It is not only an economic system, it is also a social, political, and moral philosophy.

Socialism is especially poorly understood in the United States. Often simply equated with Marxism, socialism is a buzz word sometimes used to discredit otherwise legitimate ideas and proposals. Opponents of the 1994 proposals for a national health system in the U.S., for example, dismissed it as "socialized medicine," as if to suggest that if an institution is associated with socialism it is wrong on its face. From the beginning we must keep in mind that while a particular kind of socialism was envisioned by Marx, his is just one variant of that ideology. All Marxists are socialists, but not all socialists are Marxists.

Socialism can be divided into three basic features. Two of them *ownership of production* and establishment of **the welfare state,** are mechanical and are not necessarily related to each other. The third, however, belief in **the socialist intent,** is the most fundamental aspect of socialism and must exist together with one or both of the mechanical features; otherwise, true socialism cannot be said to exist.

Ownership of Production

The concept of public ownership and control of the major means of production is a fundamental principle of socialism. The traditional way to socialize an economy is by **nationalization.** Nationalization occurs when the government expropriates—takes over the ownership of—an industry. In the Soviet Union and other communist states the former owners were not usually paid for their property. Government officials claimed that the property really belonged to the workers and that the owners had used it to exploit them; therefore, no payment was necessary. In noncommunist socialist states, however, expropriated properties are usually purchased at a fair price.

In Western societies nationalized industries are usually managed by boards or commissions appointed by government officials but insulated in some way from political pressure; that is, the commissioners are usually appointed to office for a specific term and may be removed only by parliamentary or congressional vote. Some good examples of this kind of arrangement are the Tennessee Valley Authority, the British Broadcasting Corporation, and the United States Postal Service.

In the few remaining communist countries (the People's Republic of China, Cuba, and Vietnam, for example), a government owned industry is more likely to be closely connected to the society's political leaders than is true in noncommunist countries. No attempt is made to separate the government from the industry because communists do not see the value of such a separation. Noncommunists usually try to differentiate between the political and economic functions of society. In a Marxist state, however, ideology teaches that politics results from economic conditions and that both are inseparable parts of the same historical development. Any attempt to separate one from the other is a bad error in policy or a deliberate attempt by the rulers to trick the ruled.

Although it is the traditional method of socializing the economy, nationalization has gradually lost favor in the Western states, and a different form of socialization has developed. Following the Scandinavian model, socialists in the advanced Western states have increasingly turned to **cooperatives** as a means of socializing the economy. A cooperative enterprise is made up of individuals who collectively own the enterprise. They share in both the work and the profits. Usually they elect a board of directors to manage the enterprise. Such cooperatives can become quite extensive. For instance, a village that owned a fleet of fishing boats could expand by buying a cannery, which would become part of the cooperative's assets. With part of the profits from these two *productive co-ops*, the village could buy large quantities of groceries, clothing, hardware, and so forth and create its own *consumer cooperative*, making the best possible price available to its members by buying in volume. Almost any kind of enterprise can be collectivized in this way; there are even cooperative banks similar to our own credit unions.

Cooperatives were developed because serious problems with nationalization became apparent as various enterprises were expropriated by the state. To begin with, not all enterprises can be operated as well under a nationalized structure as in a less centralized system. The size and remoteness of the central government are major drawbacks. No matter how well intentioned it may be, the bureaucracy necessary to run a nationalized enterprise tends to be insensitive to the consumers' needs and to the dynamics of the market itself. Indeed, it has become obvious to many socialists that some enterprises work poorly when they are not privately owned. These pragmatic individuals support socializing only those industries which function best under collective management, leaving the rest to private enterprise. The cooperative is an attempt to combine the virtues of private motivation with the benefits of collective ownership.

The political limitations of nationalization are perhaps even greater than its economic problems. When a large part of society's production, exchange, distribution, and employment is controlled by the government, the latter's involvement in the lives of individuals is greatly increased. Totalitarian states are born out of such enormous power. Any free society must be very cautious of centralized power. In addition, free people must be wary of placing all their productivity in the hands of government. To whom would they turn for settlement of economic disputes if all enterprises were owned by the state?

When socialization has been used, however, the cooperative has worked best with the middle to light industries. Retail sales, appliance manufacturing and servicing, and housing construction are examples of industries that have succeeded in a cooperative setting. Heavy industry and certain nationwide services are usually better socialized by the nationalization process. Basic industries such as weapons production, utilities, transportation, and communication are too vital and perhaps too big to work well under the cooperative structure. Some other industries, such as automobile manufacture, energy production, insurance, and metal production, may also be best suited to nationalization.

Socialist countries not only differ on the method of socializing the economy but also vary greatly in the degree to which their economies are socialized. Just as socialists long ago abandoned the simplistic view that nationalization is the only true method of establishing socialism, so too have they learned that many industries are best run and most productive when left in the private sector. A statement adopted by the Socialist International in 1951 reads, in part:

> Socialist planning does not presuppose public ownership of all the means of production. It is compatible with the existence of private ownership in important fields, for instance, in agriculture, handicraft, retail trade, and small and middle sized industries.

Of all the socialist societies, only the communists saw total socialization as the ultimate goal. In the past two decades, however, even the communist states began to experiment with some limited forms of market economics. The most resistant to change is Cuba, but now Fidel Castro himself has found it necessary to change some economic policies, if only slightly so far. In all other socialist countries, regardless of how long socialist governments have held power, large portions of the economy remain under private ownership.

Cornelius Vanderbilt   Museum of the City
of New York

The Welfare State

Production, however, is not the central economic focus of socialist thinking. Much more important to the socialist than production is the distribution of the goods and services produced in the society.

To the capitalist, private property is the reward for individual effort and economic achievement. Consequently, wealthy people are treated with respect, implying that somehow they have accomplished something particularly virtuous. During the 1920s, this country's most capitalist era, people held the titans of industry in great awe. Moguls such as Ford, Vanderbilt, Rockefeller, Mellon, Insull, Morgan, and Harriman were considered heroes to be admired and emulated.

A value system that puts wealth on such a pedestal is not likely to look on poverty with much understanding. The stigma of being poor or even only unemployed was very real during this era. However, also during the 1920s the United States witnessed the quintessential policies of supply side and *laissez-faire* economics. Government fiscal and monetary policies were extraordinarily favorable to big business, while government regulation of the marketplace was virtually nonexistent. The result was catastrophic. The Great Depression of the 1930s saw a quarter of the work force without jobs, long lines before soup kitchens, lives ruined, and fortunes evaporated.

Dazed and disoriented, the American people were slow to realize that they were victims of an irresponsible economic system, captained by people not necessarily devoted to the public interest but rather motivated by personal benefit. Once the blinders of the *laissez-faire* myth were lifted, the public viewed society in a more realistic way and capitalism was modified, becoming more humane.

In the 1930s, President Franklin Delano Roosevelt introduced the **New Deal,** a massive reform program that injected enough socialism into the system to give capitalism a human face. While the New Dealers stopped short of nationalizing more than a handful of industries, they vigorously regulated business and encouraged workers to organize unions to bargain collectively for better wages and benefits. Their greatest attention, however, was given to creating the **welfare state** so that the wealth might be more equitably distributed throughout society and individual suffering reduced. At this time, programs were introduced that have become commonplace in the United States; social security, government price supports for agriculture, unemployment and workers' compensation, welfare programs, federal guarantees for housing loans, government insurance for savings deposits, and so on. Since the 1930s, the welfare state in this country has been expanded to include public health plans for the elderly, job training, federal aid to education, public funding for small business opportunities, and so on.

Although the United States is still far from a socialist country, the lessons of the Great Depression led the government to adopt some socialist policies in order to prevent a recurrence of the suffering encountered during the 1930s. We were not alone in this attempt, however. Indeed, many nations preceded us and went far beyond the United States in developing policies that would redistribute wealth within the society. The communist countries tried to invoke total socialism; but their efforts have failed, and their economies currently are facing collapse. More successful are the Western European countries which have nationalized their banks, utilities, transportation, and some manufacturing, while also developing extensive social welfare policies. While programs vary from country to country, every West European country except for Spain and Portugal, Western Europe's poorest, spends almost twice as much of its economic output as the United States on its social programs. West European countries provide far more generous housing subsidies, parental leave plans, grants to the poor, public health protections, educational aid, unemployment benefits, as well as a plethora of other programs.

Regardless of the specific programs used, socialism is not always completely egalitarian. It tends to narrow the gap between the haves and the have-nots. Yet, only the most fanatic socialist wants to eliminate all differences in material status. Most socialists recognize that people are different: Some are more talented or hard working than others and should be rewarded for their extra contributions. Still, they believe that all people have a right to a reasonably comfortable life, given the economy's ability to produce enough for all. Consequently, they want to eliminate poverty. Extreme wealth is not necessarily incompatible with a socialist state, however. Indeed, people with great wealth may be found in almost every socialist society.

While Western Europe has successfully reduced poverty and its accompanying social anxiety, these gains have not been achieved without great costs. The tax rates in these societies are extremely high. Indeed, the United States enjoys the lowest tax rate as a percentage of the gross national product of all industrial countries. Also, many European states are experiencing serious economic difficulties maintaining these generous social welfare benefits and are beginning to trim them. It should be noted, however, that the U.S. is also experiencing serious economic difficulties without providing its people benefits which in many European countries have virtually eliminated poverty. (See Table 9–1.)

The general economic decline of the 1990s, joined by a growing materialism among Europeans and a general disenchantment with socialism following the collapse of the Soviet Union, has led several European states to question the extent of their social welfare programs. No European state is likely to retrench enough to fall to the level of benefits provided in the United States, but the welfare state is currently in retreat across the board. This circumstance may, however, be a temporary period of adjustment rather than a permanent state of affairs.

The Socialist Intent

As explained earlier, the first two basic features of socialism (ownership of production and the welfare state) are mechanical in nature and are not necessarily related to each other. It is conceivable that a society could socialize many, or even all, of its major means of production and still avoid creat-

Table 9–1   Social Benefits, Taxes, and Debt Growth of the Industrial States

Country	Social Welfare Benefits As a % of Total Compensation*	Taxes As a % of the GNP 1988**	Growth of Debt As % of GNP 1980–1995*
Belgium	47	45	110
France	49	44	78
Germany	46	39	81
Italy	52	40	90
Japan	25	31	39
Netherlands	46	47	110
Sweden	44	53	160
United Kingdom	32	36	3
United States	25	30	68

Sources: *Organization for European Cooperation and Development, 1995.
        **Statistical Abstracts of the United States, 1994.

ing a welfare state. Although no state has yet adopted such a policy, it is possible. It is also possible for a government to establish a welfare state without, at the same time, socializing production. In fact, the United States has followed this policy since the Great Depression, although the Reagan Administration's policies slowed this trend significantly, and the new Republican majorities in Congress promise to slow it even further.

A third basic feature of socialism, unlike the first two, is essential if the system is to be truly socialist. This is the goal of setting people free from the condition of material dependence that has imprisoned them since the beginning of time.

The true socialist looks forward to a time when the productive capacity of the society will have been increased to the point at which there is abundance for all. It is hoped that this happy state of affairs, impossible in earlier times, will bring about profound changes in people's conduct, attitudes, and beliefs. In previous eras scarcity made it necessary for people to compete with one another. In this competition for goods they treated each other inhumanely in order to survive. Forced into conflict with each other in order to make a living, people became trapped in a pattern of conduct that not only was harmful to them but also prevented them from developing their nobler aspects.

Now, however, for the first time, technology has created a situation in which people can produce enough to satisfy all their basic needs. If the Industrial Revolution has indeed brought the ultimate freedom, then compulsive toil (having to work every waking hour just to survive), the jailor of humanity for millennia, has finally been conquered. People will emerge into a reformed society with new values and new modes of conduct. Competition, formerly the necessary yet destructive mode of human conduct, will become increasingly less effective than cooperation. The replacement of competition with cooperation will lead to a new era of greater productivity, thus improving the lifestyles of individuals even more.

As the general material conditions of the society improve, the specific differences in material status among individuals will decrease. Since there will be plenty for all, traditional property values such as private ownership, the use of money, and the accumulation of luxuries by one class while others live in squalor will disappear. A new society will emerge, one in which the citizens are on an equal footing with one another. As class differences begin to disappear, so too will a major source of social strife, resulting in a happier, more tranquil society. Of course, only Marxist socialists argue that *all* human strife is caused by class differences. Yet, all socialists are convinced that materialism is a major feature in social and political relationships. Removing the cause of material anxieties, therefore, greatly improves social relationships within a particular state.

The equalizing characteristic of socialism is central to our understanding of it. Socialism is an economic equivalent of democracy, if democracy can be equated with individual political equality. Hence, socialism is compatible with democracy, since it is to the individual economically what democracy is to the individual politically. The venerable British socialist and political scientist Harold Lasky once said, "Socialism is the logical conclusion of democracy." Even more extreme, some socialists claim that democracy is impossible without socialism. Money, they reason, is a major source of political power. Thus, as Rousseau argued, economic systems that distribute wealth unevenly make political equality—an inherent of democracy—impossible.

By this time the perceptive reader is probably wondering about the classification of such obviously undemocratic (in the sense of liberal democracy) systems as those of fascist, national socialist, or communist states. Clearly, these systems use socialist economic techniques such as nationalizing industries and creating the welfare state. Yet, each of these systems, in practice if not in theory, reduces human equality rather than increasing it. In each of these systems the society is highly stratified and popular government is barely a pretense, let alone a realistic goal.

In fact, these systems are not socialist in the true sense of the word because they lack the essential ingredient of socialism. They appear to be socialist because they have some socialist institutions, yet they fail the test because they do not aspire to the **socialist intent.** Rather than encouraging equality and democracy, these systems oppose the development of these concepts. They often claim to have egalitarian goals, but in fact, they are simply trying to replace old ruling classes with new ones, denying basic human equality in the process. They are, as Michael Harrington wrote, *antisocialist socialisms.*

To sum up, socialism is much more than an economic system. It goes far beyond the socialization of the economy and the redistribution of wealth. It foresees a completely new relationship among individuals based on a plentiful supply of material goods. His goal is a completely new social order in which human cooperation is the basis of conduct and productivity. Individual equality is a major feature of the new socialist order, and this social equality leads directly to a democratic political system. Furthermore, socialists argue that the elimination of material hardships will relax human tensions as never before, creating a much more pleasant atmosphere in which people can live and develop.

THE DEVELOPMENT OF SOCIALISM

As mentioned earlier, communal living predates written records. *Communism* was originally understood to refer to a rural, agrarian, locally oriented, collectivist community. By contrast, *socialism* is traditionally understood to mean the application of collective production and consumption to an entire nation. Technologically impossible before the nineteenth century, socialism became feasible only with the Industrial Revolution, when the resources for national coordination of an economy had come into existence.

From the French Revolution to Marx

The stirrings of socialism began shortly before the French Revolution. Jean Jacques Rousseau, although not a socialist, developed several ideas that became the foundation of the new ideology. You will recall from Chapter 4 that Rousseau opposed great differences in property ownership among citizens because the disparity would create unequal political powers among them. This belief, which is shared by socialists, considers economic equality fundamental to a just society. Both positions assume that only in an environment of economic equality is the full potential of each individual completely free to develop. Hence, though primarily economic in nature, socialism is also a political ideology.

Rousseau's concept of the *organic society* is even more basic to the ideology of socialism. Rousseau viewed people as individual parts of a holistic society. So complete was the union of individuals with the group that the value of their accomplishments would be measured by the amount of benefit the society derived from them. Socialism asks individuals to produce as much as they can, and in the spirit of social conscientiousness, to share their product with the society at large. By this means, it is assumed, each will get the greatest benefit, thereby creating the best possible life for all.

Influenced by Rousseau's theories, **François Noel Babeuf** (1760–1797) carried their implications to an extreme during the French Revolution. Babouvism represents the first true expression of socialism, though it is an extreme version. While their goal of abolishing all private property and setting up a socialist state in which all people were totally equal was very simplistic, the Babouvists' insight into historical trends and their perception of the future were remarkable.

Anticipating both Marx and Lenin, Babeuf founded the revolutionary socialist movement. Even as the French Revolution unfolded, he and his most famous protégé, Louis Blanqui, became convinced that yet another revolution would be required if people were to gain the true freedom desired by the Babouvists. Yet, experience taught that the ultimate revolution could probably not be trusted to ordinary people. Nor could it be expected to occur by itself. On the contrary, the social-class structure that Babeuf was so early to recognize as the foundation of the state would probably not improve if it were left to itself.

Calculating that social improvement would not necessarily result from unguided historical development, Babeuf concluded that the masses would have to be led to the revolution by an elite corps of conspirators. Once they won out over the forces of private property, they would need, according to

Babeuf, a centrally controlled economy in which the leadership "will always know what each one does, so that he will not produce too much, or too little, but the right thing." Further, the leadership clique "will determine how many citizens will be employed in each specialty . . . everything will be appropriated and proportioned in terms of present and predicted needs and according to the probable growth, and ability, of the community." Thus, Babeuf envisioned a new society, one that he hoped would be based on the principle of mutual production and voluntary sharing of the fruits of labor. Unfortunately, he did not live long enough to make more than a momentary impact of the left wing of the French revolutionaries. Falling afoul of the revolutionary leaders in France, he went to the guillotine in 1797 at the age of thirty-seven.

Utopian socialism.[1]   After Babeuf's death violent socialism became dormant, awaiting a new generation of leftist thinkers. As the time line in Figure 9–1 illustrates, the momentum passed to a far less radical group. The **utopian socialist** movement developed from a sincere desire for equity within the society and from genuine compassion for the masses at the bottom of the social structure. Members of this movement concluded that lavishing sumptuous wealth on some while allowing others to languish in squalor was immoral, since the economy produced enough for all to live comfortably if goods were distributed more evenly.

Many utopians believed that there was an ideal egalitarian social order that, if discovered and implemented, would lead humanity to a more profound level of prosperity and happiness. The value of egalitarianism was obscure to most people, they thought, because no example of a society of equals existed to prove how productive and blissful such an arrangement could be. Accordingly, the utopians decided to create small, local, communal colonies, believing such settlements would become prototypes of the new social order.

Much more important to the socialist movement than the communal experiments was that the utopians were the first to mobilize the working class. Asserting the labor theory of value, the utopians claimed that only the workers create wealth; therefore, they held that society should adjust its social, economic, and political systems to prevent unequal distribution of wealth. Utopian support of the worker against the owner gave an important boost to the development of trade unionism by giving it an economic doctrine and moral justification.

The utopian socialist movement originated with the help of two unlikely, almost unwilling, founders and a third who was more deliberate:

---

[1]The word *utopia* is taken from Sir Thomas More's philosophical romance *Utopia*, written in 1514–1516. Grounded in the philosophy of Plato and the romantic accounts of travelers like Amerigo Vespucci, More's work featured an ideal state wherein private property was abolished.

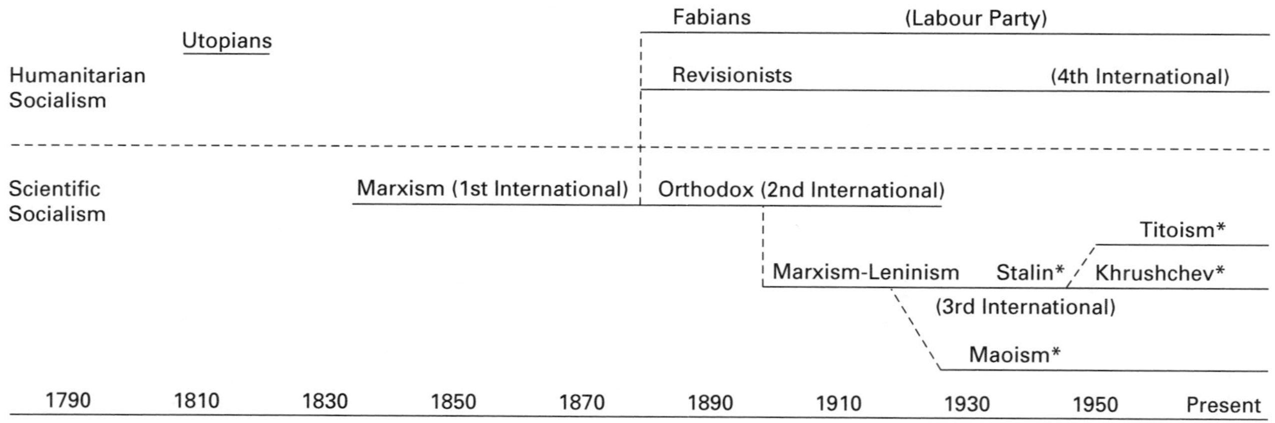

FIGURE 9-1 Time Line of the Socialist Movement. The dates are approximates, not to be viewed as exact.

Utopians

Humanitarian
Socialism

Fabians   (Labour Party)

Revisionists   (4th International)

Scientific
Socialism

Marxism (1st International)   Orthodox (2nd International)

Marxism-Leninism   Stalin*   Titoism*
                              Khrushchev*
(3rd International)

Maoism*

1790   1810   1830   1850   1870   1890   1910   1930   1950   Present

* To be discussed in Chapter 10.

Saint-Simon, Owen, and Fourier. **Claude Henri Saint-Simon** (1760–1825) is sometimes considered the founder of French socialism. Saint-Simon, however, is perhaps more socialist in the reading than in the writing. His followers read into his works a socialist content that he may not have meant to convey. Besides his wish for mutual human kindness and compassion, Saint-Simon's strongest socialist arguments were his criticisms of capitalism. Capitalism, he concluded, was wasteful because it pitted people against each other and imposed poverty on many to produce wealth for a few. Moreover, certain capitalists made profits far beyond their own productivity, a fact Saint-Simon despised, thereby making himself popular with the French working class.

As a partial solution to the evils he saw in the capitalist system, Saint-Simon proposed a centralized banking system that would make social investments. He also called for the elimination of property inheritance and supported universal education. His ideas did not become generally known until after his death, however, when a cult of admiring followers lionized him and probably credited him with beliefs he did not actually hold.

An equally enigmatic figure is the second founder of utopian socialism, **Robert Owen** (1771–1858). A self-made, wealthy industrialist, Owen was basically a conservative man who ardently supported Britain's social, political, and economic institutions. Yet, his conservatism was tempered by sincere compassion for the human suffering surrounding him. A talented administrator, he had risen from the position of clerk to that of manager of a textile plant before his twentieth birthday. He, however, was concerned about the wretched condition of his employees and became associated with Jeremy Bentham and other social reformers of the day.

Owen was strongly opposed to "dole" programs in which people were simply given money by the government or by charities. However, he realized that capitalism had to be tempered by concern for the basic humanity of people and that it could destroy human dignity when left unchecked. Further, he was unshakeably convinced that exploitation of the worker was ultimately unprofitable and that everyone would be better off if the environment were improved.

Acting on these convictions, Owen reformed the management policies of his New Lanark mill. By raising wages, encouraging trade unionism, avoiding the exploitation of women and children, encouraging universal education, and creating a company store where employees could buy goods at reduced rates, he achieved remarkable results. In less than five years, production of New Lanark had risen markedly, the workers at the mill were far better off than workers anywhere else in England, and Owen had made a fortune. This happy circumstance proved to Owen's satisfaction that, as Marx was later to contend, character was conditioned by the environment. Bad working conditions were not only immoral but simply bad business, unnecessarily depressing the workers and lowering profits as well.

Encouraged by his early success, Owen retired from his business enterprises at the age of fifty-eight and dedicated himself to popularizing and testing his controversial ideas. Traveling widely on speaking tours, he was well received in the United States, even making a speech to Congress. He opposed the imposition of socialism (a term he coined) on a people by its government and warned that people themselves had to be prepared to adopt it before it could be successful. The worst excesses of capitalism had to be curbed so that the worker would not be exploited. Owen also opposed nationalization of industries, though he favored producer cooperatives.

Like Saint-Simon, Owen was perhaps more a liberal capitalist than a true socialist. Still, he is considered the founder of British socialism, and his moderate approach set the tone for many of England's social reforms. Like most other utopian socialists, Owen was convinced that communal living was the wave of the future and that a few successful examples would prove the attractiveness of this lifestyle. So convinced was he that he invested several years of effort and his entire fortune in unsuccessful attempts to establish communes. Most noted was the effort at New Harmony, Indiana (1825–1828), purchased by Owen after another group had unsuccessfully tried to start a communal colony there. Alas, the Owenite experiment also failed.

A third influential utopian socialist was **Charles Fourier** (1772–1837). Not only was he a critic of capitalist economics, but he also became a vocal opponent of traditional institutions such as religion, marriage, and the family. Perhaps his most important criticism centered on the structure of society under capitalism. Objecting to the nation-state, Fourier envisioned a society broken up into thousands of small, politically independent, self-sustaining communal entities. These communities could associate with one another in a type of confederacy in which the fundamental independence of each unit remained unchanged. The government of the communes was to be democratic, the labor and its products being shared equally by all the members. In such a simple setting, Fourier believed, life would be pleasant and work would become an enjoyable activity in which all would take part willingly.

Although it is difficult to measure accurately, Fourier's influence was significant. Several communes based on his model were started, but each failed and was abandoned. Fourier's thought influenced many well-known socialists: Charles Dana, Horace Greeley, Nathaniel Hawthorne, and George Ripley were among his American disciples. Fourier also impressed later thinkers such as Proudhon and Marx, and his theories influenced the collectivization of farms in the Soviet Union.

Because it was a new country when utopianism became popular, the United States was often the scene of communal experiments. Here, it was thought, a new society could be founded, one that was insulated from the prejudices of the old world. Interestingly, America was regarded as the land of new opportunity and hope by socialists as well as capitalists. Although these communal experiments failed, several attained an importance beyond their role as socialist experiments. Intellectual leaders were often drawn to these societies. Important literary, technological, and scientific works were sometimes inspired by them, especially by Brook Farm in Massachusetts and by New Harmony in Indiana. Similarly, the experimental commune at Oneida, New York, became the site of America's largest flatware producer after the commune collapsed. Even so, the failure of the communes led to a general disillusionment with the theories on which they were based, and popular attention soon turned from utopianism to more practical concerns.

Important as the utopians were to the development of socialism, their influence is largely limited to their own generation and the one following. Far more important to socialist theory was Karl Marx. Since we have already discussed Marxist theory, I will limit myself to one brief point: Prior to Marx, though socialist theories differed greatly in details and structure, the basis of the proposed socialist societies had been the humanitarian hope that people would treat each other better as their material conditions improved. Furthermore, the development of socialism in any particular society was not seen as inevitable. Rather, socialism was a practice that had to be chosen by the people it was to serve. Though Marx was a compassionate person and certainly not an opponent of free choice, his conclusions were not based on a humanitarian desire for a better life. His theory postulates certain "laws" of human motivation and conduct (economic determinism and dialectic materialism); it concludes that socialism is the unavoidable goal of human historical development. Though his theory was a radical departure from the views of his predecessors, his logic and scholarship were so superior to theirs that he captivated the socialist movement until his death in 1883.

SOCIALIST THEORY AFTER MARX

When Marx died, the socialist movement no longer enjoyed the guidance of a single dominant thinker. Yet, the resulting ambiguity encouraged creativity, and eventually three distinct socialist doctrines emerged: Orthodox Marxism, Revisionism, and Marxism-Leninism.

Orthodox Marxism

Guided at first by Engels himself, the **orthodox Marxists** were led by **Karl Kautsky** (1854–1938) after Engels's death in 1895. Kautsky was a distinguished scholar but his academic skills were not matched by political acumen and he led his followers into a hopeless dilemma.

As the name implies, the orthodox Marxists clung rigidly to Marxist theory and resisted change to it. Such single-minded devotion to a set of ideas stifled imaginative thinking, ultimately spelling its doom among intellectuals and practical politicians alike. Looking forward to the revolution that would end the capitalist state forever, Kautsky's followers refused to cooperate in social reform with nonsocialist governments. This attitude badly weakened the orthodox position. Depending on the workers for support, the Kautskyists brought on their own failure by opposing programs that would improve the proletariat's lot. Desperately needing legislation on maximum hours, minimum wages, working safety, and social insurance, and caring little about the expected utopia following the proletarian revolution, the workers abandoned the orthodox Marxists for more practical political parties. Forced by the pressure of events to retreat inch by inch from his inflexible position, during the last two decades of his life Kautsky supported liberal reforms and admitted that revolution might not be necessary after all. Eclipsed by the other two socialist schools and driven from his adopted home in Vienna into exile in Amsterdam by the Nazi annexation of Austria, Kautsky died a pauper in 1938.

Revisionism

Edward Bernstein (1850–1932) was the founder of the **revisionist** school of socialist theory. Finding that several Marxist predictions did not match actual historical developments, Bernstein began to develop a revised, more moderate socialist theory. He was aided in this effort by the brilliant

Edward Bernstein (1850–1932)
Corbis-Bettmann

French socialist **Jean Jaurès** (1859–1914). Perhaps the most significant characteristic of the revisionist doctrine is that it represents the return of socialism to its original humanitarian motivations, rescuing it from the moral sterility of Marx's "scientific" socialism.

Bernstein and Jaurès were not unappreciative of Marx's contribution to socialist thinking, but they felt compelled to challenge almost every major Marxist principle. Of course, no socialist could deny the importance of economic determinism, but the revisionists believed that Marx had given it too great a role as a political stimulant. Economics, they argued, is an important motivator, but it is not the only one, nor is its impact on human motives constant, tending to decrease as people satisfy their most basic needs.

Noting that Marx had misjudged the development of capitalism, Bernstein pointed out that the capitalist class was increasing rather than decreasing, despite Marx's prediction. Literally millions of people were entering the capitalist class by buying stocks. Further, as more and more governments bowed to the demands of organized labor, wealth was becoming more evenly spread within the society and the lot of the proletariat was improving instead of growing worse.

These seeming faults in Marxist theory appeared to demand a reappraisal of the tactics socialists should use to bring about their goals. It was obvious to the revisionists that rather than racing toward inevitable self-destruction, capitalism was evolving and adjusting to new circumstances. It was becoming less exploitative and more evenhanded in the distribution of resources. Since Marx had not anticipated this development, Bernstein reasoned that it was proper for socialism to change in response to the new situation.

Revolutionary socialism began to seem inappropriate as a way of ending the evils of capitalism. Would it not be far better to develop *evolutionary* ways of achieving socialism? This speculation led Bernstein, Jaurès, and their followers to conclude that their cause would be better served by abandoning dogmatic theories and supporting pragmatic political policies designed to achieve socialism peacefully and gradually through existing European political systems—by winning elections. This adjustment introduced a very successful political movement. Nearly every non-Marxist socialist movement owes its origins to these realistic thinkers. They founded the modern *democratic socialist movement.*

Bernstein's influence did not stop at the shores of the Atlantic. Though Americans Daniel De Leon and Big Bill Haywood proposed militant socialism in their Socialist Labor Party, their efforts met with little success. But, Eugene V. Debs and Norman Thomas carried socialism to modest popularity with the revisionist approach of their Socialist party, and democratic socialism remains to this day a factor on the American left.

Although not precisely revisionist, a second development in humanitarian nonviolent socialism developed in England during the late 1800s.

Founded in the tradition of **John Stuart Mill** in 1884, the year after Marx's death, the **Fabian Society** was dedicated to bringing socialism to England.

Like Robert Owen twenty years earlier, the Fabians rejected the policy of forcing socialism on the society. They argued that socialism must be accepted from the bottom up rather than imposed from the top down. Yet, they were confident that socialism would be adopted by all freedom-loving people because they were convinced that only socialism was compatible with democracy. Consequently, if a people were committed to democracy, as the English surely were, socialism could not be long in coming.

Largely consisting of literary figures, including George Bernard Shaw, H. G. Wells, and Sidney and Beatrice Webb, the Fabian Society was particularly well suited to its task. It usually avoided direct political activity and concentrated on convincing the English people that socialism was the only logical economic system for the British nation. The Fabians carried their message to the people in pamphlets, in articles written for journals and newspapers, and in their novels and short stories. Molded as it was to the British style and temperament, Fabianism was very successful. Today's British Labour Party is the direct descendant of the Fabian movement.

Marxism-Leninism

The second son of a well-to-do Russian family, **Vladimir Ilyich Ulyanov—Lenin** (1870—1924)—appeared to have a bright future. A brilliant man who ultimately mastered nine languages, Lenin finished school with highest honors and passed the bar without ever entering law school. Lenin became a radical at an early age, and his revolutionary activities earned him imprisonment and Siberian exile at the end of the century. Allowed to have whatever books friends and family would send, Lenin, like so many other Russian revolutionaries, spent his exile studying and writing radical documents.

Released in 1900, Lenin went to Switzerland, where he was quickly included among the leadership of the Russian Marxist movement. These expatriots, given to infighting and ideological debate, gradually split into two groups: the **Mensheviks** and the **Bolsheviks.** The Mensheviks were led by the father of Russian Marxism, **Georgi Plekhanov** (1857–1918). They were roughly equivalent to the orthodox Marxists and, subscribing to Plekhanov's **Two Stage Theory,** they insisted that the dialectic had to run its course before a proletarian revolution could take place. Consequently, the revolution would not occur for a long time, since feudal Russia had to pass through the bourgeois stage before developing the proletariat that would eventually come to power. The Mensheviks called upon all socialist revolutionaries to aid the bourgeoisie in coming to power. The capitalists would then begin to exploit the masses, thus "digging their own grave" and provoking the proletarian revolution.

Vladimir Ilyich Lenin (1870–1924)
Corbis-Bettmann

The Bolsheviks, who followed Lenin, rejected Menshevik theory as too dogmatic. They argued that under certain circumstances the proletariat and the peasants could join forces, taking control of the Russian state before it had achieved the bourgeois stage. The Bolsheviks would compress, or "telescope" (as Lenin put it), the bourgeois and socialist stages into a single revolution.

The question of leadership also played a role in these disputes. Plekhanov, the dean of Russian Marxism, considered his young challenger impertinent. He insisted that the final revolution must be a massive one involving the whole society. For his part Lenin was convinced that Plekhanov lacked the imagination and spirit necessary to lead a revolution. He called for an elitist coup to seize power from the decadent Tsarist state.

Karl Marx had spent most of his time analyzing capitalism, giving relatively little attention to the coming utopia. Lenin, by contrast, more of an activist and pragmatic politician than Marx, devoted himself to developing a revolutionary doctrine and applying Marxism to a real situation. In so doing, he restored violence to the doctrine, he modified the ideas in order to answer certain apparent historical contradictions, he amended the theory so that it applied to underdeveloped states, and he filled in the blanks that Marx had left regarding the proletarian society that would exist following the revolution.

Theories of revolution and revolutionaries. You will recall that Marx encountered persecution as a young German radical and that this undoubtedly hardened him against the possibility of peaceful change. Experiencing more tolerant treatment in England during the second half of his life, he tempered his attitudes enough to suggest that revolution might not be necessary in some countries. Lenin's experience in his native land had been comparable to Marx's. Easily the most repressive government in Europe at the time, Russia brutalized its revolutionaries. Thus, Lenin drew the same conclusion as Marx: Violent revolution is the only action that will bring about meaningful change. Unlike Marx, however, Lenin never wavered from this conviction, dedicating himself single-mindedly to the cause of revolution.

Marx also taught that the revolution would take place when the workers had developed a clear awareness (class-consciousness) of the exploitation and hopelessness of their station. Galvanized in their misery, they would become a unified political force. Relying on the trade unions and other agitators to teach the workers to be conscious of the oppression they endured, Marx expected that the proletarian revolution would eventually erupt automatically, ending the bourgeois state and bringing the worker to power.

Lenin contradicted Marx on this point. He argued that the proletariat would not develop class consciousness without the intervention of a revolutionary group. Trade unions were helpful in improving the conditions of employment, but they were of no value as revolutionary agents because they did not teach the proletariat the need to bring down capitalism. Lenin believed that a different group was needed to ignite the revolution. To justify this concept, he expanded on Marx's rather unimportant theory of the **vanguard of the proletariat.** You will recall that Marx believed the vanguard could speed the approach of revolution by helping the proletariat develop class-consciousness, but he gave the vanguard no other major task. By contrast, Lenin saw the vanguard itself as the principal revolutionary agent that would overthrow the government and establish a socialist state before the proletariat developed self-awareness.

This disagreement is what lies behind an important difference in expectations between Marx and Lenin. Marx expected that the proletariat would rebel only after it had become an overwhelming majority in the society and was clearly aware of itself as a class. Consequently, he believed that the **dictatorship of the proletariat** would exist for a relatively brief period during which the small number of nonproletarians would be reeducated or eliminated, creating a classless society.

In Lenin's plan, by contrast, the vanguard would trigger a revolution long before the conditions that Marx anticipated actually existed. In this case, socialism would be imposed on the society by a minority instead of being forced upon the governing elite by the majority. Not only would socialism be hard to attain under these conditions, but the dictatorship of the proletariat would last much longer because such a huge percentage of the population would have to be "proletarianized" before the ideal society could be realized. Lenin was also very specific about the structure of his revolutionary vanguard: a *small, disciplined, totally dedicated* group. It must include only the best in the society because its job of carrying out the revolution demanded total commitment.

The vanguard of the proletariat in Russia was the Bolshevik Party (renamed the Communist Party in 1918). As implied earlier, it was to do considerably more than just carry out the revolution. You will recall that Marx's statements on the dictatorship of the proletariat were vague. One cannot be sure whether he intended the proletariat to assume the role of dictator itself until only one class existed, or if a dictator was to govern all, including the proletariat. Lenin, on the other hand, was quite specific on this subject. The vanguard of the proletariat was to become a collective dictatorship. In other words, the Bolshevik party would carry out the revolution and then impose a dictatorship on the entire society until it was prepared to enter the utopian stage. Thus, as Lenin saw it, the dictatorship of the proletariat was not to be a dictatorship *by* the proletariat but a dictatorship of Bolsheviks *over* the proletariat.

Lenin also created a structure for the vanguard of the proletariat at the international level. In 1919, he created the International Communist Movement, the **Comintern.** It was supposed to encourage socialist revolutions throughout Europe. Rebellions in Bulgaria, Hungary, and Germany were successful briefly but were eventually suppressed. These failures were a great disappointment to Lenin and his associates, who were convinced that the Bolsheviks could not stay in power long unless they received some help from the more advanced Western European countries. As it turned out, they not only sustained themselves without help from the West, but they also resisted concerted Western efforts to bring down the Soviet Union. This success, however, was achieved only at the cost of creating a totalitarian dictatorship under Joseph Stalin. As for the Comintern, while Lenin generally allowed it to function as an international revolutionary catalyst, Stalin turned it into a mere appendage of Soviet foreign policy. *Thus, socialist internationalism was overwhelmed by nationalism.*

In the short run, the efficacy of Lenin's activist and *elitist* tactics seemed borne out by the 1917 events in Russia. However, while Lenin's scheme successfully brought about the revolution, non–Marxist–Leninists argue that the recent collapse of the Soviet Union proves that Marx was in the long run correct. A successful Marxist society cannot be created by an elite group that imposes such a society on unwilling masses from the top down. Rather, it can only be successful when the people are fully prepared to accept it. Put differently, Marxism, as distinct from Marxism-Leninism, is founded on *democratic* principles, at least so far as popular acceptance is concerned.

Imperialism.   As the twentieth century began, the pressure from critics of Marxist theory became intense. Marxism was not only attacked by capitalists and conservatives but also questioned by a growing number of socialists. The core of the theory, dialectic materialism, predicted a proletarian revolution that never occurred. Indeed, as the revisionists pointed out, the conditions of labor were improving in the industrial countries, making the revolution appear to be a myth. Hard pressed to explain this seeming contradiction, Lenin studied the trends of capitalism in search of a solution to the dilemma. His conclusion was a clever analysis that went far beyond a simple rationalization of Marx's error.

Since Marx's death a new kind of capitalism had developed. As he predicted, firms became larger though less numerous, their financial needs growing along with their corporate size. But, needing vast amounts of capital to sustain their huge enterprises, the corporations became increasingly dependent on banks for financing, until the bankers themselves gained control of the monopolies. Marx had not foreseen this new financial structure, which Lenin called *finance capitalism.*

Finance capitalism marked a new, much more exploitative stage than the previous condition of *industrial capitalism.* Under these new conditions the owners of the means of production (bankers and financiers) contributed absolutely nothing to the productivity of the plants they controlled. For example, J. P. Morgan, a noted financier, created the Northern Securities Trust in the late 1800s, tying up all the major railroad trunk lines in the United States. He also put together the world's first billion-dollar corporation, United States Steel, in 1901. Morgan and his associates knew nothing at all about the railroad or steel business. Yet, by manipulating capital they gained control of two basic United States industries. Since they contributed nothing to the productivity of those two industries, the labor theory of value held that the fantastic profits of these "robber barons" were stolen from the rightful owners, the proletariat.

In addition, the very fact that the national economies were monopolizing industry was having a profound effect on the international scene. The centralization of ownership was occurring because it was becoming harder to profit from domestic markets. New markets had to be found. At the same time, Lenin believed that the ownership class had begun to realize the truth in the Marxist prediction of a revolution by a proletariat whose misery could no longer be borne. This led the owners to find new sources of cheap labor and resources. Thus, they began to *export their exploitation* through colonialism.

The foreign exploitation of which Lenin wrote began in earnest in the 1880s, too late for Marx to assess its significance. The new colonialism, which Lenin called *imperialist capitalism,* also delayed the proletarian revolution. Driven to increase profits, yet needing to protect themselves against a rebellion by their domestic proletariat, the capitalists began to exploit the labor of the colonial people. Then, to relax the tensions created by their previous domestic exploitation, the capitalists shared some of their new profits with their domestic workers. Not only was the domestic proletariat's revolutionary tension reduced by this improvement in living standards, but their virtue was corrupted. Allowing themselves to be "bought off" by profits stolen from the colonial proletariat, the domestic workers became partners in the capitalist exploitation of the unfortunate colonial people. This economic prostitution disgusted Lenin, who saw it as yet another evil policy of the capitalist enemy.

Capitalist imperialism, however, was ultimately self-destructive. Eventually all the colonial resources would be consumed by the various capitalist states. With no more colonies to subdue, the profit-hungry imperialist nations would begin to feed off each other, causing strife and conflict that would end in a general confrontation among the capitalist imperialist powers. *Imperialism,* Lenin declared in 1916, *is the final stage of capitalism.* It will ultimately lead to a conflict in which the capitalists will destroy each other. Thus Lenin concluded that World War I was a giant struggle in which the imperialist nations hoped to finally settle their colonial conflicts, and that socialists should take advantage of this conflict.

In order to take advantage of the turmoil into which the capitalist world had thrust itself, Lenin advised his fellow socialists to follow a policy of **revolutionary defeatism.** Insisting that World War I was a capitalist war, he argued that socialists should remain aloof until the capitalists defeated themselves. Only after the capitalists had become exhausted by warring with each other should the socialists step forward, united and invincible, to establish socialist states across Europe. Fired with the same nationalism and patriotic fervor as their conservative compatriots, however, most socialists did not follow Lenin's advice, preferring to cooperate with their nation's war efforts instead. Only Lenin and the other Bolsheviks, however, rejected the appeal of a nationalist war and took advantage of the chaos in Russia to overthrow the state.

While Lenin's theory of imperialism explained why the Marxist revolution had not yet occurred among the advanced industrial states in the West, there was still no answer as to why it had occurred in a fifth-rate industrial country such as Russia. Fruitful thinker that he was, Lenin again turned to imperialism for an explanation. Developing his theory of the **weakest link,** he argued that colonialism gave the advanced industrial countries a tremendous competitive advantage over the less developed, noncolonialist capitalist states. If the latter were to compete against the cheap labor and raw materials available to their imperialist opponents, they would have to exploit their own labor force even more. The increased exploitation suffered by the workers in the less advanced countries would naturally push them toward revolution at the very moment when the proletariat of the advanced capitalist countries was being "bought off" with a share of the colonialist spoils. Russia, Lenin concluded, was the weakest link in the capitalist chain, making the first Marxist revolution there quite logical.

Though most evidence indicates that Marx fully expected the revolution to begin in a developed country (perhaps Germany), the possibility of its beginning in a backward country interested him toward the end of his life. Indeed, Marx was so captivated by the revolutionary events taking place in Russia during the 1870s that he attempted to learn the Russian language to facilitate his studies. Marx expected, however, that the revolution in Russia would be a peasant uprising rather than a proletarian movement. But a peasant revolution in Russia might, Marx thought, indirectly spark a proletarian conflagration in Western Europe. "The Russian revolution," he wrote, "would give the signal to the proletarian revolution in the West." Furthermore, Marx speculated, as Lenin also later did, that if a peasant revolution in Russia helped bring socialism to the West, the West could reciprocate by helping to bring socialism to Russia.

Lenin's multipurpose theory served yet another, unanticipated function. Early to oppose colonialism, the Soviet followers of Lenin used his theory to contrast their "nonaggressive" policies with those of the "Western capitalist imperialists." Scoring heavily in the propaganda battles of the Cold War, the Soviets condemned imperialist acts and befriended the emerging Afro-Asian states. To defend against these attacks, the West answered that the Soviet policy of absorbing the satellite states of Eastern Europe after World War II was a new form of socialist imperialism. Even so, the Soviet Union benefited greatly from Lenin's theory of imperialism in a way that he had not foreseen.

Achieving the utopia.   Completing his blueprint for the practical application of Marx's sometimes vague theories, Lenin outlined the economic and political development of the future workers' paradise. The economic system to be used by the Bolshevik dictatorship of the proletariat was what Lenin called **state socialism.** According to this theory, the state was to control all elements of the economy. The workers, employees of the state, would produce a profit and the profit, or surplus value, would then be returned to the society by way of investments to increase productivity, social and governmental programs to aid and protect the citizens, and consumer goods to benefit the society.

The formula for the distribution of goods to the citizens is one that colonial Virginia's John Smith would have been proud of: *"From each according to his ability, to each according to his work."* This formula is even more practical than it appears at first glance. Marx had seen the dictatorship creating a single proletarian class imbued with the socialist ethic by one of two methods: educating the masses to convince them of the wisdom of socialism, or simply removing them from the society. Here Lenin introduced a third technique for achieving the single-class utopia. Because socialists are supposed to enjoy the process of labor, Lenin expected that they would be more productive than those who did not accept socialism. Paying workers according to the labor they performed would reward the socialists, while the slackers would be penalized for lack of productivity.

When the nonconformists had been starved into the socialist mold, all the people would be convinced of the value of labor and the utopian stage would be at hand. As more people became proletariat and socialist, class differences would diminish and strife among the people would be reduced. As human strife disappeared, the need for the state would "wither away," just as Marx had predicted. Eventually there would emerge a utopian existence in which people might live and work in peace. Sharing their labor, they would also share the fruits of their production. In the utopia the economic system would have evolved from *socialism* to *communism,* which Lenin, echoing Marx, describes as an economy in which the people give according to their abilities and take back according to their needs.

More practical (or more cynical, if you will) than Marx, Lenin contradicted him several times. More an activist than an ideologue, he was always concerned with the workability of a process, often leaving theoretical inconsistencies to sort themselves out. He ignored the democratic spirit of Marx's theory in favor of an elitist revolution, claiming that its utopian ends justified its extreme means. He violated the dialectic by demanding an early revolution, which he followed with an elitist dictatorship that Marx almost surely never intended. He used his theory of imperialism to describe a stage of capitalism not foreseen by Marx; he then used it to explain why the revolution happened first in Russia and failed to take place in the highly industrialized countries. Finally, along with state socialism, Lenin proposed a new kind of labor exploitation about which Marx would have had serious qualms. Yet, with all their twists and turns, these modifications and amendments were always intended to bring to fruition the Marxist ideal: a society at peace with itself in a world characterized by human harmony. Never losing sight of this goal, Lenin often surprised his own followers with the depth of his conviction and the totality of his Marxist commitment. However, like Marx before him, Lenin failed to foresee many of the terrible events that followed the establishment of the Soviet Union.

REVIEW

- Socialism includes three features: (1) Public ownership of production through nationalized industries or cooperatives. (2) A welfare state that assures the material well-being of the citizens. (3) And most important, the intention to improve the liberty and the well-being of all citizens, thus creating a happier, more tranquil social existence.
- Socialism can be traced to the ideas of Rousseau, who, although not a socialist, established many of its philosophical principles.
- After the Babouvists briefly demanded the violent imposition of socialism, the utopians—history's first humanitarian socialists—agreed that the only moral existence was one in which all people had enough food, housing, and clothing to assure a decent human life.

- Marx followed the discredited utopians, creating "scientific" socialism and arguing that socialism was inevitable because certain economic "laws" predisposed human historical development.
- Following Marx's death, the socialist movement split asunder into the following variants: (1) The Orthodox Marxists broached no contradiction of Marx's theory and soon became politically irrelevant. (2) The Revisionists rejected Marxism and returned to humanitarian justifications for socialism. (3) The Marxist-Leninists, led by Vladimir Lenin, explained why certain Marxist forecasts were erroneous, forsook Marx's mass approach for the tactics of elitism, truncated the dialectic with an early revolution, and modified the dictatorship of the proletariat to suit themselves.

SUGGESTIONS FOR FURTHER READING

ARCHER, ROBIN, *Economic Democracy: The Politics of Feasible Socialism.* New York: Oxford University Press, 1995.

BEAUD, MICHEL, *Socialism In the Crucible of History.* Atlantic Highlands, NJ: Humanities Press International, 1993.

BERKI, R. N., *Socialism.* New York: St. Martin's Press, 1975.

BERNSTEIN, EDWARD, *Evolutionary Socialism,* trans. E. C. Harvey. New York: B. W. Heubsch, 1909.

DERBER, CHARLES, et al., *What's Left? Radical Politics In the Postcommunist Era.* Amherst, MA: University of Massachusetts Press, 1995.

HARRINGTON, MICHAEL, *Socialism.* New York: Bantam Books, 1972.

HOLZ, HANS H., *The Downfall and Future of Socialism.* Edina, NY: M. E. Pinkham, 1992.

HORVAT, BRANKO, *The Political Economy of Socialism.* Armonk, NY: M. E. Sharpe, 1982.

MCLELLAN, DAVID, *Marxism After Marx.* London: Macmillan, 1983.

NOVE, ALEC, *The Economics of Feasible Socialism Revisited.* New York: Routledge Chapman and Hall, 1991.

SCHWEICKART, DAVID, *Against Capitalism.* New York: Cambridge University Press, 1993.

SIK, OTA, ed., *Socialism Today? The Changing Meaning of Socialism.* New York: St. Martin's Press, 1991.

YARMOLINSKY, AVRAHM, *Road to Revolution: A Century of Russian Radicalism.* New York: Collier Books, 1962.

Chapter 10

Applied Marxism: Communism

PREVIEW

Marxism has been put to a great variety of uses and has been given many different, and sometimes contradictory, interpretations. This chapter deals with the application of Marxism in four major settings: the Soviet Union, Yugoslavia, China, and Cuba.

Attempting to socialize the Soviet Union at a single stroke, Lenin saw national productivity fall to dangerous levels as the Bolsheviks fought the Russian Civil War. When the Civil War ended, Lenin reversed field, recapitalizing much of the economy with the New Economic Policy (NEP), hoping to successfully socialize the economy more gradually.

Joseph Stalin rose to power by ruthlessly purging friend and foe alike. Once in control, he revolutionized the Soviet Union by restructuring the society and creating a personal dictatorship through terrorist methods. Having weathered World War II and having successfully put the Soviet Union back on the road to economic recovery, Stalin died in 1953. Khrushchev's rise to power resulted in a liberalization program that relaxed the Stalinist totalitarian restraints. However, his economic and political reforms, together with his impulsive leadership style, resulted in his removal from power in 1964. Khrushchev's expulsion brought Leonid Brezhnev to power. His conservative policies created the stability for which many Soviets longed, but stability soon became stagnation as productivity declined, corruption increased, and spiritual malaise debilitated the Soviet public. Brezhnev's death after eighteen years in power brought a rapid succession of decrepit rulers to the Kremlin, until Mikhail Gor-

bachev, a young and energetic politician, finally came to the top. Believing that the Soviet system had to change if it was to be preserved, Gorbachev embarked on an astonishing series of liberalizing reforms, only to find himself isolated and without power when the Soviet Union collapsed after a failed coup by a cabal of hard-line communists. Russia, one of the fifteen independent states to spin out of the ruins of the former Soviet Union, is led by Boris Yeltsin. His task, transforming a socialist, totalitarian state into a market-driven, democratic society is confronted by difficulties of immense proportion.

Having come to power at the head of his own movement and without direct Soviet involvement, Josip Tito enjoyed a degree of independence from Moscow not shared by his East European colleagues. Tito struggled against the centralization of power, the over bureaucratization of the system, and the nationalistic separatism of Yugoslavia's diverse population. He encouraged a degree of local political control and of market economic activity that was unparalleled in the communist world. Yet, even the work of a political architect as wise as Tito could not overcome the imperatives of nationalism. When, twelve years after his death, the communist world in Eastern Europe collapsed, Yugoslavia came apart and descended into a frightful fraternal war. Thus, communism of even the most mild sort ultimately ended in this unhappy land.

China has developed yet another major variant of Marxism-Leninism. Modifying Marxism to fit China's rural, Asian character, Mao Tse-tung honored the peasant as he criticized the intellectual and the bureaucrat. After coming to power, Mao assumed a cautious stance at first, but eventually he introduced increasingly radical policies designed to use the masses to flout his enemies and to build a communist state. Besides identifying a dominant role in Marxism for the peasants, perhaps his greatest contribution was establishing a strategy of guerrilla warfare by which poor, backward societies could wrest themselves from the domination of more advanced powers.

Mao's death brought Deng Xiaoping to power. Embarking on a major reform program, Deng has vaulted China into a new era of economic progress, but the accompanying political stresses resulted in a bloody crackdown on students demanding faster political liberalization. Whether Deng will be succeeded by a new Maoist radicalization, conservative repression, or a new round of liberalization is impossible to predict, but current indications suggest that the liberals may prevail.

Cuba, the only communist state in the Western Hemisphere, is unusual in several ways. Being the founder of a Marxist-Leninist Cuba, Castro enjoys more personal authority than his contemporary colleagues. However, the Communist Party has less influence in Cuba than its counterparts in other communists states.

Weakened by economic failures, and isolated by American policy, Cuba was thrust into the Soviet bloc and forced to depend on Moscow for huge amounts of aid. With the collapse of the Soviet Union, its financial support was abruptly ended, and although Castro has accomplished significant social progress, his economic failures place his government in serious jeopardy. Nevertheless, Castro has evolved from a young revolutionary to an orthodox Marxist-Leninist.

The collapse of the Soviet Union and of communism throughout Eastern Europe have brought great changes. While these changes do not constitute a total rejection of socialism, they are its redefinition in that they inaugurate the abandonment of Marx's dialectics, of Lenin's notions about the inevitability of violent revolution and the imperative of single-party dominance, and of Stalin's centralized planning.

Although Leninism and Stalinism seem to have failed and socialism in general is in disarray, it is not likely that socialism is a dead issue politically. The Marxist analysis still offers much to learn, and socialism is probably too attractive an idea to be long ignored.

THE SOVIET UNION AND RUSSIA

Commenting toward the end of his life on the variety of ways his friend's theories had been interpreted, Friedrich Engels reportedly said: "Marx would not be a Marxist if he were alive today." As we have just seen, time and the influence of new generations brought about many changes in Marxist theory. Yet, varied as the interpretations were, even greater changes were made in the original theory when it was applied to practical political situations. Although many Marxist experiments have recently failed, it is important to study them and the few Marxist societies that still exist.

Lenin's Policies

War communism. Lenin immediately plunged the Soviet Union into the socialist waters. Ownership became a fluid concept as the stock market was closed, the banks were nationalized, the workers were told to take the factories and the peasants were entreated to seize the land. This abrupt plunge into socialism occurred even as Russia was still engaged in fighting World War I: Hence the name given to the era was *war communism.*

Friction between the workers and the Bolsheviks developed almost from the start. Trying to cope with an emergency situation, Lenin demanded that the economy be immediately controlled by the central government. The proletariat resisted, preferring to run the factories collectively through councils of workers. Strife on the farms was even worse as peasants resisted the confiscation of their crops and animals for the war effort. Meanwhile, any pretense of democracy was abandoned at the end of October 1917, when Lenin dissolved an elected constituent assembly in which the Bolsheviks held only a small minority of the seats. From that moment it was clear that the dictatorship of the proletariat was to function like any other dictatorship, stifling human liberties and ignoring popular preferences.

At the front the carnage of World War I was ghastly. People were fed up with the war, and Lenin knew that there was no practical alternative to making peace with the German government. Though others disagreed, Lenin insisted that peace be made at any price and justified his policy in ideological terms. Lenin argued, as he had argued before, that the conflict was a capital- ist imperialist war in which socialists had no interest. Peace negotiations were held, and the Treaty of Brest-Litovsk was signed on March 3, 1918.

Meanwhile, opponents to the Bolsheviks mobilized on every side of the Red-held territory. Wretched as it was, the suffering World War I caused Rus- sia was easily surpassed by the brutality of its civil war (1918–1921). Both sides demanded incredible sacrifices from their supporters while brutalizing their opponents. In addition to struggling against the Whites, the Bolsheviks had to contend with an invasion of Russia by Western states, including Britain, France, Italy, Japan, Canada, Poland, and the United States, a fact that did little to make the Allies popular with the new Russian rulers.

At first the Bolshevik cause seemed lost, but with great ideological re- solve and superior organizational skills they managed to rout the opposing White Armies one by one. Military victories were accompanied by economic disasters, however. Poor management and unwilling workers, together with the disruption and destruction of the war itself, combined to reduce indus- trial production to one-seventh of its prewar level by 1921. Shortages devel- oped in every conceivable item, resulting in a famine in 1920. Despite humanitarian aid from the United States, the resulting starvation claimed 5 million lives, while another 30 million suffered from malnutrition.

The NEP.   With the Civil War ending, the foreign invaders gone, the econ- omy in a shambles, and a rebellion under way in the once loyal navy, Lenin decided to take drastic steps. Accordingly, he claimed that the party had made serious errors in trying to develop a socialist state and he announced his **New Economic Policy (NEP).** Having failed in his attempt at immediate and complete socialization, he took the unexpected step of recapitalizing the bulk of the economy, calling the new system *state capitalism.* Practically everything except heavy industry, finance, communications, and transporta- tion was returned to private ownership and a market economy. Yet, Lenin in- tended the NEP to be only a temporary adjustment to restore economic order so that a better attempt to socialize the economy could be made later.

Even as Lenin relaxed his grip on the economy, however, the Bolshe- viks—by then renamed the Communist Party—began to tighten their politi- cal control over the society. Just as James Madison had stifled the American Revolution in favor of order, the leaders of the Communist Party betrayed their own revolutionary goals for the sake of power. Opposition parties were outlawed and destroyed. The trade unions were brought under state control. The national boundaries began to take shape as the Ukraine, Armenia, Geor- gia, and Azerbaijan were brought into the Union. More important, the party gradually became bureaucratically oriented instead of revolutionary in its focus.

Though the political situation was becoming more restrictive, the early

1920s was a time of great social and artistic experimentation in the Soviet Union. Egalitarianism was popular, stimulating a movement to eliminate the social institutions that imprisoned people in the bourgeois state. Free love was encouraged by Alexandra Kollontai, a leader among radical communists. Also supporting the abolition of the family, easy divorce, and abortions, she became an embarrassment to the puritanical Bolshevik leadership. Equally revolutionary experiments were made in art, film, music, education, literature, and the theater, producing some of the world's most avant-garde creations. These advances of the postwar era were later squelched by Stalin's conservative notion of *socialist realism,* which required artists to show only the good, progressive side of socialism, whether or not such idealistic examples actually existed at the time.

The NEP ended in an important feat for the Soviets. Though he died in 1924, Lenin took comfort in the knowledge that his country was well on its way toward economic recovery. Even more important, the Communist party held unchallenged power over the state, though the choice of a successor for Lenin was certainly not a foregone conclusion.

The Rise of Stalin

Upon Lenin's death the Soviet leadership was headed by a small group of men, including **Leon Trotsky** (1879–1940), a brilliant revolutionary and commissar of war, and Joseph Stalin (1879–1953), commisar of nationalities and general secretary of the Communist party. Before his death Lenin had begun to suspect Stalin's motives, correctly seeing him as a scoundrel who might destroy the revolution in his quest for personal power. Too ill to actively campaign against him, Lenin suggested in his will that Stalin be replaced. Perhaps the most fateful decision in Soviet history was made when the Central Committee (a Communist Party ruling body) decided not to publish Lenin's will.

Of the remaining leaders, Trotsky appeared the most likely to succeed Lenin. Brilliant as he was, however, Trotsky was not well liked by the other Communist party leaders, and they feared his rise to power. By contrast, the more placid, unobtrusive Stalin lacked his opponent's energy and seemed to give his colleagues little to fear. However, in underestimating Stalin, his unsuspecting rivals sealed their own fate.

Stalin's struggle with Trotsky took place between 1924 and 1928. Besides a personality clash and each man's desire to gain power, three ideological and policy issues divided them. Trotsky attacked his colleague's domination of the party, claiming that Stalin was ignoring the principle of collective leadership. The second area of disagreement between the two was Trotsky's belief that the NEP, which he never accepted, should be immediately reversed and the farms and the marketplace resocialized. Stalin opposed this rash policy, arguing instead that the NEP should be maintained

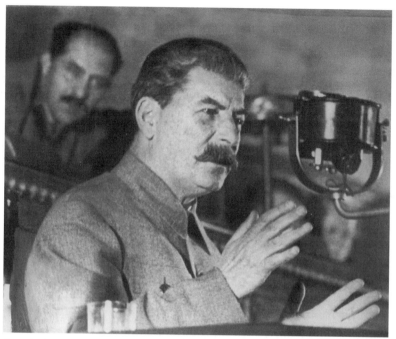

Joseph Stalin (1879–1953)   Sovfoto/Eastfoto

until the Soviet economy had regained its prerevolutionary productivity. The third important dispute is perhaps the most basic. Trotsky, always the revolutionary, deeply believed in the principle of **permanent revolution.** First implied by Marx, this theory suggests that no accommodation between socialists and capitalists can ever be made. Lenin carried this concept a step further in his theory of imperialism by claiming that the exportation of capitalist exploitation not only leads to competition between capitalist states but creates conflict between capitalist and socialist countries as well.

Not content to limit the revolution, Trotsky believed that the Bolshevik's first loyalty was not to any particular national experiment but to encouraging Marxist revolutions around the globe. Consequently, he insisted that Soviet resources should be devoted primarily to fostering revolutions abroad. Stalin preferred to dedicate all the nation's energies and resources to making the Soviet Union safe from any possible challenge. This policy of *building socialism in one country,* a consuming passion for Stalin, stemmed from his fear of *capitalist encirclement.* Western attempts to frustrate the Bolshevik rise to power, the Allied invasion in 1919 during the Russian civil war, and the Allied attempts to strangle the Soviet Union after the civil war through economic sanctions and boycotts, combined with Stalin's own paranoia, generated in him an exaggerated feeling of national peril. Stalin insisted that any large-scale attempt to ignite the world revolution must await the development of unconquerable Soviet power. Only then could enough resources be spared to bring Marxism to the rest of the world.

The policy of building socialism in one country is of the greatest ideological significance. It effectively *nationalizes Marxism-Leninism,* a result both Marx and Lenin would certainly have abhorred. This policy is of particular importance, for nationalism is the most powerful political idea of our era. Under Stalin the strongest internationalist ideology in history was completely overwhelmed by the irresistible onslaught of nationalism. Though Stalin was the first to adapt Marxism-Leninism to nationalism, later varieties of Marxism only underscore the grip in which nationalism holds it.

Stalin's Rule

In 1929, with Trotsky out of the way, Stalin decided it was time to abandon Lenin's NEP and resocialize the economy completely. Thus he initiated the first of the **five-year plans,** a crash program to modernize and industrialize the country. These programs called for the nationalization of all industries, trades, and occupations and included the collectivization of the farms. They also forced enormous sacrifices on the Soviet people so that resources could be diverted from the production of consumer goods to the military and heavy industry. The forced collectivization of the farms and the sacrifice of consumer goods caused incredible misery and millions of deaths. These ruthless policies were not without success, however. Compressing into ten years the advances other states stretched out over several decades, the first two five-year plans catapulted the Soviet Union to the status of a major industrial power.

Stalin's passion to make the Soviet Union unconquerable led him to personalize the dictatorship of the proletariat in a way Lenin would never have approved. The party became the mere servant of his will. Accumulating enormous power, Stalin became the single, unchallengeable head of the state. He increased his power over the party and the government, creating a *totalitarian state.* To accomplish this task, he used *terrorism* and the secret police, two instruments of government used by Russian rulers since the beginnings of the Russian state, but certainly never with such all-encompassing and devastating effect. On such foundations Stalin built a *personality cult* seldom equaled in history.

Stalin's megalomania inspired him to attempt the complete subjugation of the Eastern European states that fell under Soviet influence after World War II. Absorbing the devastating Nazi invasion in 1941, Soviet troops gradually pushed the Germans back to their homeland by 1944. Retreating into Germany, the Nazi armies abandoned Eastern Europe before the Soviet onslaught. One country after another fell under Soviet control, only to find that their liberation from the Nazis was simply the first step in the imposition of a new, equally severe regime. Reeling from the slaughter and pillage that caused the deaths of 26 million Soviets and destruction of a quarter of the national wealth, Stalin imposed a regime of unparalleled severity on the Eastern European countries, some of which (Bulgaria, Hungary, and Rumania) had willingly helped Hitler despoil the Soviet Union. Properly called the **satellite countries,** these states were harnessed to the Soviet reconstruction and defense effort: Stalin forced the satellites to contribute heavily to the Soviet economy and postpone their own recovery.

Khrushchev's Revisions

The long, dark rule of Stalin ended with his death in 1953 and was followed by a four-year power struggle within the top Soviet leadership. Emerging as the dominant, though never absolute, leader in the Soviet system, **Nikita Khrushchev** (1894–1971) became an important reformer. Attacking Stalin in February 1956 in a secret speech before the Twentieth Party Congress, Khrushchev listed his "crimes," many of which Khrushchev himself had helped commit. He called for the *de-Stalinization* of the Soviet Union.

Khrushchev's de-Stalinization program was part of a series of liberal reforms. The Soviet grip on the satellites relaxed, allowing them more liberty and individuality. Khrushchev even accepted Tito's declaration that there are many "different paths to socialism." To say that there was greater freedom in Eastern Europe under Khrushchev is not to suggest that there were no limits on that freedom, however. Those limits were clearly violated by the Hungarian rebellion in 1956: Soviet tanks were sent through the streets of Budapest, brutally suppressing the rebels' futile sprint for liberty.

Khrushchev's domestic reforms surpassed even his liberal policy toward the satellites. Terrorism was abandoned as a technique of governmental control. Khrushchev's adversaries were expelled from the party and the government, but they were not killed. Relaxing the government's censorship policies, Khrushchev unleashed a burst of creative energy (particularly in films and literature) that swept the country, giving vent to the genius of Boris Pasternak and Alexander Solzhenitsyn, among others. He also tried to decentralize party and government control over society.

However, his impetuous style and the failure of many of his reforms led to his undoing. Threatening the positions of older party members, pursuing agricultural reforms that failed, pounding his shoe on the podium during a United Nations speech, and retreating on the question of missiles in Cuba all weakened Khrushchev's position.

Two of Khrushchev's policies had important ideological implications. He set out on a completely new path when he realized that nuclear weapons made a general war between the Soviet Union and the United States unthinkable. Claiming that Marx could not have foreseen the development of the ultimate weapon that threatened to destroy humanity, he shifted the concept of permanent international revolution to a new arena. The two superpowers, he believed, must settle on a policy of **peaceful coexistence,** since a war between them would be suicidal and victory for either side was impossible.

This modification, however, did not mean that the struggle between the two systems was ended. "We will bury you," he shouted, by which he meant that socialism would ultimately out-compete capitalism economically, causing its demise. Hence, Khrushchev gave new meaning to the concept of permanent revolution, shifting the emphasis from violence between the two systems to economic competition. At the same time, however, he pledged Soviet aid to struggles for national liberation, especially among the emerging states.

Khrushchev's second significant ideological modification came with his announcement that the withering away of the state had begun in the Soviet Union and that the utopia would probably be achieved by 1980, when Soviet productivity had surpassed that of the United States. Clearly these predictions did not come to pass. Indeed, Soviet economic growth began to slow in the mid-1970s and the decline continued, building momentum, until the Soviet Union finally collapsed in 1991.

Further, instead of disappearing, the state became even more prominent in Soviet life after Khrushchev's demise because his successors dismantled his liberal reforms.

The Brezhnev Era and Beyond

Khrushchev was overthrown by an extremely conservative group of party leaders led by Leonid Brezhnev (1906–1982). Repelled by Khrushchev's incessant and seemingly ill-conceived reforms, the Kremlin leaders became consumed with creating stability. Stability soon transformed to political and economic stagnation, however. Job security became almost absolute from top to bottom in the society. With little danger of losing their jobs, long-time government officials became corrupt, and workers became even less conscientious than before: Absenteeism, alcoholism, shoddy production, breakage, and waste increased to serious proportions. Squeezed by low productivity and an enormous defense budget as they tried to equal the United States' military capacity, the Soviets saw shortages of staples as well as luxuries become a serious and constant problem. Shortages in state stores encouraged people to satisfy their needs illegally as the ever-present black market became pervasive throughout the society.

A spiritual malaise set in over the society and ideological conviction declined abruptly in the waning years of Brezhnev's tenure. The decline of popular resolve in response to corruption and scarcity was exacerbated by the growing gerontocracy governing the system. Few of the aging bureaucrats left their powerful positions; hence there was little upward mobility for the younger generations, and the system was sapped of the vitality it had previously enjoyed. Hope for reform dimmed as one aging, infirmed leader after another followed Brezhnev to power.

Finally, in 1985, Mikhail S. Gorbachev (born in 1931) was named General Secretary of the Communist Party. Well educated, energetic, and progressive thinking, Gorbachev believed that the moribund Soviet Union had to change if it was to survive. Beginning cautiously at first, but then quickly expanding his program, Gorbachev launched an astonishing series of reforms. Through *perestroika* (restructuring) he tried to revitalize the stalled economy by lifting from it the heavy hand of centralized control. With *glasnost* (openness) he encouraged intellectuals and even ordinary people to speak out about the system in the hope that public pressure would spur economic and structural modernization. A major factor in *glasnost* was a brutally frank exposition of the murderous policies of the Stalinist era. But this airing of past atrocities angered the hard-line party members, even as it discredited in the public eye the party itself—the mainstay of the Soviet Union. Finally, Gorbachev initiated *demokratsiya* (democratization). These reforms reorganized the government, attempting to free it from the stagnant hand of party control. It created meaningful elections in which people could choose among several candidates and numerous parties.

While professing to be a socialist to the end, Gorbachev clearly abandoned the single-party control established by Lenin and the tradition of closed government that was hallmark of Soviet government and the Tsarist government before it. Like Khrushchev, Gorbachev also tried to abandon the tightly controlled centralized Stalinist economy, but also like Khrushchev, he failed. Resisted by bureaucrats who resented the loss of power his reforms threatened, by economic managers who were wary about the amount of personal responsibility they would have to bare for production, and by the workers themselves who refused to cooperate with a policy that called upon them to work harder with no concrete assurance that their lives would improve, the economic reforms stalled. Even Gorbachev himself contributed to the failure. Perhaps stayed by the need to develop political consensus for the reforms among the party, military, police, trade unions, bureaucrats, and general public, Gorbachev hesitated taking the critical steps necessary to fully implement the economic reforms. So in the end, rather than growing, the economy continued to decline.

At the same time, the political and social reforms of *demokratsiya* and *glasnost* mobilized masses of people. Grasping the opportunity to reform themselves, the East European states—often with Gorbachev's encouragement—broke from the Soviet orbit and are now trying to develop democracies and market economies of their own. Meanwhile, Soviet politics became a tumult of people demanding change and improvement in virtually every aspect of Soviet life. Most explosive of all, however, was the question of the nationalities. The Soviet Union was a very complex society, including in its population Russians (about 52 percent) and over 100 minorities. *Glasnost* and *demokratsiya* emboldened many national minorities to demand autonomy within the Soviet state or even independence from it. Bending to these compelling demands, Gorbachev negotiated an agreement that would give the largest national minorities much more control over their political, social, and cultural lives. On the eve that the new agreement was to be signed, powerful leaders of the party, the police, the military, and the bureaucracy attempted a coup to prevent it and to reestablish traditional political control over the society. Having little public support and being opposed by the popular Russian President Boris Yeltsin, the coup failed.

While Gorbachev was returned to power, the situation for him was irreparably damaged. The national Communist party structure (the former instrument of state control) was abolished, and one by one the major national minorities declared their province to be independent from the Soviet Union. Although Yeltsin had restored Gorbachev to power, the two were longtime political rivals, and Yeltsin insisted on an independent course for Russia as well. So in late December of 1991 Gorbachev resigned the presidency of a state that had already ceased in practice to exist. Ironically, the political disillusionment that the hard-line communist plotters had sought to prevent with the coup was actually speeded by it.

Today, Yeltsin presides over Russia, and fourteen other independent countries have spun out of the former Soviet Union. The Communist Party governs none of them, but its former members—like Yeltsin himself—are still very powerful. The social and economic problems of the old Soviet Union still plague the new societies, and it will probably be decades before they are settled. Yeltsin and the other national leaders are trying to convert their economies from Stalinist centralization to market systems, but the difficulties of such transitions are daunting. Marxism-Leninism, in this part of the world, however, is abandoned.

YUGOSLAVIA

Tito's Rise to Power

Born in Croatia, **Josip Broz Tito** (1892–1980) was forced to fight on the Russian front for the Austro-Hungarian Empire during World War I. His capture made him a prisoner of war in Russia, where in 1917 the Bolsheviks took power. Fired by Marxist-Leninist doctrine, Tito became a trainee of the Comintern, returning home in 1924 to find that the Treaty of Versailles had cobbled the Balkan states together into a single entity called Yugoslavia. Without delay, Tito began organizing a communist movement in the area. The 1941 Nazi invasion of Yugoslavia found Tito in the mountains fighting the aggressor and building a communist following. At war's end, Tito was the nation's clear choice for leader. His popular support was genuine and his was the only East European state in which communism had developed on its own, not having been imposed on Yugoslavia by the Red Army. As such, Tito enjoyed a degree of authority and independence from the Soviet Union that other East European communist leaders did not.

The Evolution of Titoism

At first, Tito was among Joseph Stalin's most loyal supporters, and he established a system of economic and political controls based on the Soviet model. Yet, Yugoslav-Soviet ties were not as solid as they appeared. Stalin insisted on Soviet domination of all Eastern European states, including Yugoslavia, causing Tito serious misgivings about the wisdom of a close alliance. Therefore, he began to resist Soviet pressure to conform. Tito's resistance made Stalin even more insistent until relations between the two states were broken off in 1948. Protesting that there are many "different paths to socialism," Tito was cut adrift from the Soviet bloc. To Stalin's dismay this isolation did not lead to Tito's downfall. Instead, the Yugoslav leader pioneered the policy of nonalignment with either East or West and profited from trade with both.

By divorcing himself from the Soviet block and remaining a Marxist, Tito initiated a second communist line, one that was the most pragmatic and *least dogmatic variant of communist ideologies.* He began by warning that just as there are certain fundamental problems in capitalism, socialism is also plagued with internal difficulties that must be faced squarely if they are to be solved.

Lenin's stress on *violence* was a particular problem to Tito. He argued that although violence might have been necessary at one time, it was no longer required for socialist development. Stronger and more fully developed, socialism had gained momentum and could continue to advance without the use of force. This attitude modified the principle of permanent revolution considerably, but Tito changed it even further. Rather than constantly resisting the capitalist states, socialists should coexist with them, he believed. Moreover, he advised that when it was in their interest to do so, Marxists should cooperate actively with the capitalist world.

His fear of capitalist encirclement undiminished after the war, Stalin found Tito's moderate ideas reprehensible. He was already disturbed by Tito's doctrine of different paths to socialism. Tito had insisted that there was no single true interpretation of socialism, making it hard to justify Stalin's attempt to restrict independent socialist thought and to force compliance with Moscow's dictates.

As important as relations with Stalinism was, however, Tito's most significant ideological revision related to domestic rather than foreign policy. Having seen the Soviet Union, a revolutionary society committed to bringing socialism to the world, degenerate to a totalitarian dictatorship supported by a ponderous and exploitative bureaucracy, Tito reached the conclusion Mao Tse-tung arrived at a few years later. Tito became convinced that the greatest danger confronting socialism was not mounted by foreign capitalism. Rather, it came from within. Socialism was most jeopardized by its own tendency toward *bureaucratic rigidity.* Accordingly, Tito focused on combating the tendency of over-centralization in the regime. Since socialism requires collectivization of the society, Tito believed that conflict could be expected among several legitimate interests within the society. The most vexing of these conflicts would arise from a clash between the individual's interests and those of a society as a whole. Tito also recognized the potential for strife between the preferences of the workers and the economic goals of the state. Perhaps most important of all, however, was the contradiction he saw between the central government and the local agencies in the political arena as well as in the economic field.

Facing the problems of centralization squarely, he concluded that Marx was wrong in suggesting that the dictatorship of the proletariat would wither away as it succeeded in its task of creating the classless society. To the contrary, Tito reasoned, unless it was prevented from expanding, the bureaucracy would grow rather than disappear. Instead of evolving from state socialism to communism, as Lenin had hoped, the political system would become dominated by a bureaucracy that would end up exploiting the masses for its own sake, thus evolving a system that might be called *state capitalism.* Left untended, Tito feared that society would not evolve to the socialist utopia. Instead, he saw the state becoming an end in itself; in other words, the political system would come to resemble fascism, hardly Marx's goal.

Tito therefore resolved to decentralize the political and economic institutions in society. Under what came to be called *market socialism,* Tito decollectivized most of the farms, returning them to private ownership and control. Even more progressive, however, were the modifications he made in the industrial sector. Reversing his original preference for central control and planning of industrial output, Tito began to encourage the decentralization of industry. Always alert to the encroachments of bureaucracy on the society, he argued that in the most advanced form of socialism the workers would be in direct control of the factories. In his opinion nationalization of industries was only a first and somewhat primitive step toward socialism; *social* control rather than *state* control was the future condition of the advanced socialist societies. Accordingly, a program to return control of the plants to the workers was inaugurated. Though the program was never completely successful, it allowed workers to participate in plant management through employee-elected *worker's councils.* Guided by a general central plan, the workers councils ran the plants, making decisions about production, prices, wages, and benefits. Also, private ownership was allowed to exist side by side with public enterprise. Agricultural enterprises were largely returned to private hands. Private ownership of small businesses was not only tolerated, but it was even encouraged. Small retail shops, restaurants, repair shops, crafts, and tourist facilities were often left to private ownership. Even private foreign investment was encouraged.

Accompanying Tito's policy of economic decentralization was his determination to decentralize control of the Communist Party. Marx had argued that, as a single class evolved in society, the political institutions would whither away, leaving only an economic bureaucracy to administer the production and distribution of goods. Contradicting Marx, Tito believed that while the need for central economic control would dissipate, the party would always remain the leader and guardian of the system. Even so, Tito did not want the party to be a monolith controlled from Belgrade. Hence, he initiated steps that he hoped would leave most direct-party involvement in the citizens' lives to local party agencies.

Tito also decentralized the governmental structure. Once describing Yugoslavia as "one country with two alphabets, speaking three languages, professing four religions, made up of five nationalities in six republics," Tito moved to partition the government with federalism. The country was divided into six republics and two autonomous provinces.

Throughout Tito's life, his antibureaucratic and decentralizing policies met with mixed results. Enjoying an economic boom in the late 1950s and the 1960s, Yugoslavia suffered seriously from the worldwide economic downturn of the 1970s and followed the other East European countries into a heavy burden of international debt. Productivity declined while inflation and unemployment rose. At the same time, his governmental and party modifications encouraged divisions among Yugoslavia's feuding national minorities. These diverse groups found themselves joined in an uncomfortable union. They were unable to cooperate fully because of their traditional animosities, jealousies, cultural differences, geographical isolation, and economic disparity.

Tito's death in 1980 was greeted with deep sorrow by a fractious and impoverished state. The departure of Yugoslavia's implacable advocate for national unity left few leaders in place who were willing to look beyond petty nationalistic jealousies. As a consequence, the state, forged from the feuding and disparate peoples in the Balkans by World War I's peacemakers, began in the late 1980s to weaken.

The economic plight and growing nationalistic squabbles fed off each other, exacerbating the political crisis. As Eastern Europe began to break away from the Soviet orbit, tension mounted within Yugoslavia, with the republic of Serbia attempting to exert hegemony over the others. Resisting this ethnic imperialism, the former republics of Yugoslavia—Slovinia, Croatia, Bosnia-Herzegovina, and Macedonia—declared their independence, and a vicious, multisided civil war ensued. It is the first war fought on European soil since World War II. Led by the United States, NATO and the UN have intervened, hoping to restore peace.

Wracked by desperate bloodletting, the once-socialist economic system of these areas is a shambles. Blighted by sharp declines in productivity and astronomical inflation, people find themselves reduced to living in the basements of bombed-out buildings, bartering goods, and scratching out a living in primitive conditions.

Most frightening, the warring nationalities—Serbia in particular—have practiced policies of "ethnic cleansing." This abominable policy forces ethnic groups to abandon their ancestral homes to seek refuge in other states, thus leaving space for colonists from the conquering state to take over the vacated territory. Genocide and other heinous crimes, including death camps and systematic rape, have been alleged by each party of the dispute against the others. As in the Soviet Union, communism was able to suppress deep-rooted nationalistic hatreds for a time, but in the end, communism's failure has seen the demon of xenophobia unleashed again.

CHINA

Imperial China, one of history's most successful political systems, was based on the principles of Confucianism. Confucianism is as much a political theory as a code of moral conduct. Indeed, in this ancient philosophy moral conduct and an ordered state are equated. Confucius taught that all people should know their place and should accept it, thus maintaining a harmonious society, the most desirable state of affairs. The law, rooted in Confucian teaching, provided that the upper classes would rule and that the peasantry would obey. This sociopolitical arrangement served the Chinese remarkably well for centuries. The Chinese people enjoyed the benefits of an advanced civilization and an ordered society while the West foundered in the ignorance and social disorder of the medieval period.

Perhaps because the West was driven to improve the political and economic systems serving it, it took the initiative during the fourteenth and fifteenth centuries. For its part, Asia turned inward and became isolated from foreign influences. The Chinese placed a premium on tradition, rejecting new ideas as harmful to society.

As a result the West surpassed the East in developing modern technology and political doctrines that accommodated the changes brought about by the new economic order. As the East's resistance was worn down by the pressure of the West's technological superiority, the philosophies of the ancient regimes began to appear less viable and Western ideologies, such as nationalism and later Marxism, became more appealing. Though these Western ideas were modified somewhat, the fact remains that the East has been captivated by Western institutions, economic styles, and political idea systems.

The Belligerent Stage of the Chinese Revolution

Though its traditional power seemed antiquated, the imperial system survived foreign occupation and internal pressure for change until early in this century. The inevitable could not be avoided forever, however, and the belligerent stage of the Chinese Revolution began in 1911 and lasted until 1949.

In 1911 the Manchu Dynasty ended with the child emperor, Pu Yi, abidicating in response to overwhelming pressure. The leader of the victorious republican forces was an unimposing, idealistic man, **Dr. Sun Yat-sen**[1] (1866–1925). His ideology was a somewhat confused mixture of Western political theories, mild socialist economic ideas, and Eastern traditions. He was too idealistic and naive to understand completely the forces he had helped unleash, however, and China's needs went far beyond his simplistic solutions. In the end he was outmaneuvered by the Machiavellians surrounding him, and he spent the rest of his life struggling with autocratic elements in China.

In the meantime the Communist Party of China (CPC) was founded in 1921. Attending the first party congress was a radical young schoolteacher, **Mao Tse-tung** (1893–1976). Coming from a well-to-do peasant family, Mao pursued an education and graduated from a teacher's college in 1918. Although he began at a low rank, he attracted the attention of party superiors with his devotion to the cause, his tireless efforts as a union organizer, and his keen insight into the problems of the revolution.

For its part the Soviet Union was becoming increasingly interested in China. Lenin sent agents to coordinate the Comintern efforts in China. He favored an alliance between the CPC and the **Kuomintang** (Sun's political party) against the reactionary elements in China. More important, Stalin also supported such an alliance, actively encouraging it after Lenin became ill in 1923. Repeatedly rebuffed in his appeals for aid from the United States and Western Europe because he was a socialist, Sun Yat-sen turned to the Soviet Union for support, agreeing to the first Communist-Kuomintang alliance (1924–1927).

The purpose of the first alliance was to break the power of the reactionary warlords who controlled China's far-flung provinces. The alliance's initial success was darkened in 1925 when Sun Yat-sen died. He was suc-

---

[1]Before 1970 Chinese words in English were commonly spelled using the Wade-Giles system. In 1970 the People's Republic of China adopted the *pinyin* system, and most English publications have since adopted that format. Yet certain names like Mao Tse-tung seem strange and may not be easily recognized in the *pinyin* form (Mao Zedong). Thus, in order to keep confusion at a minimum, I am using the Wade-Giles system for historical names and the *pinyin* system for contemporary names. Also, you will note that Chinese surnames are placed in front of given names. Hence, Mao Tse-tung's surname is Mao; Deng Xiaoping's is Deng, and so forth.

ceeded by his lieutenant **Chiang Kai-shek** (1887–1975), a much more conservative leader. As world events made right-wing extremism increasingly acceptable, Chiang's Communist allies became a troublesome embarrassment. Suddenly, in 1927 he ordered his armies to attack the communists. The CPC was nearly exterminated by this treachery as Chiang slaughtered all who fell into his hands. In desperation, the communists saved themselves by fleeing the cities to seek safety in the provinces.

The ruralization of Chinese communism. Two years before the Kuomintang attacked the communists, Mao had become unhappy with the progress of the revolution. Thus, he had returned to his native Hunan province in southeastern China and studied the peasantry as a revolutionary force. In Hunan, Mao produced his first significant work, *Report on the Hunan Peasant Movement,* which called upon communists to abandon the cities for the countryside because the peasants, not the proletariat were China's true revolutionaries. With this document he laid the foundation of Maoist thought, and it, together with Chiang's betrayal and the communist failure to rouse the proletariat in the cities, ended the domination of the Soviet Union over the CPC. Though always an important factor, Stalin's influence was clearly secondary in China after 1927 as a distinctly Chinese brand of communism began to develop.

The Long March. Finally gaining an almost decisive military advantage over the communists in 1934, the Kuomintang army surrounded them and threatened their destruction. To avoid annihilation, the communists broke out of the encirclement—leaving their base behind—and fled to safety in northern China. This epic retreat, called the **Long March,** was the low point of the CPC's history and lasted a full year. About 100,000 people set out on a journey that took them 6,000 miles. Since it was more a running battle than a march, scarcely 35,000 survived. As if the hardships of the trek and attacks by the forces of Chiang and the warlords were not enough, the Long March precipitated a leadership struggle within the CPC, and Mao gained the top position in the party. Although this position did not give him absolute power, it made him dominant in the movement, a position he would hold until his death.

The march finally ended in Shensi province in north-central China, where a new base was established in 1936. Hostilities between the communists and the Kuomintang would have continued if the Japanese had not become an overriding threat in the same year. Stalin encouraged the Chinese communists to form a new alliance with the Kuomintang because he wanted to preoccupy Japan with a war in China, thus preventing it from invading the Soviet Union. This "alliance" was actually only a truce, however, permitting two antagonists to deal with a third force threatening both. Nevertheless, the war efforts of each partner were restrained, since each saved its energy for

the inevitable struggle that would take place when the Japanese were defeated.

When the Japanese were finally vanquished in 1945, the China question
emerged once again. The United States, which clearly favored the Kuomintang, tried to negotiate a coalition government between Mao and Chiang.
Ironically, Stalin, who believed that the communists could not yet defeat
Chiang, also pressured Mao to join in a coalition government. Mao and
Chiang were both convinced that they could win the struggle, however, so
they each refused to compromise. The upshot was the last phase of the belligerent period of the Chinese Revolution (1946–1949), as the two sides
locked in mortal combat. Because he had not been able to control the warlords and because his government was cruel, corrupt, and foolish, Chiang
had lost popular support. His military superiority, so obvious on paper,
melted away. Mao, on the other hand, enjoyed great popular support in the
north and considerable appeal in the south. A series of stunning defeats saw
Chiang giving ground until finally, in 1949, all was lost and he fled to the island province of Taiwan.

The Political Stage of the Revolution

The communist regime in China has been marked by a series of important, sometimes traumatic, events. Mao Tse-tung remained a radical force in
Chinese politics, often plunging China into tumultuous programs aimed at
achieving great goals for his people. When they failed, the reform periods
were followed by periods of consolidation that evolved into the staging
grounds for the next set of Mao's radical reforms. This behavior pattern was
repeated again and again, growing in intensity right up to Mao's death in
1976.

The first Five-Year Plan.   Moving quickly but cautiously, Mao struck at the
absentee landlords who dominated China's vast countryside. Knowing the
peasants would have to be led gradually to collectivized farming, he encouraged them to join the authorities in taking the land from its absent and exploitative owners. In only two years this popular policy saw most of the large
estates reduced to peasant ownership.

At the same time, Mao launched drives to increase social justices. Perhaps the most important of these campaigns was to improve the status of
women. Declaring that "women hold up half the sky," Mao demanded that
women be freed from traditional male bondage. A largely symbolic yet important step along this path was to outlaw footbinding, the brutal practice of
tightly wrapping women's feet to make them appear to be smaller.

The next task was to socialize the economy. The first **Five-Year Plan**
(1953–1957) was designed to achieve economic centralization. Its goals were

Mao Tse-tung (1893–1976)   Corbis-Bettmann

to increase heavy industrial production, socialize light industry and retail enterprises, and collectivize the farms. Though heavy industrial production improved considerably, resistance to the socialization program grew in intensity until forceful measures were used. Although the merchants and artisans were displeased by the takeover of their businesses, the greatest problems faced by the collectivization program arose on the farms. Mindful of the disastrous Soviet experience, however, the Chinese collectivized the farms more gradually. Eventually, private ownership of the land was abandoned altogether, and the peasants found themselves on giant communes.

By 1957 the goals of the first Five-Year Plan had been largely achieved, albeit painfully. Yet, political conditions within the party remained unsettled. Khrushchev's de-Stalinization campaign encouraged for a brief moment attempts at liberalizing reforms within the Soviet bloc. Meanwhile, the moderates in the CPC, the army, and the government believed that Mao had outlived his usefulness and began to maneuver for the old radical's retirement. For his part, Mao felt exposed. The adulation accorded him by the masses suddenly became uncomfortably similar to Stalin's personality cult. Wishing to disassociate himself with his former personality cult policy and hoping to outflank his moderate detractors, Mao surprised his adversaries with a sudden liberalization of his own.

The revolutionized revolution. In 1957 Mao called on the people to criticize the government and its policies and thereby stimulate the rulers to improve the system. "Let a hundred flowers bloom, let a hundred schools contend," he proclaimed, thinking that the malcontents would satisfy themselves with superficial complaints. Instead, the intellectuals took the opportunity to criticize the government, the party, and the leadership at the highest levels. Stunned by their vocal and penetrating outcries, Mao reversed himself after only two months and stifled any further criticism.

Smarting from the failure of the *Hundred Flowers Campaign,* Mao was desperate for a way to recover his fading influence. Always the revolutionary, he again took the initiative. A **Great Leap Forward** was announced, based on the twin pillars of Mao's ideology: conquering material want by applying superior willpower (a very un-Marxist idea), and overcoming technological problems by organizing the masses.

Intended to vastly increase the industrial and agricultural output of China, the Great Leap Forward was an immense failure. The society actually took several staggering steps backward. The first Five-Year Plan had centralized heavy industry. Yet, the Great Leap Forward attempted to reverse this trend. Instead of bringing the workers to the factories, the factories were carried to the workers. For example, thousands of families were given small furnaces and iron ore and urged to produce pig iron in their backyards. Unfortunately, the iron was of such poor quality that it was practically useless.

On the collective farms radicalism was also the order of the day. Attacking the family as a bourgeois institution, Mao tried to destroy it by extending communalism beyond work and ownership. Barracks were built, mess halls raised, and people encouraged to identify with the commune as a whole instead of only with the family. By 1960 all pretense that the new program was succeeding was dropped. Production had fallen drastically and famine threatened the stability of the regime. Mao's prestige reached a new low as the Great Leap Forward was abandoned. Accordingly, he announced that he would retire from government life, preferring, he said, to remain chairman of the Communist Party. "Chairman Mao," the official announcement declared, "has retired to devote his time to theoretical questions." The years between 1960 and 1966 were spent in dismantling the most radical programs of the Great Leap Forward. The backyard industries were abandoned, and the barracks and mess halls gradually disappeared from the collective farms.

Not content to allow the moderates to dominate the revolution, Mao made another radical move in 1966. Using his support in the army as a power base, he called for people to rededicate themselves to the revolution and to purge the "reactionaries" (moderates) who were destroying the movement. Thus began the **Great Cultural Revolution,** one of history's most unique and remarkable episodes. Inspired by Mao, youthful radicals formed units called the *Red Guard*. Swarming like enraged bees, the Red Guard took over party and government headquarters, schools and factories, communes and collectives. The new revolutionaries subjected officials, teachers, workers, and peasants to rump trials and condemned them for "counterrevolutionary" offenses. The turmoil spread as violence increased, destroying property, purging officials, and disrupting life. Striking out against moderation, the bureaucracy, the intellectuals, and other nonradical elements, the Red Guard made the whole society captive to its destructive fanaticism.

By 1969 the situation had become so bad that even Mao admitted things had gone too far. The army was turned on the Red Guard and order was finally restored. When the dust settled, China found itself radicalized, but bruised and bleeding as well. Productivity had plummeted again, and the government and the party were in disarray. Thousands had been purged, including **Deng Xiaoping** (born in 1904). Others, all radicals, gained power.

The moderates' fortunes, at a low ebb in 1969, began to recover gradually in the early 1970s. Despite radical demands for sacrifice, the Chinese people increasingly expected consumer goods and a better standard of living. Meanwhile the deteriorating relations with the Soviet Union required a modified foreign policy, drawing China closer to an accommodation with the United States.

Because Stalin tried to manipulate events in China for the benefit of the Soviet Union and often to the detriment of China, Mao was careful to maintain a cordial but cautious distance from the USSR. Upon Stalin's death, however, Sino-Soviet relations declined, until finally they ruptured completely. The reasons for the Sino-Soviet split are complex, including traditional Chinese-Russian territorial disputes, ideological squabbles, a personality clash between Mao and Khrushchev, and a quarrel over whether China or the USSR should presume to lead the Third World to socialist liberation. Eventually, the conflict of words erupted into a brief shooting war on the Sino-Soviet border in 1969. To compensate for its worsening relations with the Soviet Union, China dramatically improved its relations with the United States.[2]

These events enhanced the moderates' position, and, led by Chou En-lai, they were resurgent by 1974. So complete was the moderate victory that Chou was able to rehabilitate Deng Xiaoping and designate him as his successor. Yet, the moderate victory was cut short when Chou died in February 1976. Buttressed by the support of an aging Mao, the radicals, led by the now-infamous *Gang of Four*—including Jiang Quing, Mao's wife—were brought back to power, purging influential moderates, including the recently

[2]In the 1980s, however, as China and the Soviet Union embarked on similar reform programs, relations between the two socialist giants became warmer. Ironically, since the collapse of Communism in the Soviet Union and Russia's struggle to develop a market economy, China's relations with its former ideological soulmate have become even better.

restored Deng. The radicals failed to win full dominance before Mao's death in late 1976, however, and, enjoying little support besides that of "the great helmsman," they were soon vanquished.

Finally dominant, Deng and his pragmatic associates have initiated far-reaching reforms in the social structure, the legal system, the bureaucracy, the party, and especially the economy. Although resisted by the military and the radicals, these reforms have brought major improvements in China's lifestyle and constitute a rejection of the ideological extremes Mao advocated.

Reminiscent of the Soviet NEP and Tito's later policies, the Chinese leadership has returned a large part of the economy to private hands and to the market forces. Retaining most heavy industry, transportation, and communications in the hands of the state, the Chinese echo Tito in calling their ideal goal *market socialism*. Responding to critics in the 1970s who complained that the reforms were not socialist, Deng pragmatically quipped, "It does not matter if the cat is black or white as long as it catches mice."

As a result of the reforms, the communes have disappeared and peasants, farming land leased from the state, sell many of their goods on the open market. Private entrepreneurs organize small family businesses, inefficient state enterprises are allowed to go bankrupt, and state workers are paid on the basis of productivity rather than according to Mao's egalitarian policies. As a result, China's productivity has dramatically increased, fostering an economic growth rate that is among the world's highest. But these economic achievements have been accompanied by many social problems. Inflation has pushed formerly fixed prices to unprecedented heights. Many people have witnesses a distinct improvement in their lives, but others—hundreds of millions of others—remain poor. About 100 million people have become displaced. This "floating" population has forsaken the countryside and flocked to the cities looking for a better life than they could earn on the farm. Unable to employ or even house such multitudes, the cities are suffering the inevitable resulting scourge of dramatic increases in vagrancy, begging, vice, corruption, juvenile delinquency, and crimes of all sorts.

Meanwhile, a social liberalization is progressing apace. The once-puritanical society has abandoned the drab Mao suits for more colorful and fashionable clothing. Foreign films and other products are commonplace. Sexual love, once a forbidden topic, is now among the most popular themes in literature, music, and film. Even nightclubs and disco dancing are enjoyed by those who can afford them.

Again reminiscent of the Soviet NEP, although social liberalization is tolerated, political liberalization clearly remains forbidden. Since 1989, when the authorities turned the army on thousands of youthful protesters demanding representative government and an end to official corruption, the authorities have continued to punish political dissidents and steadfastly reject any suggestion that they relax their grip on the reigns of power. Indeed, in what appears to have been a definitive statement on the subject, Communist Party General Secretary Jiang Zemin introduced further economic reforms at the Fourteenth Party Congress, but, at the same time, he proclaimed that China's political goal is "absolutely not a Western, multiparty, parliamentary system."

Perhaps because of China's spectacular economic success since 1989, the public appears to have accepted its political conditions, at least for the moment. The "iron rice bowl," China's social contract, seems firmly in place. It has the people accepting political domination while the party and government provide material security.

As for Mao's image, it seems to have been rehabilitated in a curious way. Many Chinese people now treat him, in memory, as something of a patron saint. His pictures, long ignored by the public, appear again and serve as good luck charms. Private shop owners also display his picture prominently in their establishments, even though their economic pursuits are an anathema to Mao's ideology.

While dramatic systemic political change currently seems to be only a distant prospect, significant change appears to be occurring within the party and the government. Since 1992 several important hard-liners have been either removed in disgrace or retired, while moderates have seemingly strengthened their hand. Public rejoinders from party authorities have cautioned against excessive radicalism in the party and government. Also, mild but perhaps important demonstrations of independence have been seen in heretofore unprecedented divided votes in the Peoples' Congress on matters of government personnel and policy. Many authorities read these factors as indications that Deng's inevitable departure from the scene (he turned a feeble ninety-one years old in late 1995) will be followed by continued commitment to economic and social reform and that political liberalization will eventually follow.

The Principles of Maoism

Mao's major contribution to Marxism-Leninism undoubtedly was adjusting it to fit Asian culture. To accomplish this goal, he made certain modifications of the theory itself, focusing on the central concept of social class. An agrarian country lacking even the small industrial base available to Russia in 1917, China was overwhelmingly rural, and so Mao turned to the peasants for political strength.

Populism. Mao and others realized that the future of the Chinese Revolution was in the hands of the peasantry. The problem of reconciling this practical reality with Marxism inspired him to develop a unique variation on the Marxist theme. Taking a page from the Populists' book, Mao gave the peasant a leading position in the society. Of course, the peasants would eventually have to be proletarianized, but in the meantime their virtues were announced to the world in Maoist literature. Mao believed that the peasants' simple, pure character, unblemished by the evil influences of urban sophistication, was the bulwark of Chinese strength. Later, during the Cultural Revolution, he called on Chinese sophisticates to "learn from the people," as scholars, managers, public officials, and townspeople were "sent down," that is, forced to the farm to relearn basic values through hard manual labor. Millions of people were sent to the villages to toil in the fields, disrupting their lives for a decade or more.

Perhaps demonstrating that the current Chinese leadership is not so far removed from Maoism as might be wished, it exacted the same punishment on the students after the Tien An Men debacle. Thousands of students were forced to serve time on the farms, learning about the roots of China (no pun intended) before being allowed to return to their studies.

Mind over matter.   Populism poses an ideological dilemma. If the peasants are the true foundation of Chinese society, how are they to be proletarianized without destroying their positive features? Mao solved this problem by resorting to a typically Chinese, but very un-Marxist, idea. Much less an economic determinist than Marx, Mao argued that ideological purity was more important than economic training and that the proletarian mentality could be developed through educational as well as economic experience. Hence, he maintained that the peasants might be proletarianized by being taught the socialist ethic, but that they need never leave the farm to complete the transformation. This *mind-over-matter* approach occurs again and again, not only in Mao's thought but also in his policy—witness the Great Leap Forward and the Cultural Revolution. In each of these events the Chinese tried to overcome massive material problems by sheer ideological commitment and exertion.

Permanent revolution.   Easily the most radical major form of Marxism, Maoism's principle of permanent revolution makes the development of a conservative status quo impossible. You will recall that both Marx and Lenin made vague references to the concept of permanent revolution and that Trotsky actually adopted it as a major theme. Mao, however, took the notion even beyond Trotsky's position. He argued that revolution was a means by which people achieved their goals. The road to socialism, he claimed, must be constantly punctuated with violence. This conflict, after all, is the essence of the dialectic. Great progress, born of turmoil and social disruption, is an inevitable fact of life.

The same holds for socialists' relations with capitalist societies. There can never be true peace or a permanent accommodation with capitalism because the two systems diametrically contradict each other. Violent struggle between these two antagonistic systems is therefore unavoidable and can be interrupted only by brief periods of mutual restraint. Peaceful coexistence is a fantasy that can be pursued only at the risk of betraying the revolution itself.

The mass line.   Like Tito, Mao feared above all that the Chinese Revolution might fall prey to deadly institutionalization and bureaucratic inertia. Combining his theories of populism, mind over matter, and permanent revolution, Mao rejected Lenin's elitist reliance on the party to lead the revolution. Mao maintained that the people are "intrinsically red" and that given the proper ideological direction, they can be trusted to strive for revolutionary goals. Accordingly, Mao invoked the slogan "red over expert" and he called for the mobilization of the masses again and again, thus visiting a series of sociopolitical thunderbolts on the land. The antilandlord campaign (1949–1952), the first Five-Year Plan (1953–1957), the Hundred Flowers Campaign (1957), the Great Leap Forward (1958–1960), and the Great Cultural Revolution (1966–1976) were major events in which the people were mobilized to accomplish the goals of the revolution. Besides these epic movements, literally hundreds of campaigns were initiated, and indeed are still being invoked, to reach desired goals: Anti-insect and rodent campaigns, anticorruption movements, sanitary campaigns, and tree planting campaigns are examples of the frequent phenomena of Chinese life which entreat citizens to produce more, conduct themselves properly, and stamp out hazards to health.

The bourgeoisie.   When the communists came to power in 1948–1949, the economy was in a sorry state, having been battered by almost four decades of war and revolution. Regardless of Marxist doctrine, Lenin's experience with war communism had taught that immediate socialization of an economy could be dangerous. Though merchants and industrialists were not a large percentage of the population, Mao and his advisers knew that they were important to the economic stability of China, making their immediate elimination unwise. Consequently, he decided that, at least for a time, some members of the bourgeois class had to be tolerated in China.

Such a rationalization for maintaining capitalism has implications far beyond a simple pragmatic accommodation. In Mao's theory of *nonantagonistic contradictions* China was seen to be made up of four harmonious classes: the proletariat, peasantry, the petty bourgeoisie (intellectuals, artisans, and managers), and the national bourgeoisie (patriotic merchants and business owners). These diverse classes could coexist in peace because, while different, their interests were not necessarily in conflict.

By contrast, the evil elements in the society were those that exploited the Chinese people: the landlords and the *imperialist capitalists* (capitalists with foreign ties). In this theory Mao took a stance that is typical of leaders in countries that were formerly colonies. The question of class differences, the feature of utmost importance to Marx, was played down, and foreign exploitation, or imperialism, was stressed. Imperialism is a major theme in Maoist thought, as in Lenin's, though their definitions differ. To combat the evils of imperialism, Mao, like Stalin, turned to nationalism. Accordingly, although never greatly appreciated, Chinese capitalists who had no foreign dealings were tolerated, whereas those with foreign connections were persecuted. This blatant contradiction of Marxist ideals demonstrates that nationalism and anti-imperialism are powerful factors in Mao's thought. Nonetheless, when the communists thought that they had learned enough to run the privately owned enterprises themselves, even the national bourgeoisie was eliminated and the enterprises were nationalized.

Guerrilla warfare.   Perhaps the Maoist idea most widely applied is the theory of guerrilla warfare. Both Marx and Lenin believed that power could be seized at a single stroke and that the violent portion of a Marxist revolution would be very short. The two differed only on tactics, Marx believing that the revolution would happen by itself, Lenin supporting a conspiratorial approach. Mao, by contrast, argued that revolutions in the less developed world would have to extend over a long period. Lacking a doctrine to justify such a revolution, Mao developed one himself, setting down its principles in his famous work *Yu Chi Chan* (Guerrilla Warfare). In this book Mao divides guerrilla warfare into two basic parts: *military* and *political.*

Mao saw the military part of a guerrilla war as having three distinct phases. During the first phase the soldiers concentrate on building secure bases, or *safe zones,* in which to rest, refit, and train their troops. The second phase involves numerous small groups attacking the enemy by means of ambush and other guerrilla activities. The final phase begins only after victory is certain and consists of large troop maneuvers and battles similar to those of a conventional war.

The military goal of a guerrilla war is very clear. "The first law of war," Mao wrote, "is to preserve ourselves and destroy the enemy." Mao clearly warns against seeing territorial gains as a major goal. The only real objective must be to destroy the fighting capacity of the opponent. With this in mind Mao also warned that a guerrilla force should carefully choose when it fights, avoiding any battle it is unsure of winning. The only territory essential to the guerrilla is the safe zones. No other territory is worth a fight. In a guerrilla war there may be no defensive battles. If any area is given up to a superior force, with patience and cunning it will be regained later. This strategy is most clearly expressed in Mao's famous dictum, "When guerrillas engage a stronger enemy, they withdraw when he advances; harass him when he stops; strike when he is weary, pursue him when he withdraws." Of greatest importance is the guerrillas' constant field position, from which they always put pressure on the enemy. Never destroyed, always there, the guerrillas give an appearance of invincibility, humiliating the enemy, who in the eyes of the people cannot defeat a ragtag band of jungle fighters.

More important to Mao than military operations were the political activities of the guerrilla force. Mao fully expected every soldier to do more teaching than fighting. The war would be won by convincing the peasants of the rightness of the cause rather than by defeating the enemy militarily. This emphasis on converting the people is in reality another expression of the peasant-centeredness of Mao's thought. His strategy, to "surround the cities with the countryside," had little to do with actually holding territory. Rather, it was based on a desire to win the support of the peasants, thus isolating the enemy in the cities and making its defeat inevitable.

Mao was very explicit about the methods that should be used in converting the peasants. First, the soldiers must set a good example. Mao therefore banned the use of opium in the army and insisted that the troops treat the local people with respect. He also commanded that officers live no better than their troops.

When a guerrilla unit first occupied an area, it was to gain the confidence of the peasants by helping them create local governments. This would weaken their political loyalty to the enemy. Moreover, local councils would serve as a base of local resistance if the area ever had to be left to the enemy. Next, the land was to be redistributed—taken from the landlords and given to the people who farmed it—thus giving the peasants an economic stake in the guerrilla cause. Also, the guerrilla soldiers would devote a good deal of time to rebuilding the villages in order to put the peasants on an equal and friendly footing with the soldiers as they shared their labor. During this process the guerrillas would constantly teach the peasants the goals of the revolution, pointing out its benefits and reminding them of the enemy's evil policies.

By such means, Mao believed, the guerrilla force would build an invincible base of support. As peasant support grew, supplies, recruits, and information about the enemy would increase, strengthening the guerrilla units. At the same time, the enemy would grow increasingly isolated and weak as the ring around the cities became tighter and tighter, eventually stifling the enemy's initiative and sapping its power. In time the pressure would become unendurable and would bring about the enemy's collapse.

Successful not only in China, Mao's ideas on guerrilla warfare were applied throughout the developing world. Adapting Mao's military ideas to Latin American conditions, Fidel Castro seized power in Cuba and developed a unique variant of Marxism.

CUBA

In many ways Cuba is unique among Marxist-Leninist states, while in other ways its experience was anticipated in other lands, especially in China.

The Cuban Revolution

Castro, a well-educated man, began the practice of law in Havana and seemed to be on his way to becoming part of the small elite class that controlled most of the wealth in the country. However, his liberal tendencies were set in motion by the return to power of the grisly dictator Fulgencio Batista (1901–1973) after an eighteen-year absence. At the head of a tiny revolutionary group, Castro tried unsuccessfully to seize a military installation in 1953; he and his followers were easily captured and imprisoned.

Released from prison in 1955, Castro went into exile. In Mexico he trained a small group of revolutionaries to invade his homeland. In December 1956 he and his small party landed in Cuba and began to fight the government forces from a base in the Sierra Maestra Mountains. Castro began to build a following among the peasants, to whom he promised reform and land redistribution. In time his partisans took an ever-greater toll on the in-

Fidel Ruiz Castro (1927–   )   Charles Tasnadi, AP/Wide World Photos

effective Batista forces. Finally, the government collapsed, and Batista fled, leaving the capital open to Castro's occupation in December 1959.

Unquestionably a leftist, Castro was almost certainly not a Marxist during his days in the mountains. Indeed, the Cuban Marxists ignored him until very late, coming to his side, along with almost every other antigovernment group, only after he had begun to succeed. Yet, Castro was influenced from the beginning by a few committed Marxists such as the Argentine revolutionary Che Guevara (1928–1967).

His conversion to Marxism-Leninism after coming to power makes Castro unique. Cuba is the only country to become communist as a result of a movement in which the revolution was not carried out by a cadre of dedicated party members. In fact, the party and its functions are still very limited in Cuba as compared with other communist states.

Whether Castro would have created a communist system on his own is, of course, impossible to say. Certainly, Cuba would have been a socialist state. However, the hostility of the United States government toward the Castro regime from 1959 to 1961 drove Castro to seek the protection of the Soviet Union and thereby wedding Cuba to the Soviet bloc and expanding Soviet interests into the Western Hemisphere.

Once associated with the Marxist camp, Castro embarked on a number of Soviet-type, but ill-conceived, policies. Setting a goal of rapid industrialization, an almost impossible task for Cuba, the government met with one enormous disaster after another. With production falling drastically, severe rationing became necessary. The situation was so desperate that the Soviet Union had to come to Cuba's rescue with billions of dollars per year in aid.

Failing miserably in his attempt to transform Cuba into an industrial nation, Castro abruptly reversed himself, turning Cuba toward the goal of becoming a prosperous agricultural nation. In the mid-1960s he announced that by 1970 Cuba would produce ten million tons of sugar per year. This goal too proved impossible. Cuba's sugar production barely reached half the projected amount, except for the most extraordinary years.

The 1970s witnessed the development of more modest and realistic economic goals. At the same time, aided by the Soviets who bought Cuban sugar at inflated prices and sold oil to Cuba at about half the market rate, Cuba initiated policies that resulted in several important social achievements. Illiteracy was eliminated within twenty years and now free education is provided to all, a rare benefit in the region. Cubans now enjoy the best medical care and standard of health in Latin America. Housing construction has moved masses of people from hovels to sparse but adequate apartments. Full employment was achieved and the wretched poverty of prerevolutionary times has been eradicated. Hunger, until recently, had become a thing of the past. And racial equality was significantly enhanced.

Despite much progress, Cuba remained an underdeveloped country for two reasons. First, Cuban planners and economic managers have blundered repeatedly, failing to reach their goals and wasting resources. Second, policies by the United States government have consistently and deliberately impeded Cuban economic success. Since 1960 the United States has boycotted Cuba. This policy has made it very difficult for Cuba to sell its goods outside the Eastern Bloc and to modernize its industrial plant. Additionally, the United States sponsored a "secret war" against Cuba. Saboteurs and terrorists supported by the United States have infiltrated Cuba, burning sugar fields and destroying machinery, to say nothing of repeatedly trying to assassinate Castro himself. Redoubled by the Reagan and Bush administrations, until recently, these policies seemed only to have stiffened Cuban resolve against the United States—anti-Yankeeism is indeed the hallmark of Fidelismo. American militance also prompted the Castro government to militarize the society, denying Cuban people many human liberties, and it drove Cuba to even greater reliance on the Soviet Union.

With the collapse of the Soviet Union in 1991, however, Russian aid to Cuba was halted and even the Russian troops in Cuba were removed. With critical support for Cuba ended, the island nation has tumbled into an economic crisis—one that has been exacerbated by a collapse of world sugar prices. (Cuba receives 75 percent of its export income from the sale of sugar.)

Suddenly Cubans are experiencing shortages of food, soap, pharmaceuticals, paper, all manner of consumer goods, and energy. Food shortages have necessitated severe rationing of almost every staple. Unable to supplement its own modest oil production with Russian oil sold at below market price, Cuba has become a nation of bicycle riders. Its citizens are burdened by frequent, long blackouts as electricity is conserved. Before the Soviet collapse, 85 percent of Cuba's foreign trade was with the Eastern Bloc. Now its factories operate at only 20 percent of capacity.

Although Castro shouts "socialism or death," the serious economic conditions have forced him to bend. He has allowed several joint ventures with West European states, and central planning has almost become moot. To entice foreign capital investment, Castro has had to encourage tourism. This has led to legalizing the formerly reviled dollar, creating foreign currency stores that sell an abundance of products Cuban citizens cannot buy, and tolerating prostitution and other kinds of vice. Domestically the system has grudgingly been liberalized by the conversion of over 1,100 state farms into cooperatives and the sanctioning of over 140 different private enterprise occupations which now employ almost one-third of Cuba's labor force. Even so, the crisis continues to deepen and the widespread popularity Castro has traditionally enjoyed is beginning to erode. In response, Castro has begun to tighten his grip, suppressing demands for reform and warning his people of the potential for a new American invasion of the island.

Fidelismo

Similar to Mao, Castro's ideological appeal is replete with nationalistic sentiments borne of anticolonialism. Where Mao said on the day the People's Republic of China was founded, "From today on the Chinese people have stood up. Never again will foreigners be able to trample us," Castro campaigns vitriolically against imperialism, putting special emphasis on the "colossus of the north," (the United States). In his radical early years Castro tried to ignite revolutions throughout Latin America by training revolutionaries and sending them to troubled Latin American countries. These moves failed, however, and Castro was rejected and isolated by his Latin American colleagues. The discovery of Soviet missiles on Cuban bases discredited him further in their eyes.

After the 1960s Castro increasingly portrayed himself as a leader of the "establishment" communist world. Far from being a placid leader, he sent Cuban troops to aid some African countries. It is alleged that he was the source of Soviet arms flowing to Central American leftist rebels in the 1980s; and Castro continues to condemn Yankee imperialism vociferously. Yet, his demeanor is considerably less truculent than in early years.

Politically, the Cuban regime is unique among communist states in two related ways. First, because Castro became a Marxist-Leninist only after he had come to power, the Communist Party was organized as an instrument of state control only after the revolution and has little identity besides that which it takes from Castro himself. Hence the party's grasp on the Cuban regime is tenuous at best. Although its members head the various public groups like the press, the trade unions, and the social services, the party seems not yet to have established itself as the legitimate organ of authority in Cuba. Accordingly, popular commitment to the party as the instrument of power is not keen.

Second, although Cuba's current problems have to some extent hampered public support for Castro more than any other contemporary communist leader, Castro still enjoys enormous personal support. Not unlike Lenin, Tito, Kim Il Sung of North Korea, Ho Chi Min of North Vietnam, and Mao, Castro is seen as the personification of a popular revolution. Similar to his predecessors, Castro has immense charisma that assures him of a great personal following.

These political circumstances offer both worrisome and happy prospects. Not having established its legitimacy beyond Castro's personal leadership, the Communist Party may find it difficult to retain control, or at least to assure an ordered transfer of power, when Castro dies. It is true that Castro's brother, Raoul, is his chosen successor and that he and two other Castro family members hold seats on Cuba's fifteen-member Politburo. Yet, like the Communist Party itself, Raoul Castro owes the largest measure of his power to his association with Fidel. It is not at all clear that Raoul or the party will be able to step into Fidel's shoes without considerable difficulty. This is not to imply, however, that the Cuban people will completely forsake socialism when Castro is removed from the scene. The social progress made by Cuba under Castro will not be lightly abandoned.

The record of Castro's regime is mixed. Despite continuing economic problems and concerted U.S. policies to impede its success, the revolution has achieved important social progress for its people. Advances made in education, public health, and racial equity have been significant. At the same time, however, the regime is guilty of official corruption, stubborn policy stupidity, and serious human rights abuses. Public pressure for change has mounted since the 1991 Soviet collapse, and Castro has found it necessary to modify his formerly intransigent support of Soviet-style socialism. Not only have some limited market reforms been allowed, but the state has even relaxed its restrictions against religious worship and political criticism. Even so, Cuba seems to be trying to follow the Chinese example of encouraging economic change, albeit in a very limited way at this stage, while maintaining strict political controls. Once seen as the *enfant terrible* of the socialist world, Castro's current lonely defense of orthodox Marxism-Leninism makes him one of the last stalwarts of the "true faith." Given Cuba's current deep economic crisis and in light of the developments in the rest of the Marxist-Leninist world, one wonders how long Castro's island of communism can endure the blows of this decade's hurricane of political change.

SOCIALISM RETURNING

When, at the turn of the decade, the edifices of communism collapsed one by one, some people in the West predicted that socialism was doomed forever. They expected that Marxism-Leninism in China and Cuba and Stalinism in North Korea would inevitably follow the examples of the Soviet Union and Eastern Europe.

Indeed, these predictions may still come to pass. The rigidity of Cuba and North Korea seem to assure that dramatic change awaits. Similarly, Vietnam also appears destined for significant transformation. China, on the other hand, may be able to continue expanding its reforms until its system bears little resemblance to its communist past. Yet, the passing from the world screen of Marxism-Leninism, Stalinism, Titoism, and Maoism does not at all assure that socialism itself will disappear. Indeed, recent events in the former Soviet Union and in Eastern Europe indicate quite the reverse.

Almost every country that spun off from the former Soviet Union is now governed by a former communist party member. This includes Russia, and even Lithuania, the province that led the others in the march toward national independence. Similarly, most of the East European countries, including Poland, Hungary, Bulgaria, and Rumania, have abandoned right-of-center governments and returned power to socialists. Even in the former East Germany, the Social Democratic Party—the former Communist Party renamed—has attracted a significant following.

Whether this apparent rebirth of socialism in Europe will itself last for long, it is almost certain that socialism will endure as a major social and political objective for a number of reasons.

To begin with, few societies are as suited as the United States to the uncertainties and insecurities of individualism. After having enjoyed the certainty of free education, universal medical care, and social protection against the ravages of old age, it is unlikely that many societies will willingly give them up. And if economic reality for a time forces a society to forego these amenities, they will almost certainly be reinstituted when they can be afforded. By contrast, the United States' current growing infatuation with right wing individualism seems to be moving cross-current of a cautious but definite leftward shift elsewhere in the world.

Marxism-Leninism and other forms of radical socialism may be ended for good—although not even this can be concluded for sure—but socialism, the proposition that all people have the right to a decent human life and to be protected by society from the aggressions of those more economically powerful than themselves, is not likely to be extinguished. Whether socialism's most idealistic promises are possible or not, the fact is that government can do things that no individual can duplicate with comparable effects. It has the power to regulate private firms, thus preventing their profit-driven excesses and even assuring competition itself. The government can inspect food, certify safe drugs and implements, protect labor, clean the environment, manage finance, and perform a panoply of other services for society that might be ignored without government intervention.

Quite apart from these mundane chores, the welfare state and the socialist ethic are too attractive to be long ignored. In fact, if socialism did not already exist, it would certainly soon be invented. Socialism's basest imperatives hearken to opportunistic politicians and its highest principles speak to the best in humanity. What politician can long neglect the temptation to buy popularity and votes by offering state-supported material security to the people, and what even moderately compassionate individual can long turn away from the less fortunate? Whether socialism is the result of the inexorable forces of history or the imperatives of human morality, whether society's plenty is to be produced and distributed by a centrally controlled bureaucracy or by some other means, the socialist intent continues as an ideal and human beings shall still seek a social and political formula to assure that each of their kind shall have and that none shall have not.

The economics of mutual protection seem less in question than its politics. While communism has presented a formidable, yet unsuccessful challenge to liberal democratic systems, the twentieth century has witnessed a second major challenge to liberal democracy, this time from the reactionary side of the spectrum. Unlike radicalism, fascism and national socialism reject democracy altogether, advocating a political and social order based on elitism, war, and domination—reminiscent of former eras. How these retrogressive ideologies attracted such large followings is the subject of the next chapter.

REVIEW

- Lenin at first tried to completely socialize Soviet society, but found that the process required more time, whereas Stalin resumed total socialization of the economy by using terrorist methods, liquidating enemies and promoting bureaucrats who would do his bidding.
- Khrushchev, a former henchman of Stalin, managed to end the terror but could not overcome the Stalinist bureaucratic grip on the economy.
- The Brezhnev era stultified the Soviet system, miring it in corruption and stagnation.
- Gorbachev's reforms failed to save a declining Soviet Union. It collapsed and broke into several independent states, each seeking a formula for political and economic rejuvenation.
- Fearing that the bureaucracy would smother the communist revolution, Tito embarked on a flexible approach to Marxism-Leninism. It succeeded for a time, but Tito's death was followed by an economic crisis and a civil war among Yugoslavia's national groups, ending the socialist experiment.
- Mao Tse-tung modified Marxism-Leninism to suit Asian traditions. Also wary of the stifling effects of bureaucracy, Mao emphasized peasant values and ideological commitment. His guerrilla warfare tactics have been used by many people in the underdeveloped world to promote leftist insurgencies.
- Mao's death brought the moderates to power. Although they have made many significant economic changes, they have so far hesitated at pursuing political liberalization.
- Castro has accomplished many important social reforms in Cuba. However, denied Soviet aid since 1991, Cuba's economy is reaching a crisis point. Castro's Marxism-Leninism is heavily infused with nationalism and anticolonialism.
- Marxism-Leninism and Stalinism have each been largely discredited. Socialism, however, continues and is expected to gain adherents because its goals are so attractive.

SUGGESTIONS FOR FURTHER READING

ADELMAN, JONATHAN R., *Torrent of Spring: Soviet and Post-Soviet Politics.* New York: McGraw-Hill, 1995.

BARADAT, LEON P., *Soviet Political Society,* 3rd ed, Englewood Cliffs, NJ: Prentice Hall, 1992.

BIALER, SEWERYN, *Stalin's Successors.* New York: Cambridge University Press, 1982.

CARRÈRE D'ENCAUSSE, HÉLÈNE, *The End of the Soviet Empire*. New York: Random House, 1993.

COHEN, STEPHEN F., *Rethinking the Soviet Experience*. New York: Oxford University Press, 1985.

GORBACHEV, MIKHAIL S., *Perestroika*. New York: Harper & Row, 1987.

GRIFFITH, SAMUEL B., *Mao Tse-tung: On Guerrilla Warfare*. New York: Praeger, 1961.

HINTON, HAROLD C., *An Introduction to Chinese Politics*. New York: Praeger, 1973.

HSU, ROBERT C., *Economic Theories In China*. New York: Cambridge University Press, 1991.

KAPLE, DEBORAH A., *Dream of a Red Factory: The Legacy of High Stalinism In China*. New York: Oxford University Press, 1994.

LENIN, V. I., *State and Revolution*. New York: International Publishing, 1943.

MOODY, PETER R., JR., *Chinese Politics After Mao*. New York: Oxford University Press, 1983.

OPPENHEIMER, ANDRES, *Castro's Final Hour*. New York: Simon & Schuster, 1992.

REMNICK, DAVID, *Lenin's Tomb: The Last Days of the Soviet Empire*. New York: Random House, 1993.

ROZMAN, GILBERT, ed., *Dismantling Communism*. Washington, DC: Woodrow Wilson Center Press, 1992.

SINGLETON, FRED, *Twentieth-Century Yugoslavia*. New York: Columbia University Press, 1976.

SHORT, MARGARET I., *Love and Religion In Marxist Cuba*. New Brunswick, NJ: Transaction, 1993.

TOWNSEND, JAMES R., *Politics in China*. Boston: Little, Brown, 1974.

TROTSKY, LEON, *The Permanent Revolution*. trans. Max Shachtman. New York: Pioneer, 1931.

VON RAUCH, GEORG, *A History of Soviet Russia*, 6th ed. New York: Praeger, 1972.

WOODWARD, SUSAN L., *Socialist Unemployment: The Political Economy of Yugoslavia*. Ewing, NJ: Princeton University Press, 1995.

YAN SUN, *The Chinese Reassessment of Socialism*. Ewing, NJ: Princeton University Press, 1995.

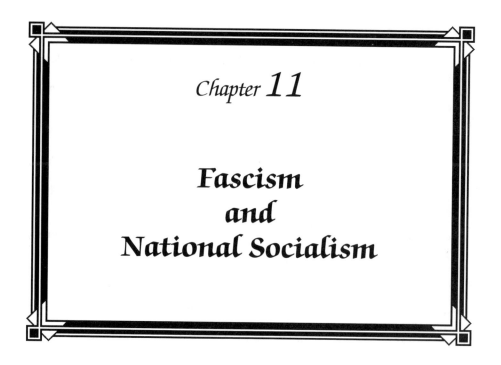

Chapter 11

Fascism
and
National Socialism

PREVIEW

The social stress created by rapid industrialization and urbanization together with the economic and political turmoil at the end of World War I caused the collapse of capitalism and the rejection of democracy in both Italy and Germany. The resulting political vacuum was filled by charlatans whose ideas constituted reactionary rejections of modern institutions and values. Men like Mussolini and Hitler called upon their people to forsake reason and prudence, to follow their leaders with unquestioned obedience toward mythical, irrational, and inevitably disastrous goals.

Forming totalitarian states—states in which individualism, human rights, and peace were viewed with disdain—the reactionary leaders built war machines and practiced imperialistic expansion, thus embroiling the world in the greatest human conflict yet experienced. The myths of the state or of the volk were used to mobilize people into a frenzy of bigotry, carnage, and genocide. The veracity of the myths were of little consequence, for they were used only as a means for motivation.

Under fascism and National Socialism, the shattered economies of Italy and Germany were revitalized and committed to rejuvenating their military ranks, which had been humiliated during World War I. Once built anew, the martial institutions became the principal instruments of domestic control and of international conquest and imperialism, subjecting weaker states to the role of satellites, servants of their political masters. The conquered people felt the whip of fascism and Nazism. They were impressed into slave labor for the good of the fatherland. Yet, even this bestial treat-

ment was restrained as compared with the penalties meted out to those who were viewed as a threat to the new order. Leftists, lunatics, Gypsies, and especially Jews were systematically brutalized and killed.

Mussolini's fascism and Hitler's National Socialism were actually reactionary movements because they rejected the values and aspirations that had developed in Western civilization over the millennia. In their place warrior states substituted practices that denied human dignity and justified unspeakable horrors. To make matters worse, these primitive impulses were exemplified by leaders who brooked no contradiction, no check.

Reactionary extremism did not die in 1945 with Hitler and Mussolini. It has reemerged from time to time, most recently in the early 1990s in Europe, although it now appears that improved economic and social conditions have reduced its appeal there for the moment. By contrast, racism, Christian fundamentalist fanaticism, and phobic attitudes about the government have combined with anxious economic circumstances to foster resurgences of the Ku Klux Klan and neo-Nazism in America. Additionally, the militant civilian militias expound violent, xenophobic, and antigovernment ideas and they blatantly threaten to immerse society in bloody conflict.

THE FAILURE OF DEMOCRACY AND CAPITALISM

It has been said that the rise of fascism and Nazism occurred because liberal democracy and capitalism failed to meet the needs of the people in some industrial states. If democracy did fail, it obviously did not fail everywhere, nor was the failure fatal. Yet, the fact remains that millions of people found that democracy did not provide the policies and solutions so desperately needed in the troubled 1920s and 1930s. Instead, they turned to fascism and National Socialism. Accordingly, we must study these reactionary ideologies, coming to better understand their causes so that they can be avoided in the future.

The Development of Fascism and National Socialism

Though the historical and philosophical roots of fascism and Nazism can be traced back to ancient times, the conditions in which they finally emerged were created by two contemporary events: the Industrial Revolution and World War I (the Great War, as it was then called). The full impact of industrialization was first felt during the Great War. Warfare, once the business of kings and mercenary armies, was democratized as citizens were mobilized for a total war effort. Millions of people were marched to the front, armed with new weapons of unequaled killing capacity. Hideous slaughter ensued as each nation applied the full weight of its technology, energies, resources, and inventiveness to the war.

Expecting a short war, both sides were surprised to find that a stale-mate had been reached. Their initial surprise evolved into disappointment and eventually into bitterness as the cruel reality of their situation became clear. Favoring the doctrine of attack (what the French called *élan*), generals carelessly hurled troops at defenders whose withering machine gun and ar-tillery fire cut them down as they became entangled in barbed wire. Think-ing that victory would go to the side that pressed the attack, but confronted with invincible defenses, military tacticians squandered human life in sense-less battles such as Verdun, where almost 1 million men fell in a battle that lasted for five months.

The folly of the Great War was made all the more painful by its irony. Technology had created a plenty never before possible, promising to elimi-nate poverty, and yet the world's most advanced nations poured their trea-sures into a European bloodbath. Similarly, as technology made possible a new mobility that freed people from their provincial bonds, the civilized world found itself engaged in a horrifying stationary slaughter. While the world's youth was dying in the rat-infested trenches of France, large num-bers of people came to the realization that science and technology, long con-sidered the solution to all human problems, often created at least as many new problems as they solved.

These disillusioned people entered the 1920s confused and cynical about their previous beliefs, and the postwar world did nothing to restore their confidence. Though the war had marked the end of monarchy as an im-portant political institution, replacing it with democracy, conditions in Eu-rope seemed even more uncertain than they had been under the previous order. Though industrialization had greatly increased productivity, it also tended to centralize wealth. Economic instability increased: Inflation was made worse by unemployment, and personal security evaporated. Millions of people felt defenseless against forces they had never known before and over which they had no control. Enticed from the farms to the cities by jobs that soon evaporated, they found themselves trapped in situations they did not understand and from which they were powerless to free themselves. Turning to government for help, they found their disillusionment changed to despair as it became obvious that no assistance would be forthcoming from that quarter.

Equally confused by the chaos surrounding them, the parliamentary leaders also lacked solutions. Some politicians desperately tried to restore or-der and prosperity, while others simply looked for scapegoats. Regardless of their motives, they all became involved in endless debating, bickering, buck-passing, name-calling, and irresponsible procrastination. Popular faith in democracy collapsed as people lost confidence in themselves and in the con-cept of self-government. Many, having abandoned religion for the new god, science, had been encouraged to support democratic government as a result.

Now, however, science was discredited, as was the idea of self-government, and it seemed to this confused and bitter generation that there was no truth left. Is it any wonder that many people put their last faith in the reactionary "flimflam men," men who promised everything to everyone, who simplified life's bewildering complexity by focusing all the blame on a single cause (such as another race or an opposing ideology)? Is it hard to understand why societies that had tried to find rational solutions and failed would willingly abandon thought and blindly attach themselves to people who claimed that they alone could find the truth? In an era when morality had been assaulted by war, poverty, national humiliation, and defeat—when rural values had been destroyed by urbanization—when people were so overwhelmed by the complexity of industrialized living that they began to question even their own self-worth, is it so unlikely that millions of people could become convinced that right and wrong were meaningless and that action was the only true value? Plausible or not, this is exactly what happened, and the world paid an enormous price for its mistake.

Mussolini

Italy, which suffered from almost all the conditions described above, was a prime candidate for fascism. A poor country, Italy joined the war in 1915, on the side of the Allies. But the strain of maintaining a total war effort was too great for this weak kingdom. Massive social and economic dislocation plagued the country, causing serious political problems.

The war's end found Italy in a desperate circumstance. Embarrassed by a poor military showing and by political weakness, the Italians demanded territorial concessions for their part in the war. After all, they had been on the winning side. When they were denied these expansionist claims, they felt betrayed by their allies.

As the veterans returned home, they found few jobs awaiting them, their meager benefits consumed by inflation, and their families displaced. Angry and disgruntled, they became increasingly hostile. With a wary eye on the Soviet Union, where the Bolsheviks were expropriating private property, and anxious about the veterans' discontent, wealthy industrialists and landowners began to fear that a Marxist revolution was brewing, especially since socialism was already popular with Italian labor.

Into this tumultuous situation stepped the unprincipled opportunist **Benito Mussolini** (1883–1945). Born the year Marx died, Mussolini overcame the terrible poverty of his childhood, obtained an education, and became a teacher. Drawn to leftist politics by his father's influence, Mussolini joined the Socialist party. He soon gravitated to the extreme left wing of the party and set out to become its leader. Since he was always able to convince himself of the rightness of his position, Mussolini's socialism was probably sincere enough until it became a political liability. He campaigned actively against militarism and condemned nationalism as a relic of a bygone era that should be replaced by internationalism.

Though a socialist, Mussolini consistently rejected egalitarianism as far as leadership was concerned. Heavily influenced by the works of the French philosopher **George Sorel** (1847–1922), Mussolini believed that great historical events were set in motion by the initiative and leadership of a small number of people. Although the masses were expected to progress to new historical eras, they could do so only if they were led by people who were more intelligent and daring than they. This elitism found him agreeing with Lenin's elitist revolutionary ideas during his socialist period. Even after he had abandoned the left, elitism remained a major principle of Mussolini's fascism.

Rising to the editorship of *Avanti,* a leading socialist newspaper, Mussolini used it to increase the popularity of his cause. Yet the elections of 1913, the year immediately preceding the beginning of World War I, denied the socialists a majority of parliament. Its disappointing showing in the elections contributed to Mussolini's growing suspicion that socialism was incapable of unifying his people. Further, since he was personally defeated, Mussolini came to regard elections as an absurd way to choose leadership. Accordingly, with the outbreak of World War I in August 1914 Mussolini carefully observed the political trends as they developed.

Following the traditional policy of the Second International, the Italian socialists campaigned heavily for Italian neutrality. Indeed, of all the national parties in Western Europe, the Italian socialists were perhaps the most loyal to the principle of internationalism. For his part Mussolini, in typical fashion, threw himself into the neutralist campaign with all his might, accusing any colleague who did not completely agree with him of betraying the cause. Although the government hesitated to enter the war, the popularity of this policy melted away as Italy became infected by the war fever that had swept through all of Europe by late August of 1914. Impressed by this change, Mussolini became alert to the potential power of nationalism. Finally, in October 1914, after only two months of war, Mussolini stunned his newspaper's readers by completely contradicting his previous stand and demanding that Italy enter the war. This reversal cost him the editorship of *Avanti* and his party membership.

Quickly finding wealthy interests that would support his newfound militarist and imperialist views, Mussolini organized a newspaper of his own. However, his new pursuits were cut short by the draft; he was severely wounded at the front and discharged upon his recovery in 1917. Still driven by the need to excel, Mussolini became involved in the politics of the war.

A secret treaty bringing Italy into the war had promised it large concessions in what later became northern Yugoslavia and is now the independent country of Slovenia. But this spoil was denied to Italy at war's end in the

Benito Mussolini (1883–1945)
Corbis-Bettmann

name of Woodrow Wilson's principle of national self-determination. Italian public opinion became outraged by the Allies' refusal to honor their wartime promise. This humiliation, together with declining social, economic, and political conditions, gave Mussolini the opportunity he needed. He founded a political party, the Fascist party, offering something to everyone. Supporting an eight-hour day, elimination of class privileges, universal suffrage, and tax advantages, he hoped to attract veterans, labor, and the middle class. Yet, his new party failed to win a single seat in parliament in the 1919 elections.

Twice humiliated at the polls, *Il Duce* (the leader), as his followers were now calling him, focused his appeal on the right-wing issues so popular among Italy's wealthy classes, hoping that with their support he could increase his strength through ample funding rather than by appealing to the unresponsive lower classes. By advocating *laissez-faire* and opposing the rash of strikes that had swept the land, he drew increasing numbers of wealthy industrialists to his side. Though he publicly condemned anarchy, he used money from his new friends to outfit a gang of thugs who attacked other street gangs supporting republican or communist ideologies. These *Black Shirts* vandalized, terrorized, and bullied, occasionally taking control of municipal governments by force. Paralyzed by this violence, the government did little to combat the fascists. Often sympathetic police would either aid them in their fights against the leftists or refuse to interfere with their violent activities.

In the elections of 1921 the fascist fortunes improved slightly with the victory of thirty-five seats in the parliament. Still, this was far from a parliamentary majority. With his third defeat Mussolini began to openly belittle the electoral process. Claiming that the vote was too insignificant to legitimize power, he suggested that only force could put a true leader into power, and what the fascists lacked in votes they made up for in brute power. Thus, Mussolini began his move toward revolution, bragging that he would one way or the other compel the government to cede him control.

A master of bluster and bluff, Mussolini laid his plans for the coup that would bring him to Rome. From Naples he demanded that the government be given to him, warning that he would seize it otherwise. Three days later, on October 27, 1922, his supporters were ordered to take over local governments, communication and transportation centers, and other strategic points. At the same time, between 8,000 and 30,000 people (estimates vary widely) marched on Rome to demand a fascist government. The government finally decided to restore order by using the army, but King Victor Emmanuel, hoping to save his throne, refused to approve the order calling out the troops. Poorly organized and led, the fascists could easily have been stopped at this point. However, because a fainthearted king tried to preserve his obsolete crown, the fascist prevailed. Two days after the march began, Mussolini received an invitation from the king to form a government. Accordingly, *Il Duce* assumed power, though he later admitted that he actually had no specific plans or solutions for the country's woes at that point.

Lacking a specific program or even an ideology, he began to react to circumstances, adopting ideological principles afterwards to justify his policies. Hence, fascism was not created as a coherent, logical theory of government. It was, instead, a collection of rationalizations for policies adopted in reaction to various political problems as they arose. The motivation for these reactions was almost always to increase the personal power of the leader within the state. Almost never positive, the method used to increase the leader's power usually played on the fears and hatreds of the masses, focusing their attention on real or, more often, imagined evils in the society and encouraging them to vent their anxieties in cruel and ignoble ways.

Hitler

At the end of World War I Germany was in even worse shape than Italy. The **Treaty of Versailles** imposed a harsh peace settlement on defeated Germany, unjustly assigning it total blame for the war. Consequently, Germany was forced to give up large amounts of territory to the victorious Allies, who also required ridiculously high war reparation payments. Fearing a revival of German military power, the Allies also imposed severe limits on German armament.

The turmoil that followed on the heels of defeat plunged Germany into a five-year period of economic and political chaos. Unemployment reached a high mark and inflation was rampant. Treated as outcasts and bewildered by their economic plight, the German people began to turn to extreme political movements for solutions: the Nazi Party among them.

The moderate **Weimar Republic** found coping with the tumultuous social, economic, and political problems very difficult. Although conditions improved somewhat in the mid-1920s, and the Weimar government looked as if it might succeed, the Great Depression struck in 1929, plunging Germany again into political and economic turmoil; a chaos exacerbated by the oppressive war reparations Germany was forced to pay. This time the democracy did not survive and the state fell into the hands of an evil genius: **Adolf Hitler** (1889–1945).

The son of a minor customs official, Hitler had an undistinguished childhood during which he apparently developed an exaggerated sense of German nationalism. Wanting desperately to become an artist, he went to Vienna in 1906, where he remained for seven years, experiencing only rejection, poverty, and humiliation. Ignored by the city's leading art schools, Hitler was soon reduced to painting houses, hanging wallpaper, designing postcards, and taking charity to avoid starvation. During his Viennese period Hitler was influenced by the anti-Semitism that was widespread at the time.

Adolf Hitler (1889–1945)   AP/Wide World Photos

An easy target for unreasoning hatred, Jews were blamed for every possible misfortune. Though he would exploit Germanic anti-Semitism to advance his political ambitions, there is no convincing evidence that Hitler's hatred and suspicion of the Jews was merely a political tactic. On the contrary, in his last days he took comfort in the grisly realization that, though the Third Reich had failed, a "better, purer" Europe would evolve because he had exterminated 6 million Jews.

Leaving Vienna for Munich in 1913, Hitler welcomed World War I and joined the German army in 1914. Fighting with distinction, he was severely wounded by poison gas, was decorated, and spent the last months of the war convalescing. Not having witnessed Germany's domestic turmoil or the collapse of the army at the front, Hitler readily joined the large number of people who claimed that the war was not actually lost, that Imperial Germany was instead betrayed by the "Jew-democrats."

In Munich at war's end, Hitler joined a tiny reactionary political party. Easily dominating the other six members, Hitler quickly became the leader of the organization, which called itself the **National Socialist German Workers (Nazi)** Party. Appealing to the dissatisfied elements of Bavarian society, Hitler soon built a following and attracted some important military people to his cause. Seeing Mussolini rise to power in Italy and the Weimar government at a low ebb, he attempted to seize the Munich government in 1923, planning to march from there to Berlin and bring down the Republic. Failing to get military support, Hitler's attempted coup, known as the "Beer Hall Putsch," was easily put down; it ended in his arrest and trial.

Because he still enjoyed the sympathy of some powerful authorities, Hitler received only a five-year sentence, of which he served less than a year. He was given fairly comfortable quarters at Landsberg fortress and spent his imprisonment writing his political ideology. This book, *Mein Kampf* (My Struggle), stated the basic principles of Nazi ideology several years before Hitler came to power, and even before Mussolini had developed his own ideology completely. A rambling tirade full of irrational outbursts and torrential verbosity, it is nevertheless a reliable guide to the Nazi policies that extended over the next two decades. Unfortunately, few people took the book seriously, discounting it as the rantings of a malcontent ne'er-do-well. Yet, fantastic as it seemed at the time, we now know that Hitler not only meant what he wrote but he was able to make it happen.

When Hitler emerged from prison in 1924, he found the country on the road to economic recovery. The new prosperity quieted the political unrest, and the Nazi movement lost popularity. Undeterred, Hitler worked tirelessly to organize the party. Interest in extremist politics was renewed in 1929 as the nation sank into the depths of the Great Depression. Seizing the opportunity to exploit the discontentment born of hard times, Hitler spoke out against the "treacherous Jewish democrats and communists." Passions flared on all sides; armed thugs were sent into the streets to do battle with each other.

Hitler's force, patterned on Mussolini's Black Shirts, called itself the *Storm Troopers (SA)*, or *Brown Shirts*.

Meanwhile the Nazi Party, heavily financed by wealthy industrialists, made significant gains at the polls. In 1928 the Nazis held only seven seats in the 608-member Reichstag (the national legislature), but the elections of 1932 gave them 230 seats, the largest bloc of votes in that body. The centrist parties lost power as the communists and other leftist parties also gained larger numbers of seats. Political chaos continued, and governmental indecision became chronic as street violence increased. Finally, thinking they could control Hitler, the conservatives in the government persuaded President Paul von Hindenburg, a heroic general in World War I, to appoint the Nazi leader chancellor (head of government) in 1933.

Badly underestimating their new chancellor, the conservatives were overwhelmed by Hitler's audacity. He outmaneuvered his rivals in a series of swift, decisive acts. Only a month before the elections in March 1933, the Reichstag building was destroyed in a fire set by the Nazis but which Hitler claimed was started by the communists. Whipping up a hysterical backlash among the people, the chancellor filled the German jails with leftist "traitors" to the Fatherland. His plan succeeded completely: The people flocked to the Nazi banner, giving Hitler a clear majority in the Reichstag.

After this move Hitler quickly consolidated his power. Statutes were passed outlawing opposition parties, strikes, and demonstrations. The Reichstag all but voted itself out of existence by giving legislative authority to Hitler's hand-picked cabinet. Von Hindenburg died the following year, and the *Führer* (leader), as Hitler's followers called him, assumed the office of president as well as chancellor and required all military personnel to take an oath of personal allegiance to him. Thus his power was complete. Adolph Hitler had become the totalitarian dictator of the Third Reich scarcely a decade following Mussolini's success in Italy.

FASCIST AND NAZI IDEOLOGY

Although Hitler articulated his ideology in *Mein Kampf* before he came to power, whereas Mussolini fashioned his after taking control, neither theory was developed into a logical whole. Rather, their principles evolved from pragmatic responses to various issues the leaders faced, guided by a reactionary rejection of the most fundamental principles current in Western civilization: human dignity, the right to freedom, human equality, rationalism, objective truth, and the desirability of peace in human relationships.

National Socialism and fascism are, beyond question, closely related; indeed, they share such concepts as irrationalism, totalitarianism, elitism, militarism, and imperialism. Yet, they differ in several important respects. Due to their philosophical and intellectual traditions, the German people were prepared for a much more complete acceptance of reactionary irrationalism than the Italian people were. Italian fascism[1] employed the corporate state economy, a phenomenon which never fully developed in Germany. And perhaps most important, Hitler focused on racism, while Mussolini emphasized the more abstract theory of the state. Although in 1938 Mussolini belatedly tried to incorporate racism into his ideology in an effort to ingratiate himself with the Führer, it never really gained much importance among Italians.

Irrationalism

Fascism and National Socialism are reactionary ideologies because they reject the most fundamental contemporary features of Western civilization, hearkening back to values that prevailed in former eras. Since the Enlightenment, as we have already learned, Western civilization has been based on the assumption that people are intelligent beings who can use reason to improve their lives. Indeed, reason is a major characteristic that distinguishes human beings from lower forms of life. The upshot of this emphasis on rationalism was the development of science and technology. Though science has brought us many advantages, perhaps its greatest benefit is the ability to determine objective truth. The scientific method has given us a way to discover the secrets of the universe and better understand the physical world, revealing facts that can be proved.

Fascism and National Socialism reject objective science and reason. Life is so complex and so unpredictable, they argue, that it cannot be understood by ordinary people. Objective truth is either a hoax or unimportant because the really important truths defy rational understanding, being random facts with no logical relationship to one another. Those who believe in reason, therefore, are deluding themselves and grasping at false reality. Reason, Mussolini said, is "barren intellectualism," lacking true meaning. The ordinary mind is not fertile; it is a wasteland full of mirages that give only illusions of reality.

Truth is a subjective quality, available only to a few gifted people whose *will*, or spirit, or personality, is greater than that of the masses. Those with superior will perceive a higher truth than others. They instinctively realize the

---

[1]Besides Fascist Italy and Nazi Germany, various authorities have listed the following as fascist states: Japan during the 1930s and 1940s, Spain under Francisco Franco, Portugal under Antonio Salazar, Argentina under Juan Peron (1946–1955), Greece during the late 1960s, Uganda under Idi Amin, Chile under Augusto Pinochet, and South Africa during the time of apartheid. Because fascism is a very unpopular term, such regimes did not openly claim to be fascist. For this reason, and because of the vagueness of the ideology itself, it is hard to say with certainty that all these states qualify as fascist regimes. Without question, however, these countries and several others, including Nationalist China, South Korea, and Paraguay, demonstrated fascist tendencies during important times in their recent histories.

right, and those who are not so gifted should listen to them, having faith in their leaders' intuitions and following their orders. One should note, however, that not even the specially gifted people in society realize truth through their intellect or through any other controllable ability. Instead, the source of the higher truth is instinct. The gifted ones simply *know* the truth, acting as neutral conveyers of the righteous energy, from its source to the society.

Selectively citing the theories of Plato, Rousseau, Hegel, and many other philosophers to justify his ideas, Mussolini turned to Georges Sorel to support his notion of irrationalism. Sorel had developed a theory suggesting that myth (accepted ideas that cannot be proved or disproved) can be used with great political effect. It can unite and motivate the masses, turning millions of individuals into a single entity by giving them a belief to cling to and a goal to work toward.

It was Mussolini and Hitler, however, who used the myth to the greatest political advantage. Mussolini demanded that his audience have faith in the Italian myths, abandoning other loyalties for this higher reality. "We have created our myth," he shouted. "The myth is a faith, it is passion. It is not necessary that it be a reality. It is reality by the fact that it is a goal, a hope, a faith. . . ." Myth, therefore, though it could not be scientifically or objectively proved, was true simply because it existed and served a purpose.

The purpose of myth was to mobilize the masses and channel them into a course of action. Again relying on irrationalism for support, Mussolini argued that the goal of an action was really unimportant. Meaning came from the action itself rather than from its goal. Action, he said, is its own justification; the struggle is as important as the truth or myth that motivated the masses.

Hence, Mussolini admitted that the main goal of his movement was simply to stir the people up and set them on a course of action that might have no provable value. Contemptuous of intellectual conviction, he demanded emotional commitment. "Feel, don't think" was his command to followers. Desiring only emotional responses, both he and Hitler used every available technique to ignite emotional outbursts among their people.

Largely ignoring the written word, Mussolini and Hitler much preferred live speeches in which they could use their considerable rhetorical talents, never giving their audience time to think about the true significance of their inflammatory words. The microphone, it is said, became the technology of fascism. It brought the fanatic leaders to previously unparalleled numbers of people. Encouraged to let their emotions outstrip rational restraints, the crowds would be brought to a frenzy, crying, shouting, chanting, and applauding on cue. Such was the hysterical substance of two societies that tried to rule the world.

German mythology. Strong as irrationalism became in Italian fascism, long traditions of mythology and philosophy made it far more potent in Germany.

Mythology, or folklore, has always played an important part in the German culture. Tales of the glorious Teutonic peoples have long been the subject matter of storybooks, serious drama, and family entertainment. The theme most often portrayed in German myth is that of the *volk* and its mystical powers. The concept of *volk* has no exact equivalent in English. More than just people or folk, *volk* refers to an inner quality or power residing in the German people. The **volkish** *essence* is a power possessed by the German people, yet one that goes beyond them as well. It is a spirit, an invincible, invisible force that is constantly engaged in struggle and conflict but emerges victorious after each battle.

Though the volkish essence is part of the German people, it can also be considered part of the German geography. In a mystical communion the people draw strength and courage from nature. Implying that the country is blessed with mysterious, inexplicable powers, German mythology gives particular attention to the deep forest. Mist, which shrouds reality, is also a favorite source of power in these stories. Early mornings—crisp, fresh, quiet, still somewhat vague to the mind after a night's sleep—play an important part in these popular legends. Perhaps most vital of all, however, is the soil. Giver of life, mother of plenty, the soil has unmatched mystical properties that nourish and enliven the German people and their volkish essence.

Mythology and reality thus were never completely separated in the German mind. When in the nineteenth century some philosophers and artists began to lionize mythological figures as *the* source of reality, many people were quick to take up the theme. The philosopher Friedrich von Schilling (1775–1854) managed to attract a following among the early German romanticists, including the famed author Goethe. Von Schilling argued that there was a direct relationship between people and their myths, that mythology unified people, actually creating a social and political unit out of otherwise separate and diverse persons. "A nation," Schilling wrote, "comes into existence with its mythology." Mythology was a "collective philosophy" that expressed the national ethic.

Richard Wagner (1813–1883), a master of the epic drama, gave myth added respectability when he brought it to life in his spectacular operas. Leading a group of artists and scholars in what amounted to a Teutonic fetish, Wagner established an intellectual community at Bayreuth that idealized the Germanic people by romanticizing their history and dramatizing their myths. Ancient heroes such as Brünhilde, Hegan, and Kriemhild were immortalized on the German operatic stage. Most important of all was **Siegfried,** the big, blond warrior who rose above mortal standards of right or wrong and triumphed in his effort to dominate. Hitler later became ecstatic when he heard Wagnerian music and made Siegfried the central hero of the Nazi state. Claiming that the Führer was actually the embodiment of the Teutonic essence and was destined to lead Germany to greatness, Hitler forged a link between himself and the ancient German myth.

Besides teaching the glory of struggle and the destiny of Germany to surpass all other nations, this flirtation with mythology encouraged a turn toward barbarism and a renunciation of Western civilization. Physical strength was prized, as was glorious death. In addition, the exaltation of Teutons or **Aryans** was soon turned into a justification for unbelievably brutal racism.

German irrationalist philosophical tradition. Unlike the Italians, who were forced to rely largely on foreigners for most of the philosophical basis of fascism, the Nazis drew from a rich store of irrationalist theory that had accumulated in Germany during the nineteenth century. This was not limited to mythology. A number of German thinkers began to seek explanations of life and nature in areas quite beyond the reach of human reason. However, it is important to note that many of these philosophers' theories were deliberately distorted by the Nazis to give an aura of philosophical respectability to their beliefs.

Johann Fichte (1762–1814), an early German nationalist, wanted to see the numerous German principalities united into a single, powerful teutonic state. Fichte argued that the German people were destined for greatness. Led by a small elite, they would eventually dominate the globe because theirs was a superior race. They would establish a new and more perfect order in which the Germans would rule the lesser races while the leadership elite stood above ordinary morality, tolerating no opposition.

Heinrich von Treitschke (1834–1896), an otherwise obscure writer, was rescued from oblivion by Nazi theorists because, like Fichte, his reactionary ideas suited their cause. Following Fichte's theme, he claimed that the Germans were a superior race. He also adopted philosopher Georg Hegel's nationalist idea that the state was the platform on which the human drama, the dialectic of history, was played out. Yet, von Treitschke went far beyond Hegel, claiming that people were merely servants to the state and must obey the orders of their political superiors without hesitation. Thinking, he believed, was a futile waste of the ordinary person's time. The leaders supplied the thought while less gifted people simply followed directions.

Important as these philosophers were to the Nazis, two others were even more central to Hitler's ideology. **Arthur Schopenhauer** (1788–1860) expressed irrationalist philosophy perhaps more starkly than any other major philosopher. To Schopenhauer life was the product of uncontrollable, inexplicable impulse, and it was therefore unintelligible and incomprehensible. He called the mysterious energy randomly motivating history the *will*. The will, Schopenhauer argued, had no purpose or cause and was unbounded by space or time. It was a blind, erratic, unpredictable force that manifested itself in the physical world but could not be analyzed rationally.

Beyond the reach of human reason, the will that produced all physical and intellectual reality made life meaningless. Finding no meaning or rational

pattern in life, people were fools to try to resist the will. Any rational explanation of life was artificial, since the will is a senseless fury, a force with no
justification. Since their source cannot be understood, the conditions of life
cannot be improved by human effort. Life is only a meaningless struggle and
resistance is pointless. Faced with such uncontrollable and incomprehensible
power, people have no alternative but to submit and let the will have its way.

Most important of all philosophers to the Third Reich was **Friedrich
Nietzsche** (1844–1900). At the outset it must be noted that Nietzsche would
certainly not have been a follower of Hitler. Though he was neither a German
chauvinist nor an anti-Semite, his theories were misinterpreted to serve the
Nazi cause. Greatly influenced by both Schopenhauer and Wagner, Nietzsche wrote about a race of supermen who would someday rule the earth.
Nietzsche used the word *übermensch*, which may be translated as "over-
man." By this he meant a race of people who were stronger and more righteous than the human beings of his generation.

Nietzsche argued that Schopenhauer was mistaken when he said that
life was a meaningless struggle. The meaning of life was actually to be found
in the struggle itself. Conflict purified humanity because it strengthened the
survivors and destroyed the weak, parasitic members of the society. Rather
than being a meaningless force, Schopenhauer's will was purposeful. It was
a **will to power,** a force that stimulated people to fight and to dominate. Human domination, the will to power, therefore becomes the highest moral expression in life. Accordingly, any attempt to protect the weak or the helpless
is immoral. Not surprisingly, Nietzsche found his society corrupted by
schemes and plots to protect the weak and the unfit. Especially corrupt, in his
mind, were Christianity and democracy. Christianity wrongly shielded the
weak from their superiors; democracy favored mediocrity and penalized the
excellent. Rather than freeing people, these two institutions created an enslaving pseudo morality. Consequently, Nietzsche proposed a "transvalua-
tion" of societal norms. In place of the Christian values of peace, humility,
charity, and compassion, Nietzsche demanded eternal struggle, arrogance,
selfishness, and ruthlessness. Instead of the democratic virtues of equality,
fairness, and happiness, he insisted upon an autocracy of strength, deceit,
and pain. Anticipating the end of a world dominated by Christian values, Nietzsche defiantly proclaimed "God is dead."

Such a world, he believed, would produce a new race of supermen,
"magnificent blond brutes" who would eventually replace the weaker human specimens common in his time. Admiring the Spartan life, Nietzsche argued that people should be hard on themselves as well as ruthless toward
others. Pain should not be avoided but rather sought out because it tough-
ened people and strengthened them for the battle. Power, Nietzsche said,
was its own justification: "Might makes right." When those with the greatest
will to power dominated all others, the most perfect possible existence
would have been achieved.

Hitler's attraction to Nietzsche's belief that the strong should be free to dominate the weak became clear very early in his career. In 1926 he said,

> It is evident that the stronger has the right before God and the world to enforce his will. History shows that the right as such does not mean a thing, unless it is backed up by great power. If one does not have the power to enforce his right, that right alone will profit him absolutely nothing. The stronger have always been victorious. The whole of nature is a continuous struggle between strength and weakness, an eternal victory of the strong over the weak. All nature would be full of decay if it were otherwise.

He returned to this theme when he said,

> The fundamental motif through all the centuries has been the principle that force and power are the determining factors. All development is struggle. Only force rules. Force is the first law. A struggle has already taken place between original man and his primeval world. Only through struggle have states and the world become great. If one should ask whether this struggle is gruesome, then the only answer could be: For the weak, yes, for humanity as a whole, no.
>
> World history proves that in the struggle between nations, that race has always won out whose drive for self-preservation was the more pronounced, the stronger. . . . Unfortunately, the contemporary world stresses internationalism instead of the innate values of race, democracy and the majority instead of the worth of the great leader. Instead of everlasting struggle the world preaches cowardly pacifism, and everlasting peace. These three things, considered in the light of their ultimate consequences, are the causes of the downfall of all humanity. The practical result of conciliation among nations is the renunciation of a people's own strength and their voluntary enslavement.

Racism

Although racism is not an important factor in fascism, nothing is more central to Nazism. Anti-Semitism stretches far back into German history, but before the twentieth century, it was no more virulent in Germany than in France, Russia, Spain, and most other European countries. It is true that German myth and philosophy had long stressed the virtues of Germanic peoples as compared with other groups. Yet, this history of ethnocentrism was not the source of Nazi anti-Semitism. Strange as it may seem, Hitler based his racial theories on the works of a Frenchman and an Englishman. In the nineteenth century the study of linguistics and anthropology had revealed that the languages of many people in Europe and central Asia were related. Though the evidence at the time was sparse, scientists assumed that these related languages had a common origin, and many scholars began referring to these supposed people—people who have not even yet been proved to exist—as *Aryans*. These discoveries sparked several theories about the histories of the various peoples in Europe. One of the strangest of all was developed by a French count, **Arthur de Gobineau** (1816–1882). This intelligent noble-man, who had served as secretary to the brilliant social observer Alexis de Tocqueville, was eventually sent to Germany as a diplomat. Greatly influ-enced by the German people, Gobineau developed a theory of racial superi-ority that was to have a profound impact on German history.

Basically, Gobineau argued that the Aryans had been a nomadic people superior to all other races. At various times they had imposed their will on inferior peoples and had established new civilizations. Unfortunately, the Aryans tended to intermarry with the inferior races, causing the decline of each of these civilizations as their purity became corrupted.

Though the Aryans, blond and blue eyed, had at one time wandered from the north across Europe and Central Asia, by the nineteenth century miscegenation had caused most of their descendants to lose their superiority. Indeed, there was only one area left in which the Aryan blood was pure enough to offer hope for a revival of human civilization. Extending across northwestern Europe, Gobineau's Aryan heaven included Ireland, England, Northern France, the Benelux countries, and Scandinavia. Yet, the purest strain of all, Gobineau said, was the German people. Though none of the re-maining Aryans could claim to have no trace of inferior blood, the German people were the least mixed racially. This genetic purity gave them an ad-vantage over all other people in fostering the next advanced civilization. This would be possible, however, only if the Germans and other Aryan peoples protected their racial purity against further miscegenation. Not surprisingly, these ideas were ignored throughout most of Europe but they became very popular in Germany.

Among the Germans who were deeply affected by these theories was the great composer Richard Wagner. Wagner's importance in popularizing and dramatizing German myth has already been mentioned, but his contri-bution to Nazi ideology is far more significant. In Wagner, three of the major foundations of Nazi ideology—mythology, irrationalism, and racism—are brought together. Wagner had known and admired Schopenhauer and had been briefly associated with Nietzsche. In addition, the German composer had met Gobineau and been deeply influenced by his ideas. Under Wagner's leadership the artistic and intellectual colony at Bayreuth became the center of German irrationalism and racism: The site was made a national shrine when Hitler came to power.

The Bayreuth ethic was carried into the next generation by a German-ized Englishman, **Houston Stewart Chamberlain** (1855–1927). The son of a British admiral and a nephew of the British prime minister, Neville Chamber-lain, this troubled intellectual was attracted to Bayreuth and attached himself to the Wagner household. He became an ardent supporter of Wagner and in 1908, years after Wagner's death, Chamberlain married his daughter Eva.

Chamberlain combined Teutonic mythology, German philosophical ir-rationalism, and Gobineau's racial theories, achieving in literature what

Wagner had tried to accomplish musically. He argued that the Aryan race had created all the world's civilizations, but that each of these advances had been lost as a result of the impurity produced by interbreeding. Chamberlain believed that all races were impure and mixed except the Germans, who were Aryan and good, and the Jews, who were completely evil. History was simply a struggle between the Aryan good and the Jewish evil.

With the "truth" established, the road to the salvation of humanity became obvious. The German people must protect and increase their racial purity and avoid interbreeding with Jews at all costs. This purification, he suggested, would be accomplished when a great leader emerged among the Germans to show them the way. Having set out on a course of deliberate racial purification, the German Aryans would prove their superiority by conquering the world.

These ideas were an instant success in Germany. Kaiser Wilhelm II became an enthusiastic admirer of Chamberlain, and the two men were soon close friends. During World War I Chamberlain supported the German war effort in the hope that it would lead to the Teutonic conquest of the world. After Germany's defeat Chamberlain's fortunes declined, but his belief that a leader would arise to guide a racially pure Germany to world domination never dimmed. So it was that in 1923, when Adolf Hitler was still an obscure politician, Chamberlain recognized his destiny and predicted that Germany would soon find its true master. Thus, the tradition begun in prehistory was passed through Gobineau, Wagner, and Chamberlain, and was finally adopted by Hitler as the basis of his political theory.

This long tradition of Teutonic superiority, expressed in German mythology, irrationalism, and racism, combined with the hardship and humiliation of the interwar era, made Germany an easy prey for the Nazi movement, and Germanic racism became the centerpiece of Hitler's regime. Following Chamberlain's theories closely, Hitler claimed that history was simply a struggle for domination among the various races in the world. The villain in this drama was the Jew. Hitler used the Jews to his own political advantage, blaming all of Germany's problems on them. His hatred and contempt for the Jews is frightening. "The Jew," he said,

> . . . is a maggot in a rotting corpse; he is a plague worse than the Black Death of former times; a germ carrier of the worst sort; mankind's eternal germ of disunion; the drone which insinuates its way into the rest of mankind; the spider that slowly sucks people's blood out of its' pores; . . . the typical parasite; a sponger who like a harmful bacillus, continues to spread; the eternal bloodsucker; . . . the people's vampire.

Hitler divided the people of the world into three racial categories. The *culture-creating* race was of course the Aryans. This group included the English, Dutch, and Scandinavians, but these peoples were less pure than, and hence inferior to, the German people. These Aryan people, he claimed, were responsible for creating every civilization in the history of the world. Specifically, he argued that the civilizations of India, Persia, Egypt, Greece, and Rome were Aryan creations. Since all cultural achievements were supposedly the products of Aryan peoples, and since Hitler believed that the Germans were the purest Aryans, he saw them as the only hope for humanity. "Man," he said, "owes everything that is of any importance to the principle of struggle and to one race which has carried itself forward successfully. Take away the Nordic Germans and nothing remains but the dance of apes."

Below the Aryans were the *culture-bearing* races such as the Asians, Latins, and Slavs. These peoples were racially inferior; they could not spawn a new culture, but they could maintain a civilization as long as they did not allow their blood to be corrupted by inbreeding with the lower forms of humanity. The last group, the *culture-destroying* races, included Gypsies, Negroes, and Jews. Because of their destructive tendencies these people were thought to be subhuman. They alone were responsible for the decline of the great civilizations.

Race, the dominant feature of national socialist ideology, was used to explain all aspects of the society. The *volk,* cradled in the German soil, was united in a common destiny: to win the struggle against the evils of the world. Because the Aryan blood was the strongest, the impurities among the German people could be eliminated by strictly avoiding miscegenation. A nation of supermen—of Siegfrieds, if you will—could be created by breeding racially pure people, thus producing Nietzsche's "magnificent blond brutes."

Everything must bend to the imperative of racial superiority. The inferior people of the world must be made to understand and accept their subordination to the master race. If they resist, they must be crushed and forced to comply, for such is the destiny of the world. "Jewish institutions" such as communism and democracy must be destroyed because they protect the weak and thus encourage decay. Objective science also fell victim to racism. "We think with our blood" was the proud, irrationalist slogan of the Third Reich. Hitler and his colleagues rejected any knowledge that did not prove Teutonic racial superiority. "Science," he said, "like every other human product, is racial and conditioned by blood." Accordingly, a new German culture—art, biology, architecture, anthropology, history, genetics, religion—sprang up, all based on Germanic strength and superiority. Even food raised on German soil was considered superior in taste and nutrition. If others failed to recognize the truth of German supremacy, it was because non-Germans did not have the superior understanding of the world enjoyed by Teutonic peoples.

Much of this would be laughable if German racism had not been taken to other, more pathological, extremes. Racial purity was used as an excuse for sterilizing thousands of people who were mentally or physically lame.

Ghastly experiments were performed on "subhuman" people to satisfy morbid Nazi "scientific" curiosity. Millions were marched into forced labor and often were literally worked to death, while others were executed for political and racial crimes, or just because they were either too sick, too young, or too old to work. Most horrifying of all, 9 million people, two-thirds of them Jews, were systematically murdered in the extermination camps that dotted the landscape of Hitler's empire. The stench of rotting flesh and burning bodies filled the air as Hitler pursued his "final solution" to the Jewish question.

Totalitarianism

A totalitarian state is a dictatorship in which the political leaders control every institution in the society and use them for political purposes as well as for the functions for which they are ostensibly designed. Hence, a totalitarian dictator dominates not only the government and political parties, but also the labor unions, churches, media, education, social institutions, and cultural and artistic displays. All aspects of society controlled by the state are used as mechanisms of political manipulation.

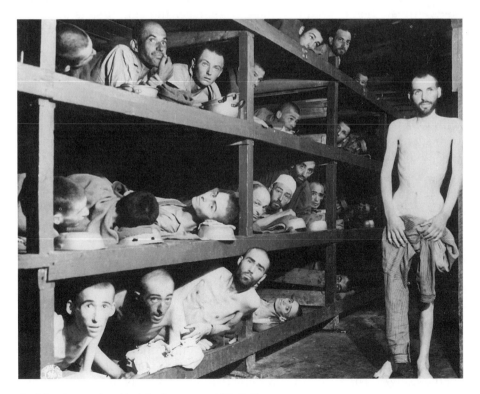

Jewish prisoners in a Nazi death camp.   UPI, Bettmann

The term "totalitarianism" was coined by Mussolini, and he also developed most completely the philosophical justification for it. Even so, his inability to subject the Catholic Church to his will—he was only able to force the church into an uneasy stalemate with his regime—prevented him from exercising totalitarian power in Italy. On the other hand, Hitler was able to do in practice what Mussolini could complete only in theory.

Theory of the state.   Although Mussolini failed to create a completely totalitarian state, he cannot be accused of failing to try. To justify the accumulation of such a huge amount of power in the hands of the state, Mussolini turned again to the German philosopher Georg Hegel. As we saw in Chapter 8, Hegel believed that history was the unfolding of God's plan. The nation-state was the stage on which God's plan was enacted. As the vehicle of God's will, the state had uncommon value, and its people should dedicate themselves to it. The people in the state, also part of God's plan, must take their identity from the state. Like Rousseau, Hegel argued that people derive meaning only through service to the state and that they become free only when they become subject to it. Yet, Hegel did not propose a totalitarian state. Instead, he believed that there were many human pursuits that were not political and that, while people should dedicate themselves to the state in political matters, the state should not interfere in nonpolitical affairs.

Selecting the parts of this theory that suited him and ignoring the rest, Mussolini transformed it into what is today called **statism.** The state had mystical properties; it was at the center of life, with incomparable purpose and meaning. Speaking to a Catholic society, Mussolini used a vocabulary with which Italians could easily identify. Only the state gave human beings their identity, he claimed, and only through it could they reach the "higher life," a condition he never specifically described.

Making use of the **organic theory of the state,** Mussolini argued that although the state was made up of individuals, it took on an importance that was much greater than the sum of its individual parts. As the cells of the body each contribute to a life far greater than their own, so too the state becomes a living being with an importance far beyond that of its individual members. Just as each individual has a personality and a will, the state draws from each, developing a personality and a will of its own. Having the greater will, the state rightfully dominates the individuals within it. The **will of the state** has such power over the society that it actually becomes the measure of all value, virtue, and wisdom. It is the "will of wills," the "good of goods," and the "soul of souls."

Faced with such horrendous power, the individual would be foolish to resist the will of the state. People must conform completely if they are to fulfill themselves. The state can make any demand, give any order, require any sacrifice, and the individual must obey. The power of the state is total, and the loyalty and commitment of the individual must be total. As Mussolini put it, "Everything for the state; nothing against the state; nothing outside the state."

Being the "creator of right" and the "good of goods," the state can tolerate no resistance. Conceiving of a society in which all people had functions—some great, some modest—Mussolini believed that all persons must perform to their maximum for the state, no more and no less. Those who did not meet their obligations were of little value to the society and could be removed. Such total subordination of people and human rights to a nonhuman institution flies in the face of the advances of humanity over the past several hundred years and is another reason for fascism's reputation as a reactionary ideology. Yet, the reward for compliance with the will of the state was great indeed. The "higher life" offered the purest, most "heroic" existence possible, even promising immortality in an indirect way. "The State," Mussolini wrote, "is not only present, it is also past, and above all future."

Unlike fascism, Nazi ideology gave the state only secondary importance. It was not seen as the central object in Germany; rather racial purity was most important. The state was only the arena in which the race built its strength and identified its leadership. In foreign affairs the state was the vehicle through which the superior race governed its inferiors. In short, states were jurisdictions into which various races were divided, but the races were of prime importance, not the states.

The combination of absolute political power with modern technology produced a totalitarian Nazi state. Structurally, the Nazi government was very similar to the Italian regime, but unlike Mussolini, Hitler was able to carry the totalitarian ideal to fruition. The traditional German state (that is, provincial) governments of Saarland and Bavaria, for example, were dissolved, and power was centralized in Berlin. At the same time, the Reichstag gave up its legislative power to the cabinet, which was headed by the Führer himself. The laws and courts were politicized, along with the military and the civil police. The Gestapo, a secret police force, established a reign of terror that has rarely been equaled.

To augment the power of his governmental institutions, Hitler mounted the most extensive propaganda campaign in the history of the world. With the expert help of his propaganda minister Joseph Goebbels, Hitler converted every possible medium into a political tool. He used every available technique to get his message across. He destroyed all books and films that opposed his views; he politicized every textbook, newspaper, magazine, novel, movie, radio program, and musical score. Manipulating all the information that reached the people, he followed the formula he had set forth in *Mein Kampf*: Keep the message simple, with little regard to its veracity, and repeat it again and again. A master showman, he manipulated people through extravagant, carefully orchestrated mass rallies, using symbols, insignia, regalia, color, emotional outbursts, and patriotic passion to induce collective hysteria. Thus, he spurred the German people to levels of barbarity and fanaticism seldom, if ever, matched in modern times.

Elitism

Again referring to Hegel, who argued that people are not equal and that the leaders of society are its heroes and therefore not subject to ordinary moral restraints, Mussolini and Hitler developed theories of *elitism*. People, they argued, are quite obviously unequal: Some are more intelligent, some are stronger, some are more talented, some are more attractive. To act as though people are equal is to ignore the obvious and to fatally deny a basic fact of nature.

Although people vary greatly, they all have an obligation to perform: to serve the state in Italy or the *volk* in Germany. Yet, being unequal, they cannot each make the same level of contribution—some are able to contribute more and some less—and citizens cannot rightfully expect to be rewarded equally for unequal contributions. Therefore, those who give the greatest service deserve the greatest benefit.

Both Mussolini and Hitler envisioned a highly stratified society with each person making his or her maximum contribution. As we have already learned, those who failed to fulfill their potential would be done away with. By the same token, if all did what they were best suited for, the best possible society would result. If, for example, the most able carpenters were allowed to build and the most talented bankers could bank and the most gifted teachers were assigned to the classroom, the society would profit from the best possible construction, finance, and education.

The same logic was applied to society's most important endeavor: government. Rejecting democracy as a sham founded on the false premise of human equality, Mussolini and Hitler were contemptuous of the masses—each referring to the people as "the herd." Political power must be left to the elite in society if it is to enjoy excellent government. Democracy, it was suggested, reduced government to the lowest common denominator.

Obviously referring to the Fascist party, Mussolini suggested that in the ideal system the best citizens would emerge. They would be the people most in tune with the will of the state. Relying on racism, Hitler suggested the same dynamic, except that the German elite would be those who enjoyed the greatest amount of the volkish essence.

And, they declared, just as there are some people in society who are better than others, so too there is a single person who is qualified above all, and that person should be given total deference as the infallible leader. Truly good people in society would easily recognize their betters and defer to them without qualm.

Il Duce and the *Führer* were endowed with innate power: It could not be acquired. Their claim to power rested in their intuitive, unreasoned oneness with the will of the state or the will of the *volk*. It was not something that could be understood rationally or controlled; it simply existed. Mussolini said that the leader is "the living sum of untold souls striving for the same goal"; he is the embodiment of the state itself. And the Nazi philosopher Ernst Hubber said,

> the Führer is no 'representative' of a particular group whose wishes he must carry out. He is no 'organ' of the state in the sense of a mere executive agent. He is rather himself the bearer of the collective will of the *volk*. In his will the will of the *volk* is realized. He transforms the mere feelings of the *volk* into a conscious will.

Thus, the leader was the indispensable and infallible conduit of the nation's will. He (it was assumed the leader would be male) crystallized and articulated the will of the state or *volk* and was therefore to be relied upon for the most authoritative expression of truth. Accordingly, the leader was to receive complete obedience. The people were not to question the leader's commands since his will was actually that of the society itself. To cement the point early in life, Italian schoolchildren were required to begin each day with the assertion "Mussolini is always right!"

The Corporate State

Fascist totalitarianism and elitism manifest themselves economically in the **corporate state.** Though Mussolini announced it as a unique economic system, the corporate state was actually borrowed from other idea systems. Again drawing on the theories of Georges Sorel, Mussolini used **syndicalism** as the basic structure of his economic system. Actually a radical who would certainly have rejected fascism, Sorel was the foremost philosopher of syndicalism, which would restructure society around giant trade unions. Sorel's movement was basically democratic because he expected that the syndicates would be popularly governed. You will recall that **Pierre Joseph Proudhon** also advocated syndicalism.

Mussolini stood this concept on its head, reversing the power flow. Instead of the people running for government through the syndicates, Mussolini intended that the *government would control the people through the trade unions.* The corporate state was based on a foundation of *syndicates* (trade unions) to which both workers and owners belonged. Strikes and boycotts being illegal, the syndicates were supposed to settle disputes between management and labor. By the same token, prices, profit margins, production standards, and the like were set by the state, leaving very few important decisions to the owners. In fact, though the Italian economy was privately owned, it was actually completely controlled by the state. Membership in the syndicates was technically voluntary, but everyone had to pay dues, and all were bound by the agreements they reached.

The local syndicates were brought together in regional federations, which, in turn, were organized at the national level. Every industry, syndicate, and regional federation was attached to one of twenty-two "corporations." Actually official agencies of the government rather than private firms, the Italian corporations governed the industries, owners, and workers in the economy. The heads of the corporations were members of the National Council of Corporations, by which the economy was centrally controlled and directed. The members of the National Council of Corporations automatically became members of the Chamber of Fasces and Corporations, Italy's highest governing body, which was, of course, headed by *Il Duce* himself. To be assured of absolute obedience at every level, the state appointed the heads of all the corporations, regional federations, and syndicates. Through this process Rome directly controlled the economy.

Besides serving as a tool for directing the economy, however, the corporate state was the primary means by which the state controlled its citizens. Through this mechanism almost every aspect of daily existence was controlled. Jobs, wages, fringe benefits, social programs, housing, retail goods, recreation, entertainment, and education were all part of this elaborate organization.

The corporate state was also the only vehicle for "valid" popular political comment. Convinced that general policy is too complex a matter for ordinary people, fascists discouraged popular comment on most political affairs. Maintaining that people are suited by nature to different status levels in life and are not qualified to hold valid political opinions on all subjects, fascism limited individuals' political comments to areas in which they had occupational interests. Consequently, farmers were supposed to make formal political statements only in relation to agricultural policy, while masons could discuss political questions only in relation to the construction industry, and autoworkers could speak out only on issues directly connected with their occupation. Only the elite, or the party members, were qualified to comment on general political questions, and even they were limited by their party rank. At any rate, the questions of popular political activities is an academic one, since the people were seldom given a real opportunity to express their views on political questions.

By these means the state controlled and regulated almost every conceivable social, economic, and political activity of its citizens. This made it relatively easy for the government to reward supporters and punish dissidents. Along with the party and the police, the corporate state was Mussolini's principal mechanism for creating and maintaining control.

Unlike the Italians, the Germans did not establish a corporate state, though there was considerable talk about doing so in the early days of the regime. The economy was tightly controlled by three super agencies. Industrial production was managed by the Estate of Industry and Trade, and the agricultural sector was controlled by the German Food Estate. As in Italy, strikes and boycotts were made illegal and the trade unions were dissolved. In their place Hitler created the Labor Front, a federation of worker and professional associations. Through these mechanisms all economic functions were manipulated by the state.

Imperalism

As we have seen, Mussolini and Hitler viewed society in terms of conflict. Good combated evil, strength fought weakness, purity struggled with decadence. Just as people within society vied with each other for power, so too should nations compete with each other for dominance, until the strongest national will reigned supreme. Mussolini, in an ethnocentric fury, claimed that just as people within society were not equal, states and their wills were not equal, and justice demanded that the most powerful will of the state should achieve supremacy over all others. Applying his racist theories, Hitler concluded the same. Since the German *volk* enjoyed the purist blood, they had the right to impose their will on all lessor races. To shirk this responsibility would be to deny destiny, rejecting rightful heritage, and thus betraying the natural order of things.

Imperalism (one nation dominating others) became the paramount mission for both societies. Exerting power over others within a society is a vital function of those who are best able to rule; imperialism is simply an extension of this principle to a higher, more important level of human relationship. Imperalism, Mussolini claimed, is the most advanced form of this natural regulator, which he called "the will to power." "The highest expression of human power," he said, "is Empire."

Arguing that the "higher life" is possible only when the greatest will dominates all lesser personalities, Mussolini gave imperalism a moral justification. In *The Doctrine of Fascism*, written in 1932, he said, "For Fascism the tendency to empire, that is to say, to the expansion of nations, is a manifestation of vitality; its opposite, staying at home, is a sign of decadence: people who rise or re-rise are imperalist, people who die are renunciatory."

As one might expect, Mussolini saw Italy as an imperialist state. Once great, Italy was regaining its status as a world power. Accordingly, Mussolini assigned it the task of recreating the Roman Empire. This goal became the national myth, stimulating the Italian nation to action. The absurdity of equating modern Italy with ancient Rome was ignored, since as we have already seen, fascists consider the veracity of a myth unimportant; its value is in spurring people to activity.

Hitler's justification of imperialism was basically the same as Mussolini's except that the Nazi dictator substituted the will of the *volk* for the will of the state. Believing that the strong must dominate the weak in an ongoing process of Social Darwinism, Hitler lusted for territorial acquisition. Sending out an ominous warning of this suicidal tendency in 1929, Hitler said,

> If men wish to live, then they are forced to kill others. . . . As long as there are peoples on this earth, there will be nations against nations and they will be forced to protect their vital rights in the same way as the individual is forced to protect his rights. . . . There is in reality no distinction between peace and war. . . . One is either the hammer or the anvil. We confess that it is our purpose to prepare the German people again for the role of the hammer.

Thus, each expansionist dictator threw his war machine against his weak adversaries even as Britain, France, and the United States appeased them in an effort to placate the aggressive titans. Italian armies were sent to conquer Abyssinia (Ethiopia), Albania, and Greece, while Hitler's *blitzkrieg* (lightning war) was hurled against Poland, and *fifth column* (collaborationist) reactionary movements seemed to rise everywhere. Finally, France and England resolved to allow no more aggression, and World War II began in 1939.

Militarism

The tool of fascist and Nazi imperialism is of course militarism. Yet, according to these ideologies, war is actually much more than simply a means of asserting the national will: War is the prime goal. Rather than something to be used only as a last resort, war is a spiritually creative and positive feature of life. It should occur often and should never be avoided merely to achieve peace. A particular war is ended when the superior national will has dominated its adversaries. Peace is not a positive condition but rather an interlude between national struggles for imperial dominance. Indeed, permanent peace is equated with cowardice and is not to be tolerated because it robs society of its vitality. "Fascism," Mussolini wrote,

> believes neither in the possibility nor the utility of perpetual peace. It thus repudiates the doctrine of Pacifism—born of a renunciation of the struggle and an act of cowardice in the face of sacrifice. *War alone brings up to its highest tension all human energy and puts the stamp of nobility upon the people who have the courage to meet it.* (Emphasis added.)

For Hitler's part, he chose to express the same sentiment with the racist attitudes of von Treitschke. War, von Treitschke believed, was good in itself because states, like people, were driven to dominate each other and warfare was the process by which national domination was achieved. Hence, war was a normal condition of human life. "That war should ever be banished from the world," von Treitschke wrote, "is not only absurd, but profoundly immoral." Permanent peace, he argued, would be a crime, and societies that wanted peace were obviously decaying. The entire society was therefore channeled into preparation for war. Every possible pursuit, be it school, work, pleasure, or whatever, served a martial purpose.

Struggle, conflict, fight, discipline, courage, obedience, the holiness of heroism, are among the terms that occur often in fascist literature. Dueling, swordsmanship, pistolry, riding, uniforms, weapons, discipline, and other martial trappings were valued. Masculinity and virility were prized, women being confined to the kitchen and domestic duties. "War," Mussolini said, "is the most important thing in a man's life as maternity is in a woman's."

Fascism's and national socialism's attempt to create *warrior states* is an important reason they are classified as reactionary ideologies. Denying the value of peaceful and friendly human relationships amounts to favoring a return to an ancient era during which those who were physically strong dominated everyone else and people were judged and ranked by their ability to fight. Accordingly, martial activities, emotional causes, and domination become the goals of such a society, whereas values like human refinement, rationality, culture, peace, equality, and brotherhood are rejected.

Despite all the rhetoric and emotionalism of these assertions, perhaps the essence of fascism and national socialism was captured in the fascist slogan "Believe, Obey, Fight!" Nothing better expresses the irrationalism, elitism, militarism, or contempt for the masses so prominent in these ideologies. This simple phrase says it all. It demands blind faith rather than intelligent commitment, it insists that people follow the orders of their superiors without hesitation, and it pits people against each other for no other reason than love of struggle itself.

Romantic, emotional, and violent creeds based on a militant rejection of the modern rational and scientific world, these reactionary movements offer little save the perverted sense of glory derived from annihilation and carnage. In a sentence which surely would have enjoyed Hitler's agreement, Mussolini said "Fascism brings back color, force, the picturesque, the unexpected, the mystical; in short, all that counts in the soul of the crowds."

CONTEMPORARY FASCIST AND NEO-NAZI MOVEMENTS

Chile and South Africa, the two states most closely associated with contemporary fascism have recently each moderated considerably. Chile's right-wing dictator, Augusto Pinochet, finally stepped down and after over a decade-and-a-half of iron-gripped political control, a democratically elected government is back in power. In South Africa even more dramatic change has occurred. Former President Fredrick W. de Klerk, bowing to the inevitable, but demonstrating significant statesmanship in the process, dismantled the infamous practices of severe racial segregation known as *apartheid*. To seal the change, de Klerk brought forward a new constitution, one giving South Africa's black population (three-fourths of the people in that land) the vote for the first time in modern history. As a result, a new government was elected, one dominated by black people, and Nelson Mandela, South Africa's gentle but irrepressible conscience for so long, became president of the Republic. Regrettably, however, right-wing extremism is still widespread in both societies and reactionary elements resort to violence to resist democratic trends and policies.

Meanwhile, fascism's popularity seemed to take a serious upturn in the early 1990s. Fueled by a global recession, neo-Nazi and other hate groups rapidly climbed in number and, unfortunately, in European public acceptance. Right-wing extremists were elected to the parliaments of Germany, France, Belgium, and Sweden. In Italy, a neo-fascist party even headed a right-wing coalition government in 1994, and the neo-fascist Liberal Democratic Party of Vladimir Zhirnovsky won the largest percentage of votes in Russia's 1993 parliamentary elections and the second largest number of votes in the parliamentary election of 1995.

The collapse of the Soviet Union and the Communist bloc in Eastern Europe caused immigrants to stream into the wealthy Western European countries, thus exacerbating public anxiety about the future and feeding the growth of right-wing reaction. Acts of violence against foreigners and Jews increased across Europe and racist inspired vandalism became a matter of concern. Many countries passed laws tightening up on the numbers of immigrants they would allow to enter their territories. France even went so far as to create a special police agency to focus on its problems with illegal immigration.

By the mid-1990s, however, the sharp right turn of many of Europe's societies seems to have abated. The neo-fascist government of Italy failed after only a few months, moderate people in each society mobilized to protest right-wing extremism, the sixtieth anniversary of Hitler's rise to power in 1993, and the 1995 fiftieth anniversary of the liberation of more than 300 Nazi concentration camps served as sobering reminders of the horrors incumbent in policies inspired by fear and hatred. Furthermore, the economic conditions improved in both Eastern and Western Europe, causing a reduction in Eastern emigration and a reduction in Western social anxiety.

Right-wing extremism in the United States.   The situation has not yet resolved itself in the United States, however. A complicated combination of factors has given birth to a rather widespread and deeply rooted resurgence of right-wing extremism.

The collapse of the Soviet Union has eliminated a traditional negative focal point of the extreme right. With that external danger removed, those Americans who tend to look for sources of great evil in their midst have come to see the federal government as a threatening and oppressive force which must be resisted; violently, if necessary. This political paranoia, fed by exaggerated notions of individual rights and xenophobic Christianity, has often been reinforced and strengthened by alliance with profound racial hatreds brought to new pitch by the enormous increase recently in immigration from Latin America and Asia. Accordingly, traditional right-wing extremist groups like the Ku Klux Klan, the American Nazi Party, and the John Birch Society have rapidly developed new vitality and memberships. At the same time, these movements have changed with the times and evolved new ideological doctrines that resonate with new generations of Americans.

Joining these more traditional hate groups are new organizations with similar extremist leanings. Racist *skinhead* groups attract young people who use anti-Semitism and anti-African-American or anti-Hispanic vitriol and violence as vents for their frustrations. Also, the recent profusion of militant civilian militia groups has complicated and heightened the lethal potential of right-wing extremism in the United States.

Analyzing the ideology of the recently popular strains of American right-wing extremism is difficult because not all groups agree about their goals. Common themes among all of them, however, can be identified. They include a black-and-white view of the world in which the players are either good or bad; the certainty that Christian fundamentalist ideas are true and constitute the foundation of a good society; a belief that people have a right to absolute sovereignty—thus, they and their property are virtually sacrosanct and government regulation and taxation are unwarranted intrusions on the sacred rights of the individual; a profound sense of foreboding about the future, punctuated by the belief that sinister forces are controlling society and are sapping it of its goodness and vitality; the persuasion that the nation's strength rests with its fundamental values and that evil people are destroying the moral fiber of the society; the conviction that the good people must be ever vigilant against unceasing and insidious efforts of the sinister forces to infiltrate and destroy the organizations that the good people use to identify and resist the bad; the commitment to defending their liberties with violence if necessary; and finally, the belief that life is only meaningful when struggle against the ingrained enemy is occurring. Norman Olson, a Baptist minister and a founder of the Michigan Militia defiantly said in a recent recruiting video,

> I say to you faint-hearted, if you love wealth more than liberty, if you love the quiet tranquility of servitude more than the animating contest of freedom, then go home in peace, we ask neither your counsel nor your arms.
>
> Bow down and lick the hands that feed you. May your chains rest lightly on your shoulders.[2]

---

[2]James Risen, "Militias Rely on Networks of Fiery Right," *The Los Angeles Times*, April 30, 1995.

These ideas are not new in the American experience. Exaggerated notions about personal liberty, mistrust of government, and beliefs of racial and moral superiority have been present since the earliest days of colonial America. Even political paranoia is no stranger to our shores: consider the various nativist movements in the last century, the great Red Scare of 1919, and the McCarthy hysteria of the 1950s. Indeed, one could conclude that Americans tend to be relatively susceptible to right-wing extremist movements.

The specific beliefs of today's right-wing extremists are a bit more difficult to set forth. White supremacism is a very strong factor among most extremist groups, yet there are a few that specifically disavow this bias. Most extremist groups view environmentalism as an unwarranted and dangerous threat to individual and property rights, but there are a few that call for an end to both racial pollution and environmental pollution in America. A militant opposition to taxation is not only a very common stance among these groups, but it is also among the oldest specifically identified evils in the movement. Gun control legislation is also a very common evil, so far as these groups are concerned. Indeed, if there are two specific policies with which these groups find themselves most at odds, they are taxes and gun control legislation. In a more general sense, socialism and liberalism seem to be used as catchalls for whatever is suspicious or bad.

An example of this sweeping condemnation and the extreme right's fuzzy equation of Americanism and Christianity can be seen in this rambling statement of Bob Lord, the leader of Pennsylvania's Keystone Militia. Lord asserted that what America needed was

> . . . a return to a type of government and type of morality America was founded upon. The values are, in other words, Christian values. . . . Another way of putting it is that we're standing our ground against socialism. . . . This is what is motivating the militia movement—that government is taking control of our lives in every extent, so that we feel we are becoming a socialist country.[3]

Although the concept of an international conspiracy to control the globe is well worn on the extreme right, the *New World Order* has arisen as a villain unique to this era. Ironically, the term was first used by Adolf Hitler, an earlier reactionary, but the term was recently resurrected by President George Bush at the end of the Cold War. Although Hitler's reference was to a world dominated by Nazi supermen, Bush used it in a more hopeful way. He described a world in which peace and economic prosperity was the norm. Left with no villain when the Soviet Bloc collapsed, however, right-wing extremists searched almost desperately for a new bad guy because, as was explained in Chapter 6, conspiratorialists are fixated on the belief that someone evil is about to take over society and enslave the innocent.

[3]Bill Steigerwald, "Spotlight Costs Sobering Glare on U.S. Militias," *The Los Angeles Times,* May 6, 1995.

Robbed of the "evil empire" for a villain, American reactionaries took up cudgels against the New World Order. Although a precise definition of the nature of the adversary has yet to be explained, the New World Order, it is suggested, is code for a massive conspiracy that threatens civilization. The people perpetrating this potential holocaust are described variously, depending on which extremist group is giving the warning to resist. Yet to be vanquished communists are sometimes suggested as the villains. Then, of course, there are other old standbys including Jews, international bankers, the United Nations, and foreigners of one kind or another. And, of course, it is often suggested that the identity of the evil ones is not yet known but that it is well known that they do exist and portend imminent danger.

Another unusual feature of this eclectic ideology is that the United States government has become a willing participant in these deadly efforts to subvert the society. As mentioned above, suspicion of the government has long been a tenet in American politics, but the suspicion is usually born of a contempt for bureaucracy and as defense against individual politicians who may trounce on the people's rights in pursuit of their own selfish ambitions, or that some evil people—the communists for example—have infiltrated the government and want to use power for nefarious reasons. The current reactionary phobia about the government, by contrast, is founded on a much more sweeping fear. They believe that the government's authority is totally evil and cannot be reconciled with individual freedom or with God's true will; that they are so incompatible as to be mutually exclusive. Thus, these reactionaries see themselves as soldiers in a righteous cause. They are called by a higher power to resist satanic control and they seem almost to welcome an apocalyptic fate in resisting evil.

About a year before she was shot to death in a 1992 standoff with federal agents at Ruby Ridge, Idaho, Vicky Weaver addressed two letters to "The Queen of Babylon" and mailed them to the United States Attorney's office in Boise. "A long forgotten wind is starting to blow," she wrote.

> "Do you hear the approaching thunder? . . . The stink of your lawless government has reached Heaven, the abode of Yahweh or Yahshua. Whether we live or whether we die, we will not bow to your evil commandments."[4]

There is little or no recognition in this ideology that government does at least some good things, and the extremist firebrands offer no coherent suggestion for what institutions society might use to resolve its problems in the absence of government. (These blind spots are particularly ironic since several leaders of this movement, including Randy Weaver who battled with federal agents on Ruby Ridge and Jack Maxwell Oliphant of Arizona, who is among the founders of one of the first militant civilian militias, the Arizona

[4]Kim Murphy, "Both Sides Still Wrestling With Horrors of Ruby Ridge," *The Los Angeles Times*, August 20, 1995.

Patriots, have long depended on social security checks and other government assistance for their economic well-being. Weaver is now financially independent, having been given a $3 million settlement by the government for
the shootings of his son and wife during the Ruby Ridge standoff.)

Convinced as they are that the government is conspiring to enslave
them, these reactionaries often oppose government policies as plots to unjustly seize the individual's liberties. The things that have been pointed to as
repressive range from local zoning laws to the North American Free Trade
Agreement (NAFTA), from city decisions to fluoridate drinking water to the
monetary policies of the Federal Reserve Board. Moreover, the federal government is often seen as willing agents of the UN, or some other equally
threatening international group, in plots to demolish U.S. power and to surrender the society to them.

The origins of the reactionary movement that currently has become so
prominent in the U.S. can be traced back at least to the 1970s. William L.
Pierce, a former professor of physics at Oregon State University, wrote a
novel entitled *The Turner Diaries*. Self-published under the pen name of Andrew Macdonald, the book calls for violence against blacks, Jews, journalists,
liberals, immigrants, gun control advocates, the federal government, its
agents, and anyone else who supports it.

The FBI suspects that the book, which the agency refers to as "a blueprint for revolution," was used as a model for at least one terrorist escapade
in which a man stole $500,000 at gunpoint and later died in a standoff with
police. The money, it is believed, was to be used to fund the overthrow of the
government. The book, which calls for cutting the throats of newspaper edi-
tors and which imagines Jews being herded off to a remote canyon—reminiscent of the Babiy Yar massacre in which the Nazis murdered over 100,000
Ukrainian Jews during World War II—also describes bombing an FBI building with a car bomb made of ammonia nitrate fertilizer. Such a bomb was
used in 1995 to demolish a federal building in Oklahoma City. The blast took
the lives of almost 200 people.

Also in the 1970s the *Posse Comitatus* was organizing in the Midwest. It
was violently opposed to the federal government and to taxes. The group became increasingly active until its leaders were either jailed or killed in shoot-
outs with the police. The economic and social insecurities of the 1980s gave
additional impetus to right-wing extremism. Traditional groups like the Ku
Klux Klan and American Nazis rose to new prominence. Some of the nation's
youth followed their seniors organizing into racist *Skinhead* groups that have
sometimes attacked ethnic minority people on the streets.

With more permanent and formal structures the White Aryan Resistance (WAR) and the Aryan Nations have established themselves and serve
as propaganda vehicles and organizational advisers to a profusion of right-
wing groups. WAR was founded by Tom Metzger in Southern California.
Using considerable political savvy and electronic and print media skills,

Metzger has become something of a guru to violent reactionaries. His literature and broadcasts extol white supremacism and advocate violent attacks on Jews and blacks. Answering his call, some skinheads have attacked and even killed innocent people. Recently, members of the Fourth Reich Skinheads were arrested as they developed plans to ignite a race war by murdering Rodney King (the African American brutally beaten in a 1993 confrontation with the Los Angeles police) and bombing a prominent black church in Los Angeles during services.

The Aryan Nations, the political wing of the Church of Jesus Christ Christian, is headquartered in Idaho. A paramilitary affiliate, The Order, assassinated a Jewish Colorado radio talk show host and engaged in a crime spree before being brought down in the mid-1980s. The movement's founder, Rev. Richard Grint Butler, has an office adorned with pictures of Adolf Hitler and situated inside a compound which has signs warning, "Whites Only." The sect believes in "Christian Identity" which holds that the Jews are impostors and that the whites are the real descendants of the Israelites and are thus the true chosen people. This sect, which also believes that bar codes on food products are a Jewish plot to poison whites, had an influence on Randy Weaver and his wife.

Posted along State Highway 99 in California's great central valley, this sign graphically expresses the militant antitax and violence-prone stances of the extreme right-wing. Additional signs in the same general area along this stretch of highway express other extremist sentiments: "Get your Alternate I.D.: Learn to be free," the alternate ID is supposed to be used to evade income taxes. "Keep Your Car Use A BAR," a BAR is a Browning Automatic Rifle, and "Follow Jesus Or Go To Hell."

The militant civilian militia movement became popular in the 1990s. Now boasting hundreds of groups, the greatest militia activity is found in Florida, Montana, Michigan, California, and Arizona, but these paramilitary groups have been formed in virtually every state. Their avowed purpose differs from group to group and ranges from an extremist neighborhood watch to militant neo-Nazi, Christian fundamentalist fanaticism.

Their movement has been encouraged by a wide range of people, from short-wave broadcaster Mark Koernke, a janitor in Michigan, to radio talk-show host G. Gordon Liddy. Liddy is a former FBI agent and was convicted of participating in the Watergate break-in in 1972. Following his term in the federal penitentiary he became a vociferous federal government foe who calls for violent resistance against federal agents. He once publicly advised that, since federal agents wear bullet-proof vests, people should aim for the head in order to bring them down.

Paralleling the militia groups are the "Common Law courts." These groups are populated by private citizens who claim the right to literally take the law into their own hands. The Freemen, who in 1996 barracaded themselves in a Montana farmhouse against state agents and the FBI trying to arrest them on charges of fraud and tax evasion, are partisans of this view. Using tortured interpretations of the common law, the U.S. Constitution, and the Bible, they claimed to be exempt from federal and state law.

Descending from the Posse Comitatus and led by some former Posse members, these kangaroo courts claim the authority to overrule the government's judiciary. Espousing an eccentric theory of constitutional law that includes the belief that the "original" Thirteenth Amendment, which allegedly outlawed lawyers, has been suppressed. This group claims that there are about 100 Common Law Courts in thirty states. They encourage people to renounce any further financial responsibility for debts. They also have tried and convicted in absentia certain real jurists whose rulings they opposed. They have attempted to intimidate jurists by summoning them to appear before them, by sending judges threatening letters, and, in one case, by attempting to assassinate a Missouri highway patrol officer.

Although they are spread throughout the country and they are becoming increasingly militant and open about their beliefs, the number of people engaging in the militias and similar movements is still fairly small, estimated at about 30,000 in July of 1995. The number of neo-Nazis and Klansmen is probably roughly the same proportion. Yet, there are some much more mainline manifestations of growing right-wing extremism. The former Grand Wizard of the KKK, the viciously racist David Duke, was elected to the Louisiana state legislature in 1989, and in 1992 he ran as a candidate for the Republican Party nomination for president. In 1995, following the murder of a black couple by two openly white supremacist soldiers from Fort Bragg, North Carolina, the Army announced the opening of a general investigation of violent racism in its ranks.

Meanwhile, incidences of vandalism and violence against African Americans and Jews are occurring with increasing frequency across the country. Whether these episodes are the short-lived manifestations of a fleeting fad, or whether they are harbingers of a new prominence for Nazism in this country is, as yet, impossible to say. What can be concluded, however, is that reactionary extremism is far from a dead issue as we move toward the twenty-first century. Indeed, something of a fascist rebirth might also be occurring among societies in the Third World, to which we now turn our attention.

REVIEW

- The economic collapse in Europe following World War I caused severe trauma and insecurity. Playing on national fears, Mussolini and Hitler rose to power on militaristic, reactionary platforms.
- Nazis and fascists have similar views, except that fascists revere the state and Nazis hold up the *volk* as the source of truth and justice.
- These reactionaries claim that life's complexities exceed the capacity of human reason to deal with them.
- The Nazis believe that all good is the product of the Aryan race and that other races are inferior.
- Fascists and Nazis argue that most people are base and unworthy but that a few superior people among them are conduits for the national will.
- They call on people to give absolute and unquestioned obedience and loyalty to the leaders among them, thereby creating the totalitarian state.
- The fascists organized society into a syndical corporate state in which all people were given functions that they were obliged to perform. The Nazis, though less stringently organized, demanded no less commitment from their people.
- Just as they insisted on elitism within their nations, the Nazis and fascists claimed that some nations were superior to others, thus justifying the subordination of weaker nations to the stronger. This imperialistic drive was backed up by the glorification of war.
- Neo-Nazism and racism, together with militant opposition to the government and taxes, are on a dramatic increase in the United States.

SUGGESTIONS FOR FURTHER READING

BAYNES, NORMAN H., ed., *The Speeches of Adolf Hitler.* London: Oxford University Press, 1942.

CARSTEN, F.L., *The Rise of Fascism.* Berkeley, CA: University of California Press, 1982. First published in 1967.

DENNIS, L., *The Coming American Fascism.* New York: Gordon Press, 1994.

FERRAROTTI, FRANCO, *The Temptation to Forget: Racism, Antisemitism, Neo-Nazism.* Westport, CT: Greenwood Press, 1994.

GREGOR, A. JAMES, *Fascism: The Classic Interpretation of the Interwar Period.* Morristown, NJ: General Learning Press, 1973.

———, *Fascism: The Contemporary Interpretation.* Morristown, NJ: General Learning Press, 1973.

GRIFFIN, ROGER, *The Nature of Fascism.* New York: St. Martin's Press, 1991.

HALPERIN, S. WILLIAM, *Mussolini and Italian Fascism,* ed. Louis L. Snyder. Princeton, NJ: Van Nostrand, 1964.

HITLER, ADOLF, *Mein Kampf,* trans. Ralph Manheim. Boston: Houghton Mifflin, 1943.

MUSSOLINI, BENITO, *Fascism: Doctrine and Institutions.* New York: Howard Fertig, 1968.

O'SULLIVAN, NOEL, *Fascism.* London: J. M. Dent, 1983.

ROEPKE, WILHELM, *The Social Crisis of Our Time.* New Brunswick, NJ: Transaction Press, 1991.

SHIRER, WILLIAM L., *The Nightmare Years, 1930–1940.* Boston: Little, Brown, 1984.

SHIRER, WILLIAM L., *The Rise and Fall of the Third Reich.* New York: Simon & Schuster, 1960.

Chapter *12*

Ideologies
in
the Third World

PREVIEW

While the various Third World countries voice their unique qualities, they tend to exhibit certain ideological traits in common. Being divided along tribal, cultural, religious, and ethnic lines, many newly independent states have adopted an exaggerated nationalistic or even statist posture in attempts to unify the diverse elements within their society and to secure the state's interests against foreign aggression, real or imagined. In the past decade, many underdeveloped states have experimented with democracy, but the lack of political and economic stability threatens these efforts. Struggling against extreme overpopulation, crushing poverty, and neocolonial exploitation, most Third World states find socialism to be compatible with their world views since the individualism and aggressiveness of capitalism repel many. Still, even before the collapse of the Soviet Union, few in the Third World were enthusiastic for communism.

Holding a different perspective than the capitalist or the communist states, Third World countries tend to evolve unique political and economic systems. Liberal democracy, while tried by some countries, is generally considered impractical in most of these struggling societies, while totalitarian dictatorship is also rejected. Hence, many Third World countries are governed by paternalistic authoritarian rulers. Lacking the individual freedom of the liberal democracies, these systems, sometimes referred to as "guided democracies," vest powerful political controls in the hands of their leaders while denying them complete authority over other elements in the society. Under the most pleasant circumstances, some Third World states may gradually improve their economic and political systems enough to maximize the benefits for all their citizens. Yet, in other cases, the combination of authoritarianism and nationalism may doom their people to fascist equivalents. At the same time, the growing popularity of religious fundamentalism in the Muslim world engenders reactionary revolutionary movements that would see modern political systems replaced by theocracies.

THIRD WORLD DEFINED

To this point we have, with but few exceptions, studied the ideologies that relate to the industrialized nations of the world. Such an approach is completely appropriate given the relationship between modern ideologies and the Industrial Revolution. There are, however, a large number of countries that have yet to undergo the Industrial Revolution, but having not yet developed an industrial base does not prevent these nations from feeling the consequences of industrialization. Indeed, these societies have been very dramatically affected by its economic and political implications.

The term one normally hears in reference to these unmodernized states is the **Third World.** Doubtless, this term was not created by the underdeveloped countries themselves, since it implies a subordination to the other two worlds. In fact, the term has gained currency among the Western industrialized community, which refers to itself as the "First World." While the Soviet bloc existed, the West sometimes referred to it as the "Second World." In any event, the term *Third World* is generally used today to describe the "have-not" nations, and so will it be applied here as well. Among the Third World states are Bolivia and Nicaragua, Nigeria and Ghana, Somalia, Libya and Syria, Burma, Indonesia and Malaysia, and many other small, underdeveloped nations.

As with all generalizations, the term Third World suggests a uniformity that in reality does not exist. Including the majority of the world's nations and a huge number of people and cultures, the Third World is composed of a bewildering diversity that virtually defies adequate generalization. There are similarities within the Third World, however, and perhaps the most comprehensive similarity among these countries is poverty. The Malthusian calamity of population growth far exceeding the food supply is pressing hard on this sector of the world. Accordingly, feeding the multitudes is the most important preoccupation of many Third World governments. At the same time, however, some of the Third World countries have recently acquired vast wealth through the production and sale of oil. Hence, even in its most obvious commonality—poverty—the Third World is fraught with contradictions and exceptions.

As difficult as it is to generalize about the Third World without hopelessly distorting the subject, this must be done if such an important element in the world community is not to be ignored. The following, therefore, is intended to be a broad approach to the politics and ideologies prominent among the world's underdeveloped countries.

POLITICS OF THE THIRD WORLD

Essentially, the modern world has seen two periods of colonial expansion, each fundamentally representing the economically advanced powers forcing their domination over other parts of the world. The first colonial era spanned the period from 1492 to about 1785. During this time the trading countries of Portugal, Spain, France, England, and the Netherlands established some outposts in Africa, dominated the Indian subcontinent, and also established themselves in the East Indies and in some port cities in China and Japan. But the most extensive colonization was in the newly discovered Western Hemisphere. The colonies produced some precious metals, gems, and items of trade; but essentially they were consigned the task of providing agricultural goods to their European masters. While private fortunes were made, the military and administrative costs of maintaining the colonies proved to be bur-

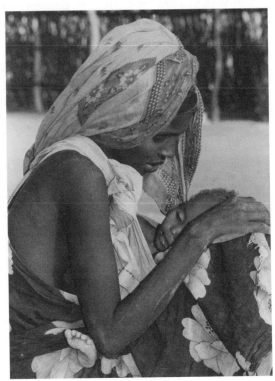

A worried Somalian mother comforts her starving child. Mike Theiler, Reuters. Corbis-Bettmann

densome for the European governments. Gradually, as Spain, Portugal, and the Netherlands declined in power; as France was vanquished by England from North America and India; and when England lost its most prized colony to the American Revolution, colonialism came to be viewed askance, causing almost a century to pass in which relatively little more colonial expansion took place.

The second era of colonial growth ran from 1875 to the 1950s. Driven by the wish to feed their newly industrialized economies with cheap raw materials and labor, England, France, Belgium, Italy, and Germany began colonial expansion anew, rushing to take as much of Africa as they could; and, joined by Russia, the United States, and Japan, they also invaded large parts of Asia. By 1914, with the exception of most of Latin America (which had won its independence from Spain and Portugal) and Canada, Australia, and New Zealand (which had become independent from England) virtually all the world had succumbed to the industrial powers.

In their rush to collect colonies, the industrial powers warred not only with their hapless captives but also with each other. For example, Japan fought with China (1894–1895); the United States warred with Spain (1898); Russia and Japan fought over Manchuria and Korea (1904–1905); and finally, all of the industrial powers entered in the titanic bloodletting of World War I, which was in part motivated by colonial competition. The interwar years saw the rise of totalitarianism and a new spate of colonialism by Italy, Germany, and Japan, even as the Soviet Union expanded westward, taking the Baltic states and parts of Finland and Rumania.

To the industrialized nations, World War II is viewed as a struggle to conquer the chauvinistic ideologies of fascism, National Socialism, and Japanese militarism. With the war's end, the industrialized world put its faith in international cooperation; the United Nations, after all, promised security as a reward for such cooperation. Soon, however, the industrialized world found itself split again, divided ideologically in the Cold War. To the people in the world's colonies, however, World War II was seen as something more than a struggle against fascism. Abandoned during the war to the advancing Axis armies (Germany, Italy, and Japan) or left to fend for themselves by their preoccupied masters, the colonies saw an awakening of *nationalism* among their peoples.

As the advanced states became polarized ideologically, aligning themselves with one of the two great superpowers, the United States or the Soviet Union, the colonial countries went a third way: toward independence. Nationalist movements in the colonies organized to resist continued colonial rule by the industrial powers. Except for India where Mahatma Gandhi used passive resistance to compel independence, long and bloody wars of national liberation were fought to loosen the colonialists' grip on Asia and Africa.

Without question, the most striking political reality among Third World countries is their enthusiastic nationalism. Used as the rallying cry to drive the hated colonial powers out, nationalism assumed enormous authority in the Third World. Nationalism's importance in the newly emerged states is especially great because they have suffered a severe identity crisis. In addition to the wretched economic exploitation of the colonial peoples, the industrial powers also practiced cultural imperialism. Impelled by racism and paternalism, they denigrated the languages, customs, and religions of their colonial charges. The imperial powers paid scant attention to traditional tribal boundaries when they staked out their empires, they ignored the histories of the people they conquered, and they taught that European ways were good and that local traditions were backward.

Thus, when the former colonies emerged as independent states, they found themselves comprised of varieties of tribes, social structures, and cultures and were confused and disoriented about themselves. Grasping for unifying themes, their leaders have pursued contradictory policies of lionizing the traditional languages, art, religions, and cultures, while at the same time championing national unity. Moreover, the weight of nationalism in the Third World is compounded by the insecurity of its leaders. New to independence and power, they are anxious to prove the legitimacy of their rule. This concern often leads them beyond occasional assertion of their national interests to bravado and bombast in world arenas such as the United Nations.

The exaggerated nationalism in the Third World is also a by-product of anticolonialist emotions. Having experienced the humiliating exploitation of colonialism, the people of the emerging states will not be denied their independence. Yet, the power that foreign investors will have in many developing countries, called **neocolonialism** (dollar, yen, pound, franc, mark diplomacy), frightens the Africans, Asians, and Latin Americans. At the same time, they lack the funds for domestic capital investment and, therefore, are forced to encourage foreign investment, even though experience has painfully taught that foreign influence can become oppressive. Understandably, this dilemma makes the people of developing countries defensive about their status in world affairs.

While nationalism is used to unify the people in the Third World countries, several factors in these societies also tend to divide them. More often than not, Third World states are composed of a number of different tribal, ethnic, cultural, and religious groups. Forging these diverse people into a single nation requires more than geographic proximity or political and economic necessity. The citizens of these states may be oriented entirely toward their own villages and feel little identification with their newly named country or its government.

In such circumstances leaders use patriotic appeals to awaken national awareness in the minds of their provincial citizens. They often warn that a neighboring regime may take advantage of the new state or that a former colonial oppressor wants to reestablish its control; such warnings are intended to galvanize nationalist spirit. Frequent use of this technique has contributed to strong nationalistic ideologies among the emerging states.

At the same time, however, a true and deeply felt nationalistic attachment cannot be created by such techniques. Nationalism, as explained in Chapter 3, is based on a very personal identification with one's nation-state. For nationalism to develop, a nation must already exist. Shared traditions, history, and territory, while not essential, are very helpful in building a nation. Often the colonial experience has failed to make a unified group out of the various peoples thrown together by European rule and later by independence. Too often a Third World country becomes an independent state without a nation to serve as its foundation. Nigeria, for example, Africa's most populous country, is comprised of at least ten major ethnic groups, including the Hausa-Fulani, the Yoruba, the Igbo, and the Nupe. The cultural and religious differences among Nigeria's people are so strong that civil war and military dictatorship are common. While not yet as politically chaotic, South Africa, Africa's most commercially advanced society, also finds itself torn asunder. Not only is it split along lines of color; black, coloreds, whites, and South Asians, but the black population (about two-thirds of the total) is divided among several important tribes. The Xhosa, Zulu, Swazi, Ndebele, Sotho, Tswana, and Venda each have different religions, languages, and histories which make creating nationhood extraordinarily difficult. The same could be said of many other countries in Africa, Asia, and Latin America.

Unifying these diverse societies is a monumental political task. The collapse of the Soviet Union has, in fact, complicated the effort in that the titanic struggle between East and West is no longer a factor. Hence, it no longer distracts peoples' attention. Consequently, people of the Third World have become even more focused on their own economic, social, and political difficulties. Moreover, the world seems to be evolving from one dominated by military confrontation to one absorbed in economic competition: a struggle for which most of the Third World is poorly suited.

This situation creates a political paradox. Not only must the emerging states maintain their independence, sometimes against incredible economic and political odds, but at the same time they must also build a nation. Hence, though the emerging states are often the strongest supporters of nationalism in international affairs, they also often suffer the greatest disunity and separatism within their own borders.

Disunity within Third World countries is matched by parochialism in international affairs. Although several attempts have been made to create regional international unions, none have succeeded very well. Driven by nationalistic jealousies and historical differences, the Arab states have consistently faltered in efforts to coalesce into larger political units. The Organization of African Unity has seldom been more than a forum in which the various members vent their frustrations, rarely being able to agree on united action. And the Organization of American States, perhaps the most successful of Third World organizations, because it makes no pretense at establishing permanent political unity, is often criticized as being a puppet of the United States.

In the Muslim world the situation is even more complex, with three different factions vying for support. Oil-rich Saudi Arabia, Kuwait, and the United Arab Emirates struggle to hold together their lucrative monarchies in the face of increasingly strong demands for social and political change. Modernists, like Maummar Quaddafi and the Ba'th parties of Syria's Hafiz al-Assad and Iraq's Saddam Hussein each separately call for Arab unity. They propose to coalesce the traditions of Islam with socialism, but these leaders also impose upon their people heavy-handed despotisms. Finally, there are the religious fundamentalists. Demanding that all political and social systems be subordinated to the dictates of religious leaders, these theocrats are gaining enormous influence. The success of the Ayatollah Khomeini in establishing a theocracy in Iran in 1979 and the growing disorder in the rest of the Middle East ranging from riots in Turkey, to assassinations of major political leaders in Egypt, Algeria, and Israel, to a nasty and lethal civil war in Algeria, all speak to the growing political potency of Islamic fundamentalism. Indeed, it is the most virulent reactionary movement in the world today.

Rather than uniting the Muslim people, the awakening of Islam has become the catalyst for bloody divisions in the Third World, as the civil strife in Lebanon, the war between Iraq and Iran, and the Persian Gulf War have shown. Moreover, the collapse of the Soviet Union resulted in its Muslim republics becoming independent. These areas, containing some 50 million people, are torn by civil strife as they try to find their way toward sovereignty in a confusing and dangerous political environment.

Sadly, caught in a murderous cross fire among those who wish to prevent change, those who wish modernization, and those who demand that the clock be turned backward, the Middle East squanders its youth and resources in desperate struggles with the shattering realities of the late twentieth century.

Religion is also playing a major role in the politics of other parts of the Third World. Cypress continues to be divided among its Greek Christians and Turkish Muslims. In Sri Lanka, Christians war with Buddhists. On the subcontinent, strained relations persist between Muslim Pakistan and Hindu India; and within India itself, Sihks and Hindus have come to bloody clashes over religious, economic, and political issues.

In Latin America, a quite different phenomenon is occurring. Inspired by European liberalism and even Marxism, some Roman Catholic clerics and lay people are becoming political activists in struggles to combat poverty, ignorance, and powerlessness among the masses. Hearkening to the trumpet call of *liberation theology,* these leftists decry the exploitation of capitalism and neocolonialism and insist that the Church lead the poor in efforts to restructure their societies, and redistribute wealth and power more equitably. Socialist in concept and sometimes Marxist in rhetoric, this movement has achieved significant followings in Guatemala, El Salvador, Nicaragua, Peru, Brazil, Chile, and Colombia.

In the late 1800s, the Church abandoned its previous posture in focusing only on the spiritual needs of its flock, while remaining uninvolved in social and political questions. Instead, today it recognizes the validity of the Church's engaging in a broader mission. Pope Leo XIII (1878–1903), the greatest of modern pontiffs, wrote a number of public letters (encyclicals) at the turn of the century. These appeals called for social justice (at the time, the primary focus of these thoughts was Europe) and nurtured the Christian socialist movement in Europe, which saw a connection between the egalitarian goals of humanitarian socialism and the teachings of Christ. Following a conservative resurgence in the Church's focus during the first half of the twentieth century, in the 1960s it gave new impetus to its social and political role with a new set of encyclicals emanating from the work done at the Second Vatican Council (1962–1965) and with subsequent papal comments condemning economic and social exploitation of the poor. While other religions in other areas have also moved toward taking a greater part in redressing the social conditions of the world's poor, the Catholics in Latin America, albeit not unanimously, have taken the leadership. But the Vatican has greeted these activists with ambiguous feelings. Pope John Paul II is genuinely committed to social and economic egalitarianism and to an activist Church, but he recoils from the Marxist tendencies of some zealots. Accordingly, he has supported efforts of Latin America priests and nuns to combat poverty and political oppression, but he has condemned their involvement in revolutionary and other directly political activities.

ECONOMICS OF THE THIRD WORLD

As pointed out at the beginning of this chapter, poverty is probably the most common single feature in the Third World. In fact, the situation is becoming very complicated and potentially catastrophic. The ongoing population explosion combined with a lack of capital, changing economic conditions, and a clear decline in the food supply are creating increasingly hopeless circumstances and potentially explosive political conditions in the Third World.

A United Nations study estimates that the total world population reached 1 billion people in 1830. By 1930 it stood at 2 billion, thirty years later it was 3 billion, and in 1986 it had reached 5 billion. In 1996 the world population is above 6 billion people, and if the current growth rate continues, the world population will multiply by 124 times by the year 2150, reaching 694 billion. Most of the population growth is occurring in the Third World. It is estimated that between 1995 and 2030, the world population will increase by 2.6 billion people, with a growth rate of 1 percent in Europe, 24 percent in North America, 47 percent in Asia, 52 percent in Central and South America, and, in Africa, a whopping 116 percent.

This "population time bomb" will soon absorb the attention of the world's policy makers. "Before this decade (the 1990s) is over," said Lester Brown, president of the Worldwatch Institute, "food security may replace military security as a principal preoccupation of governments." This startling change of focus is seemingly inevitable because, as Thomas Malthus had foreseen, the food supply cannot possibly keep up with the population increase.[1]

Already, according to the World Health Organization (WHO), one billion people live in abject poverty, 800 million suffer chronic hunger, 36,000 die of hunger related diseases daily, and 2 billion live in dangerously unsanitary conditions. For fifty years the world's supply of grain, meat, and fish increased, but in the 1990s the UN Food and Agriculture Organization reports dramatic declines in the production of each of these staples. Overfishing has rendered virtually every commercial species of fish dangerously close to depletion. Overgrazing, soil erosion, and urbanization have stunted the growth of commercial herds of beef, sheep, and pork. Desertification, soil depletion, overuse of fertilizers, and—perhaps most startling of all—a growing scarcity of fresh water has reduced grain production almost 10 percent.

In 1996, the worldwide average per capita economic production was estimated to be at $4,600. But, of course, the wealth is very unevenly distributed. The United States produces a per capita gross national product (GNP) of $25,860. The figure is highest in Luxembourg at $39,850. Looked at differently, the people in the eighteen richest countries comprise 13 percent of the world's population, but they account for over 60 percent of the world's per capita income. By contrast, sixty-four of the world's poorest countries produce a per capita income of less than $725, with Mozambique the lowest at $80. Put even more dramatically, the 358 billionaires in the world control as much wealth between them as is owned by the poorest 45 percent of the world's total population.

---

[1]It should be noted that the population explosion has not occurred because the fertility rate has increased around the globe. The number of births per woman has been brought down in the last forty years. However, modern medicine has expanded the life expectancy so greatly that it easily overwhelms the gains made in the declining fertility rate. This fact is true even though 12.2 million children under the age of five years die each year of diseases that are easily treated, such as cholera, measles, pneumonia, and shengella.

Clearly, political tranquillity is closely related to economic well-being. The people of the Third World, in their multitudes, see their lives becoming more and more hopelessly bound to the squalor that surrounds them. Simple expedience, one might think, dictates that the economically advanced countries would increase their efforts to help the Third World cope with the declining economic conditions. Instead, the very magnitude of the problem, the occurrence of seemingly insoluble crises like those in Rwanda and Somalia, and economic reversals encountered by the wealthy countries have led to what some observers call "compassion fatigue." Canada, Japan, Western Europe, and the United States have significantly reduced the amount of money they give to foreign aid in the Third World, thus exacerbating the suffering plaguing these countries.

Meanwhile, the Third World's own approach to economics is heavily influenced by cultural proclivities and traditional practices. Largely eschewing individualism, communal or tribal values are revered. Indeed, many cultures condemn the accumulation of individual wealth. These beliefs tend to make capitalism unattractive in the Third World. In addition, capitalism does not recommend itself to former colonial peoples who have seen firsthand the exploitation and humiliation imperialism brought.

The Third World is prone to rely on socialism for its economic salvation. This is ironic since, as we learned in Chapter 9, socialism is usually not successful in poor, agrarian countries, since socialism needs to be able to spread out industrial wealth if it is to improve the material conditions of most people in society.

Preference for socialism does not, however, attract the Third World to Marxism. Except for the resonance caused by Lenin's condemnation of imperialism, few Third World countries, other than China, Cuba, North Korea, and Vietnam have adopted Marxism. This is so not only because the collapse of the Soviet Union has discredited the ideology, but also because the social class conflict stressed in Marxism is just as foreign to the Third World as is the competitive individualism of the West. Further, those in the Third World who have managed to develop a nationalistic spirit are more likely to see their compatriots as members of a single exploited group and to see foreigners, not the local bourgeoisie, as exploiters.

Likewise, European socialism offers serious contradiction to the ideologies and beliefs of the Third World. European socialist traditions are heavily identified with internationalism. National boundaries, it is supposed, are artificial divisions among people who are far more similar than they are different. Clearly, the nationalistic attitudes in the Third World contradict socialist internationalism. Indeed, some observers suggest that the combination of socialism and exaggerated nationalism, or militaristic statism, accounts for the former Ugandan regime of Idi Amin, Qaddafi's Libya, Hussein's Iraq, and

Assad's Syria, as well as several other Third World regimes that resemble fascist or even Nazi states. Liberal institutions such as individual freedom and opposition parties are not tolerated by many Third World leaders, who see such tendencies as dangerously divisive.

Even in other less extreme systems the contradiction between socialism and nationalism is also apparent. Perhaps the best explanation for this contrariety is that the traditional tribal customs of many Third World cultures are communal. Consequently, in the emerging states socialism is often an extension of the tribal-communal ethic to the nation as a whole rather than a commitment to traditional socialist goals. Socialism is seen in the Third World as a means by which to equalize the wealth somewhat. But more important, it is regarded as an instrument with which to engender unity among the people. Hence it is used primarily as a political device. The socialist intent, explained in an earlier chapter, plays only a secondary role among many Third World states.

There are, however, some socialist experiments in the Third World that are genuinely devoted to the economic and social objective of improving the status of all people in the society. Unfortunately, none of these have been successful yet. The experiment with *ujamaa* (familyhood) villages in the United Republic of Tanzania is a case in point. Devised by President Julius K. Nyerere, this program attempted to weld African tradition with socialist goals and, uncommonly, it focused on agricultural development rather than industrialization.

Similar in some ways to the Scandinavian cooperatives and to Mao's communes, Nyerere's communal farms were organized around the extended family. Private ownership of land was eschewed; the group collectively controlled land and produced goods both for its own use and for the market. These familial collectives were to strive for self-sufficiency, providing for their own needs and caring for those in the family who could not work. While major trade and financial concerns were nationalized and managed by the central government, the focus of the economic system rested in the agrarian villages.

Well meaning though it was, the *ujamaa* experiment failed. The crushing poverty of Tanzania, the depressed world market for its goods, the inefficiency and corruption of its political system, and the hesitance of its people to cooperate with a system offering future benefits but few immediate rewards, all combined to defeat the experiment's objectives. Indeed, the economic plight of most Third World countries causes serious questions about the sanguine effect of virtually any effort to modernize and create prosperity.

Most newly emerged states are plagued by illiteracy, cultural traditions that stand in the way of modernization, few skilled or college-educated people, a lack of experienced civil servants, little modern technology, a small number of natural resources, and scarce domestic capital. Often the problems of Third World countries are made worse by economic dependence upon a single cash crop, such as peanuts, bananas, or sugar.

The feelings of poverty are increased by the awareness, made possible by modern communications systems, that other societies enjoy great wealth and luxurious lifestyles. Television, radio, the press, and films bring distant societies into clearer focus than ever before. The world's have-nots are now painfully cognizant that others enjoy a bounty far exceeding their own meager existence. It would be unnatural for the have-nots to recognize the chasm dividing them from the haves and not want to cross over to the land of plenty.

Indeed, the have-nots are demanding "their share" of the world's material goods with ever-increasing assertiveness, and these demands are creating great tension in world politics. The pressure on national leaders to produce instant prosperity is often disastrous because such demands are impossible to satisfy. The inevitable failure of the leaders to meet the needs of the impatient citizens leads to conflict, resulting in either a rapid succession of unstable governments or in dictatorship imposed by force.

Meanwhile colonialism has taken on several new faces as it has become more sophisticated to meet the needs of the current era. Though the former colonial powers no longer send troops and bureaucrats to physically govern the developing countries, they have found other ways of controlling them. *Neocolonialism,* in which the industrialized countries own large shares in the basic industries of the Third World countries, is one example. Foreign aid, which often has political strings attached, is another way of manipulating these capital-hungry and technology-starved countries, luring them into economic arrangements similar to colonialism. Often referred to as "dollar diplomacy," this phenomenon has been aptly described as imperialism without colonialism.

Perhaps the greatest threat of all to the Third World countries' independence is the role of international corporations in the political affairs of the emerging states. With annual revenues larger than the national budget or even the gross national product of many of the countries in which they do business, these corporations often operate without meaningful legal restraints, protected by their corporate structure and wealth.

The power relationship between the international corporations and the host countries is frequently so uneven that the developing nations find themselves needing the companies more than the companies need them, and they are forced to sell their labor and resources at what they consider unfair rates. Once a corporation has made heavy investments in a Third World country, it understandably becomes interested in its politics. This interest sometimes leads to improper involvement in the domestic and international political affairs of the host country, evoking charges of oppression, exploitation, and neocolonialism. One need only recall the well-publicized involvement of In-

Saddam Hussein (1937–) Jim
Hollander, Reuters. Corbis-
Bettmann

ternational Telephone and Telegraph (ITT) in the 1973 fall of Chilean president Salvador Allende to appreciate the disquiet the Third World feels when
its destiny is manipulated by these corporate giants.

THIRD WORLD DEMOCRACIES AND DICTATORSHIPS

Over the past decade and a half, as the Soviet Union declined and finally collapsed, several Third World countries have entered into the process of trying
to create democratic systems. Yet, even as the Western democracies have become victorious over their communist adversaries, the prospects for democracy in the underdeveloped world seem to be dimming. Late in 1995,
Freedom House, an independent institution that monitors the status of
democracy in the world, decried the reemergence of authoritarian regimes in
the Third World.

Although many factors such as national tradition and cultural habits
are important, the most fundamental source of the problems plaguing the
fledgling democratic states is economics. Perhaps more than any other political system, democracy depends for success on wealth. For example, in 1996

all but three (Saudi Arabia, Kuwait, and the United Arab Emirates) of the twenty-four richest countries were democratic. By contrast, of the forty-two poorest countries only two (India and Sri Lanka) enjoyed democratic systems.

Democracy, with its need for tolerance and its requirement for public consensus, often does not fare well during periods of severe economic privation. Consequently, the worldwide economic problems of the early 1990s has placed in jeopardy several Third World democratic experiments. Ironically, the same economic conditions have reduced the ability of the wealthy industrial states to help the jeopardized Third World democracies. Currently, many of Africa's twenty fledgling democracies seem on the verge of collapse, and several Asian countries—including India—have tightened control over individual liberties. Right-wing authoritarian regimes are also beginning to reappear in Latin America and the same seems to be threatening in several countries in Eastern Europe and the former Soviet Union—perhaps even in Russia itself.

In this century, we have seen communism rise and fall, colonialism vanquished, and fascism/Nazism come and go. Democracy and market economies have survived and they have gained adherents, causing many to rejoice. If, however, the current economic difficulties are not overcome, soon a new era of social insecurity could cause old demons—or perhaps yet to be imagined totalitarian ideologies—to arise.

Regardless of what fate awaits the struggling Third World democracies, the fact is that most Third World states eschew liberal democratic institutions. Most Third World societies believe that the individualism and competitiveness of liberal democracy are incompatible with their culture and traditions.

Still, democracy remains a popular term, and every existing state somehow identifies with it. The term **guided democracies** is often applied to the centralized systems that tend to develop among Third World states. A euphemism for **authoritarian dictatorship,** this concept is worth some study. Unlike a **totalitarian state,** in which a ruler controls every aspect of the society—be it cultural, economic, historical, social, or political—an authoritarian dictatorship is less complete. While the authoritarian dictator is in firm control of the political system, he or she has less control over other aspects of the society and is checked by other institutions, such as the church, the military, or a property-holding class.

As pointed out in Chapter 10, the various communist states tended toward totalitarianism as a result of a mixture of ideological dogmatism, Stalinist influence, and Western hostility. Interestingly, most underdeveloped states are no more attracted to totalitarianism than they are to liberal democracy. The centralization of all power in the hands of a small group would be difficult in many technologically backward countries. More important, however, the enormous variety of tribal loyalties, religious beliefs, and traditional attitudes found in many of the Third World states makes national identification shaky and totalitarianism impractical. Recalling the Indonesian experience with the leftist policies of the former Sukarno government, President Suharto recently said,

> We have taken a path that corrects the mistakes we made in adopting open democracy and communism based on class conflict. They may work in other countries but liberalism and communism don't work here.

Guided democracy gets its name from the authoritarian administration of "democratic" policies. In the developing countries political power tends to become centralized for three basic reasons. First, the communal spirit of tribalism encourages a collective rather than a competitive approach. Second, the politically aware people in a Third World state often united in a single movement organized to liberate the society from colonial control. When a single movement did evolve, it became easier to centralize power. Since these movements usually benefited from experienced, politically aware, and popular leadership, they often remained in existence after the state won its independence and tended to dominate the political system.

Third, faced with serious political and economic conditions, together with urgent demands for material progress, many Third World leaders have been forced into a corner. When the government fails to overcome the problems of the new nation, the response of the impatient masses is often violent and negative. The ruling group must then choose between riding out the period of disorder, taking the chance that the resultant chaos will bring about their fall from power or even lead to foreign intervention, and dealing with the dissidents sternly, thereby stifling free political expression. A brief glance at many governments in Africa and Asia will reveal a clear preference for the latter policy. Hence, most Third World societies are "guided" by an authoritarian government supported by and often controlled by the military. How can such a system be considered democratic?

The argument is that the people in a developing country are basically united. Although some rule while others are ruled, and while they are divided by tribal, cultural, ethnic, and religious differences, still they remain in the same social group. Regardless of the present status of any individual, all have shared the experience of exploitation by the country's former colonial masters.

True or not, this concept of the basic equality of all the citizens of a Third World country has great political resonance. It tends to legitimize the ruler's power and gives an aura of democratic respectability to the government even as dissent is muffled. Coming from the same origins as the people, the rulers suggest that they are united by common interests and goals. This makes the system democratic in the eyes of some of its citizens. Though most of the people have had little say in developing the nation's policies, they still consider the system democratic. To do otherwise, it is argued, would be to put democratic procedures above the ultimate democratic goal: the common good. Though this vision of democracy is unlike the ideals of the liberal industrial states of the West, we must remember that no society has a monopoly on the political dictionary; hence, other countries' definitions of democracy may legitimately differ from our own.

REVIEW

- The *Third World* is a term used to signify the wretchedly poor preindustrial societies of the world, although some of their number have recently become extremely wealthy through the exploitation of their oil reserves.
- Most Third World countries were colonies that suffered exploitation (many still do) at the hands of the industrial world.
- Often divided internally by tribal, ethnic, cultural, and religious differences, Third World countries are united by vitriolic anticolonialism and by appeals to extreme nationalism.
- The Muslim states are among the most complex in the Third World, finding themselves torn between archaic conservative monarchies, modernizing despots, and reactionary religious fundamentalists.
- While some societies are experimenting with liberal democracy and market economics, their desperate economic circumstances threaten to cause failure. Many Third World states are ruled by authoritarian cliques that apply modified socialist institutions and expound nationalism in regimes that are uncomfortably similar to fascism.

SUGGESTIONS FOR FURTHER READING

BOFF, LEONARDO, *Church, Charisma and Power.* New York: Crossroad, 1985.

COHEN, ROBIN, and HARRY GOULBOURNE, eds., *Democracy and Socialism in Africa.* Boulder, CO: Westview Press, 1991.

ESCOBAR, ARTURO, *Encountering Development: The Making and Unmaking of the Third World.* Ewing, NJ: Princeton University Press, 1994.

FERNANDEZ, ELEAZAR S., *Toward a Struggle.* Maryknoll, NY: Orbis Books, 1994.

KEE, ALISTAIR, *Marx and the Failure of Liberation Theology.* Valley Forge, PA: Trinity Press International, 1990.

MAHAN, BRIAN, and L. DALE RICHESIN, eds., *The Challenge of Liberation Theory.* Maryknoll, NY: Orbis Books, 1978.

MAZRUI, ALI A., and MICHAEL TIDY, *Nationalism and New States in Africa from About 1935 to the Present,* London: Heinemann, 1984.

OTTAWAY, DAVID, and MARINA OTTAWAY, *Afro-Communism.* New York: Afrikana, 1981.

POURGERAMI, ABBAS, *Development and Democracy in the Third World.* Boulder, CO: Westview Press, 1991.

SCHUBECK, THOMAS L., *Liberation Ethics, Models and Norms.* Minneapolis, MN: Augsburg Fortress Press, 1993.

SIMON, JULIAN, *Population and Development in Poor Countries.* Ewing, NJ: Princeton University Press, 1992.

SISK, TIMOTHY D., *Democratization In South Africa: The Elusive Social Contract.* Ewing, NJ: Princeton University Press, 1994.

STODDARD, PHILIP, DAVID C. CUTHELL, and MARGARET W. SULLIVAN, eds., *Change and the Muslim World.* Syracuse, NY: Syracuse University Press, 1981.

VON DER MEHDEN, FRED R., *Politics of the Developing Nations.* 2nd ed. Englewood Cliffs, NJ: Prentice Hall, 1973.

YOUNG, CRAWFORD, *Ideology and Development in Africa.* New Haven, CT: Yale University Press, 1982.

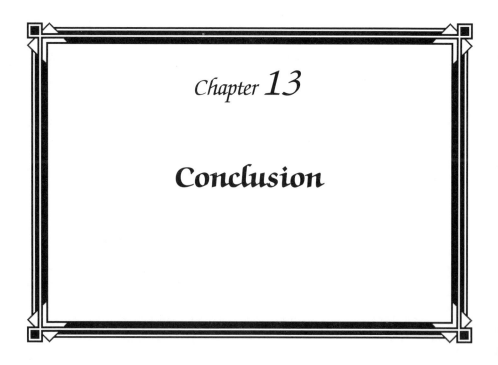

Chapter 13

Conclusion

The world is not only what we have made it but is also a product of earlier generations' efforts. "Today is the child of yesterday," as the Arabs put it. Thus, to fully grasp the present, we must first understand the past. The great thinkers wrote what they did because they had unusual talents, but they were also strongly influenced by their times. Locke, Madison, Bakunin, Marx, Mill, Hitler, Mao, and all the others can be fully appreciated only in the light of their historical, intellectual, political, social, and economic circumstances. Yet, although these ideologues were influenced by situations particular to their respective ages, they each responded to a common phenomenon—modernization.

The most fundamental feature of this era, the event that has done more to distinguish this period in history from all others and has contributed most heavily to shaping our environment, is the Industrial Revolution. Industrialization is the latest stage in the chain reaction begun by the scientific method and its application to technology. The shift from making things by hand to mechanized production changed the world dramatically. The reaction to industrialization varied among observers. Some, like Adam Smith, reveled in its potential benefits; others, including Marx, argued that people were robbed of their skills and reduced to being mere tenders of machines, but he looked forward to improved social conditions with the equal distribution of the newly produced bounty; and still more, Hitler for instance, turned the new productivity into a frightful killing machine in an ironic effort to return the world to primitive social values.

As the ideologues struggled with the larger question of social development, the masses met industrialization as individuals. People faced new social problems as they found themselves packed into cities far removed from the families and land with which they had previously been so intimately involved. New goods in unimagined abundance tended to become an end in themselves; people increasingly turned away from spiritual satisfaction and justification, looking to materialism as the standard by which actions and ideas were judged.

At the same time, new ideas began to develop and to exercise a great impact on politics. Modern ideas of human equality, individual freedom, and democracy developed currency. But these new ideas were applied differently by different people at various times. John Locke and Adam Smith, ignoring equality, exalted individual freedom. Rousseau and Marx equated freedom with equality and economic well-being and turned many liberal ideas to radical extremes. The anarchists saw human liberty impeded by society's institutions and they demanded that government be abandoned. Humanitarian socialists insist that liberal democratic institutions be set the task of distributing wealth on a more equal basis, and the people of the Third World, facing insoluble problems of overpopulation and crushing poverty, demand that they be allowed to share the bounty created by the industrialization.

The changes brought about by the Industrial Revolution confronted humanity with some very hard choices. Political problems have become more serious as history has pushed us beyond feudalism toward popularly based social and political structures. Politics truly came into its own in our age. Once the sole province of a tiny elite, government has become the concern of all people regardless of their social status, gender, or race. As technology expanded and people became involved in governing themselves and as new ideologies were met with resistance by those seeking to maintain the status quo and others trying to reverse the progressive trend of history, enormous struggles developed leading to World War I and World War II. Following the defeat of Hitler and Mussolini the world gravitated to a Cold War in which the industrial states polarized on an East-West axis, while the southern societies—the Third World—charted a nonaligned course.

The collapse of the Soviet Union introduced a new ideological ambiguity to world politics. Russia, Eastern Europe, and Central Asia at first abandoned socialism for the market, yet many of those states quickly restored the socialists when the complexity and trauma of transforming to a market economy became apparent. Although most of their governments could not be considered democratic today, they certainly fall short of the totalitarian regimes that formerly governed them. Whether the political structures of the states comprising the former Soviet Bloc continue to moderate or will once again harden into dictatorship is impossible to know.

The West, ostensibly the victor of the Cold War, ironically seems disoriented now that its once implacable foe is no more, and the West is curiously indecisive about its future. Meanwhile, the Third World continues to grapple with problems that seem more insurmountable with each new day.

The ideological convictions of the post–World War II world are now being questioned on all sides; certainty is, at least for the moment, ended. The current failure of our ideologies to sufficiently simplify and clarify contemporary politics has delivered us to the current point of indecision and questioning. The failure of the far left is fresh in mind; conservatism seems unlikely to become more than it ever was, a short-sighted justification for sustaining the power elite; liberal democracy, at the moment of its seeming triumph, appears hesitant and faltering. On the other hand, the failure of the far right is but a distant memory in the minds of some, whereas to others it is a vaguely perceived historical curiosity. Its appeal to base emotionalism and fear is most acute in times of ambivalence, ambiguity, and confusion. While alarm at the possibility of a resurgence of reactionary extremism is certainly premature, its prospects should at least be sobering, given the ambivalence of today's politics.

Whether progressive or reactionary, the ideologies people espouse are responsible—at least in part—for the ambiguous situation in which we now find ourselves. Their imperfections have encouraged tragic wastes of resources and energy, yet they are also necessary statements of political aspirations. While they have embroiled the world in devastating conflicts, they have also been the inspiration for some of our most noble and most admirable social accomplishments.

Hence, the record of ideologies is mixed. They cannot be roundly condemned nor can they be uniformly applauded. Good or bad, political ideologies are a fact of modern life. They exist and they exercise immense impact on our lives. Accordingly, we dare not ignore them. Instead, we must understand them if we are to grasp the full significance of our social and political existence.

Many people feel that it is enough simply to cope with life's problems; understanding them is too much to expect. Nevertheless, some individuals have put much effort into rationalizing the world and understanding its relationship to their lives. Whether we are indeed intelligent enough to grasp the meaning of life, to know truth, and to be just, are questions that will continue to be asked and may perhaps never be answered. What is certain is that we have tried and that while our efforts have fallen short of complete success, they have, at the same time, escaped total failure. What, therefore, remains for us but continuing the quest?

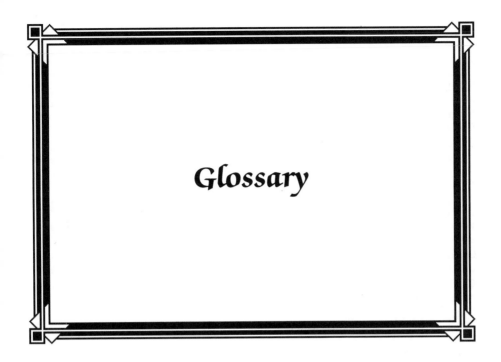

Glossary

Anarchism   An ideology opposed to all or much of institutionalized government. Some anarchists want to free the individual so that he or she can make the greatest possible personal advancement; they are the *individual anarchists*. Others hope to free people so that they can make their greatest possible contribution to society as a whole; they are the *social anarchists.*

Aryans   In Nazi ideology, a race of people who have the best of all human qualities and are the creators of all culture. Science has so far failed to find any proof that this race ever existed.

Authoritarian dictatorship   A dictatorship in which the government has an extraordinary amount of control over society's political institutions (the police, the courts, the military), but does not control every major institution in society as does a totalitarian dictator.

Babeuf, François Noel (1760–1797)   A brilliant revolutionary socialist who talked about creating the workers' revolution as early as the 1790s.

Bakunin, Mikhail (1814–1876)   The founder of violent anarchism. He also competed with Marx for control of the international socialist movement.

Bentham, Jeremy (1748–1832)   The creator of utilitarianism and the founder of modern liberalism. He was also an important force in Britain's early nineteenth-century reform movement.

Bernstein, Edward (1850–1932)   A revisionist socialist. See also *Revisionism.*

Bolsheviks   Followers of Lenin who believed that violence was necessary to bring about socialism and that Russia could be taken in a coup led by them. The Bolsheviks were renamed the Communist party after they came to power in Russia.

Bourgeoisie   The wealthy merchant and professional class that became the dialectical challenge to the feudal society.

Brezhnev, Leonid (1906–1982)   Replaced Nikita Khrushchev as General Secretary of the Soviet Communist Party in 1964. He was the USSR's most powerful leader until his death and his policies are primarily responsible for the demise of the Soviet Union.

Burke, Edmund (1729–1797)   An Irish-born British parliamentarian and the father of modern conservative philosophy. His ideas contributed heavily to neoclassical democratic theory, especially in making the property right a dominant theme. He thought that the people ought to be ruled by a benevolent aristocracy elected by them.

Calhoun, John C. (1782–1850)   A philosopher for the Southern cause before the Civil War. He believed that the national government should be greatly limited in its powers over the states.

Capitalism   An economic system first conceived of by Adam Smith. It is based on individual competition in an unregulated market place.

Castro, Fidel Ruiz (born in 1927)   A Cuban revolutionary and the founder of the present Cuban regime.

Chamberlain, Houston Stewart (1855–1925)   A friend and later the son-in-law of Richard Wagner who shared Wagner's anti-Semitic views and developed a theory based on those views.

Checks and balances   Madison's plan of government, in which each branch of government has the power to influence the others, but no single branch can become too powerful. In addition, through staggered terms of office, indirect elections, and a specific election date, Madison hoped to prevent a permanent majority from controlling the government.

Coalition government   When no single party wins a majority of seats in parliament, sometimes two or more parties will unite to form a government. Such unions are usually unstable and short-lived.

Collective responsibility   In the parliamentary-cabinet system, the notion that the members of the cabinet share responsibility for the government's successes and failures.

Comintern   An organization, also called the Third International, created by Lenin to stimulate communist revolutions throughout the world.

Communism   A very old term that originally meant a local communal relationship among a small number of people. Today it refers to a system based on Marxist-Leninist ideology.

Compulsive toil   A term Marx used to describe Locke's notion of a condition in which people had to work every waking hour just to make ends meet. While Locke and Marx appreciated work, they resented people being forced into compulsive toil, thinking that it denied them sufficient time to refine their humanity.

Concurrent majorities   John C. Calhoun's argument that there is not just one majority, but, rather, several majorities that should all agree to a policy before it is put into effect.

Concurrent powers   Used in the federal system of the United States, these powers are exercised by both the state and national governments at the same time. If the two conflict, the laws of the national government prevail.

Confederate system   A compact among several sovereign states. A confederacy exists to achieve certain goals, and any member state, being sovereign, may secede from it at any time.

Conservative   A person who is satisfied with the system as it is and tends to resist change. Some conservatives, realizing that things could be improved, will accept gradual, very superficial, and progressive change. Property rights tend to be very important to conservatives.

Conservative theory of representation   A system in which an elite group is chosen by the people to govern them. Yet while public officials should try to represent their constituents' interest, the people cannot compel them to vote in a particular way.

Conspiratorial theory   The theory that a small group of powerful people are secretly controlling the political and economic events in a country. The militant civilian militia movement, popular among some in the U.S. today, is an excellent example of the conspiratorial theory.

Convention, nomination by   A nomination procedure in which the candidate must receive a certain number of delegate votes at a nominating convention.

Cooperatives   Enterprises that are owned and operated by their members, who all participate in the enterprise directly.

Corporate state   The economic system used by fascist Italy. The society was organized into syndicates (unions), regional organizations, and national corporations controlled by the state. Though industry was privately owned, production and prices were controlled by the state through the national corporations; strikes and boycotts were outlawed.

de Tracy, Antoine Louis Claude Destutt (1754–1836)   A French scholar who coined the term *ideology,* calling it the "science of ideas."

Deng Xiaoping (born in 1904)   A pragmatic reformer who presently enjoys great power in China. Twice purged from the leadership by the radicals, Deng has managed to survive Mao and is responsible for the present modernization of China.

Dewey, John (1859–1952)   The philosopher of the New Deal. He called upon people to use their reasoning ability and their control of government to create a better life. He argued that truth was constantly changing and that no institution should be maintained if it was no longer useful. His ideas about social change are often called *social engineering.*

Dialectic   George Hegel's concept that historical progress is achieved through conflict between the existing order and challenges to that order.

Dialectic materialism   The Marxist theory of history, which suggests that human progress has resulted from struggle between the exploiters and the exploited. This dynamic, Marx argued, would inevitably lead to socialism.

Dictatorship   See *Authoritarian* and *Totalitarian.*

Dictatorship of the proletariat   A temporary tyranny of the workers that would follow the revolution and last until all nonproletarian classes had been removed, at which time the state would wither away and a democratic utopia would evolve.

"Different paths to socialism"   The slogan under which Tito led Yugoslavia away from Stalin's domination. Tito claimed that each state had to find its own way to socialism.

Direct democracy   A system in which there is no elected legislature and people make the laws themselves.

Divine right of kings theory   The belief that the king had been chosen by God to rule.

Divine theory of the state   The belief that God has chosen one people above all others, and that, therefore, the state governing the chosen ones is allowed to do things to other people that could not be morally justified otherwise.

Division of labor   Economic specialization that Marx claimed led to the creation of private property, social classes, and human exploitation.

Economic determinism   The belief that all social and political features are conditioned by the economic environment.

Elite theorism   A theory suggesting that the political system is controlled by a relatively small number of people who head important interest groups.

Elitism   The assumption that some people are more deserving and qualified than others and that they ought to govern.

Engels, Friedrich (1820–1895)   The son of a wealthy Prussian textile manufacturer who became a close friend of Marx in 1844 and remained his collaborator and benefactor until Marx died in 1883.

Fabianism   Founded in 1884, the Fabian society was a British socialist movement in the tradition of John Stuart Mill and Robert Owen. The Fabians argued for socialism in a democratic society, insisting that it must be adopted peacefully and gradually.

Federalism   A system of government developed in the United States that divides the powers of government between the states and the national levels.

Federalist Papers   A series of articles written by James Madison, Alexander Hamilton, and John Jay, during 1787 and 1788, urging New Yorkers to ratify the proposed federal Constitution.

Fidelismo   Castro's adaptation of Marxism, which combines dialectic and idealistic rhetoric with anti-Yankee policies to create the new Cuba.

Five-Year plans   Plans that direct a state's production and distribution of goods and services over a five-year period; introduced by Stalin in 1929 to replace Lenin's NEP. Also used in China.

Force theory of the state   The belief that the state was created by the forceful conquest of some people by others. One group supporting this theory held that the use of force was evil, while a second group saw force as a positive feature of society.

Foundation of the society (as used by Marx)   Marx argued that economics was the foundation of any society. This economic base was composed of the *means of production* (resources and technology) and the *relations of production* (ownership). The economic base preconditioned the rest of the society (*the superstructure*).

Fourier, Charles (1772–1837)   A utopian socialist. See also *Utopian socialism.*

Functional representation   A system that gives legislature representation to institutions such as the Church, universities, trade unions, corporations.

General election   An electoral contest between candidates for public office.

General will   The all-powerful authority of Rousseau's organic society. The General Will is created by the majority when it is acting in the best interests of all people.

Gobineau, Arthur de (1816–1882)   A French noble who tried to prove that the French aristocracy was superior to the peasantry and should therefore rule France. In doing so he claimed that the Aryan race was superior to all others. His theories became the foundation of Nazi racism.

Godwin, William (1756–1836)   Once a protestant minister, Godwin eventually became an atheist and founded anarchism.

Goldman, Emma (1869–1940)   The leading anarchist in American history. Sometimes known as "Red Emma."

Gorbachev, Mikhail S. (born in 1931)   General Secretary of the Communist party of the Soviet Union from 1985 until its collapse in 1991. Gorbachev tried to prevent the Soviet collapse by initiating a series of stunning reforms, but his efforts failed. Even so, he will probably be recorded as one of the twentieth century's most important leaders.

Great Cultural Revolution (1966–1969)   A revolution in which the radicals in China were unleashed against the moderate bureaucrats and intellectuals. The radicals favored greater personal sacrifice and stronger commitment to the goals of the revolution, while the moderates wanted to produce more consumer goods.

Great Leap Forward (1958–1961)   An attempt to bring China into the modern industrial age through maximum use of the vast Chinese labor force; it failed miserably.

Green, Thomas Hill (1836–1882)   A liberal philosopher who wrote about freedom in a positive rather than a negative sense. He argued that the government should actively try to provide a good life for its citizens. His ideas offered an early justification for the welfare state, and his work directed liberalism away from solitary individualism and toward collectivity.

Guided democracies   Third World dictatorships in which the leaders claim to be carrying out the popular will.

Hegel, Georg Wilhelm Friedrich (1770–1831)   A German political philosopher whose ideas were not only important in their own right but which also greatly influenced both Marx and Mussolini.

Hitler, Adolf (1889–1945)   A German revolutionary leader and the founder of the ideology of National Socialism and the Nazi state.

Hobbes, Thomas (1588–1679)   A social contract theorist who claimed that people had created an ordered society by surrendering their rights to a king.

Human rights   The rights listed in the Declaration of Independence and guaranteed in the Constitution of the United States. The question of whether or not property should be considered a human right is a subject of debate between liberals and conservatives.

Ideology   Any of a number of action-oriented, materialistic, popular, and simplistic political theories that were originally developed as an accommodation to the social and economic conditions created by the Industrial Revolution.

Il Duce   The Italian title for supreme leader, as used by Mussolini.

Imperialism (as used by Lenin)   The most advanced state of capitalism. It followed the stages of industrial capitalism and finance capitalism and represented the exportation of exploitation.

Imperialist capitalists   Members of the Chinese bourgeoisie who had ties to foreign nations. They were held to be the most dangerous element in the society and were quickly eliminated after the communists came to power.

Industrial Revolution   A period beginning in the eighteenth century that consisted of several phases: Handcrafted goods produced in cottages or small shops gave way to mechanization (goods produced by machines). Labor then became concentrated in factories and cities. This phase was followed by *automation* (production of goods with machines powered by steam, gasoline, coal, running water, or electricity rather than by humans or animals). Today the United States has reached the *cybernetic* level, in which machines are run by other machines.

Iron law of oligarchy   Robert Michels's theory that only a very few people are active in any organization and that they therefore gain control of the organization. This theory supports the argument that a small elite actually governs the United States.

Iron law of wages   David Ricardo's argument that the capitalist would pay the worker no more than a subsistence wage.

Irrationalistism   The belief that human reason has definite limits and that people must depend on phenomena that are beyond reason for the explanation and solution of some of their problems.

Jaurès, Jean (1859–1914)   A revisionist socialist. See also *Revisionism.*

Jefferson, Thomas (1743–1826)   An American statesman and philosopher in the classical democratic tradition of Locke and Rousseau. He argued for a government that was much more directly controlled by the people than the one proposed in the federal Constitution.

Kautsky, Karl (1854–1931)   A German Marxist who became the leader of the Orthodox Marxists following Engels's death.

Khrushchev, Nikita (1894–1971)   The successor of Stalin and a political reformer in the Soviet Union.

Kropotkin, Prince Peter (1842–1921)   A scientist and a communistic anarchist.

Kuomintang   A Chinese nationalist political party founded by Dr. Sun Yat-sen and taken over by Chiang Kai-shek after Sun's death.

Labor theory of value   A theory espoused by David Ricardo and amplified by Marx. It suggested that the true value of any item was determined by the amount of labor it took to produce it.

Laissez-faire   The belief held by John Locke, Adam Smith, and David Ricardo that government should stay out of economic matters. This concept is fundamental to capitalism.

Lenin,Vladimir (Nikolai) Ilyich (1870–1924)   A Russian revolutionary who first adapted Marxism to a practical political situation; the founder of the Union of Soviet Socialist Republics.

Liberal   A person who favors rapid, substantial, and progressive change in the existing order. Liberals usually use legal means to achieve their goals. The *classic liberals* believed in human reason; to them property was a human right. *Contemporary liberals* reject natural law and count property among the social rights.

Liberal theory of representation   The belief that people should be able to compel their elected representatives to vote in a particular way.

Liberation theology   A movement centered primarily in the Roman Catholic Church in Latin America. Priests, nuns, and lay persons are committed to a socially and politically active Church to bring economic improvement, social advancement, and political power to the poor.

Locke, John (1632–1704)   A social contract theorist and the leading philosopher of classical liberal democracy. He argued that people had created government to serve their needs and that most of the time government should have very little power over the individual.

Long March (1934–1935)   A massive retreat by the Chinese communists from southern to northern China. A power struggle took place during the march, with Mao emerging as the dominant Chinese political figure.

Lumpenproletariat   Vagabonds, prostitutes, and other social outcasts whom Bakunin wanted to mold into a revolutionary force.

Madison, James (1751–1836)   the founder of the American federal system. He believed that people were rather base by nature and that governmental institutions should turn the people's vices into virtues. Hence, he designed a system of separate and diffuse powers with institutions that would check and balance each other.

Malthus, Thomas (1766–1834)   An English economist who postulated that since population increases more rapidly than does food, calamity awaits those nations that do not exercise "moral restraint." His *Essay on the Principle of Population* was very controversial as well as influential. Malthus's work enjoyed wide impact, even influencing Charles Darwin's theory of natural selection.

Maoism   Marxist ideology heavily influenced by populism and traditional Chinese values. Like the ideologies of other developing countries, Maoism is at least as concerned with the problem of imperialist expansion by the advanced states as with the struggle between social classes within the society.

Mao Tse-tung (1893–1976)   A Chinese revolutionary and political leader. He founded the People's Republic of China and adapted Marxism to an Asian peasant society.

March on Rome   A 1922 demonstration in which several thousand supporters of Mussolini marched on Rome to demand that he be given power. The indecisive Italian political leaders became confused and frightened, and finally invited Mussolini to form a government.

Mass Line   A Maoist doctrine calling upon the masses of China to carry out the goals of the revolution.

Marx, Karl (1818–1883)   A scholar and the leader of the international socialist movement. He developed a theory of historical development—Marxism—based on the assumption that economic factors were the primary human motivation and that history was propelled by struggle among competing social classes.

Mensheviks   Followers of Georgi Plekhanov (1857–1918), who believed that socialism would come to Russia only after the nation had been transformed into a capitalist state.

Mercantilism   An economic theory prominent in the 1600s and 1700s. Nations practicing mercantilism used economic monopolies and colonial exploitation in efforts to increase their wealth and political power. Today's vestiges of mercantilism are called "economic nationalism."

Mill, John Stuart (1806–1873)   A British writer who contributed greatly to the development of democratic socialism by questioning the assumptions that people are naturally selfish and that government should have no economic role.

Moderate   A person who is basically content with the system but sees some flaws in it. Accordingly, a moderate will accept a small amount of progressive change.

Moral absolutism   The belief that there is a set of absolute truths that apply equally to all people. Natural law is an example of these presumed truths.

Moral relativism   The belief that truth at any given time is subject to the needs of society.

Multimember district   An electoral district in which several people are elected to office. A system of proportional representation is usually employed to distribute the votes in these districts, thus encouraging the development of a multiparty system.

Multiparty system   A system in which there are several political parties that enjoy significant strength. This system gives the clearest voice to minority opinions but in doing so destroys the majority. Coalition governments and governmental instability may result from the absence of a majority. In addition, the multiparty system demands a certain flexibility that is not possible in a presidential-congressional system.

Mussolini, Benito (1883–1945)   An Italian revolutionary, the originator of fascism and the leader of the Italian fascist state.

Myth   An idea that is believed but cannot be proved. The concept of myth as a political tool was developed by Georges Sorel, who suggested the use of myth to stimulate mass action. The validity of the myth was unimportant as long as it resulted in the desired action.

Narodniki   Russian Populists of the late nineteenth century.

Nation   A sociological term used to refer to a group of people who share a common language, ethnic relationship, culture, or history. The term does not necessarily have a political meaning.

Nationalism   The ideology of the nation-state; the most powerful political idea to emerge in the past 300 years.

Nationalization   Government expropriation of an industry and the later operation and control of that industry by the government.

National Socialist German Workers party   The official name of the Nazi party.

Natural law   Rules in nature governing human conduct that can be discovered through the use of human reason.

Natural theory of the state   The belief that people are political as well as social animals and can develop their humanity only within the context of the state.

Neocolonialism   A condition in which wealthy nations gain control of developing states of making vast economic investments in those states.

New Deal   The 1930s policies of Franklin Delano Roosevelt which tempered capitalism with government regulation of business, collective bargaining for labor, and welfare state institutions including social security, housing loan guarantees, and welfare programs for the needy.

New Economic Policy (NEP)   The failure of War Communism, in which the Soviets tried to rapidly socialize the economy, caused Lenin to initiate the NEP in 1921 to rebuild the economy. Retail, small factories, and agriculture were returned to private ownership; while finance, heavy industry, foreign trade, transportation, and communications remained under state control. Although the NEP revitalized the economy, it was ended by Stalin in 1929 with the introduction of the planned economy.

Nietzsche, Friedrich (1844–1900)   A German philosopher who thought that power and strength were desirable qualities that justified all things.

Nihilism   An anarchist theory of the mid-1800s; its goal was the complete destruction of society.

Nullification   Calhoun's theory that the state legislatures could vote to void a national statute within their jurisdiction.

Organic theory of the state   The belief that the state is similar to a living organism and that people are the cells of that organism.

Original donation theory   The belief that God gave Adam the power to rule the state and that all later kings were his heirs.

Orthodox Marxists   A group of socialists led by Engels and Karl Kautsky who followed the teachings of Marx without significant deviation. The movement was never very successful because of its rigid dogmatism.

Owen, Robert (1771–1858)   A self-made industrialist who recoiled at the suffering capitalism caused ordinary people. Wanting to reform capitalism, he became a utopian socialist and actually coined the term *socialism*.

Parliamentary-cabinet system   A system in which the people elect the legislature, which then chooses a leader who is appointed prime minister by the head of state. The head of state also appoints members of the legislature to the cabinet on the recommendation of the prime minister. The cabinet acts as a plural executive, and its members stand (or fall) together on the government's policies.

Passive obedience theory   Calvin's theory that people should obey the king because his power came from God.

Patriotism   An act or gesture of loyalty or commitment to the nation-state.

Peaceful coexistence   Khrushchev's policy of accommodation with the West, based on the recognition that neither side could win a nuclear war.

Permanent revolution   A theory, supported by Leon Trotsky and Mao Tse-tung, that favored revolution as the best way to achieve meaningful reform even after Marxists have taken power.

Plekhanov, Georgi (1857–1918)   The founder of Marxism in Russia, Plekhanov broke with Lenin over differences regarding the dialectic and revolutionary tactics. His ideas became the foundation for the Menshevik movement.

Pluralism   A decision-making process in which the people's interests are represented by various interest groups; governmental policy is a compromise between the competing interests of those groups.

Plurality   The largest number of votes cast. A plurality is distinct from a majority because it need not be over half; it is simply the most votes.

Popular sovereignty   The belief that the people are the sole source of political power; a fundamental idea in liberal democracy.

Positivist law   Bentham's theory that the law should serve the people's interests and should be changed when it fails to do so.

Presidential-congressional system   A system used in the United States in which the executive and the legislature are elected separately, resulting in less interdependence between the two branches than in other systems. Officials are elected to uninterruptable terms, a fact that adds stability to the system but tends to reduce popular control over the government.

Primary election   An election in which candidates are nominated for public office.

Principle democrats   Those who believe that the process of making decisions is only part of democracy. More important are the basic goals of democracy, such as the freedom and independence of the individual.

Process democrats   Those who argue that democracy is simply a process by which decisions are made on a popular basis.

Proletariat   Industrial workers who, according to Marx, are exploited by capitalists and are supposed to rebel and eventually create a communist democratic utopia.

Proportional representation   A method of awarding legislative seats to parties or candidates in relation to the proportion of the vote won.

Proudhon, Pierre Joseph (1809–1865)   A leading anarchist socialist, sometimes called the founder of modern anarchism.

Radical   A person who wants immediate, profound, and progressive change in the existing order. Some radicals insist that violence is the only way to bring about meaningful change; pacifist radicals, by contrast, oppose violence altogether.

Radical theory of representation   A theory that rejects elected representatives and holds that people should represent themselves in the policy-making process.

Rationalism   The belief that human problems can be solved through the use of human reason.

Reactionary   A person who would like to see the existing order reversed and favors substituting earlier political institutions for the contemporary system.

Reactionary theory of representation   A theory stating that the monarch and parliament should represent the people's interests as they see them without necessarily consulting the people.

Republic   Also called indirect democracy or representative government, a republic is a system in which the people elect representatives to make laws for them. Traditionally the term has meant nonmonarchial government.

Revisionism A movement led by Edward Bernstein (1850–1932) and Jean Jaurès (1859–1914) that challenged almost every major principle of Marxism. Abandoning scientific socialism, the revisionists returned humanitarianism to a central place in socialist theory.

Revolution A profound change in the social, political, economic, and cultural patterns of a given society that need not be violent but often is.

Revolutionary defeatism A policy of neutrality favored by Lenin, who believed that World War I was a war of capitalist imperialism. He hoped that when the war was over the socialists could seize control from the exhausted capitalist governments.

Ricardo, David (1772–1823) An English economist who applied the capitalistic theories of Adam Smith to the British economy. He is particularly noted in articulating the "iron law of wages" and for his contribution to the theory of profit—"the leavings of wages" as he called it. His major work, *The Principles of Political Economy and Taxation,* earned him the title of the "Newton of economies."

Rousseau, Jean Jacques (1712–1778) A social contract theorist and founder of modern radical thought. He argued that people are free only when they subordinate their own interests to those of the group.

Rural Soviets Communist bases of power in the rural provinces of China during the Chinese revolution.

Saint-Simon, Claude Henri (1760–1825) A utopian socialist. See also *Utopian socialism.*

Satellite countries A term used to refer to the East European countries that were controlled by the Soviet Union during the Stalinist period.

Schopenhauer, Arthur (1788–1860) A German philosopher who thought that life was a meaningless struggle beyond human understanding.

Scientific socialism The term used by its supporters to describe Marxism; they called it scientific because it was based on certain principles of human conduct that Marxists believed were inviolable laws.

Secret war against Cuba During the 1960s the Central Intelligence Agency funded, trained, armed, and directed Cuban exiles in order to perpetrate acts of sabotage and terrorism against Castro's Cuba. This campaign included numerous attempts to assassinate Fidel Castro.

Self-alienation, theory of Marx's belief that bourgeois exploitation alienated the workers from themselves in three ways: (1) by making the conditions of labor so harsh that workers were forced to hate their jobs; (2) by forcing the workers to sell the product of their labor at much less than its inherent value; and (3) by robbing the workers of their skills through mechanization.

Separation of powers The distribution of the powers of the national government among three branches: legislative, executive, and judicial.

Siegfried The idealization of the Aryan superman. Richard Wagner immortalized this character in his operas, and Hitler made him the symbol of the Nazi racial ideal.

Single-member district An electoral district in which only one person is elected to office. Since only one person can be elected, those who voted for the losers go unrepresented. Used in the United States, this electoral system also tends to favor a single or two-party system while working against a multiparty system.

Single-party system A system in which only one party has a reasonable chance of gaining control of the government. Although it can easily be used to create a dictatorship, it may exist in a democracy as well.

Smith, Adam (1723–1790) A Scottish scholar, he is considered the founder of economics. With the 1776 publication of *The Wealth of Nations,* he first articulated the basic principles of capitalism.

Social anarchism   Wants to free people from government and other institutional restraints so that they will be able to make their greatest possible contribution to society.

Social contract theory   The notion, outlined by Hobbes, Locke, Rousseau, and others, that people joined together in a contract to create a government that would protect them from the tyranny of the state of nature.

Social Darwinism   A theory developed by Herbert Spencer, who claimed that the wealthy were superior to others and therefore benefited society more than others. Coining the phrase "survival of the fittest," Spencer argued that the wealthy should succeed while the poor should perish because this would strengthen the human race.

Socialism   The application of communistic principles to a national economy. Socialism developed only after the Industrial Revolution increased productivity enough to make it possible to provide plenty for everyone.

Socialist ethic   The hope that true socialists will enjoy work and will voluntarily share the product of their labor with the whole community.

Socialist intent   A moral goal that must exist for a system to be truly socialist. This goal is to free people from material need, allowing them to develop and refine themselves as human beings.

Sorel, Georges (1847–1922)   A French philosopher who developed the ideology underlying syndicalism and encouraged the use of myth as a tool of mass politics. Though Sorel was a leftist, his ideas were adapted and modified by Mussolini.

Sovereign   The highest legal authority in a given society. The term is sometimes used to refer to a monarch.

Spencer, Herbert (1820–1903)   The founder of Social Darwinism, Spencer claimed that the wealthy were the select of nature and had a right to accumulate wealth at the expense of inferior beings. Spencer, not Charles Darwin, coined the phrase "survival of the fittest."

Stalin, Joseph (1876–1953)   A Bolshevik conspirator who succeeded Lenin and became the unquestioned leader of the Soviet Union. Although he made the Soviet Union a first-rate military and industrial power while successfully defeating the Nazi invasion, he imposed a cruel totalitarian system on his country, executing or imprisoning millions of people.

State   A political term that includes people, territory, sovereignty, and government. In the United States of America the term has also been used to refer to what are actually provinces.

State socialism   Lenin's theory that in preparation for the communist utopia, the socialist state will exploit the proletariat and share the proceeds among all the people in proportion to their productivity. The guiding slogan would be "from each according to his ability, to each according to his *work*."

Statism   The concept that the state is the focal point of human existence and that all citizens should therefore give it absolute obedience.

Stirner, Max (1806–1856)   A leading individualist anarchist. He encouraged each person to ignore society and to focus only on the self; what he called "ownness."

Sun Yat-Sen (1866–1925)   A Chinese physician and revolutionary leader. He inspired the movement that eventually led to the ouster of the Chinese Emperor in 1911.

Superstructure   All elements, according to Marx, that are built on the economic foundation of the society, including art, values, government, education, ideology, and the like.

Supply-side economics   Pursued by Republican Presidents in the 1920s and again by Ronald Reagan in the 1980s, this policy reduces taxes and government regulation for large corporations while increasing government subsidies and other support for big business.

Surplus value, theory of Marx's argument that the capitalist forced the workers to surrender their product for less than its true worth. The difference between the workers' wages and the true value of the item was the "surplus value" or profit.

Syndicalism A radical theory suggesting that trade unions should become the primary social and political units in the society.

Third World Usually found in Africa, Asia, and Latin America, these states often have marginal economies and are noted for their anticolonialism and nationalism.

Tito, Josip Broz (1892–1980) A Yugoslavian political and revolutionary leader.

Titoism A pragmatic approach to Marxism that is basically antibureaucratic and led Yugoslavia to a mixed economy.

Tolstoy, Count Leo (1828–1910) A famed author and pacifist anarchist.

Totalitarian state A state in which the government controls the economic, social, and cultural as well as political aspects of a society. Totalitarianism was not possible before the development of twentieth-century technology.

Trotsky, Leon (1879–1940) A brilliant Bolshevik revolutionary who was Lenin's intellectual equal but was no match for Stalin's ruthlessness; he suffered exile and was finally assassinated at Stalin's order.

Two-party system A system in which the bulk of the vote is consistently divided between two major parties. Though this system has the advantage of loyal opposition, the views of the minority rarely get a fair hearing.

Two-stage theory A question asked by some Marxists, including Lenin, as to whether or not a feudal society must pass through the capitalist stage of the dialectic to reach the communist stage.

Two-swords theory The belief that spiritual and secular powers are both essential and should not be held by a single person.

Ujamaa Meaning familyhood, this policy of Julius K. Nyerere of the United Republic of Tanzania attempted to raise the social and economic conditions of the people by creating self-sufficient familial agrarian collectives.

Unitary system A system of government that centralizes all governmental power in the national government.

Utilitarianism Bentham's philosophy that the government should do whatever would produce the greatest happiness for the greatest number of people.

Utopian socialism A humanitarian movement that unsuccessfully tried to create ideal socialist experiments that would be imitated by the rest of the society.

Vanguard of the proletariat (as used by Lenin) A small, dedicated elite of professional revolutionaries who would lead the proletariat to socialism through revolution. The Bolsheviks were the Russian vanguard and the Comintern, the internal vanguard.

Vanguard of the proletariat (as used by Marx) Those who, because of their superior intellect, could recognize the coming of socialism. Marx expected them to awaken the proletariat's class consciousness and thus stimulate the revolution.

Versailles, Treaty of The treaty ending World War I. It imposed very harsh conditions on Germany and was blamed by Hitler for Germany's severe postwar problems.

Volk The German people. See also *Volkish essence.*

Volkish essence A mystical power within the German people that supposedly makes them superior to all others.

Wagner, Richard (1813–1883)   An operatic composer who popularized German mythology and the foundation for anti-Semitism.

War communism (1917–1921)   A period in which Lenin tried to totally socialize the Soviet Union. The experiment ended in failure, and Lenin was forced to shift to his new economic policy (NEP).

Warsaw Pact   A military alliance of communist countries similar to the North Atlantic Treaty Organization (NATO). It is now defunct.

Weakest-link theory   Lenin's theory that Russia was the weakest link in the capitalist chain because it had exploited its workers mercilessly to make up for the advantages enjoyed by the imperialist capitalists. This increased exploitation pushed the Russian proletariat to revolution before the proletarian classes of the more advanced industrial states.

Weimar Republic   The democratic government of Germany that existed before Hitler came to power. Although Hitler destroyed the Weimar government when he came to power, he never actually eliminated its constitution.

Welfare state   A society that provides a large number of social programs for its citizens, including social security, publicly supported education, public assistance for the poor, and public health services.

Will of the state   The fascist belief that the state is a living being with a will or personality of its own. The will of the state is more powerful than that of any person or group within the state and must be obeyed without question.

Will to power   An uncontrollable force that inspired people to try to dominate one another. Nietzsche argued that this force was the primary motivator of human history.

Work, theory of   Marx's belief that work was a form of self-creation and self-expression and was therefore good.

Yeltsin, Boris (born in 1931)   Once a leader in the Communist party of the Soviet Union, Yeltsin resigned from the party and eventually became the president of Russia. Yeltsin was a major player in the events that led ultimately to the collapse of the Soviet Union.

Index